The Economics and Ethics of Private Property

Studies in Political Economy and Philosophy

Second Edition

The Mises Institute dedicates this volume
in deepest gratitude to
Douglas French and Deanna Forbush
And in honor of Murray N. Rothbard.

The Economics and Ethics of Private Property

Studies in Political Economy and Philosophy

Second Edition

Hans-Hermann Hoppe

Ludwig
von Mises
Institute

AUBURN, ALABAMA

To Murray N. Rothbard

CONTENTS

Preface to the Second Edition

The first edition of *The Economics and Ethics of Private Property*, published in 1993, has been out of print for several years. For some time and from many sides I have been urged to prepare a new edition, and Llewellyn Rockwell has graciously offered the Ludwig von Mises Institute to serve as its publisher.

The Economics and Ethics of Private Property was dedicated to my teacher and mentor, Murray N. Rothbard, with whom I had been closely associated during the last ten years of his life, first as a visiting scholar at the Brooklyn Polytechnic Institute in New York City and after 1986 as a colleague at the University of Nevada, Las Vegas. The year 2005 marks the tenth anniversary of Rothbard's death. Thus, it seemed a most appropriate time to honor Murray anew with this second edition.

The present edition of *The Economics and Ethics of Private Property* is enlarged. It adds four articles written after the original publication of the book but related thematically to its central subject matter of the economic and ethic rationale of the institution of private property—chapters 6, 7, 8, and 15. The opportunity of a new edition has also been used to make significant editorial improvements and revisions.

Hans Hermann Hoppe
Las Vegas, Nevada, 2005

Preface to the First Edition

The collapse of socialism across Eastern Europe—as manifested most dramatically by the events of the forever memorable November 9, 1989, when the Germans of East and West reunited, moved and overjoyed, on top of the Berlin Wall—has added more support and urgency to the central thesis of this volume than I had ever hoped for.

Whether the following studies deal with economic topics such as employment, interest, money, banking, business cycles, taxes, public goods, or growth; with philosophical problems as the foundations of knowledge, and of economics and ethics in particular; or the reconstruction and theoretical explanation of historical and sociological phenomena such as exploitation, the rise and fall of civilizations, international politics, war, imperialism, and the role of ideas and ideological movements in the course of social evolution—each ultimately contributes to but one conclusion: The right to private property is an indisputably valid, absolute principle of ethics and the basis for continuous "optimal" economic progress. To rise from the ruins of socialism and overcome the stagnation of the Western welfare states, nothing will suffice but the uncompromising privatization of all socialized, that is, government, property and the establishment of a contractual society based on the recognition of the absoluteness of private property rights.

◆   ◆   ◆

In writing the following studies I received help from many sides. Special thanks go to my wife Margaret, who again took on the task of de-Germanizing my English; to Llewellyn H. Rockwell, Jr., president of the Ludwig von Mises Institute, and to Burton S. Blumert, president of the Center for Libertarian Studies, for their continuing support of my work; and to my friend David Gordon, for his numerous invaluable suggestions and comments.

My largest debt is to Ludwig von Mises and Murray N. Rothbard, the twentieth century's two greatest—though much neglected—economists and social philosophers. While I never met Ludwig von Mises, and indeed had not heard of his name until after his death, I am fortunate to have been closely associated with Murray Rothbard for the past six years, first in New York City, and since 1986 as colleagues at the University of Nevada, Las Vegas. Apart from the intellectual debt that I owe him, words cannot express my personal gratitude. His wisdom, insight, kindness, enthusiasm, and unflagging encouragement have been a continuous inspiration to me. It is, therefore, to him that this volume is dedicated.

Hans-Hermann Hoppe
Las Vegas, Nevada, 1993

Part One

ECONOMICS

Fallacies of the Public Goods Theory and the Production of Security

In 1849, at a time when classical liberalism was still the dominant ideological force and "economist" and "socialist" were generally considered antonyms, Gustave de Molinari, a renowned Belgian economist, wrote,

> If there is one well-established truth in political economy, it is this: That in all cases, of all commodities that serve to provide for the tangible or intangible need of the consumer, it is in the consumer's best interest that labor and trade remain free, because the freedom of labor and trade have as their necessary and permanent result the maximum reduction of price. And this: That the interest of the consumer of any commodity whatsoever should always prevail over the interests of the producer. Now, in pursuing these principles, one arrives at this rigorous conclusion: That the production of security should in the interest of consumers of this intangible commodity remain subject to the law of free competition. Whence it follows: That no government should have the right to prevent another government from going into competition

[Reprinted from the *Journal of Libertarian Studies* 9, no. 1 (Winter 1989).]

4 The Economics and Ethics of Private Property

with it, or require consumers of security to come exclusively to it for this commodity.[1]

He comments on this whole argument by saying, "Either this is logical and true, or else the principles on which economic science is based are invalid."[2]

There is apparently only one way out of this unpleasant (for all socialists, that is) conclusion: to argue that there are particular goods to which for some special reasons the above economic reasoning does not apply. It is this that the so-called public goods theorists are determined to prove.[3] However, I will demonstrate that in fact no such special goods or special reasons exist, and that the production of security in particular does not pose a problem any different from that of the production of any other good or service, be it houses, cheese, or insurance. In spite of its many followers, the whole public goods theory is faulty, flashy reasoning, riddled with internal inconsistencies, non sequiturs, appealing to and playing on popular prejudices and assumed beliefs, but with no scientific merit whatsoever.[4]

What, then, does the escape route that socialist economists have found in order to avoid drawing Molinari's conclusion look like? Since Molinari's time it has become more common to answer yes to

---

[1]Gustave de Molinari, *The Production of Security*, trans. J. Huston McCulloch (New York: Center for Libertarian Studies, Occasional Paper Series No. 2, 1977), p. 3.

[2]Ibid., p. 4.

[3]For various approaches of public goods theorists, see James M. Buchanan and Gordon Tullock, *The Calculus of Consent* (Ann Arbor: University of Michigan Press, 1962); James M. Buchanan, *The Public Finances* (Homewood, Ill.: Richard Irwin, 1970); idem, *The Limits of Liberty* (Chicago: University of Chicago Press, 1975); Gordon Tullock, *Private Wants, Public Means* (New York: Basic Books, 1970); Mancur Olson, *The Logic of Collective Action* (Cambridge, Mass.: Harvard University Press, 1965); William J. Baumol, *Welfare Economics and the Theory of the State* (Cambridge: Harvard University Press, 1952).

[4]See on the following, Murray N. Rothbard, *Man, Economy, and State* (Los Angeles: Nash, 1970), pp. 883ff.; idem, "The Myth of Neutral Taxation," *Cato Journal* (1981); Walter Block, "Free Market Transportation: Denationalizing the Roads," *Journal of Libertarian Studies* 3, no. 2 (1979); idem, "Public Goods and Externalities: The Case of Roads," *Journal of Libertarian Studies* 7, no. 1 (1983).

the question of whether there are goods to which different sorts of economic analyses apply. As a matter of fact, it is almost impossible to find a single contemporary economics textbook that does not stress the vital importance of the distinction between private goods, for which the truth of the economic superiority of a capitalist order of production is generally admitted, and public goods, for which it is generally denied.[5] Certain goods or services (including security) are said to be special because their enjoyment cannot be restricted to those who have actually financed their production. Rather, people who do not participate in financing them also draw benefits from them. Such goods are called public goods or services (as opposed to private goods or services, which exclusively benefit those people who actually pay for them). Because of this special feature of public goods, it is argued, markets cannot produce them, or at least not in sufficient quantity or quality; hence, compensatory state action is required.[6]

---

[5]See for instance, William J. Baumol and Alan S. Blinder, *Economics, Principles and Policy* (New York: Harcourt, Brace, Jovanovich, 1979), chap. 31.

[6]Another frequently used criterion for public goods is that of "nonrivalrous consumption." Generally, both criteria seem to coincide: When free riders cannot be excluded, nonrivalrous consumption is possible; and when they can be excluded, consumption becomes rivalrous, or so it seems. However, as public goods theorists argue, this coincidence is not perfect. It is, they say, conceivable that while the exclusion of free riders might be possible, their inclusion might not be connected with any additional cost (the marginal cost of admitting free riders is zero, that is), and that the consumption of the good in question by the additionally admitted free rider will not necessarily lead to a subtraction in the consumption of the good available to others. Such a good would be a public good, too. And since exclusion would be practiced on the free market and the good would not become available for nonrivalrous consumption to everyone it otherwise could—even though this would require no additional costs—this, according to statist-socialist logic, would prove a market failure, i.e., a suboptimal level of consumption. Hence the state would have to take over the provision of such goods. (A movie theater, for instance, might be only half full, so it might be "costless" to admit additional viewers free of charge, and their watching the movie also might not affect the paying viewers; hence the movie would qualify as a public good. Since, however, the owner of the theater would be engaging in exclusion, instead of letting free riders enjoy a "costless" performance, movie theaters would

The examples given by different authors of alleged public goods vary widely. Authors often classify the same good or service differently, leaving almost no classification of a particular good undisputed, which clearly foreshadows the illusory character of the whole distinction.[7] Nonetheless, some examples that enjoy particularly popular status as public goods are the fire brigade that stops a neighbor's house from catching fire, thereby letting him profit from my fire brigade, even though he did not contribute anything to financing it; or the police that, by walking around my property scare away potential burglars from my neighbor's property as well, even if he did not help finance the patrols; or the lighthouse, an example particularly dear to economists,[8] that helps a ship find its way even though the ship's owner did not contribute a penny to its construction or upkeep.

Before continuing with the presentation and critical examination of the theory of public goods, I will investigate how useful the distinction between private and public goods is in helping decide what should be produced privately and what should be provided by the state or with state help. Even the most superficial analysis could not fail to point out that using the alleged criterion of inexcludability, rather than presenting a sensible solution, would get one into deep trouble. While at least at first glance it seems that some of the state-provided goods and services might indeed qualify as public goods, it certainly is not obvious how many of the goods and services that are actually produced by states could come under the heading of public goods. Railroads, postal services, telephone, streets, and the like seem to be goods whose usage can be restricted to the persons who actually finance them, and hence appear to be private goods. And the same seems to be the case regarding many aspects of the multidimensional good "security": everything for which insurance could be taken out would have to qualify as a private good. Yet this does not

---

be ripe for nationalization.) On the numerous fallacies involved in defining public goods in terms of nonrivalrous consumption see notes 12 and 17 below.

[7]On this subject Walter Block, "Public Goods and Externalities."

[8]See for instance Buchanan, *The Public Finances*, p. 23; Paul Samuelson, *Economics* (New York: McGraw Hill, 1976), p. 166.

suffice. Just as many state-provided goods appear to be private goods, so many privately produced goods seem to fit in the category of a public good. Clearly my neighbors would profit from my well-kept rose garden—they could enjoy the sight of it without ever helping me garden. The same is true of all kinds of improvements that I could make on my property that would enhance the value of neighboring property as well. Even those people who do not throw money in his hat can profit from a street musician's performance. Those fellow passengers on the bus who did not help me buy it profit from my deodorant. And everyone who ever meets me would profit from my efforts, undertaken without their financial support, to turn myself into a most lovable person. Now, do all these goods—rose gardens, property improvements, street music, deodorants, personal improvements—since they clearly seem to possess the characteristics of public goods, then have to be provided by the state or with state assistance?

As these examples of privately produced public goods indicate, there is something seriously wrong with the thesis of public goods theorists that public goods cannot be produced privately, but instead require state intervention. Clearly they can be provided by markets. Furthermore, historical evidence shows us that all of the so-called public goods that states now provide have at some time in the past actually been provided by private entrepreneurs or even today are so provided in one country or another. For example, the postal service was once private almost everywhere; streets were privately financed and still are sometimes; even the beloved lighthouses were originally the result of private enterprise;[9] private police forces, detectives, and arbitrators exist; and help for the sick, the poor, the elderly, orphans, and widows has been a traditional concern of private charity organizations. To say, then, that such things cannot be produced by a pure market system is falsified by experience a hundredfold.

Apart from this, other difficulties arise when the public-private goods distinction is used to decide what and what not to leave to the market. For instance, what if the production of so-called public goods

---

[9]See Ronald Coase, "The Lighthouse in Economics," *Journal of Law and Economics* 17 (1974).

did not have positive but had negative consequences for other people, or if the consequences were positive for some and negative for others? What if the neighbor whose house was saved from burning by my fire brigade had wished (perhaps because he was overinsured) that it had burned down; or my neighbors hate roses, or my fellow passengers find the scent of my deodorant disgusting? In addition, changes in the technology can change the character of a given good. For example, with the development of cable TV a good that was formerly (seemingly) public has become private. And changes in the laws of property—of the appropriation of property—can have the very same effect of changing the public-private character of a good. The lighthouse, for instance, is a public good only insofar as the sea is publicly (not privately) owned. But if it were permitted to acquire pieces of the ocean as private property, as it would be in a purely capitalist social order, then as the lighthouse shines over only a limited territory, it would clearly become possible to exclude nonpayers from the enjoyment of its services.

Leaving this somewhat sketchy level of discussion and looking into the distinction between private and public goods more thoroughly, we discover that the distinction turns out to be completely illusory. A clear-cut dichotomy between private and public goods does not exist, and this is essentially why there can be so many disagreements on how to classify a given good. All goods are more or less private or public and can—and constantly do—change with respect to their degree of privateness/publicness as people's values and evaluations change, and as changes occur in the composition of the population. In order to recognize that they never fall, once and for all, into either one or the other category, one must only recall what makes something a good. For something to be a good it must be recognized and treated as scarce by someone. Something is not a good as such, that is to say; goods are goods only in the eyes of the beholder. Nothing is a good unless at least one person subjectively evaluates it as such. But then, when goods are never goods-as-such—when no physico-chemical analysis can identify something as an economic good—there is clearly no fixed, objective criterion for classifying goods as either private or public. They can never be private or public goods as such. Their private or public character depends on how few or how many people consider them to be goods, with the degree to which they are private or public changing as these evaluations change and range from one to infinity. Even seemingly completely private things like the interior of my apartment or the color of my underwear can thus become public goods as soon as somebody else starts caring about them.[10] And seemingly public goods, like the exterior of my house or the color of my overalls, can become extremely private goods as soon as other people stop caring about them. Moreover, every good can change its characteristics again and again; it can even turn from a public or private good to a public or private bad or evil and vice versa, depending solely on the changes in this caring or uncaring. If this is so, then no decision whatsoever can be based on the classification of goods as private or public.[11] In fact, to do so it would become necessary to ask virtually every individual with respect to every single good whether or not he happened to care about it—positively or negatively and perhaps to what extent—in order to determine who might profit from what and who should therefore participate in the good's financing. (And how could one know if they were telling the truth?) It would also become necessary to monitor all changes in such evaluations continuously, with the result that no definite decision could ever be made regarding the production of anything, and as a consequence of a nonsensical theory all of us would be long dead.[12]

---

[10]See, for instance, the ironic case that Block makes for socks being public goods in "Public Goods and Externalities."

[11]To avoid any misunderstanding here, every single producer and every association of producers making joint decisions can, at any time, decide whether or not to produce a good based on an evaluation of the privateness or publicness of the good. In fact, decisions on whether or not to produce public goods privately are constantly made within the framework of a market economy. What is impossible is to decide whether or not to ignore the outcome of the operation of a free market based on the assessment of the degree of privateness or publicness of a good.

[12]In fact, then, the introduction of the distinction between private and public goods is a relapse into the pre-subjectivist era of economics. From the point of view of subjectivist economics, no good exists that can be categorized objectively as private or public. This is essentially why the second proposed criterion for public goods—permitting nonrivalrous consumption (see note 6 above)—breaks down too. For how could any outside observer determine whether or not the admittance of an additional free rider at no charge would not indeed lead to a subtraction in the consumption of a good to others? Clearly there is no way

But even if one were to ignore all these difficulties and were willing to admit, for the sake of argument that the private-public good distinction does hold water, the argument would not prove what it is supposed to. It neither provides conclusive reasons why public goods—assuming that they exist as a separate category of goods—should be produced at all, nor why the state rather than private enterprises should produce them. This is what the theory of public goods essentially says, having introduced the aforementioned conceptual distinction: The positive effects of public goods for people who do not contribute anything to their production or financing proves that these goods are desirable. But evidently they would not be produced, or at least not in sufficient quantity and quality, in a free, competitive market, since not all of those who would profit from their production would also contribute financially to make the production possible. In order to produce these goods (which are evidently desirable, but would not be produced otherwise), the state must jump in and assist in their production. This sort of reasoning, which can be found in almost every textbook on economics (Nobel laureates not excluded)[13] is completely fallacious on two counts.

---

that he could objectively do so. In fact, it might well be that one's enjoyment of a movie or of driving on a road would be considerably reduced if more people were allowed in the theater or on the road. Again, to find out whether or not this is the case one would have to ask every individual—and not everyone might agree (what then?). Furthermore, since even a good that allows nonrivalrous consumption is not a free good, as a consequence of admitting additional free riders "crowding" would eventually occur, and hence everyone would have to be asked about the appropriate "margin." In addition, my consumption may or may not be affected depending on who it is that is admitted free of charge, so I would have to be asked about this, too. And finally, everyone might change his opinion on all of these questions over time. It is thus in the same way impossible to decide whether or not a good is a candidate for state (rather than private) production based on the criterion of nonrivalrous consumption as on that of nonexcludability (see also note 17 below).

[13]See Paul Samuelson, "The Pure Theory of Public Expenditure," *Review of Economics and Statistics* (1954); idem, *Economics*, chap. 8; Milton Friedman, *Capitalism and Freedom* (Chicago: University of Chicago Press, 1962), chap. 2; F.A. Hayek, *Law, Legislation and Liberty* (Chicago: University of Chicago, 1979), vol. 3, chap. 14.

For one thing, to come to the conclusion that the state has to pro-vide public goods that otherwise would not be produced, one must smuggle a norm into one's chain of reasoning. Otherwise, from the statement that because of some special characteristics they have, certain goods would not be produced, one could never reach the con-clusion that these goods *should* be produced. But with a norm required to justify their conclusion, the public goods theorists clearly have left the bounds of economics as a positive, *wertfrei* science. Instead they have moved into the realm of morals or ethics, and hence one would expect to be offered a theory of ethics as a cognitive discipline in order for them to do legitimately what they are doing and to justifiably derive their conclusion. But it can hardly be stressed enough that nowhere in public goods theory literature can anything that even faintly resembles such a cognitive theory of ethics be found.[14] Thus it must be stated at the outset, that public goods theorists are

---

[14]Economists in recent years, particularly the Chicago School, have been increasingly concerned with the analysis of property rights. Harold Demsetz, "The Exchange and Enforcement of Property Rights," *Journal of Law and Economics* 7 (1964); idem, "Toward a Theory of Property Rights," *American Economic Review* (1967); Ronald Coase, "The Problem of Social Cost," *Journal of Law and Economics* 3 (1960); Armen Alchian, *Economic Forces at Work* (Indianapolis: Liberty Fund, 1977), part 2; Richard Posner, *Economic Analysis of the Law* (Boston: Brown, 1977). Such analyses, however, have nothing to do with ethics. On the contrary, they represent attempts to substitute economic effi-ciency considerations for the establishment of justifiable ethical principles [on the critique of such endeavors see Murray N. Rothbard, *The Ethics of Liberty* (Atlantic Highlands, N.J.: Humanities Press, 1982), chap. 26; Walter Block, "Coase and Demsetz on Private Property Rights," *Journal of Libertarian Studies* 1, no. 2 (1977); Ronald Dworkin, "Is Wealth a Value," *Journal of Legal Studies* 9 (1980); Murray N. Rothbard, "The Myth of Efficiency," in Mario Rizzo, ed., *Time Uncertainty and Disequilibrium* (Lexington, Mass.: D.C. Heath, 1979). Ultimately, all efficiency arguments are irrelevant because there simply exists no nonarbitrary way of measuring, weighing, and aggregating individual utilities or disutilities that result from some given allocation of property rights. Hence any attempt to recommend some particular system of assigning property rights in terms of its alleged maximization of "social welfare" is pseudo-scientific hum-bug. See in particular, Murray N. Rothbard, *Toward a Reconstruction of Utility and Welfare Economics* (New York: Center for Libertarian Studies, Occasional

misusing whatever prestige they might have as positive economists for pronouncements on matters on which, as their own writings indicate, they have no authority whatsoever. Perhaps, though, they have stumbled on something correct by accident, without having supported it with an elaborate moral theory? It becomes apparent that nothing could be further from the truth as soon as one explicitly formulates the norm that would be needed to arrive at the conclusion that the state has to assist in the provision of public goods. The norm required to reach the above conclusion is this: whenever one can somehow prove that the production of a particular good or service has a positive effect on someone else but would not be produced at all or would not be produced in a definite quantity or quality unless certain people participated in its financing, then the use of aggressive violence against these persons is allowed, either directly or indirectly with the help of the state, and these persons may be forced to share in the necessary financial burden. It does not need much comment to show that chaos would result from implementing this rule, as it amounts to saying that anyone can attack anyone else whenever he

---

Paper Series No. 3, 1977); also Lionel Robbins, "Economics and Political Economy," *American Economic Review* (1981).

The "Unanimity Principle" which Buchanan and Tullock, following Knut Wicksell (*Finanztheoretische Untersuchungen*, Jena: Gustav Fischer, 1896), have repeatedly proposed as a guide for economic policy is also not to be confused with an ethical principle proper. According to this principle only such policy changes should be enacted which can find unanimous consent—and that surely sounds attractive; but then, *mutatis mutandis*, it also determines that the status quo be preserved if there is less than unanimous agreement on any proposal of change—and that sounds far less attractive, because it implies that any given, present state of affairs regarding the allocation of property rights must be legitimate either as a point of departure or as a to-be-continued-state. However, the public choice theorists offer no justification in terms of a normative theory of property rights for this daring claim as would be required. Hence, the unanimity principle is ultimately without ethical foundation. In fact, because it would legitimize any conceivable status quo, the Buchananites' most favored principle is no less than outrightly absurd as a moral criterion. See on this also Rothbard, *The Ethics of Liberty* chap. 26; idem, "The Myth of Neutral Taxation," pp. 549f.

Whatever might still be left for the unanimity principle, Buchanan and Tullock, following the lead of Wicksell again, then give away by reducing it in effect to one of "relative" or "quasi" unanimity.

feels like it. Moreover, as I have demonstrated in detail elsewhere[15] this norm could never be justified as a fair norm. To argue so, in fact to argue at all, in favor of or against anything, be it a moral, nonmoral, empirical, or logico-analytical position, it must be presupposed that contrary to what the norm actually says, each individual's integrity as a physically independent decision-making unit is assured. For only if everyone is free from physical aggression by everyone else could anything first be said and then agreement or disagreement on anything possibly be reached. The principle of nonaggression is thus the necessary precondition for argumentation and possible agreement and hence can be argumentatively defended as a just norm by means of a priori reasoning.

But the public goods theory breaks down not only because of the faulty moral reasoning implied in it. Even the utilitarian, economic reasoning contained in the above argument is blatantly wrong. As the public goods theory states, it might well be that it would be better to have the public goods than not to have them, though it should not be forgotten that no a priori reason exists that this must be so of necessity (which would then end the public goods theorists' reasoning right here). For it is clearly possible, and indeed known to be a fact, that anarchists exist who so greatly abhor state action that they would prefer not having the so-called public goods at all to having them provided by the state.[16] In any case, even if the argument is conceded so far, to leap from the statement that the public goods are desirable to the statement that they should therefore be provided by the state is anything but conclusive, as this is by no means the choice with which one is confronted. Since money or other resources must be withdrawn from possible alternative uses to finance the supposedly desirable public goods, the only relevant and appropriate question is

---

[15]Hans-Hermann Hoppe, "From the Economics of Laissez Faire to the Ethics of Libertarianism," in Walter Block and Llewellyn H. Rockwell, Jr., eds., *Man, Economy, and Liberty: Essays in Honor of Murray N. Rothbard* (Auburn, Ala.: Ludwig von Mises Institute, 1988); infra chap. 8.

[16]See on this argument Rothbard, "The Myth of Neutral Taxation," p. 533. Incidentally, the existence of one single anarchist also invalidates all references to Pareto optimality as a criterion for economically legitimate state action.

whether or not these alternative uses to which the money could be put (that is, the private goods which could have been acquired but now cannot be bought because the money is being spent on public goods instead) are more valuable—more urgent—than the public goods. And the answer to this question is perfectly clear. In terms of consumer evaluations, however high its absolute level might be, the value of the public goods is relatively lower than that of the competing private goods because if one had left the choice to the consumers (and had not forced one alternative upon them), they evidently would have preferred spending their money differently (otherwise no force would have been necessary). This proves beyond any doubt that the resources used for the provision of public goods are wasted because they provide consumers with goods or services that at best are only of secondary importance. In short, even if one assumed that public goods that can be distinguished clearly from private goods existed, and even if it were granted that a given public good might be useful, public goods would still compete with private goods. And there is only one method for finding out whether or not they are more urgently desired and to what extent, or *mutatis mutandis*, if, and to what extent, their production would take place at the expense of the nonproduction or reduced production of more urgently needed private goods: by having everything provided by freely competing private enterprises. Hence, contrary to the conclusion arrived at by the public goods theorists, logic forces one to accept the result that only a pure market system can safeguard the rationality, from the point of view of the consumers, of a decision to produce a public good. And only under a pure capitalist order could it be ensured that the decision about how much of a public good to produce (provided it should be produced at all) would be rational as well.[17] No less than

---

[17]Essentially the same reasoning that leads one to reject the socialist-statist theory built on the allegedly unique character of public goods as defined by the criterion of nonexcludability, also applies when, instead, such goods are defined by means of the criterion of nonrivalrous consumption (see notes 6 and 12 above). For one thing, in order to derive the normative statement that they *should* be so offered from the statement of fact that goods that allow nonrivalrous consumption *would not* be offered on the free market to as many consumers as

a semantic revolution of truly Orwellian dimensions would be required to come up with a different result. Only if one were willing to interpret someone's "no" as really meaning "yes," the "nonbuying of something" as meaning that it is really "preferred over that which the nonbuying person does instead of nonbuying," of "force" really

---

could be, this theory would face exactly the same problem of requiring a justifiable ethics. Moreover, the utilitarian reasoning is blatantly wrong, too. To reason, as the public goods theorists do, that the free-market practice of excluding free riders from the enjoyment of goods that would permit nonrivalrous consumption at zero marginal costs would indicate a suboptimal level of social welfare and hence would require compensatory state action is faulty on two related counts. First, cost is a subjective category and can never be objectively measured by any outside observer. Hence, to say that additional free riders could be admitted at no cost is totally inadmissible. In fact, if the subjective costs of admitting more consumers at no charge were indeed zero, the private owner-producer of the good in question would do so. If he does not do so, this reveals that the costs for him are *not* zero. The reason may be his belief that to do so would reduce the satisfaction available to the other consumers and so would tend to depress the price for his product; or it may simply be his dislike for uninvited free riders as, for instance, when I object to the proposal that I turn over my less-than-capacity-filled living room to various self-inviting guests for nonrivalrous consumption. In any case, since for whatever reason the cost cannot be assumed to be zero, it is then fallacious to speak of a market failure when certain goods are not handed out free of charge. On the other hand, welfare losses would indeed become unavoidable if one accepted the public goods theorists' recommendation of letting goods that allegedly allow for nonrivalrous consumption to be provided free of charge by the state. Besides the insurmountable task of determining what fulfills this criterion, the state, independent of voluntary consumer purchases as it is, would first off face the equally insoluble problem of rationally determining *how much* of the public good to provide. Clearly, since even public goods are not free goods but are subject to "crowding" at some level of use, there is no stopping point for the state, because at any level of supply there would still be users who would have to be excluded and who, with a larger supply, could enjoy a free ride. But even if this problem could be solved miraculously, in any case the (necessarily inflated) cost of production and operation of the public goods distributed free of charge for nonrivalrous consumption would have to be paid for by taxes. And this then, i.e., the fact that consumers would have been coerced into enjoying their free rides, again proves beyond any doubt that these public goods, too, are of inferior value from the point of view of consumers to the competing private goods that they now no longer can acquire.

meaning "freedom," of "noncontracting" really meaning "making a contract" and so on, could the public goods theorists' point be "proven."[18] But how then could we be sure that they really mean what they seem to mean when they say what they say, and do not rather mean the exact opposite, or do not mean anything with a definite content at all, but are simply babbling? We could not. Murray N. Rothbard is thus completely right when he comments on the endeavors of the public goods ideologues to prove the existence of so-called market failures due to the nonproduction or a quantitatively or qualitatively "deficient" production of public goods. He writes,

---

[18]The most prominent modern champions of Orwellian double talk are Buchanan and Tullock (see their works cited in note 3 above). They claim that government is founded by a "constitutional contract" in which everyone "conceptually agrees" to submit to the coercive powers of government with the understanding that everyone else is subject to it too. Hence government is only *seemingly* coercive but *really* voluntary. There are several evident objections to this curious argument. First, there is no empirical evidence whatsoever for the contention that any constitution has ever been voluntarily accepted by everyone concerned. Worse, the very idea of all people voluntarily coercing themselves is simply inconceivable, much in the same way as it is inconceivable to deny the law of contradiction. For if the voluntarily accepted coercion is voluntary, then it would have to be possible to revoke one's subjection to the constitution, and the state would be no more than a voluntarily joined club. If, however, one does not have the "right to ignore the state"—and that one does not have this right is, of course, the characteristic mark of a state as compared to a club—then it would be logically inadmissible to claim that one's acceptance of state coercion is voluntary. Furthermore, even if all this were possible, the constitutional contact could still not claim to bind anyone except the original signers of the constitution.

How can Buchanan and Tullock come up with such absurd ideas? By a semantic trick. What was "inconceivable" and "no agreement" in pre-Orwellian talk is for them "conceptually possible" and a "conceptual agreement." For a most instructive short exercise in this sort of reasoning in leaps and bounds, see James Buchanan, "A Contractarian Perspective on Anarchy," in idem, *Freedom in Constitutional Contract* (College Station: Texas A&M University Press, 1977). Here we learn (p. 17) that even the acceptance of the 55 mph speed limit is possibly voluntary (Buchanan is not quite sure) since it ultimately rests on all of us conceptually agreeing on the constitution, and that Buchanan is not really a statist, but in truth an anarchist (p. 11).

[s]uch a view completely misconceives the way in which economic science asserts that free-market action is *ever* optimal. It is optimal, not from the standpoint of the personal ethical views of an economist, but from the standpoint of free, voluntary actions of all participants and in satisfying the freely expressed needs of the consumers. Government interference, therefore, will necessarily and always move *away* from such an optimum.[19]

Indeed, the arguments supposedly proving market failures are nothing short of patently absurd. Stripped of their disguise of technical jargon all they prove is this: A market is not perfect, as it is characterized by the nonaggression principle imposed on conditions marked by scarcity, and so certain goods or services that could only be produced and provided if aggression were allowed will not be produced. True enough, but no market theorist would ever dare deny this. Yet, and this is decisive, this "imperfection" of the market can be defended, morally as well as economically, whereas the supposed "perfections" of markets propagated by the public goods theorists cannot.[20] It is also true that a termination of the state's current practice of providing public goods would imply some change in the existing social structure and the distribution of wealth. Such a reshuffling would certainly imply hardship for some people. As a matter of fact, this is precisely why there is widespread public resistance to a policy of privatizing state functions, even though in the long run overall social wealth would be enhanced by this very policy. Surely, however, this

---

[19]Rothbard, *Man, Economy, and State*, p. 887.

[20]This, first of all, should be kept in mind whenever one has to assess the validity of statist-interventionist arguments such as the following, by John Maynard Keynes ("The End of Laissez Faire," in idem, *Collected Writings*, London: Macmillan, 1972, vol. IX, p. 291):

The most important Agenda of the state relates not to those activities which private individuals are already fulfilling but to those functions which fall outside the sphere of the individual, to those decisions which are made by no one if the state does not make them. The important thing for government is not to do things which individuals are doing already and to do them a little better or a little worse: but to do those things which are not done at all.

This reasoning not only *appears* phony, it truly is.

fact cannot be accepted as a valid argument demonstrating the failure of markets. If a man has been allowed to hit other people on the head and is now not permitted to continue with this practice, he is certainly hurt. But one would hardly accept that as a valid excuse for upholding the old (hitting) rules. He is harmed, but harming him means substituting a social order in which every consumer has an equal right to determine what and how much of anything is produced, for a system in which some consumers have the right to determine in what respect other consumers are not allowed to buy voluntarily what they want with the means justly acquired by them and at their disposal. Certainly, such a substitution would be preferable from the point of view of all consumers as voluntary consumers.

By force of logical reasoning, one must accept Molinari's conclusion that for the sake of consumers, all goods and services be provided by markets.[21] It is not only false that clearly distinguishable

---

[21]Some libertarian minarchists object that the existence of a market presupposes the recognition and enforcement of a common body of law, and hence a government as a monopolistic judge and enforcement agency. (See, for example, John Hospers, *Libertarianism* [Los Angeles: Nash, 1971]; Tibor Machan, *Human Rights and Human Liberties* [Chicago: Nelson-Hall, 1975].) Now it is certainly correct that a market presupposes the recognition and enforcement of those rules that underlie its operation. But from this it does not follow that this task must be entrusted to a monopolistic agency. In fact, a common language or sign-system is also presupposed by the market; but one would hardly think it convincing to conclude that hence the government must ensure the observance of the rules of language. Like the system of language, then, the rules of market behavior emerge spontaneously and can be enforced by the "invisible hand" of self-interest. Without the observance of common rules of speech, people could not reap the advantages that communication offers, and without the observance of common rules of conduct, people could not enjoy the benefits of the higher productivity of an exchange economy based on the division of labor. In addition, as I indicated above, independent of any government the nonaggression principle underlying the operation of markets can be defended a priori as just. Moreover, as I will argue in the conclusion of this chapter, it is precisely a competitive system of law-administration and law-enforcement that generates the greatest possible pressure to elaborate and enact rules of conduct that incorporate the highest degree of *consensus* conceivable. And of course the very rules that do just this are those that a priori reasoning establishes as the logically necessary presupposition of argumentation and argumentative agreement.

categories of goods exist, which would render special amendments to the general thesis of capitalism's economic superiority necessary; even if they did exist, no special reason could be found why these supposedly special public goods should not also be produced by private enterprises, since they invariably stand in competition with private goods. In fact, in spite of all the propaganda from the public goods theorists, the greater efficiency of markets as compared with the state is increasingly realized with respect to more and more of the alleged public goods. Confronted daily with experience, hardly anyone seriously studying these matters could deny that nowadays markets could produce postal services, railroads, electricity, telephone, education, money, roads and so on more effectively than the state, i.e., more to the liking of consumers. Yet people generally shy away from accepting in one particular sector what logic forces upon them: in the production of security. Hence, for the rest of this chapter I will turn my attention to explaining the superior functioning of a capitalist economy in this particular area—a superiority whose logical case has already been made by now, but which shall be rendered more persuasive once some empirical material is added to the analysis and it is studied as a problem in its own right.[22]

---

[22]Incidentally, the same logic that would force one to accept the idea of the production of security by private business as economically the best solution to the problem of consumer satisfaction also forces one, so far as moral-ideological positions are concerned, to abandon the political theory of classical liberalism and take the small but nevertheless decisive step (from there) to the theory of libertarianism, or private property anarchism. Classical liberalism, with Ludwig von Mises as its foremost representative in the twentieth century, advocates a social system based on the nonaggression principle. And this is also what libertarianism advocates. But classical liberalism then wants to have this principle enforced by a monopolistic agency (the government, the state)—an organization, that is, which is not exclusively dependent on voluntary, contractual support by the consumers of its respective services, but instead has the right to unilaterally determine its own income, i.e., the taxes to be imposed on consumers in order to do its job in the area of security production. Now, however plausible this might sound, it should be clear that it is inconsistent. Either the principle of nonaggression is valid, in which case the state as a privileged monopolist is immoral, or business built on and around aggression—the use of force and of noncontractual means of acquiring resources—is valid, in which case one must

How would a system of nonmonopolistic, competing producers of security work? It should be clear from the outset that in answering this question one is leaving the realm of purely logical analysis and hence the answers must lack the certainty, the apodictic character of pronouncements on the validity of the public goods theory. The problem faced is precisely analogous to that of asking how a market would solve the problem of hamburger production, especially if up to this point hamburgers had been produced exclusively by the state and hence no one could draw on past experience. Only tentative answers could be formulated. No one could possibly know the exact structure of the hamburger industry—how many competing companies would come into existence, what importance this industry might have compared to others, what the hamburgers would look like, how many different sorts of hamburgers would appear on the market and perhaps disappear again because of a lack of demand, and so on. No one could know all of the circumstances and the changes that would influence the very structure of the hamburger industry—changes in the demands of various consumer groups, changes in technology, changes in the prices of various goods that affect the industry directly or indirectly, and so on. It must be stressed that although similar issues arise concerning the private production of security, this by no means implies that nothing definitive can be said. Assuming certain general conditions of demand for security services (conditions that more or less realistically reflect the world as it presently is) what can and will be said is how different social orders of security production,

---

toss out the first theory. It is impossible to sustain both contentions and not to be inconsistent unless, of course, one could provide a principle that is more fundamental than both the nonaggression principle and the states' right to aggressive violence and from which both, with the respective limitations regarding the domains in which they are valid, can be logically derived. However, liberalism never provided any such principle, nor will it ever be able to do so, since, to argue in favor of anything presupposes one's right to be free of aggression. Given the fact then that the principle of nonaggression cannot be argumentatively contested as morally valid without implicitly acknowledging its validity, by force of logic one is committed to abandoning liberalism and accepting instead its more radical child: libertarianism, the philosophy of pure capitalism, which demands that the production of security be undertaken by private business too.

characterized by different structural constraints under which they have to operate, will respond differently.[23] Let me first analyze the specifics of monopolistic, state-run security production, for at least in this case one can draw on ample evidence regarding the validity of the conclusions reached and then compare this system with what could be expected if it were replaced by a nonmonopolistic one.

Even if security is considered to be a public good, in the allocation of scarce resources it must compete with other goods. What is spent on security can no longer be spent on other goods that also might increase consumer satisfaction. Moreover, security is not a single, homogeneous good, but rather consists of numerous components and aspects. There is not only prevention of crime, detection of criminals, and enforcement of the law, but there is also security from robbers, rapists, polluters, natural disasters, and so on. Moreover, security is not produced in a "lump," but can be supplied in marginal units. In addition, different people attach different importance to security as a whole, and also to different aspects of the whole thing, depending on their personal characteristics, their past experiences with various factors of insecurity, and the time and place in which they happen to live.[24] Here I address the fundamental economic problem of allocating scarce resources to competing uses, how can the state—an organization not financed exclusively by voluntary contributions and the sales of its products but rather partially or even wholly by taxes—decide how much security to produce, how much of each of its countless aspects, to whom and where to provide how much of what? The answer is that it has no rational way to decide this question. From the point of view of the consumers, its response to their security demands must be considered arbitrary. Do we need one policeman and one

---

[23]On the problem of competitive security production, see Gustave de Molinari, *Production of Security*; Murray N. Rothbard, *Power and Market* (Kansas City: Sheed Andrews and McMeel, 1977), chap. 1; idem, *For A New Liberty* (New York: Macmillan, 1978), chap. 12; W.C. Woolridge, *Uncle Sam the Monopoly Man* (New Rochelle, N.Y.: Arlington House, 1970), chaps. 5–6; Morris and Linda Tannehill, *The Market for Liberty* (New York: Laissez Faire Books, 1984), part 2.

[24]See Manfred Murck, *Soziologie der Öffentlichen Sicherheit* (Frankfurt: Campus, 1980).

judge, or 100,000 of each? Should they be paid $100 a month or $10,000? Should the policemen, however many we might have, spend more time patrolling the streets, chasing robbers, and recovering stolen loot, or spying on participants in victimless crimes such as prostitution, drug use, or smuggling? And should the judges spend more time and energy hearing divorce cases, traffic violations, cases of shoplifting, and murder, or antitrust cases? Clearly, all of these questions must be answered somehow because as long as there is scarcity and we do not live in the Garden of Eden, the time and money spent on one thing cannot be spent on another. The state must answer these questions, too, but whatever it does, it does it without being subject to the profit-and-loss criterion. Hence, its action is arbitrary and necessarily involves countless wasteful misallocations from the consumer's viewpoint.[25] Independent to a large degree of

---

[25]To say that the process of resource allocation becomes arbitrary in the absence of the effective functioning of the profit-loss criterion does not mean that the decisions that somehow have to he made are not subject to any kind of constraint and hence are pure whim. They are not, and any such decisions face certain constraints imposed on the decision maker. If, for instance, the allocation of production factors is decided democratically, then it evidently must appeal to the majority. But if a decision is constrained in this way or if it is made in any other way, it is still arbitrary from the point of view of voluntarily buying or not-buying consumers.

Regarding *democratically* controlled allocations, various deficiencies have become quite evident. As, for example, James Buchanan and Richard E. Wagner write (*The Consequences of Mr. Keynes* [London: Institute of Economic Affairs, 1978], p. 19):

> Market competition is continuous; at each purchase, a buyer is able to select among competing sellers. Political competition is intermittent; a decision is binding generally for a fixed number of years. Market competition allows several competitors to survive simultaneously. . . . Political competition leads to an all-or-nothing outcome. . . . In market competition the buyer can be reasonably certain as to just what it is that he will receive from his purchase. In political competition, the buyer is in effect purchasing the services of an agent, whom he cannot bind. . . . Moreover, because a politician needs to secure the cooperation of a majority of politicians, the meaning of a vote for a politician is less clean than that of a "vote" for a private firm.

consumer wants, the state-employed security producers instead do what they like. They hang around instead of doing anything, and if they do work they prefer doing what is easiest or work where they can wield power rather than serving consumers. Police officers drive around a lot, hassle petty traffic violators, spend huge amounts of money investigating victimless crimes that many people (i.e., nonparticipants) do not like but that few would be willing to spend their money on to fight, as they are not immediately affected by them. Yet with respect to what consumers want most urgently—the prevention of hardcore crime (i.e., crimes with victims), the apprehension and effective punishment of hard-core criminals, the recovery of loot, and the securement of compensation of victims of crimes from the aggressors—the police are notoriously inefficient, in spite of ever higher budget allocations.

Furthermore, whatever state-employed police or judges happen to do (arbitrary as it must be), they will tend to do poorly because their income is more or less independent of the consumer's evaluations of their services. Thus one observes police arbitrariness and brutality and the slowness in the judicial process. Moreover, it is remarkable that neither the police nor the judicial system offers consumers anything even faintly resembling a service contract in which it is laid down in unambiguous terms what procedure the consumer can

---

See also James M. Buchanan, "Individual Choice in Voting and the Market," in idem, *Fiscal Theory and Political Economy* (Chapel Hill: University of North Carolina Press, 1962); for a more general treatment of the problem Buchanan and Tullock, *The Calculus of Consent.*

What has commonly been overlooked, though—especially by those who try to make a virtue of the fact that a democracy gives equal voting power to everyone, whereas consumer sovereignty allows for unequal "votes"—is the most important deficiency of all: Under a system of consumer sovereignty people might cast unequal votes but, in any case, they exercise control exclusively over things that they acquired through original appropriation or contract and hence are forced to act morally. Under a democracy of production everyone is assumed to have something to say regarding things one did not so acquire; hence, one is permanently invited thereby not only to create legal instability with all its negative effects on the process of capital formation, but, moreover to act immorally. See on this also Ludwig von Mises, *Socialism* (Indianapolis: Liberty Fund, 1981), chap. 31.

expect to be set in motion in a specific situation. Rather, both operate in a contractual void that over time allows them to change their
rules of procedure arbitrarily and that explains the truly ridiculous
fact that the settlement of disputes between police and judges on the
one hand and private citizens on the other is not assigned to an independent third party, but to another policeman or judge who shares
employers with one party—the government—in the dispute.

Third, anyone who has seen state-run police stations and courts,
not to mention prisons, knows how true it is that the factors of production used to provide us with such security are overused, badly
maintained, and filthy. Since no one using these factors of production
actually owns them (no one can sell them and privately appropriate
the receipts from sale) and losses (and gains) in the value embodied
in the capital used are thus socialized, everybody will tend to increase
his private income resulting from the use of the factors at the expense
of losses in capital value. Hence, marginal cost will increasingly tend
to exceed the value of marginal product, and an overutilization of
capital will result. And if, in an exceptional case, this happens not to
be so and an overutilization should not be apparent, then this has
only been possible at costs that are comparatively much higher than
those of any similar private business.[26]

Without a doubt, all of these problems inherent in a system of
monopolistic security production would be solved relatively quickly
once a given demand for security services was met by a competitive
market with its entirely different incentive structure for producers.
This is not to say that a "perfect" solution to the problem of security
would be found. There would still be robberies and murders; and not
all loot would be recovered nor all murderers caught. But in terms of

---

[26]Sums up Molinari, *Production of Security*, pp. 13–14,

If . . . the consumer is not free to buy security wherever he pleases,
you forthwith see open up a large profession dedicated to arbitrariness and bad management. Justice becomes slow and costly, the
police vexatious, individual liberty is no longer respected, the price of
security is abusively inflated and inequitably apportioned, according
to the power and influence of this or that class of consumers.

consumer evaluations the situation would improve to the extent that the nature of man would allow it to improve. First, as long as there is a competitive system (i.e., as long as the producers of security services depend on voluntary purchases, most of which probably take the form of service and insurance contracts agreed to in advance of any actual "occurrence" of insecurity or aggression), no producer could increase its income without improving services or quality of product as perceived by the consumers. Furthermore, all security producers taken together could not bolster the importance of their particular industry unless, for whatever reasons, consumers indeed started evaluating security more highly than other goods, thus ensuring that the production of security would never take place at the expense of the non- or reduced production of, let us say, cheese, as a competing private good. In addition, the producers of security services would have to diversify their offerings to a considerable degree because a highly diversified demand for security products among millions and millions of consumers exists. Directly dependent on voluntary consumer support, they would immediately be hurt financially if they did not appropriately respond to the consumers' various wants or change in wants. Thus every consumer would have a direct influence, albeit small, on the output of goods appearing on or disappearing from the security market. Instead of offering a uniform "security packet" to everyone, a characteristic of state production policy, a multitude of service packages would appear on the market. They would be tailored to the different security needs of different people, taking account of different occupations, different risk-taking behavior, different needs for protection and insurance, and different geographical locations and time constraints.

But that is far from all. Besides diversification, the content and quality of the products would improve, too. Not only would the treatment of consumers by the employees of security enterprises improve immediately, the "I-could-care-less" attitude, the arbitrariness and even brutality, the negligence and tardiness of the present police and judicial systems would ultimately disappear. Since policemen and judges would be dependent on voluntary consumer support, any instances of maltreatment of consumers, of impoliteness or ineptness could cost them their job. Further, the peculiarity that the settlement of disputes between a client and his business partner is invariably entrusted to the latter's judgment, would almost certainly disappear from the books, and conflict arbitration by independent parties would become the standard offered by producers of security. Most importantly, in order to attract and retain customers the producers of such services would have to offer contracts that would allow the consumer to know what he was buying and enable him to raise a valid, intersubjectively ascertainable complaint if the actual performance of the security producer did not live up to the contract. More specifically, insofar as they are not individualized service contracts where payment is made by a customer to cover his own risks exclusively but are rather insurance contracts that require pooling one's own risks with those of other people, contrary to the present statist practice these contracts most certainly would no longer contain any deliberately built-in redistributive scheme favoring one group of people at the expense of another. Otherwise, if anyone had the feeling that the contract offered to him required him to pay for other people's peculiar needs and risks—factors of possible insecurity, that is, that he did not perceive as applicable to his own case—he would simply reject signing it or discontinue his payments.

Yet when all this is said, the question will inevitably surface. "Wouldn't a competitive system of security production necessarily result in permanent social conflict, in chaos and anarchy?" Several responses can be made to this question. First, it should be noted that such an impression would by no means be in accordance with historical, empirical evidence. Systems of competing courts have existed at various places (e.g., in ancient Ireland or at the time of the Hanseatic League) before the arrival of the modern nation state, and as far as we know they worked well.[27] Judged by the then existent crime rate (crime per capita), the private police in the so-called Wild West (which incidentally was not as wild as some movies imply) were relatively more

---

[27]See the literature cited in note 22; also Bruno Leoni, *Freedom and the Law* (Princeton, N.J.: D. Van Nostrand, 1961); Joseph Peden, "Property Rights in Celtic Irish Law," *Journal of Libertarian Studies* 1, no. 2 (1977).

successful than today's state-supported police).[28] And turning to contemporary experience and examples, millions and millions of international contracts exist even now—contracts of trade and travel—
and it certainly seems to be an exaggeration to say, for instance, that
there is more fraud, more crime, more breach of contract there than
in domestic relations. And this, it should be noted, without there
being one big monopolistic security producer and lawmaker. Finally
it is not to be forgotten that even now in a great number of countries
there are various private security producers alongside the state: private investigators, insurance detectives, and private arbitrators. Their
work seems to confirm the thesis that they are more, not less, successful in resolving social conflicts than their public counterparts.

However, this historical evidence is very much subject to dispute,
in particular regarding whether any general information can be
derived from it. Yet there are systematic reasons, too, why the fear
expressed by the question is not well-founded. Paradoxical as it may
seem, establishing a competitive system of security producers implies
erecting an institutionalized incentive structure to produce an order
of law and law-enforcement that embodies the highest possible
degree of consensus regarding the question of conflict resolution.
Such a structure will tend to generate less rather than more social
unrest and conflict than would occur under monopolistic auspices.[29]
In order to understand this paradox, it is necessary to take a closer
look at the only typical situation that concerns the skeptic and that
allows him to believe in the superior virtue of a monopolistically
organized order of security production: when a conflict arises
between A and B, both are insured by different companies and the
companies cannot come to an immediate agreement regarding the
validity of the conflicting claims brought forward by their respective
clients. (No problem would exist if such an agreement were reached
or if both clients were insured by one and the same company—at

---

[28]See Terry L. Anderson and Peter J. Hill, "The American Experiment in
Anarcho-Capitalism: The *Not* So Wild, Wild West," *Journal of Libertarian
Studies* 3, no. 1 (1980).

[29]On the following, see Hans-Hermann Hoppe, *Eigentum, Anarchie, und
Staat* (Opladen: Westdeutscher Verlag, 1986), chap. 5.

least the problem then would not be different in any way from that emerging under a statist monopoly.) Would not such a situation always result in a shoot-out? This is highly unlikely. First, any violent battle between companies would be costly and risky, in particular if these companies had reached a respectable size (which would be important for them to have in order to appear as effective guarantors of security to their prospective clients in the first place). More importantly, under a competitive system with each company dependent on the continuation of voluntary consumer payments, any battle would have to be deliberately supported by each and every client of both companies. If there were only one person who withdrew his payments because he was not convinced a battle was necessary in the particular conflict at hand, there would be immediate economic pressure on the company to look for a peaceful solution to the conflict.[30] Hence any competitive producer of security would be extremely cautious about engaging in violent measures in order to resolve conflicts. Rather, to the extent that it is peaceful conflict resolution that consumers want, each and every security producer would go to great lengths to provide it to its clients and to establish in advance, for everyone to know, to what arbitration process it would be willing to submit itself and its clients in case of a disagreement over the evaluation of conflicting claims. And as such a scheme could appear to the clients of different firms to be working only if there were agreement among them regarding such arbitrational measures, a system of law governing relations between companies that would be universally acceptable to the clients of all of the competing security producers would naturally evolve. Moreover, the economic pressure to generate rules representing a consensus on how conflicts should be handled is even more far-reaching. Under a competitive system, the independent arbitrators

---

[30]Contrast this with the state's policy of engaging in battles without having everyone's deliberate support because it has the right to tax people; and ask yourself if the risk of war would be lower or higher if one had the right to stop paying taxes as soon as one had the feeling that the states' handling of foreign affairs was not to one's liking.

who would be entrusted with the task of finding peaceful solutions to conflicts would be dependent on the continued support of the two disputing companies insofar as the companies could and would select different judges if either one of them were sufficiently dissatisfied with the outcome of the arbitration work. Thus, these judges would be under pressure to find solutions to the problems handed over to them that, this time not with respect to the procedural aspects of law but its content, would be acceptable to all of the clients of the firms involved.[31] Otherwise one or all of the companies might lose customers, thus inducing those firms to turn to different arbitrators the next time they are in need of one.[32]

But wouldn't it be possible under a competitive system for a security producing firm to become an outlaw company—a firm, that is, which, supported by its own clients, started aggressing against others? There is certainly no way to deny that this might be possible, though again it must be emphasized that here one is in the realm of empirical social science and no one could know such a thing with certainty. And yet the tacit implication that the possibility that a security firm could become an outlaw company somehow indicates a severe deficiency in the philosophy and economics of a pure capitalist social order is fallacious.[33]

---

[31]And it may be noted here again that norms that incorporate the highest possible degrees of consensus are, of course, those that are presupposed by argumentation and whose acceptance makes consensus on anything at all possible, as indicated above.

[32]Again, contrast this with state-employed judges who, because they are paid from taxes and so are relatively independent of consumer satisfaction, can pass judgments that are clearly not acceptable as fair by everyone; and ask yourself if the risk of not finding the truth in a given case would be lower or higher if one had the possibility of exerting economic pressure whenever one had the feeling that a judge who one day might have to adjudicate in one's own case had not been sufficiently careful in assembling and judging the facts of a case, or simply was an outright crook.

[33]See on the following in particular Rothbard, *For A New Liberty*, pp. 233ff.

First, it should be recalled that any social system, a statist-socialist order no less than a pure market economy, is dependent for its continued existence on public opinion and that a given state of public opinion at all times delimits what can or cannot occur as well as what is more or less likely to occur. The current state of public opinion in West Germany, for instance, makes it highly unlikely or even impossible that a statist-socialist system of the current Soviet type could be imposed on the West German public. The lack of public support for such a system would doom it to failure and make it collapse. It is even more unlikely that any attempt to impose a Soviet-type order could ever hope to succeed among Americans, given American public opinion. Hence, in order for us to see the problem of outlaw companies correctly, the above question should be phrased as follows: How likely is it that any such event would occur in a given society with its specific state of public opinion? Formulated in this way, it is clear that the answer would have to be different for different societies. For some, characterized by socialist ideas deeply entrenched in the public, there would be a greater likelihood of the reemergence of aggressor companies, and for other societies there would be a much smaller chance of this happening. But then, would the prospect of a competitive system of security production in any given case be better or worse than that of the continuation of a statist system? Let us look, for instance, at the present-day United States. Assume that by a legislative act the state had abolished its right to provide security with tax funds and a competitive system of security production was introduced. Given the state of public opinion, how likely then would it be that outlaw producers would spring up, and what if they did? Evidently, the answer would depend on the reactions of the public to this changed situation. Thus, the first reply to those challenging the idea of a private market for security would have to be: What about you? What would your reaction be? Does your fear of outlaw companies mean that you would then go out and engage in trade with a security producer that aggressed against other people and their property, and would you continue supporting it if it did? Certainly the critic would be much muted by this counterattack. But more important than this is the systematic challenge implied in this personal counterattack. Evidently, the described change in the situation would imply a change in the cost-benefit structure that everyone would face once he had to make his decisions. Before the introduction of a competitive system of security production, it had been legal to participate in and support (state) aggression. Now such an activity would be illegal. Hence, given one's conscience, which makes each decision appear more or less costly (i.e., more or less in harmony with one's own principles of correct behavior), support for a firm engaging in the exploitation of people unwilling to deliberately support its actions would be more costly than before. Given this fact, it must be assumed that the number of people (including even those who otherwise would have readily lent their support to the state) who would now spend their money to support a firm committed to honest business would rise wherever this social experiment was tried. In contrast, the number of people still committed to a policy of exploitation—of gaining at the expense of others—would fall. How drastic this effect would be would of course depend on the state of public opinion. In the example at hand—the United States, where the natural theory of property is extremely widespread and accepted as a private ethic, the libertarian philosophy being essentially the ideology on which the country was founded and that led it to the height it reached[34]—the effect would naturally be particularly pronounced. Accordingly, security producing firms committed to the philosophy of protecting and enforcing libertarian law would attract the greatest bulk of public support and financial assistance. And while it may be true that some people, and among them especially those who have profited from the old order, might continue their support of a policy of aggression, it is very unlikely that they would be sufficient in number and financial strength to succeed in doing so. Rather, the likely outcome would be that the honest companies would develop the strength needed—alone or in a combined effort and supported in this effort by their

---

[34]See Bernard Bailyn, *The Ideological Origins of the American Revolution* (Cambridge, Mass.: Harvard University Press, 1967); Jackson Turner Main, *The Anti-Federalists: Critics of the Constitution* (Chapel Hill: University of North Carolina Press, 1961); Murray N. Rothbard, *Conceived in Liberty* (New Rochelle, N.Y.: Arlington House, 1975–1979).

own voluntary customers—to check any such emergence of outlaw
producers and destroy them wherever and whenever they came into
existence.[35]

---

[35]Naturally, insurance companies would assume a particularly important
role in checking the emergence of outlaw companies. Note Morris and Linda
Tannehill (*The Market of Liberty*, pp. 110–11):

> Insurance companies, a very important sector of any totally free econ-
> omy, would have a special incentive to dissociate themselves from any
> aggressor and, in addition, to bring all their considerable business
> influence to bear against him. *Aggressive violence causes value loss*,
> and the insurance industry would suffer the major cost in most such
> value losses. An unrestrained aggressor is a walking liability, and no
> insurance company, however remotely removed from his original
> aggression, would wish to sustain the risk that he might aggress
> against one of its own clients next. Besides, aggressors and those who
> associate with them are more likely to be involved in situations of vio-
> lence and are, thus, bad insurance risks. An insurance company
> would probably refuse coverage to such people out of a foresighted
> desire to minimize any future losses which their aggression might
> cause. But even if the company were not motivated by such foresight,
> it would still be forced to rate their premiums up drastically or cancel
> their coverage altogether in order to avoid carrying the extra risk
> invoked in their inclination to violence. In a competitive economy, no
> insurance company could afford to continue covering aggressors and
> those who had dealings with aggressors and simply pass the cost on to
> its honest customers; it would soon lose these customers to more rep-
> utable firms which could afford to charge less for their insurance cov-
> erage.

2

The Economics and Sociology of Taxation

A s the title of the chapter indicates, I have set myself two goals. First, I want to explain the general economic effect of taxation. This part of the chapter represents a praxeological analysis of taxation and as such should not be expected to go much beyond what has already been said by other economists.

More originality might be found in the second part, where I will try to answer the question: why is there taxation; and why is there always more of it? Answering such questions is not the task of economic theory but of praxeologically informed and constrained sociological or historical interpretations and reconstructions, and from the very outset much more room for speculation in this field of intellectual inquiry exists.

I.

To say there is nothing new to be stated regarding the economic effects of taxation is not to say that what there *is* would not be news to many. In fact, after surveying several popular economics textbooks it would seem that what I have to say is news to most of today's economists and students of economics. Insofar as these texts deal with the

[Reprinted from the *Journal des Economistes et des Etudes Humaines* 1, no. 2 (1990.)]

economic effects of taxation at all, beyond a purely descriptive presentation of various tax-schemes and their historical development[1],
they are almost completely silent on the question of what the general
effects of taxation are. Moreover, what in their discussion of the
problem of tax-incidence these texts then say about the economic
effects of specific forms of taxation is invariably flawed.

However, this state of affairs merely reflects a process of intellectual degeneration. As early as 150 years ago almost everything that
should be understood today about the economics of taxation had
been correctly and convincingly stated by such a prominent figure in
the history of economics as Jean Baptiste Say in his *Treatise on Political Economy*.

In contrast to today's textbook writers, who assign the discussion
of taxation to arbitrary places within the overall architectonic of their
books, from the beginning Say correctly locates the phenomenon
under the general heading "Of the Consumption of Wealth."

He then unmistakenly identifies and explains taxation as an attack
on and punishment of the acquisition and production of property,
which necessarily leads to a reduction in the formation of wealth
embodied in such property and to a lowering of the general standard
of living.

Notes Say:

> It is a glaring absurdity to pretend, that taxation contributes to
> national wealth, by engrossing part of the national produce, and
> enriches the nation by consuming part of its wealth.[2]

> Taxation is the transfer of a portion of the national products from
> the hands of individuals to those of the government, for the pur-
> pose of meeting public consumption or expenditure. Whatever be
> the denomination it bears, whether tax, contribution, duty, excise,
> custom, aid, subsidy, grant, or free gift, it is virtually a burden

---

[1]Exclusively descriptive analyses of taxation are given, for instance, by Paul
Samuelson, *Economics*, 10th ed. (New York: McGraw Hill, 1976), chap. 9;
Roger L. Miller, *Economics Today*, 6th ed. (New York: Harper and Row, 1988),
chap. 6.

[2]Jean Baptiste Say, *A Treatise on Political Economy* (New York: Augustus M.
Kelley, 1964), pp. 446–47.

imposed upon individuals, either in a separate or corporate character, by the ruling power for the time being, for the purpose of supplying the consumption it may think proper to make at their expense; in short, an impost, in the literal sense.[3]

Since such fundamental insights seem to have been forgotten, or at least no longer appear obvious today, let me, as my first task, present anew a praxeological account and explanation for Say's central argument and its validity, and in so doing refute some popular "counterarguments" claiming to show that taxation need not obstruct the formation of property and wealth. In light of this general explanation, I will then demonstrate the fundamental logical fallacy in the standard textbook analysis of tax-incidence.

That taxation—foremost and above all—is and must be understood as a means for the destruction of property and wealth-formation follows from a simple logical analysis of the meaning of taxation.

Taxation is a coercive, non-contractual transfer of definite physical assets (nowadays mostly, but not exclusively money), and the value embodied in them, from a person or group of persons who first held these assets and who could have derived an income from further holding them, to another, who now possesses them and now derives an income from so doing. How did these assets come into the hands of their original owners? Ruling out that this was the outcome of another previous act of taxation, and noting that only those assets can be taxed that have not yet been consumed or whose value has not yet been exhausted through acts of consumption (a tax-gatherer does not take away another man's garbage but rather his still valuable assets!), three and only three possibilities exist: They come into one's possession either by one's having perceived certain nature-given goods as scarce and having actively brought them into one's possession before anyone else had seen and done so; by having produced them by means of one's labor out of such previously appropriated goods; or through voluntary, contractual acquisition from a previous appropriator or producer. Only through these types of activities is one capable

---

[3]Ibid., p. 446; on Say's economic analysis of taxation see also Murray N. Rothbard, "The Myth of Neutral Taxation," *Cato Journal* (Fall, 1981), esp. pp. 551–54.

of acquiring and increasing valuable—and hence taxable—assets. Acts of original appropriation turn something which no one had previously perceived as a possible source of income into an income-providing asset; acts of production are by their very nature aimed at the transformation of a less valuable asset into a more valuable one; and every contractual exchange concerns the change and redirection of specific assets from the hands of those who value their possession less to those who value them more.

From this it follows that any form of taxation implies a reduction of income a person can expect to receive from original appropriation, from production, or from contracting. Since these activities require the employment of scarce means—at least time and the use of one's body—which could be used for consumption and/or leisure, the opportunity cost of performing them is raised. The marginal utility of appropriating, producing, and contracting is decreased, and the marginal utility of consumption and leisure increased. Accordingly, there will be a tendency to shift out of the former roles and into the latter ones.[4]

Thus, by coercively transferring valuable, not yet consumed assets from their producers (in the wider sense of the term including appropriators and contractors) to people who have not produced them, taxation reduces producers' present income and their presently possible level of consumption. Moreover, it reduces the present incentive for future production of valuable assets and thereby also lowers future income and the future level of available consumption. Taxation is not just a punishment of consumption without any effect on productive efforts; it is also an assault on production as the only means of providing for and possibly increasing future income and consumption expenditure. By lowering the present value associated with future-directed, value-productive efforts, taxation raises the effective rate of time preference, i.e., the rate of originary interest and, accordingly, leads to a shortening of the period of production and provision and so exerts an inexorable influence of pushing mankind into the

---

[4]See on this also Murray N. Rothbard, *Man, Economy, and State* (Los Angeles: Nash, 1970), chap. 12.8; idem, *Power and Market* (Kansas City: Sheed Andrews and McMeel, 1977), chap. 4, 1–3.

direction of an existence of living from hand to mouth. Just increase taxation enough, and you will have mankind reduced to the level of barbaric animal beasts.

Straightforward as such reasoning may seem, there are a number of popular objections raised against it. For instance, from the side of economists who falsely conceive of economics as an empirical science that produces nothing but hypothetical explanations which invariably must be tested against empirical evidence in order to be validated (analogous to the situation in the natural sciences), the following argument is frequently heard: Empirically, it has been observed repeatedly that a rise in the level of taxation was actually accompanied by a rise (not a fall) in GNP or other measures of productive output; hence, the above reasoning, however plausible, must be considered empirically invalid. In fact, some empiricists of this sort go even further and make the stronger claim that taxation actually helps increase the standard of living as evidenced by the fact that some countries with once low standards of living and low levels of taxation now enjoy a much greater wealth with much higher taxes.

Both objections are simply confused. Experience cannot beat logic, and interpretations of observational evidence which are not in line with the laws of logical reasoning are no refutation of these but the sign of a muddled mind (or would one accept someone's observational report that he had seen a bird that was red and non-red all over at the same time as a refutation of the law of contradiction rather than the pronouncement of an idiot?).

As regards the stronger thesis, it is nothing but a beautiful illustration of the ever so attractive *post hoc ergo propter hoc* fallacy. From the fact that the correlated events of high taxation and wealth were to be observed later than those of low taxation and wealth it is inferred that increased taxation increases wealth. Yet to reason in this way is about as convincing as the argument—justly ridiculed by Say— that one can observe rich men consuming more than poor ones; therefore, their high level of consumption must be responsible for the fact that they are rich.[5] Just as it follows from the meaning of

---

[5]See Say, *A Treatise on Political Economy*, p. 448.

consumption that this is impossible and that, on the contrary, the rich are not rich because of their high level of consumption but because they previously abstained from consumption and engaged instead in value-productive actions, so it follows from the meaning of taxation that mankind cannot have prospered because of higher levels of taxation but despite such a fact.

The weaker thesis—that experience would at least disprove any claim of a relationship between taxation and productive output that was negative by necessity—is also off the mark. The praxeological reasoning presented above does not at all rule out what empiricist economists falsely interpret as a refutation. In this earlier discussion the conclusion had been reached that the effect of taxation is a relative reduction in the production of valuable assets—a reduction, that is, as compared with the level of output that would have been produced had there been no taxation at all or had the level of taxation not been raised. Nothing was said or implied with respect to the absolute level of the output of valuable assets. As a matter of fact, absolute growth of GNP, for instance, is not only compatible with our earlier praxeological analysis, but can even be seen as a perfectly normal phenomenon to the extent that advances in productivity are possible and actually take place. If it has become possible through improvements in the technology of production to produce a higher output with an identical input (in terms of cost), or a physically identical output with a reduced input, then the coincidence of increased taxation and an increased output of valuable assets is anything but surprising. However, this does not in the least affect the validity of what has been stated about relative impoverishment resulting from taxation. With a given state of technological knowledge, though it may change over time, and taxation being what it is (a punishment of value-productive efforts), the level of productive output must be lower than the one that could have been attained with the same knowledge and no or lower taxation. Statistical studies here are entirely beside the point: they can neither help strengthen it, nor can they ever be used to weaken it.

Another theoretical objection which enjoys some popularity is that imposing or raising taxes leads to a reduction of income derived from the assets taxed; that this reduction raises the marginal utility of such assets as compared to what can be derived from other forms of activity; and thus, instead of lowering it, taxation actually helps increase the tendency to engage in production. For the usual case of taxing money assets this is to say that taxes reduce monetary income which raises the marginal utility of money, and this in turn increases the incentive to attain monetary returns. This argument, to be sure, is perfectly true as far as it goes. However, it is a misconception to believe that it does anything to invalidate the relative impoverishment thesis that I have advanced. First of all, in order to keep the record straight it should be noted that even if it were true—as the just presented argument seems to suggest, albeit falsely as we will see— that increased taxation does not lead to a relatively lower output of valuable assets produced since it spurs a proportional increase in workaholism, it is still the case that the income of value-productive individuals has fallen. Even if they produce the same output as previously, they can only do so if they expend more labor now than before. Since any additional labor expenditure implies forgone leisure or consumption (leisure or consumption which they otherwise could have enjoyed along with the same output of valuable assets), their overall standard of living must be lower.[6]

It now becomes apparent why the assumption that taxation can leave the productive output of valuable assets unaffected and exclusively cripple consumption is fatally flawed. If taxation reduces one's income (which includes that derived from present consumption and leisure), and given the universal fact of time preference, that is, that human actors invariably prefer present goods over future goods (that they cannot do without continuous consumption and can engage in lengthier, more roundabout methods of production only if a provision in the form of consumption goods has been made for the corresponding waiting period), then it necessarily follows that a person's effective rate of time preference must have been raised through this very act (the disutility of waiting must have increased), and that he will have to shorten the length of the structure of production as compared to the one that he otherwise would have chosen. Accordingly,

---

[6]See on this point also Rothbard, *Power and Market*, pp. 95f.

his output of valuable assets available at future dates will have to be lower than would be the case otherwise. If with lower or no taxation his income had been higher and his time preference schedule being given (whatever it happens to be at any particular point in time), he would have invested in lengthier production processes. As a consequence, his output of valuable future assets would have been relatively greater.[7]

---

[7]One might object here that the tax receipts will come into someone's hands—those of government officials or of governmental transfer-payment-recipients—and that their increased income, resulting in a lower effective time preference rate for them, may offset the increase in this rate on the taxpayers' side and hence leave the overall rate and the structure of production unchanged. Such reasoning, however, is categorically flawed: For one thing, insofar as government expenditure is concerned, it cannot be regarded as investment at all. Rather, it is consumption, and consumption alone. For, as Rothbard has explained,

> [i]n any sort of division-of-labor economy, capital goods are built, not for their own sake by the investor, but in order to use them to produce lower-order and eventually consumers' goods. In short, a characteristic of an investment expenditure is that the good in question is not being used to fulfill the needs of the investor, but of someone else—the consumer. Yet, when government confiscates resources from the private market economy, it is precisely defying the wishes of the consumers; when government invests in any good, it does so to serve the whims of government officials, not the desires of consumers. (*Man, Economy, and State*, pp. 816–17)

Thus, government expenditure, by definition, cannot be conceived of as lengthening the production structure and hence as counterbalancing the taxpayers' raised time preference rate.—On the other hand,

> as for the *transfer* expenditures made by the government (including the salaries of bureaucrats and subsidies to privileged groups), it is true that some of this will be saved and invested. These investments, however, will not represent the voluntary desires of consumers, but rather investments in fields of production *not* desired by the *producing* consumers. . . . Once let the tax be eliminated, and . . . the new investments called forth by the demands of the specially privileged will turn out to be *malinvestments*. (*Power and Market*, p. 98)

Consequently, transfer expenditures also cannot be conceived of as compensating for the fact that taxpayers shorten the length of the production structure. All

The error in the thesis that taxation can have a neutral effect on production lies in the fact that time preference is not taken into account. The argument presently under scrutiny is quite correct in pointing out that taxation implies a twofold signal: on the one hand the substitution effect working in favor of consumption and leisure and against work; and on the other hand the income effect of raising the marginal utility of the taxed asset. However, it is false to interpret this simplistically as a mixed bag of contradictory signals—one in favor of and one against work—so that one can then state nothing of a categorical nature regarding the effects of taxation on production, and the question of whether or not taxation provides for a lower or a higher output of valuable assets must be conceived of as an entirely empirical one.[8] For in fact, the signal of taxation is not contradictory at all once it has been recognized that it is being sent to persons whose actions are invariably constrained by time preference. For such actors there exists not only the alternative between work and no work at all but also one between producing a valuable asset in more or less time-consuming ways. Invariably, they must also choose between obtaining an asset quickly and directly, with little waiting time involved, but at the price of having to resort to less efficient methods of production (the famous fisherman who decides to use his bare hands to catch fish in order to obtain it more quickly than by going through more roundabout methods of production), or obtaining it through more productive methods but then having to wait longer for them to bear fruit (the fisherman who, lured by higher future returns,

---

such expenditures can do is to lengthen the structure of mal-production. "At any rate" concludes Rothbard,

> the amount consumed by the government insures that the effect of income taxation will be to raise time-preference ratios and to reduce saving and investment. (Ibid., p. 98)

[8]See for such—irrelevant—empirical studies regarding the relative importance of income vs. substitution effects George F. Break, "The Incidence and Economic Effects of Taxation," in *The Economics of Public Finance* (Washington, D.C.: Brookings, 1974), pp. 180ff.; A.B. Atkinson and Joseph E. Stiglitz, *Lectures on Public Economics* (New York: McGraw Hill, 1980), pp. 48ff.; Stiglitz, *Economics of the Public Sector* (New York: Norton, 1986), p. 372.

decides to endure a longer waiting period and first builds a net).
However, given these choices, the message of taxation is completely
unambiguous and unequivocal, and there can no longer be any question that the substitution effect must be thought of as systematically
dominating any income effect: If there is not only the option of having something or not having it but also of having less of something
sooner or more of it later, the double message sent through taxation
is easily integrated and translated into one: reduce the waiting time;
shorten the roundabout methods of production! By doing so, valuable assets will be obtained earlier—in line with their increased marginal utility. Simultaneously, in shortening the waiting period, more
room will be given for leisure—in line with its increased marginal
utility. By reducing the length of roundabout methods of production
the two seemingly contradictory signals stemming from taxation are
simultaneously accounted for. Contrary to any claim of a systematically "neutral" effect of taxation on production, the consequence of
any such shortening of roundabout methods of production is a lower
output produced. The price that invariably must be paid for taxation,
and for every increase in taxation, is a coercively lowered productivity that in turn reduces the standard of living in terms of valuable
assets provided for future consumption. Every act of taxation necessarily exerts a push away from more highly capitalized, more productive production processes in the direction of a hand-to-mouth-exis-
tence.

It is not difficult to illustrate the validity of these conclusions if one
considers the all-too-familiar case of taxing money assets. Such assets
are only acquired and held because they can purchase other valuable
assets at future dates. They have no own intrinsic use-value at all (as
in the case of a fiat paper money), or such use-value is insignificant
compared to the exchange-value (as in the case of the gold standard
where money also has an—albeit small—commodity value). Rather,
the value attached to them is due to their future purchasing power.
Yet if the value of money consists of representing other future available assets, the effects of taxing money becomes clear immediately.
Most importantly, along with increasing the marginal utility of leisure
or consumption, such a tax increases the marginal utility of such

future assets. This change in the constellation of incentives translates itself for an actor into increased attempts to obtain these assets more quickly, in less time-consuming production processes. The only production processes now that are systematically shorter than those of attaining future assets indirectly, via the earlier acquisition of money, are those of acquiring them through direct exchanges. Thus, taxation implies that barter trade will be substituted increasingly for the lengthier roundabout production method of monetary exchanges. But once again, resorting increasingly to barter is a regression to economic primitivism and barbarism. It was precisely because production for bartering purposes yielded an extremely low output that mankind actually outgrew this developmental stage and instead increasingly resorted to and expanded a system of production-for-indirect-exchange purposes which, while requiring a longer waiting period, renders a far larger return of ever more and different assets drawn into the cash nexus. Every act of taxation means a coerced step backward in this process. It reduces output, decreases the extent of the division of labor, and leads to a reduction in social and economic integration (which, it may be noted, could never have become worldwide, were it not for the institution of indirect monetary exchanges).

Furthermore, the general tendency towards increasingly adopting direct instead of indirect exchange mechanisms caused by every coercive seizure of money also has highly important consequences with regard to the methods of attaining money itself. Just as in the case of non-monetary assets, the increased marginal utility of money along with that of leisure-consumption also makes it relatively more attractive to acquire money in less time-consuming ways. Instead of acquiring it in return for value-productive efforts, i.e., within the framework of mutually beneficial exchanges, taxation raises the incentive to acquire it more quickly and directly, without having to go through such tediously roundabout methods as producing and contracting. On the one hand, this means that one will try more frequently to increase one's money assets by simply hiding them from the tax collector. On the other hand, a growing tendency will emerge to come into the possession of money through coercive seizure—either in the illegal form called stealing, or legally, by participating in the game called politics.[9]

Having completed this general economic analysis of the effects of taxation, which today's economic textbook writers typically prefer not to deal with at all, let me now turn to what they typically do say about the effects of taxation under the heading of tax-incidence. In light of our previous analysis it will be easy to detect the fatal flaw in such accounts. Indeed, that one should fall headlong into error in dealing with specifics if one has not bothered to study the basics can hardly come as a complete surprise.

The standard account of the problem of tax-incidence most frequently exemplified by the case of an excise or sales tax goes like this:[10] Suppose an excise or sales tax is imposed. Who must bear the burden of this? It is recognized—and I have of course no intention of disputing the validity of this—that in one sense there can be no

---

[9]Here once again what has already been explained in a somewhat different connection in note 7 above becomes evident: why it is a fundamental mistake to think that taxation might have a "neutral" effect on production such that any "negative" effects on tax*payers* may be compensated by corresponding "positive" effects on tax *spenders*. What is overlooked in this sort of reasoning is that the introduction of taxation not only implies favoring nonproducers at the expense of producers. It simultaneously changes, for producers and nonproducers alike, the cost attached to different methods of attaining an income, for it is then relatively less costly to attain an additional income through nonproductive means, i.e., not through actually producing more goods but by participating in the process of noncontractual acquisitions of already produced goods. If such a different incentive structure is applied to a given population, then the length of the production structure will necessarily be shortened, and a decrease in the output of goods produced must result. See on this also Hans-Hermann Hoppe, *A Theory of Socialism and Capitalism* (Boston: Kluwer Academic Publishers, 1989), chap. 4.

[10]See for instance William Baumol and Alan Blinder, *Economics: Principles and Policy* (New York: Harcourt Brace Jovanovich, 1979), pp. 636ff.; Daniel R. Fusfeld, *Economics: Principles of Political Economy*, 3rd ed. (Glenview, Ill.: Scott, Foresman, 1987), pp. 639ff.; Robert Ekelund and Robert Tollison, *Microeconomics*, 2nd ed. (Glenview, Ill.: Scott, Foresman, 1988), pp. 463ff. and 469f.; Stanley Fisher, Rudiger Dornbusch, and Richard Schmalensee, *Microeconomics*, 2nd ed. (New York: McGraw Hill, 1988), pp. 385f.

question that consumers must take the brunt, and invariably do. For no matter what the specific consequences of such a tax are, it must either be the case that consumers will have to pay a higher price for the same goods and their standard of living will be impaired because of this, or it must be the case that the tax imposes higher costs on producers, and consumers will then be punished because of a lower output produced. However, and it is with this that we will have to disagree sharply, it is then argued that whether or not the imposition of a tax harms consumers in the former or in the latter way is an open empirical question, the answer to which depends on the elasticity of demand for the taxed products. If the demand is sufficiently inelastic, then producers will shift the entire burden onto consumers in the form of higher prices. If it is highly elastic, then producers will have to absorb the tax in the form of higher costs of production, and if some section of the demand curve is inelastic and another elastic (this allegedly being empirically the most frequent case), then the burden somehow will have to be shared, with part of it being shifted onto consumers and another falling on producers.

What is wrong with this sort of argument? While it is couched in terms different from those used in my earlier analysis, one can hardly fail to notice that it merely restates, on a somewhat more specific level of discussion, what has already been demonstrated as false on a more general level: the thesis that taxes may or may not reduce productive output; that there is no necessary connection between taxes and productive output; and that it must be considered empirically possible that a tax may affect consumption exclusively while production remains untouched. To assume, as the textbook-account of tax-incidence does, that taxes can be shifted forward, either totally or partially, onto consumers is simply to say that a tax may not negatively affect production. For if it were possible to shift any amount of a tax forward onto consumers, that amount would represent a "non-production tax," a tax exclusively on consumption.[11]

---

[11]On the impossibility of a pure consumption tax see also Rothbard, *Power and Market*, pp. 108ff.

In order to refute the typical textbook analysis, one could simply
go back to our previous discussion that resulted in the conclusion that
any tax imposed on people constrained by time preference must
negatively affect production above and beyond any negative consequences that it implies for consumption. However, I will choose a
somewhat different route of argument here in order to make
essentially the same point and thereby establish the more specific
thesis that no amount of any tax can be shifted onto consumers. To
assume otherwise is to assume something manifestly impossible.

The absurdity of the tax-forward-shifting doctrine becomes clear
as soon as one tries to apply it to the case of a single actor who continuously acts in both roles—that of a producer and a consumer. For
such a producer-consumer, the doctrine amounts to this proposition:
If he is faced with an increase in the costs of attaining some future
good—an increase, that is, that he himself perceives as a cost-increas-
ing event—then he shifts these higher costs onto himself in such a
way that he responds by attaching a correspondingly higher value to
the good to be obtained, thereby restoring his old profit-margin, thus
leaving his role as producer unchanged and unimpaired, and requiring restrictive adjustments exclusively in his role as a consumer. Or,
formulated even more drastically, insofar as his value-productive
efforts are concerned, a tax does not make any difference for an individual, because he just starts liking the to-be-produced good correspondingly more.

Plain reasoning reveals that what generates such absurdity is a
fundamental conceptual confusion: The forward-shifting doctrine
arises from not recognizing that in one's analysis one must assume
that demand is given—and that this must be assumed because it in
fact is given at any point in time. Any analysis that loses track of this
is flawed, for if one were to assume that demand had changed, then
everything would be possible: production might increase, decrease,
or remain unchanged. If I am a producer of tea and tea is taxed and
if it is assumed that the demand schedule for tea rises concurrently,
then, naturally, it is possible that people are now willing to pay a
higher price for tea than previously. Yet this is obviously not a forward shifting of the tax but the result of a change in demand. To present this possibility under the heading of tax-incidence analysis is plain

nonsense: it is in fact an analysis of the entirely different question of how prices are affected by changes in demand and has nothing whatsoever to do with the effects of taxation. The confusion here is on as grand a scale as that which one would encounter if someone were to "refute" the statement that one apple and another make two by saying "No, I have just added another apple, and look, there are not two but three apples here." It is hard to get away with such nonsense in math; in economics a doctrine hardly less absurd is the orthodoxy.

Yet if one is logically committed to assuming demand to be given whenever one tries to answer the question whether or not a tax can be shifted forward, every tax must be interpreted as an event that exclusively affects the supply side: it reduces the supplies at the disposal of suppliers.[12] Any other conclusion would amount to a denial of what had been assumed from the outset—that a tax had indeed been imposed and perceived as such by producers. To say that only the supply curve is shifted whenever a tax is extracted (while the demand curve remains the same as before) is to say nothing else than that the entire tax-burden must in fact be absorbed by the suppliers. To be sure, the leftward shift of the supply curve would cause prices to rise and consumers would naturally be harmed by having to pay these higher prices and by only being able to afford a smaller amount of goods at such a price.[13] Yet that consumers will invariably be hurt by taxes has of course never been doubted as one should recall. However, it is a misconception to think that this higher price is a shifting of the tax burden from producers to consumers. Rather, consumers are hurt here "only" by harm being done to producers who, despite higher prices charged for their supplies, must bear the brunt.[14] One must ask oneself why, if an entrepreneur could indeed shift any amount of the tax-burden away from himself and onto consumers, he

---

[12]Baumol and Blinder, *Economics: Principles and Policy*, p. 636, present the *demand* curve as changing in response to a tax.

[13]To avoid any misunderstanding then: Insofar as the textbook analyses of tax-incidence point out this fact they are of course entirely correct. It is the interpretation of this phenomenon they give which is fundamentally confused!

[14]See on this point also Rothbard, *Man, Economy, and State*, p. 809.

would not have already done so by voluntarily imposing a tax on himself instead of waiting for the actual coercive tax to come along! The answer is clear: At all times he is constrained in his price-setting activity by the actual given demand. The price set by any entrepreneur is set with the expectation that a price higher than the one actually chosen would yield a lower total revenue. Otherwise, if he expected a higher price to bring about a larger revenue he would raise it. As long as an entrepreneur expects the demand to be inelastic within the region of any price-range under consideration, he will take advantage of this and choose the higher price. He stops raising prices and settles for a specific one because his expectations are reversed and he anticipates the demand curve above this price to be elastic. These expectations regarding inelastic and elastic portions of the demand curve are not at all changed if the entrepreneur is faced with a tax. Then as now he expects higher prices to produce revenue losses. Thus, it is obviously out of the question to argue that he could escape the burden of the tax. In fact, if as a consequence of the reduced supply the price now rises, this upward movement must be into an elastic portion of the demand curve, and the entrepreneur thus must assumedly pay the full price of it in the form of reduced revenue. Any other conclusion is logically flawed. Only if the entrepreneur expects a change in demand occurring simultaneously with taxation could he change his price without thereby incurring losses. If he expects demand to have increased, for instance, such that there will now be an inelastic rather than an elastic stretch of the demand curve above the presently going price, he will be able to raise it without punishment. Again, this is not a forward shifting of the tax. This is increased demand. With or without the tax the entrepreneur would have acted in precisely the same way. The tax has nothing to do with such price changes. In any case, the tax must be paid exclusively and in full by the suppliers of the taxed goods.[15]

---

[15]Should a tax not immediately affect supply at all, as can happen in the short run, then it follows from the above analysis that the price charged will not change at all. For to raise it in response to the tax would once again imply pushing it into an elastic region of the demand curve. In the long run the supply will have to be relatively reduced and prices must move into this region. In any case,

II.

There can be no doubt, then, that taxes invariably reduce production and with this the consumer's standard of living. Whichever way things are put, there is no escaping the conclusion that taxation is a means of obstructing the formation of wealth and thereby creating relative impoverishment.

This brings me to my second subject: the sociology of taxation. If taxation is an instrument for the destruction of wealth-formation, then the question immediately becomes pressing of how it can be explained that there is taxation; that there is ever more of it; that we have experienced, in particular during the last hundred years, a steady increase not just in the absolute but also in the relative level of taxation; and that the institutions which lead the way in this process, the tax-states of the Western World, have simultaneously assumed ever more powerful positions in the arena of international politics and increasingly dominate the rest of the world.

With these questions one leaves the realm of economic theory. Economics answers the question "What is the consequence if taxation is introduced?" It deduces its answer from an understanding of the meaning of action and the meaning of taxation as a particular type of action. Why there is taxation is the subject matter of psychology, history, or sociology. Economics, or rather praxeology, recognizes that all actions are determined by ideas, correct or incorrect, good or bad. But it does not attempt to explain what these ideas are and how people come to hold or change them. Rather, it assumes them to be given and aims at explaining the logical consequences that flow from acting upon them, whatever they are. History and sociology ask what these ideas are, how people come to entertain them, and why they act the way they do.[16]

---

no forward shifting takes place. See on this also Rothbard, *Man, Economy, and State*, pp. 807ff.; idem, *Power and Market*, pp. 88ff.

[16]To make this distinction between economics and history or sociology is not to say, of course, that economics is of no importance for these latter disciplines. In fact, economics is indispensable for all other social sciences. While the reverse is not the case, economics can be developed and advanced without historical or

On a highly abstract level the answer to the question why there is steadily increasing taxation is this: The root cause for this is a slow but dramatic change in the idea of justice that has taken place in public opinion.

Let me explain. One can acquire property either through homesteading, production, and contracting, or else through the expropriation and exploitation of homesteaders, producers, or contractors. There are no other ways.[17] Both methods are natural to mankind. Alongside production and contracting there has always been a process of nonproductive and noncontractual property acquisitions. Just as productive enterprises can develop into firms and corporations, so can the business of expropriating and exploiting occur on a larger scale and develop into governments and states.[18] That taxation as such exists and that there is the drive toward increased taxation

---

sociological knowledge. The only consequence of doing so is that such economics would probably not be very interesting, as it would be written without consideration of real examples or instances of application (as if one were to write on the economics of taxation even though there had never been an actual example of it in all of history), for it would formulate what could not possibly happen in the social world, or what would have to happen provided that certain conditions were in fact fulfilled. Thus, any historical or sociological explanation is logically constrained by the laws as espoused by economic theory, and any account by a historian or sociologist in violation of these laws must be treated as ultimately confused. On the relationship between economic theory and history see also Ludwig von Mises, *Theory and History* (Auburn, Ala.: Ludwig von Mises Institute, 1985); Hans-Hermann Hoppe, *Praxeology and Economic Science* (Auburn, Ala.: Ludwig von Mises Institute, 1988).

[17]See on this also Franz Oppenheimer, *The State* (New York: Vanguard Press, 1914) esp. pp. 24–27; Rothbard, *Power and Market*, chap. 2; Hoppe, *A Theory of Socialism and Capitalism*, chap. 2.

[18]On the theory of the state as developed in the following see—in addition to the works cited in note 17—in particular Herbert Spencer, *Social Statics* (New York: Schalkenbach Foundation, 1970); Auberon Herbert, *The Right and Wrong of Compulsion by the State* (Indianapolis: Liberty Fund, 1978); Albert J. Nock, *Our Enemy, the State* (Tampa, Fla.: Hallberg Publishing, 1983); Murray N. Rothbard, *For a New Liberty* (New York: Macmillan, 1978); idem, *The Ethics of Liberty* (Atlantic Highlands, N.J.: Humanities Press, 1982); Hans-Hermann Hoppe, *Eigentum, Anarchie und Staat* (Opladen: Westdeutscher Verlag, 1987); Anthony de Jasay, *The State* (Oxford: Blackwell, 1985).

should hardly come as a surprise. For the idea of nonproductive or noncontractual appropriations is almost as old as the idea of productive ones, and everyone—the exploiter certainly no less than the producer—prefers a higher income to a lower one.

The decisive question is this: what controls and constrains the size and growth of such a business?

It should be clear that the constraints on the size of firms in the business of expropriating producers and contractors are of a categorically different nature than those limiting the size of firms engaged in productive exchanges. Contrary to the claim of the public choice school, government and private firms do not do essentially the same sort of business. They are engaged in categorically different types of operations.[19]

---

[19]This central idea of the public choice school has been expressed by its foremost representatives as follows:

> Both the economic relation and the political relation represent co-operation on the part of two or more individuals. The market and the state are both devices through which co-operation is organized and made possible. Men co-operate through exchange of goods and services in organized markets, and such co-operation implies mutual gain. The individual enters into an exchange relationship in which he furthers his own interest by providing some product or service that is of direct benefit to the individual on the other side of the transaction. At base, political or collective action under the individualistic view of the State is much the same. Two or more individuals find it mutually advantageous to join forces to accomplish certain common purposes. In a very real sense, they "exchange" and devote resources to the construction of the common good. (James M. Buchanan and Gordon Tullock, *The Calculus of Consent* [Ann Arbor: University of Michigan Press], p. 192)

Surely, the most amazing thing about such a "new theory of politics" is that anyone takes it seriously. Remarks Joseph A. Schumpeter on such views:

> The theory which construes taxes on the analogy of club dues or the purchase of the service of, say, a doctor only proves how far removed this part of the social sciences is from scientific habits of mind. (*Capitalism, Socialism and Democracy* [New York: Harper, 1942], p. 198)

And H.L. Mencken has this to say regarding a thesis such as Buchanan's and Tullock's:

The size of a productive enterprise is constrained on the one hand by consumer demand (which imposes a definite limit on the total revenue attainable), and on the other hand by the competition of other producers, which continuously forces each firm to operate with the lowest possible costs if it wishes to stay in business. For such an enterprise to grow in size the most urgent consumer wants must be served in the most efficient ways. Nothing but voluntary consumer purchases support its size.

The constraints on the other type of firm, of government or the state, are altogether different. For one thing, it is absurd to say that its size is determined by demand in the same sense as the size of a private firm is determined by demand. One cannot say, by any stretch of the imagination, that the homesteaders, the producers, and the contractors who must surrender part of their assets to a government have demanded such a service. Instead, they must be coerced into accepting it, and this is conclusive proof of the fact that the service is not actually in demand at all. Hence, demand cannot be considered as a limit on the size of government. Insofar as it grows, the state grows by acting in open *contradiction* to demand.

The state is also not in the same way constrained by competition as is a productive firm. Unlike such a firm, the state must not keep its

------

The average man, whatever his errors otherwise, at least sees clearly that government is something lying outside him and outside the generality of his fellow men—that it is a separate, independent and often hostile power, only partly under his control, and capable of doing him great harm. . . . Is it a fact of no significance that robbing the government is everywhere regarded as a crime of less magnitude than robbing an individual, or even a corporation? . . . When a private citizen is robbed a worthy man is deprived of the fruits of his industry and thrift; when the government is robbed the worst that happens is that certain rogues and loafers have less money to play with than they had before. The notion that they have earned that money is never entertained; to most sensible men it would seem ludicrous. They are simply rascals who, by accidents of law, have a somewhat dubious right to a share in the earnings of their fellow men. When that share is diminished by private enterprise the business is, on the whole, far more laudable than not. (*A Mencken Chrestomathy* [New York: Vintage Books, 1949] pp. 146–47)

cost of operation at a minimum but can operate at above-minimum costs because it is able to shift its higher costs onto competitors by taxing or regulating their behavior. Thus, the size of the state also cannot be considered as constrained by cost competition. Insofar as it grows, it does so in spite of the fact that it is *not* cost-efficient.

This, however, is not to say that the size of government is not constrained at all and that the historical fluctuations in the size of states are mere random walks. It only states that the constraints on the firm "government" must be fundamentally different.

Instead of being constrained by cost and demand conditions, the growth of an exploitative firm is constrained by public opinion:[20] It is not voluntarily supported, but by its very nature employs coercion. On the other side of the same coin, coercion implies creating victims, and victims are not supporters but active or passive resisters of a firm's size. It is conceivable that this resistance can be lastingly broken by force in the case of one man, or one group of men, exploiting one or maybe two or three others, or another group of roughly the same size. It is inconceivable, however, to imagine that force alone can account for the breaking down of resistance in the actually familiar case of small minorities operating their business of expropriating and exploiting populations tens, hundreds, or thousands of times their size.[21] For this to happen, such a firm must have public support in addition to its coercive force. A majority of the population must accept its operations as legitimate. This acceptance can range from active enthusiasm to passive resignation. But there must be acceptance in the sense that a majority must have given up the idea of

---

[20]See on this also Murray N. Rothbard, "The Anatomy of the State" in idem, *Egalitarianism as a Revolt Against Nature and Other Essays* (Washington, D.C.: Libertarian Review Press, 1974), esp. pp. 37–42.

[21]It might be thought that the government could accomplish such a feat by merely improving its weaponry: by threatening with atomic bombs instead of with guns and rifles, so to speak. However, since realistically one must assume that the technological know-how of such improved weaponry can hardly be kept secret, especially if it is in fact applied, then with the state's improved instruments for instilling fear the victims' ways amid means of resisting improve as well. Hence, such advances must be ruled out as an explanation of what must be explained.

actively or passively resisting any attempt to enforce nonproductive and noncontractual property acquisitions. Instead of displaying outrage over such actions, of showing contempt for everyone who engages in them, and of doing nothing to help make them successful (not to mention actively trying to obstruct them), a majority must actively or passively support them. Only in light of this can it be explained how the few can govern the many. State-supportive public opinion must counterbalance the resistance of victimized property owners to the extent that active resistance appears futile.

The state of public opinion also imposes a constraint on the size of the state in another respect. Every firm in the large-scale business of property expropriation must naturally aim to be a monopolist in a definite territory, for one can only prosper in such a business so long as there is something that can be expropriated. However, if competition were allowed in the business of expropriating, there would obviously be nothing left to take. Hence, in order to stay in business, one must be a monopolist.

Even if there is no internal competition, competition between governments operating in *different* territories still exists, and it is this competition that imposes severe limits on the size of government. On the one hand, it opens up the possibility that people may vote with their feet against a government and leave its territory if they perceive other territories as offering less exploitative living conditions. Naturally, each state must see this as a crucial problem, for it literally lives off a population, and any population loss is thus a loss of potential state-income.[22] Again, the state of public opinion is of utmost importance for maintaining exploitative rule. Only if the state succeeds in generating the impression in the general public that that state's own territory compares favorably, or at least tolerably well with others will it be able to secure and expand its position.

Public opinion also plays a decisive role in the case of interstate aggression. While not a logical necessity, the nature of a state as an exploitative enterprise still makes it highly likely (not the least

---

[22]Witness the all-too-numerous states that go so far as to shoot everyone down without mercy who has committed no other sin than that of trying to leave a territory and move elsewhere!

because of the just addressed problem of population movements) that it will become engaged in aggression against a "foreign" territory, or that it must defend itself against such aggression from other states.[23] Moreover, in order to emerge successfully from such interstate wars or warlike actions, a state must be in command of sufficient (in relative terms) economic resources that alone make its actions sustainable. However, these resources can only be provided by a productive population. Thus, to secure the means necessary to win wars and avoid being confronted with slackening productive outputs while at war, public opinion again turns out to be the decisive variable controlling the size of government. Only if popular support for the state's war exists can it be sustained and possibly won.

Finally, the state of public opinion limits the size of government in yet a third way. While the state maintains its position vis-à-vis the exploited population through coercion and the successful management of public opinion, to maintain its own internal order, which regulates the relationships between the various branches of government and its employees, there is nothing else at its disposal but public opinion, for clearly, no one outside the state exists who could enforce its internal rules upon it. Rather, the enforcement must be accomplished exclusively by means of supportive public opinion among state employees themselves in the various branches of government.[24] That is, the president cannot coerce the general to go to war—in fact, the greater physical strength would probably be on the general's side; and the general in turn cannot coerce his soldiers to do the fighting and killing—in fact, they could smash him anytime. President and general can only succeed because of favorable

---

[23]On the intimate relationship between state and war see the important study by Ekkehart Krippendorff, *Staat und Krieg* (Frankfurt/M.: Suhrkamp, 1985); also Charles Tilly, "War Making and State Making as Organized Crime" in Peter Evans et al., eds., *Bringing the State Back In* (Cambridge: Cambridge University Press, 1985).

[24]This insight (which refutes all talk about the impossibility of anarchism in showing that intra-governmental relations are, in fact, a case of—political— anarchy) has been explained in a highly important article by Alfred G. Cuzán, "Do We Ever Really Get Out of Anarchy," *Journal of Libertarian Studies* 3, no. 2 (1979).

intrastate public opinion, and only insofar as the overwhelming majority of the state employees at least passively supports their actions as legitimate. If, in the various branches of government, a large majority of them were strictly opposed to the enforcement of presidential policy, it could not be put into action successfully. The general who thinks most of his troops consider the war illegitimate or who thinks that the Congress, the IRS, the large majority of public educators and the so-called social services regard such actions as outrageous and to be openly opposed, would face an impossible task even if he himself supported the presidential command.[25]

> Wherever earthly governments are established or exist, anarchy is officially prohibited for all members of society, usually referred to as subjects or citizens. They can no longer relate to each other on their own terms. . . . Rather, all members of society must accept an external "third party"—a government—into their relationships, a third party with the coercive powers to enforce its judgments and punish detractors. . . . However, such a "third party" arrangement for society is non-existent among those who exercise the power of government themselves. In other words, there is no "third party" to make and enforce judgments among the individual members who make up the third party itself. The rulers still remain in a state of anarchy *vis-à-vis* each other. They settle disputes *among themselves*, without regard for a Government (an entity outside themselves). Anarchy still exists. Only whereas without government it was market or natural anarchy, it is now a *political* anarchy, an anarchy inside power. (Cuzán, pp. 152–53)

[25]One of the classic expositors of this idea is David Hume. In his essay, "Of The First Principles of Government," he writes:

> Nothing appears more surprising to those, who consider human affairs with a philosophical eye, than the easiness with which the many are governed by the few; and the implicit submission, with which men resign their own sentiments and passions to those of their rulers. When we enquire by what means this wonder is effected, we shall find, that as FORCE is always on the side of the governed, the governors have nothing to support them but opinion. It is therefore, on opinion only that government is founded; and this maxim extends to the most despotic and most military governments, as well as to the most free and most popular. The soldan of EGYPT, or the emperor of ROME, might drive his harmless subjects, like brute beasts, against their sentiments and inclination: but he must, at least, have led his

With public opinion rather than demand and cost conditions thus identified as the constraining force on the size of government, I return to my original explanation of the phenomenon of ever-increasing taxation as "simply" a change in prevailing ideas.

If it is public opinion that ultimately limits the size of an exploitative firm, then an explanation of its growth in purely ideological terms is justified. Indeed, any other explanation, not in terms of ideological changes but of changes in "objective" conditions must be considered wrong. The size of government does not increase because of any objective causes over which ideas have no control and certainly not because there is a demand for it. It grows because the ideas that prevail in public opinion of what is just and what is wrong have changed. What once was regarded by public opinion as an outrage, to be treated and dealt with as such, has become increasingly accepted as legitimate.

What has happened regarding the general public's conception of justice?[26]

In the aftermath of the fall of the Roman empire, Western Europe gradually fell into a highly anarchic system of territories ruled by small-scale feudal governments. Facilitated by this international anarchy, which tended to reduce each individual government's internal power and ease population movements,[27] and nourished by the

---

mamalukes, or *praetorian bands*, like men, by their opinion. (*Essays, Moral, Political and Literary* [Oxford: Oxford University Press, 1971], p. 19)

[26]See on the following in particular also Murray N. Rothbard, "Left and Right: The Prospects for Liberty" in idem, *Egalitarianism as a Revolt Against Nature and Other Essays.*

[27]The importance of international anarchy for the erosion of feudalism and the rise of capitalism has been justly emphasized by Jean Baechler, *The Origins of Capitalism* (New York: St. Martin's Press, 1976), esp. chap. 7. He writes: "The constant expansion of the market, both in extensiveness and in intensity, was the result of an absence of a political order extending over the whole of Western Europe" (p. 73). "The expansion of capitalism owes its origin and *raison d'etre* to political anarchy. . . . Collectivism and state management have only succeeded in school textbooks" (p. 77).

All power tends toward the absolute. If it is not absolute, this is because some kind of limitations have come into play . . . those in the

ideology of natural law and natural rights, which emerged as an increasingly powerful theory within the intellectual elite of the Catholic Church, man's unmistakable instinct that only private property is compatible with one's nature as a rational being took effect.[28] Small centers developed where governmental power had been whittled away to a degree heretofore unknown: the cities of northern Italy, most notably Venice, those of the Hanseatic League, such as Lübeck and Hamburg, and those of Flanders and the Low Countries, in particular Antwerp and Amsterdam. There, the feudal ideas of bondage, of servitude, and of a hierarchically stratified society of rigidly separated classes was supplanted by public opinion that instead supported freedom, equality, property rights, and contractual relations. This public opinion steadily gained momentum with a continuous influx of new population, inspired by similar ideas and

---

positions of power at the center ceaselessly tried to erode these limitations. They never succeeded, and for the reason that also seems to me to be tied to the international system: a limitation of power to act externally and the constant threat of foreign assault (the two characteristics of a multi-polar system) imply that power is also limited internally and must rely on autonomous centers of decision-making and so may use them only sparingly. (p. 78)

[28]The central characteristic of the modern natural law tradition (as represented by St. Thomas Aquinas, Luis de Molina, Francisco Suarez, and the late sixteenth century Spanish Scholastics, and the Protestant Hugo Grotius) was its thorough rationalism: its idea of universally valid, absolute, and immutable principles of human conduct that are—ultimately independent of any theological beliefs—to be discovered by and founded in and reason alone. "Man," writes Frederick C. Copleston, [*Aquinas* (London: Penguin Books, 1955), pp. 213–14]

cannot read, as it were, the mind of God . . . (but) he can discern the fundamental tendencies and needs of his nature, and by reflecting on them he can come to a knowledge of the natural moral law. . . . Every man possesses . . . the light of reason whereby he can reflect . . . and promulgate to himself the natural law, which is the totality of the universal precepts of dictates of right reason concerning the good which is to be pursued and the evil which is to be shunned.

On the origin and development of the natural rights doctrine and its idea of justice and property (including all the statist failings and slips of its aforementioned heroes) see Richard Tuck, *Natural Rights Theories* (Cambridge: Cambridge University Press, 1979); on the revolutionary character of the idea of natural law

attracted by the unrivaled prosperity that freedom was proving itself capable of producing.[29]

However, the ideas of human rationality, freedom, and private property were not yet widespread enough. Rooted only in a few dispersed areas, the more or less distant feudal powers that naturally

---

see Lord (John) Acton, *Essays on Freedom and Power* (Glencoe, Ill.: Free Press. 1948); as an eminent contemporary natural rights philosopher see Henry Veatch, *Human Rights* (Baton Rouge: Louisiana State University Press, 1985).

[29]On the rise of the cities see C.M. Cipolla, *Before the Industrial Revolution: European Society and Economy 1000–1700* (New York: Norton, 1980), chap. 4. Europe around 1000, writes Cipolla,

> was poor and primitive . . . made up of numberless rural microcosms—the manors. . . . Society was dominated by a spirit of resignation, suspicion, and fear toward the outside world. . . . The arts, education, trade, production, and the division of labor were reduced to a minimal level. The use of money almost completely disappeared. The population was small, production meager, and poverty extreme. . . . The prevailing ideas reflected a brutal and superstitious society— fighting and praying were the only respectable activities. . . . Those who labored were regarded as despicable serfs. . . . In this depressed and depressing world, the rise of cities between the tenth and thirteenth centuries represented a new element which changed the course of history. (p. 144)

> At the root of urban growth was a massive migratory movement. (p. 145)

> The town was to the people of Europe from the eleventh to the thirteenth centuries what America was to Europeans in the nineteenth century. The town was the "frontier," a new and dynamic world where people felt they could break their ties with an unpleasant past, where people hoped they could find opportunities for economic and social success, where sclerotic traditional institutions and discriminations no longer counted, and where there would be ample reward for initiative, daring, and industriousness (p. 146). In the feudal world, a vertical arrangement typically prevailed, where relations between men were dictated by the concepts of fief and service; investiture and homage; lord, vassal, and serf. In the cities, a horizontal arrangement emerged, characterized by cooperation among equals. (p. 148)

See also Henri Pirenne, *Medieval Cities* (Princeton, N.J.: Princeton University Press, 1952), chap. 5; Michael Tigar and Madeleine Levy, *Law and the Rise of Capitalism* (New York: Monthly Review Press, 1977).

recognized such developments as a threat to their own stability could once again reassemble strength. By consolidating their territories in a long process of interfeudal struggles and warfare into large-scale states and thereby concentrating and centralizing their forces, they were able to succeed in crushing the competition of the idea of freedom blossoming in just a few places and reimpose their exploitative rule over such areas with increased strength. The age of absolutism had set in, and with it the age of a feudal super-power, the monarchy, which successfully centralized the system of feudal exploitation over territories that for the first time reached the size of familiar modern nation states. With absolutism taking hold, the competitive territories of free cities were again forced into economic decline and stagnation, which in some cases lasted for centuries.[30]

Yet this victory did not defeat the ideas of freedom and private property. On the contrary, these ideas found ever more powerful expression and increasingly inspired public opinion. Influenced by the continuously advanced natural rights tradition, another secularized intellectual tradition emerged and captivated minds: The tradition of what later became known as classical liberalism and was even more decisively centered around the notion of individual freedom and property and devoted to its intellectual justification.[31] In addition,

---

[30]See on this Carolyn Webber and Aaron Wildavsky, *A History of Taxation and Expenditure in the Western World* (New York: Simon and Schuster, 1986), pp. 235–41; Pirenne, *Medieval Cities*, pp. 179–80, pp. 227f.

[31]As the outstanding champion of this tradition see John Locke, *Two Treatises of Government*, ed. Peter Laslett (Cambridge: Cambridge University Press, 1960).

> [E]very man has a property in his own person. This nobody has any right to but himself. The labour of his body and the work of his hands, we may say, are properly his. Whatsoever then he removes out of the state that nature hath provided, and left in it, he hath mixed his labour with, and joined to it something that is his own, and thereby makes it his property. It being by him removed from the common state nature placed it in, it hath by his labour something annexed to it that excludes the common right of other men. For this labour being the unquestionable property of the labourer, no man but he can have a right to what that is once joined to. (p. 305)

stimulated by the recent experiences of unrivaled prosperity achieved under conditions of freedom and contractualism, the development of economic thinking took great strides. The then orthodox statist doctrines of mercantilism, cameralism, and *Polizeiwissenschaft* became intellectually demolished by a swelling number of new political economists who systematically explained, with great thoroughness and comprehensiveness, the indispensable role of private property and contractualism for the process of production and wealth formation and who accordingly hailed a policy of radical laissez-faire.[32]

From about 1700 onward, public opinion was captivated by these ideas to such an extent that revolutionary conditions emerged within the absolutist monarchies in Western Europe. England had already gone through a number of revolutions during the seventeenth century that severely shattered the powers of the absolutist state. The eighteenth century ended with the cataclysmic events of the American and French revolutions. Then until about the mid-nineteenth century a constant series of upheavals gradually stripped away governmental exploitation to an all-time low all over Western Europe.

The idea that had conquered public opinion and that had made this reduction of governmental power possible was that individual freedom and private property are just, self-evident, natural, inviolable and holy, and that any invader of such rights, a governmental agent no less (or even more so) than a private offender, should be regarded and treated as a contemptuous outcast.

See also Ernest K. Bramsted and K.J. Melhuish, eds., *Western Liberalism* (London: Longman, 1978).

[32]See on these developments of economic theory Marjorie Grice-Hutchinson, *The School of Salamanca: Readings in Spanish Monetary History* (Oxford: Clarendon Press, 1952); Raymond de Roover, *Business, Banking, and Economic Thought* (Chicago: University of Chicago Press, 1974); Murray N. Rothbard, "New Light on the Prehistory of the Austrian School" in Edwin Dolan, ed., *The Foundations of Modern Austrian Economics* (Kansas City: Sheed and Ward, 1976); on the outstanding contributions in particular of Richard Cantillon and A.R.J. Turgot see *Journal of Libertarian Studies* 7, no. 2 (1985) (which is devoted to Cantillon's work) and Murray N. Rothbard, *The Brilliance of Turgot* (Auburn, Ala.: Ludwig von Mises Institute, Occasional Paper Series, 1986); see also Joseph A. Schumpeter, *A History of Economic Analysis* (New York: Oxford University Press, 1954).

With each successful step towards liberation, the movement grew stronger. In addition, the so-called Industrial Revolution that had been ushered in by these ideological changes and that had brought about unheard of economic growth rates, sustaining for the first time a steadily increasing population and gradually but continuously raising the general standard of living, created an almost unbounded optimism.[33] To be sure, in Western Europe there was still plenty of feudal and absolutist despotism left even during the first half of the nineteenth century when the ideology of freedom and private property and of anti-statist vigilance reached its highest level of popularity, but progress toward an ever farther-reaching erosion of the exploitative powers of government and toward freedom and economic prosperity seemed almost unstoppable.[34] In addition, there now

---

[33]On the Industrial Revolution and its misinterpretation by the orthodox (school-book) historiography see F.A. Hayek, ed., *Capitalism and the Historians* (Chicago: University of Chicago Press, 1963).

[34]In fact, though the decline of liberalism began around the mid-nineteenth century, the optimism that it had created survived until the early twentieth century. Thus, John Maynard Keynes could write [*The Economic Consequences of the Peace* (London: Macmillan, 1919)]:

What an extraordinary episode in the economic progress of man that age was which came to an end in August 1914! The greater part of the population, it is true, worked hard and lived at a low standard of comfort, yet were, to all appearances, reasonably contented with this lot. But escape was possible, for any man of capacity or character at all exceeding the average, into the middle and upper classes, for whom life offered, at a low cost and with the least trouble, convenience, comforts, and amenities beyond the compass of the richest and most powerful monarchs of other ages. . . . But, most important of all, he [man] regarded this state of affairs as normal, certain, and permanent, except in the direction of further improvement, and any deviation from it as aberrant, scandalous, and avoidable. The projects and politics of militarism and imperialism, of racial and cultural rivalries, of monopolies, restrictions, and exclusion, which were to play the serpent to this paradise, were little more than the amusements of his daily newspaper, and appeared to exercise almost no influence at all on the ordinary course of social and economic life, the internationalization of which was nearly complete in practice. (pp. 6–7)

existed an independent America, free of a feudal past and with hardly any government at all, that assumed a role similar to that of the free cities of the middle ages: of serving as a source of ideological inspiration and a center of attraction but on a much larger scale.[35]

Today, little is left of this ethic of private property and its anti-government vigilance. Although they now take place on a much grander scale, governmental appropriations of private property owners are overwhelmingly regarded as legitimate. There is no longer a general public opinion that regards government as an antisocial institution based on coercion and unjust property acquisitions, to be opposed and ridiculed everywhere and at all times on principled grounds. No longer is it generally regarded as morally despicable to propagate or, even worse, to actively participate in the enforcement of acts of expropriation, and no longer is it the general opinion that one would not have any private dealings whatsoever with people who engaged in such activities.

For a similar account see also J.P. Taylor, *English History 1914–15* (Oxford: Clarendon Press, 1965), p. 1.

[35]Characterizing nineteenth-century America Robert Higgs (*Crisis and Leviathan* [New York: Oxford University Press, 1987]) writes:

> There was a time, long ago, when the average American could go about his daily business hardly aware of the government—especially the federal government. As a farmer, merchant, or manufacturer, he could decide what, how, when, and where to produce and sell his goods, constrained by little more than market forces. Just think: no farm subsidies, price supports, or acreage controls; no Federal Trade Commission; no antitrust laws; no Interstate Commerce Commission. As an employer, employee, consumer, investor, lender, borrower, student, or teacher, he could proceed largely according to his own lights. Just think: no National Labor Relations Board; no federal consumer "protection" laws; no Securities and Exchange Commission; no Equal Employment Opportunity Commission; no Department of Health and Human Services. Lacking a central bank to issue national paper currency, people commonly used gold coins to make purchases. There were no general sales taxes, no Social Security taxes, no income taxes. Though governmental officials were as corrupt then as now—maybe more so—they had vastly less to be corrupt with. Private citizens spent about fifteen times more than all governments combined. (p. IX)

On the contrary, instead of being laughed off the stage or met with open hostility or passive indignation, such people are respected as decent and honest men. The politician who actively supports a continuation of the ongoing system of non-contractual property taxation and regulation or who even demands its expansion is treated everywhere with respect, rather than contempt. The intellectual who justifies taxation and regulation receives recognition as a deep and profound thinker in the public eye, instead of being exposed as an intellectual fraud. The IRS agent is regarded as a man doing a job just as legitimate as yours and mine, and not as an outcast that no one wishes to have as a relative, friend, or neighbor.

How could government accomplish such a feat and bring about a change in public opinion that removed the former constraint on its size and instead allowed (and still allows) it to grow in absolute as well as relative terms?[36]

There can be no doubt that the key element in this turn-around of public opinion that started to take hold in Western Europe around the mid-nineteenth century, around the turn of this century in the U.S., and then at a steadily accelerating pace everywhere after World War I[37] has been the emergence of attractive new—implicitly or explicitly—statist ideologies.

In fact, states have always been aware of the decisive importance of state-supportive ideologies for stabilizing and increasing their exploitative grip on a population, and in this knowledge they have always made attempts to exert their control, above all, over the institutions of education. Even at their weakest, it should appear natural to see them give particular attention to "correct" ideological instruction and to concentrate whatever is left of their power on the destruction of

---

[36]On the following see in particular A.V. Dicey, *Lectures on the Relation Between Law and Public Opinion in England* (New Brunswick, N.J.: Transaction Books, 1981); Elie Halevy, *A History of the English People in the 19th Century*, 2 vols. (London: Benn, 1961); W.H. Greenleaf, *The British Political Tradition*, 3 vols. (London: Methuen, 1983–87); Arthur E. Ekirch, *The Decline of American Liberalism* (New York: Atheneum, 1976); Higgs, *Crisis and Leviathan*.

[37]On the worldwide excesses of statism since World War I see Paul Johnson, *Modern Times: The World from the Twenties to the Eighties* (New York: Harper and Row, 1983).

all independent institutions of learning and their take-over into the states' monopolistic hands. Accordingly, in order to regain the upper hand in the permanent struggle of ideas, since the mid-nineteenth century a steady process of nationalizing or socializing schools and universities (with one of the most recent examples being the unsuccessful attempt by the Mitterand government to crush France's Catholic schools) and lengthening the period of compulsory schooling has taken place.[38]

Yet pointing out this and the related facts of an increasingly close alliance between state and intellectuals[39] and the latter's rewriting history in line with statist ideologies merely puts the problem into focus. Indeed, when one hears about the state's take-over of the system of education, must one not immediately ask how it could succeed in doing so if public opinion were really committed to a private property ethic?! Such a take-over presupposes a change in public opinion. How, then, was this accomplished, especially in view of the fact that such a change implies the acceptance of manifestly wrong ideas and thus can hardly be explained as an endogenously motivated process of intellectual advancement?

It would seem that such a change toward falsehood requires the systematic introduction of exogenous forces: A true ideology is capable of supporting itself merely by virtue of being true. A false one needs reinforcement by outside influences with a clear-cut, tangible impact on people in order to be capable of generating and supporting a climate of intellectual corruption.

It is to these tangible, ideology-supporting and reinforcing factors that one must turn to understand the decline of the private property ethic and the corresponding rise of statism during the last 100 to 150 years.[40]

---

[38]On the relation between state and education see Murray N. Rothbard, *Education, Free and Compulsory: The Individual's Education* (Wichita, Kans.: Center for Independent Education, 1972).

[39]On the relation between state and intellectuals see Julien Benda, *The Treason of the Intellectuals* (New York: Norton, 1969).

[40]On the following see in particular Hoppe, *Eigentum, Anarchie, und Staat*, chaps. 1, 5; idem, *A Theory of Socialism and Capitalism*, chap. 8.

I will discuss four such factors and explain their corruptive function for public opinion. All are changes in the organizational structure of the state. The first one is the state's structural adjustment from a military or police state toward a redistributive one. (The prototype of such an organizational change is the often copied Prussia under Bismarck.) Instead of a governmental structure that is characterized by a small ruling class that uses its exploitatively appropriated resources almost exclusively for pure governmental consumption or for the maintenance of its military and police forces, states now increasingly engage in a policy of actively buying support among the people outside of the governmental apparatus itself. Through a system of transfer payments, grants of privilege to special clients, and governmental production and provision of certain "civilian" goods and services (as for instance education), the population is made increasingly dependent on the continuation of state rule. People outside the governmental apparatus increasingly have a tangible financial stake in its existence and would be harmed, at least in the short run and in parts of their existence, if the government were to lose power. Quite naturally, this dependency tends to reduce resistance and increase support. Exploitation may still seem reprehensible, but it is less so if one also happens to be someone who at least on some fronts is a legal benefactor of such actions.

In recognition of this corruptive influence on public opinion, then, states increasingly become engaged in redistributive policies. The share of government expenditure for civilian spending compared to military spending and pure government consumption increases. The latter expenditures can still increase steadily in absolute terms, and they have indeed done so practically everywhere to this day, but they lose importance everywhere relative to expenditures allocated to redistributionist measures.[41]

Depending on the particular conditions of public opinion, such redistributionist policies typically simultaneously assume one of two forms and frequently, as in the case of Prussia both: On the one hand

---

[41]On this trend see Webber and Wildavsky, *A History of Taxation and Expenditure in the Western World*, pp. 588f.; on redistribution in general see also de Jasay, *The State*, chap. 4.

the form of *Sozialpolitik*, of so-called welfare reforms, generally involving an income redistribution from the "haves" among producers to the "have-nots," and on the other hand that of business cartelizations and regulations, generally implying a redistribution from productive "have-nots" or "not-yet-haves" to the established "already-haves." With the introduction of a *Sozialpolitik* an appeal is made to egalitarian sentiments and a substantial part of it can be corrupted into accepting state exploitation in exchange for the state's enforcement of "social justice." With the introduction of a policy of business cartelization and regulation one appeals to conservative feelings, particularly among the bourgeois establishment, and it can be brought to accept the state's noncontractual appropriations in exchange for its commitment to the preservation of a status quo. Egalitarian socialism and conservatism are thus transformed into statist ideologies. They compete with each other in the sense that they advocate somewhat different patterns of redistribution, but their competitive efforts converge and integrate in joint support for statism and statist redistribution.

The second structural adjustment aiding in the roll-back of the private property ethic is a change in states' constitutions. In response to the challenge of the private property ethic, states change their constitutions from a monarchic autocracy or an aristocratic oligarchy to the now familiar type of a so-called liberal democracy.[42] Instead of being an institution which restricts entry into itself and/or into particular governmental positions through a system of caste or class legislation, a state constitution is adopted which in principle opens every government position to everyone and grants equal and universal rights of participation and competition in the making of state-policy. Everyone—not just the "nobility"—now receives a legal stake in the state, and resistance to its rule tends to reduce accordingly. While exploitation and expropriation may have seemed bad, they seem much less so, mankind being what it is, once one is given the chance to participate in its process, and while the ambitions of potential

---

[42]On this trend see Reinhard Bendix, *Kings or People* (Berkeley: University of California Press, 1978).

power-wielders within the general public previously must have been frustrated, now there is an institutionalized outlet for them.

In paying the price of democratizing its constitution, the state corrupts substantial parts of public opinion into gradually losing sight of the fundamental fact that an act of exploitation and expropriation is in all appearances and consequences the same no matter how and by whom it is decided and enforced. It lures them instead into accepting the view that such acts are legitimate as long as one is guaranteed a say over them somewhere along the line and could somehow somewhere participate in the selection of the state-personnel.[43]

This corruptive function of democratization as a stimulus for the resurgence of state power has been described with great perceptiveness by Bertrand de Jouvenel:

> From the twelfth to the eighteenth century governmental authority grew continuously. The process was understood by all who saw it happening; it stirred them into incessant protest and to violent reaction. In later times its growth has continued at an accelerated pace, and its extension has brought a corresponding extension of war. And now we no longer understand the process, we no longer protest, we no longer react. The quiescence of ours is a new thing, for which Power has to thank the smoke-screen in which it has wrapped itself. Formerly it could be seen, manifest in the person of the king, who did not disclaim being the master he was, and in whom human passions were discernible. Now, masked in anonymity, it claims to have no existence of its own, and to be but the impersonal and passionless instrument of the general will. But that is clearly a fiction. . . . Today as always Power is in the hands of a group of men who control the power house. . . . All that has changed is that it has now been made easy for the ruled to change the personnel of the leading wielders of Power. Viewed from one angle, this weakens Power, because the wills that control a society's life can, at the society's pleasure, be replaced by other wills,

---

[43]On the social psychology of democracy see Gaetano Mosca, *The Ruling Class* (New York: McGraw Hill, 1939); H.L. Mencken, *Notes on Democracy* (New York: Knopf, 1926); on the tendency of democratic rule to "degenerate" to oligarchic rule see Robert Michels, *Zur Soziologie des Parteiwesens* (Stuttgart: Kroener, 1957).

in which it feels more confidence. But, by opening the prospect of Power to all the ambitious talents, this arrangement makes the extension of Power much easier. Under the *ancien régime*, society's moving spirits, who had, as they knew, no chance of a share of Power, were quick to denounce its smallest encroachment. Now, on the other hand, when everyone is potentially a minister, no one is concerned to cut down an office to which he aspires one day himself, or to put sand in a machine which he means to use himself when his turn comes. Hence it is that there is in the political circles of a modern society a wide complicity in the extension of Power.[44]

The other two adjustments made by the state in order to overcome its lowest point of popularity and rise to its present size have to do with interstate relations. For one thing, as explained earlier and just mentioned again by de Jouvenel, states qua monopolistic exploiters tend to get involved in interstate warfare. With their internal exploitative power weak, the desire to compensate for these losses by external expansion rises. However, this desire is frustrated by a lack of internal support. The support is created through a policy of redistribution, industrial regulation, and democratization. (In fact, states that do not adopt these measures are bound to lose in any long-lasting warfare!) It is this support that is used as a springboard for a realization of the state's expansionist desires.

This newfound support takes advantage of the fact that redistribution, regulation, and democratization imply a greater tangible identification of the population with a specific state and thus almost automatically lead to an increase in protectionist if not open antagonistic attitudes toward "outsiders" and that in particular state-privileged producers are by nature hostile to "foreign" competition. This support is transformed by the state and its intellectual bodyguards into a frenzy of nationalism and provides the intellectual framework for the integration of socialist-egalitarian, conservative, and democratic sentiments.[45]

------

[44]Bertrand de Jouvenel, *On Power* (New York: Viking Press, 1949), pp. 9–10.

[45]On nationalism, imperialism, colonialism—and their incompatibility with classical liberalism—see Ludwig von Mises, *Liberalism* (San Francisco: Cobden

Backed by such nationalism, states begin on their expansionist course. For more than a century an almost uninterrupted series of wars and imperialist expeditions set in, each one more brutal and destructive than the previous one, with always greater involvement of the non-combative population, culminating in World War I and II but not ending with this. In the name of the socialist, conservative, or democratic nation, and by means of warfare, states have expanded their territories to sizes compared to which even the Roman Empire appears insignificant, and have actually wiped out or brought under foreign rule a steadily increasing number of culturally distinct nations.[46]

However, not only external expansion of state power is brought about by the ideology of nationalism. War as the natural outgrowth of nationalism is also the means of strengthening the state's internal powers of exploitation and expropriation. Each war is also an internal emergency situation, and an emergency requires and seems to justify the acceptance of the state's increasing its control over its own population. Such increased control gained through the creation of emergencies is reduced during peacetime, but it never sinks back to its pre-war levels. Rather, each successfully ended war (and only successful governments can survive) is used by the government and its intellectuals to propagate the idea that it was only because of nationalistic vigilance and expanded governmental powers that the "foreign aggressors" were crushed and one's own country saved, and that this successful recipe must then be retained in order to be prepared for the next emergency. Led by the just proven "dominant" nationalism, each successful war ends with the attainment of a new peacetime high of governmental controls and thereby further strengthens a government's appetite for implementing the next winnable international emergency.[47]

Press, 1985); idem, *Nation, State and Economy* (New York: New York University Press, 1983); Joseph A. Schumpeter, *Imperialism and Social Classes* (New York: World Publishing, 1955); Lance E. Davis and Robert A. Huttenback, *Mammon and the Pursuit of Empire: The Political Economy of British Imperialism 1860–1912* (Cambridge: Cambridge University Press, 1986).

[46]See Krippendorff, *Staat und Krieg*; Johnson, *Modern Times*.

[47]This process is the central topic of Higgs, *Crisis and Leviathan*.

Each new period of peace means a higher level of governmental interference as compared with the previous one: internally in the form of increased restrictions on the range of choices that private property owners are allowed to make regarding their own property; and externally, as regards foreign relations, in the form of higher trade barriers and of increasingly severe restrictions on population movements (most notably on emigration and immigration). Not the least because it is based on increased discrimination against foreigners and foreign trade, any such peace contains the increased risk of the next international conflict, or pressures the affected governments into negotiating bi- or multilateral interstate-agreements aimed at cartelizing their respective power structures and thereby jointly exploiting and expropriating each other's populations.[48]

Finally, the fourth adjustment is made necessary by the other three, and again because of the ongoing process of interstate competition, crises, and warfare. It is less of the state's own making than are redistribution, democratization, and war-making—just as it is not of its own making that there *is* interstate-competition at all. Rather, in fashionable Hayekian terminology, it is the unintended consequence of the fact that short of one state's domination of the entire world (which is, of course, every state's dream!) the continued existence of other states keeps exerting a significant constraint on each state's size and structure.

Whether intended or unintended, this structural adjustment must also be noted if one wishes to fully understand the development that has led to the present world of statism. It is also only by mentioning this adjustment that the question why it is specifically the *tax*-state that has risen to world dominance is finally answered.

It is easy enough to explain how through a series of nationalistic wars during the nineteenth and twentieth century the states of Western Europe and North America could come to dominate the rest of the world and leave their imprint upon it. Notwithstanding the presently

---

[48]The most vicious of such agreements is very likely that of restricting entry for noncriminal persons wanting to immigrate into a given territory—and the chance for those living in this territory to offer employment to them—and of extraditing them back to their home-countries.

booming cultural relativism, the reason for this is the simple fact that these states were the outgrowth of societies with a superior intellectual tradition—that of Western rationalism—with its central ideas of individual freedom and private property, and that this tradition had laid the foundation for the creation of economic wealth far exceeding that existing anywhere else. Because they parasitically drew on such superior economic wealth, it is not at all surprising that these states were then able to battle all others victoriously.

It is also obvious why with the remarkable exception of a number of Pacific countries most of these defeated and reconstituted non-Western states have to this day utterly failed to significantly improve their international stature or even match that of the Western nation states, and have in particular failed to do so after having reached political independence from Western imperialism. With no endogenous tradition of rationalism and liberalism to speak of, such states naturally felt inclined to imitate or adopt the "victorious" ideological imports of socialism, conservatism, democratism, and nationalism, the very ideologies to which these countries' intellectual elite had been exposed almost exclusively during their studies at the universities of Oxford and Cambridge, London, Paris, Berlin, Harvard, and Columbia. As a matter of course, a brew of such each-and-all statist ideologies, unconstrained by a significant tradition of private property ethic, spells economic disaster, and such a fact more or less rules out any prominent role in international politics.[49]

Yet what—and it is the answer to this that is somewhat less obvious—if the Western states fight each other? What determines the success in these conflicts, and what is bound to cause defeat?

Naturally, redistribution, democratization, and nationalism cannot be cited again here, for assumedly these states have already

---

[49]On the problem of the so-called Third World see Peter T. Bauer and B.S. Yamey, *The Economics of Under-Developed Countries* (London: Nisbet and Co., 1957); P.T. Bauer, *Dissent on Development* (Cambridge, Mass.: Harvard University Press, 1972); idem, *Equality, The Third World and Economic Delusion* (Cambridge, Mass.: Harvard University Press, 1981); Stanislav Andreski, *The African Predicament* (New York: Atherton Press, 1969); idem, *Parasitism and Subversion* (New York: Pantheon, 1966).

adopted such policies in order to regain internal strength and prepare for interstate warfare in the first place. Rather, just as it is the
relatively stronger tradition of private property ethic that is responsible for these states' dominance over the non-Western world, so,
ceteris paribus, is a relatively more liberal policy responsible for their
long run success in the struggle for survival among the Western states
themselves. Among them, those states which have adjusted their
internal redistributionist policies so as to decrease the importance of
a conservatively minded policy of economic regulations relative to
that of socialistically inclined policy of taxation tend to outstrip their
competitors in the arena of international politics.

Regulations through which states either compel or prohibit certain exchanges between two or more private persons as well as acts of
taxation are invasions of private property rights. In pursuing both
types of redistributionist policies, the states' representatives increase
their own income at the expense of a corresponding income reduction for someone else. However, while by no means less destructive
of productive output than taxation, regulations have the peculiar
characteristic of requiring the state's control over economic
resources in order to become enforceable without simultaneously
increasing the resources at its disposal. In practice, this is to say that
regulations require the state's command over and expenditure of
taxes, yet regulations produce no monetary income for the state but
only income in the form of the satisfaction of pure power lust (as
when A, for no material gains of his own, outlaws that B and C
engage in mutually beneficial trade with each other). On the other
hand, taxation and a redistribution of tax revenue according to the
principle "from Peter to Paul" increases the economic means at a
government's disposal at least by its own "handling-charge" for the
act of redistribution but may produce no other satisfaction (apart
from the increased appreciation by the Pauls) than that of actually
possessing certain economic resources and being able to expend
them according to its own whims.[50]

---

[50]On regulation and taxation as different forms of aggression against private
property and their economics and sociology see Rothbard, *Power and Market*;
Hoppe, *A Theory of Socialism and Capitalism*.

Clearly, interstate conflicts and war require economic means, and even more resources the more frequent and longer-lasting such events are. In fact, those states which control more ample economic resources expendable on a war-effort will *ceteris paribus* tend to be victorious. Hence, since a policy of taxation, and taxation without regulation, yields a higher monetary return to the state than a policy of regulation, and of taxation cum regulation, states must willy-nilly move in the direction of a comparatively deregulated economy and a comparatively pure tax-state in order to avoid international defeat.

It is this relative advantage in international politics of the tax-state over the regulatory state that explains the rise of the U.S. to the rank of the world's foremost imperial power.[51] It also explains the defeat of such highly regulatory states as Nazi-Germany and Fascist-Italy, the relative weakness of the Soviet Union and its allies as compared to the NATO-alliance, and the recent simultaneous moves toward economic deregulation and increased levels of imperialist aggression of the Reagan and, to a lesser extent, the Thatcher governments.

This concludes my praxeologically informed sociological account of the evolution of the present statist world and the rise, in particular, of the modern tax-state. Based on such an understanding let me end with just a few brief remarks of how it is possible to overcome the tax-state.

It cannot be fought by a simple boycott, as could a private business, because an institution devoted to the business of expropriating and exploiting does not respect the negative verdict revealed by boycotts. It also cannot simply be fought by countering its aggression with defensive violence because the state's aggression is supported by public opinion. Thus, overcoming it depends on a change in public opinion. The private property ethic—the idea that private property is a just institution and the only means of creating economic prosperity, and the view of the state as an outcast institution that is destructive of wealth formation, must be revived and must again inspire people's

---

[51]On the imperialistic foreign policy of, in particular, the U.S. see Krippendorff, *Staat und Krieg*, chap. III, p. 1; and Rothbard, *For a New Liberty*, chap. 14.

minds and hearts. With the rampant statist ideologies of nationalism, democratism, and redistributionism (of either the socialist or the conservative kind), this may sometimes appear hopeless. However, ideas have changed in the past and can change again in the future. In fact, ideas can change instantaneously.[52] Moreover, the idea of private property has one decisive attraction: it, and only it, is a true reflection of man's nature as a rational being.[53]

---

[52]See on this also Etienne de la Boétie, *The Politics of Obedience: The Discourse of Voluntary Servitude*, ed. Murray N. Rothbard (New York: Free Life Editions, 1975).

> Resolve to serve no more, and you are at once freed. I do not ask that you place bands upon the tyrant to topple him over, but simply that you support him no longer; then you will behold him, like a great colossus whose pedestals have been pulled away, fall of his own weight and break into pieces. (pp. 52–53)

[53]On the—a prioristic—rational justification of the private property ethic see Hans-Hermann Hoppe, "From the Economics of Laissez Faire to the Ethics of Libertarianism," in Walter Block and Llewellyn H. Rockwell, Jr., eds., *Man, Economy, and Liberty: Essays in Honor of Murray N. Rothbard* (Auburn, Ala.: Ludwig von Mises Institute, 1988); idem, "The Justice of Economic Efficiency," *Austrian Economics Newsletter* (Winter, 1988); infra chaps. 8 and 9.

3

Banking, Nation States, and International Politics: A Sociological Reconstruction of the Present Economic Order

1. MONEY AND BANKING

In order to explain the emergence of barter, nothing more than the assumption of a narrowly defined self-interest is required. Insofar as man prefers more choices and goods to fewer, he will choose barter and division of labor over self-sufficiency.

The emergence of money from barter follows from the same narrow self-interest, if man is integrated in a barter economy and prefers a higher to a lower standard of living, he will choose to select and support a common medium of exchange. In selecting a money he can overcome the fundamental restriction imposed on exchange by a barter economy, i.e., that of requiring the existence of a double coincidence of wants. With money his possibilities for exchange widen. Every good becomes exchangeable for every other, independent of double coincidences or imperfect divisibilities. And with this widened exchangeability the value of each and every good in his possession increases.

[Reprinted from the *Review of Austrian Economics* 4 (1990).]

If as man is integrated in an exchange economy, self-interest com-
pels him to look out for particularly marketable goods which have
desirable money properties such as divisibility, durability, recogniz-
ability, portability and scarcity, and to demand such goods not for
their own sake but for the sake of employing them as media of
exchange. And it is in his self-interest to choose that commodity as
his medium of exchange that is also used as such most commonly by
others. In fact, it is the function of money to facilitate exchange, to
widen the range of exchange possibilities, and to thereby increase the
value of one's goods (to the extent that they are perceived as integrated in an exchange economy). Thus, the more widely a commodity is used as money, the better it will perform its monetary function.
Driven by no more than narrow self-interest, man will always prefer
a more general and, if possible, a universal medium of exchange to a
less general or nonuniversal one. For the more common the money,
the wider the market in which one is integrated, the more rational
one's value and cost calculations (from the viewpoint of someone
desiring economic integration and wealth maximization), and the
greater the benefits that one can reap from division of labor.[1]

Empirically, of course, the commodity that was once chosen as the
best-because-most-universal-money is gold. Without government
coercion gold would again be selected for the foreseeable future as
the commodity best performing the function of money. Self-interest
would lead everyone to prefer gold—as a universally used medium of
exchange—to any other money. To the extent that every individual
perceives himself and his possessions as integrated into an exchange
economy, he would prefer accounting in terms of gold rather than in
terms of any other money, because gold's universal acceptance makes
such accounting the most complete expression of one's opportunity
costs, and hence serves as the best guide in one's attempts to maximize
wealth. All other monies would be driven out of use quickly, because
anything less than a strictly universal and international money such as

---

[1]On the free-market development of money, see Carl Menger, *Principles of
Economics* (New York: New York University Press, 1976), pp. 257–85; "Geld,"
in Carl Menger, *Gesammelte Werke*, vol. IV (Tübingen: Mohr, 1970).

gold—national or regional monies, that is—would contradict the very purpose of having money in the first place. Money has been invented by self-interested man in order to increase his wealth by integrating himself into an ever-widening and ultimately universal market. In the way of the pursuit of self-interest, national or regional monies would quickly be out-competed and supplanted by gold, because only gold makes economic integration complete and markets worldwide, thereby fulfilling the ultimate function of money as a common medium of exchange.[2]

The emergence of money, of increasingly better monies, and finally of one universal money, gold, sets productive energies free that previously remained frustrated and idle due to double-coincidence-of-wants-restrictions in the process of exchanges (such as the existence of competing monies with freely fluctuating exchange rates). Under barter the market for a producer's output is restricted to instances of double want coincidences. With all prices expressed in terms of gold the producers market is oft-encompassing, and demand takes effect unrestricted by any absence of double coincidences on a worldwide scale. Accordingly, production increases—and increases more with gold than with any other money. With increased production the value of money in turn rises; and the higher purchasing power of money reduces one's reservation demand for it, lowers one's effective rate of time preference (the originary rate of interest), and leads to increased capital formation. An upward spiraling process of economic development is set in motion.

This development creates the basis for the emergence of banks as specialized money-handling institutions. On the one hand, banks come forward to meet the increasing demand for the safekeeping, transporting, and clearing of money. On the other hand, they fulfill the increasingly important function of facilitating exchanges between capitalists (savers) and entrepreneurs (investors), actually making an almost complete division of labor between these roles possible. As

---

[2]On the gold standard, see Llewellyn H. Rockwell, Jr., ed., *The Gold Standard: An Austrian Perspective* (Lexington, Mass.: D.C. Heath, 1985), Ron Paul and Lewis Lehrman, *The Case for Gold* (San Francisco: Cato Institute, 1983).

institutions of deposit and in particular as savings and credit institutions, banks quickly assume the rank of nerve centers of an economy.
Increasingly the spatial and temporal allocation and coordination of
economic resources and activities takes place through the mediation
of banks; and in facilitating such coordination the emergence of
banks implies still another stimulus for economic growth.[3]

While it is in everyone's economic interest that there be only one
universal money and only one unit of account, and man in his pursuit
of wealth maximization will not stop until this goal is reached, it is
contrary to such interest that there be only one bank or one monopolistic banking system. Rather, self-interest commands that every
bank use the same universal money—gold—and that there then be
no competition between different monies, but that free competition
between banks and banking systems, all of which use gold, must exist.
Only so long as free entry into banking exists will there be cost efficiency in this as in any other business; yet only as long as this competition concerns services rendered in terms of one and the same
money commodity will free banking actually be able to fulfill the very
function of money and banking, i.e., of facilitating economic integration rather than disintegration, of widening the market and expanding the division of labor rather than restricting them, of making value
and cost accounting more rather than less rational, and hence of
increasing rather than decreasing economic wealth. The notion of
competition between monies is a *contradiction in adjecto*. Strictly
speaking, a monetary system with rival monies of freely fluctuating
exchange rates is still a system of (partial) barter, riddled with the
problem of requiring double coincidences of wants in order for
(some) exchanges to take place. The existence of such a system is
dysfunctional of the very purpose of money.[4] Freely pursuing his own
self-interest, man would immediately abandon it—and it would be a

---

[3]On banking and in particular the different function of loan and deposit
banking, see Murray N. Rothbard, *The Mystery of Banking* (New York:
Richardson and Snyder, 1983).

[4]See Murray N. Rothbard, *The Case for a 100 Percent Gold Dollar* (Meriden,
Conn.: Cobden Press, 1984), pp. 32–34.

fundamental misconception regarding the essence of money to think of the free market not only in terms of competing banks but also in terms of competitive monies.[5] Competitive monies are not the outcome of free market actions but are invariably the result of coercion, of government imposed obstacles placed in the path of rational economic conduct.

With free banking based on a universal gold standard emerging, the goal of achieving the most cost efficient solution to coordinating and facilitating interspatial and intertemporal exchanges within the framework of a universally integrated market is accomplished. Prices for the service of safekeeping, transporting and clearing money, as well as for advancing money in time-contracts would drop to their lowest possible levels under a regime of free entry. And since these prices would be expressed in terms of one universal money, they would truly reflect the minimum costs of providing market-integrative services.

Moreover, bank competition combined with the fact that money must emerge as a commodity—such as gold—which in addition to its value as money has a commodity value and thus cannot be produced without significant cost-expenditure, also provides the best possible safeguard against fraudulent banking.

As money depositing institutions, banks—much like other institutions depositing fungible commodities yet more so in the case of banks because of the special role of the commodity money—are tempted to issue "fake" warehouse receipts, i.e., notes of deposit not covered by real money, as soon as such banknotes have assumed the role of money substitutes and are treated by market participants as unquestionable equivalents of actually deposited real money. In this situation, by issuing fake or fiat banknotes that physically cannot be distinguished from genuine money substitutes, a bank can—fraudulently and at another's expense—increase its own wealth. It can

---

[5]A highly prominent example for this misconception is F.A. Hayek, *Denationalization of Money* (London: Institute of Economic Affairs, 1976); for a critique see Murray N. Rothbard, "Hayek's Denationalized Money," *Libertarian Forum* XV, nos. 5–6 (August 1981–January 1982).

directly purchase goods with such fake notes and thus enrich itself in the same way as any simple counterfeiter does. The bank's real wealth and the wealth of the early recipients of the money increases through these purchases, and at the same time and by the same action the wealth of those receiving the new money late or not at all decreases, due to the inflationary consequences of counterfeiting. Or a bank can use such fiat money to expand its credit and earn interest on it. Once again a fraudulent income and wealth redistribution in the bank's favor takes place.[6] Yet in addition, this time a boom-bust cycle is also set in motion: Placed at a lowered interest rate, the newly granted credit causes increased investments and initially creates a boom that cannot be distinguished from an economic expansion; however, this boom must turn bust because the credit that stimulated it does not represent real savings but instead was created out of thin air. Hence, with the entire new and expanded investment structure under way, a lack of capital must arise that makes the successful completion of all investment projects systematically impossible and instead requires a contraction with a liquidation of previous malinvestments.[7]

Under the gold standard any bank or banking system (including a monopolist one) would be constrained in its own inclination to succumb to such temptations by two requirements essential for successful counterfeiting. On the one hand, the banking public must not be suspicious of the trustworthiness of the bank—that is, its anti-fraud vigilance must be low for otherwise a bank run would quickly reveal the

---

[6]On the counterfeiting process, see Rothbard, *The Mystery of Banking*, chap. IV; also Elgin Groseclose, *Money: The Human Conflict* (Norman: University of Oklahoma Press, 1934), pp. 178 and 273.

[7]On the Austrian business cycle theory, see Ludwig von Mises, *The Theory of Money and Credit* (Irvington-on-Hudson, N.Y.: Foundation for Economic Education, 1971); idem, *Human Action* (Chicago: Regnery, 1966), chap. XX; F.A. Hayek, *Monetary Theory and the Trade Cycle* (New York: Augustus M. Kelley, 1975); *Prices and Production* (New York: Augustus M. Kelley, 1967); Richard von Strigl, *Kapital und Produktion* (Vienna: Julius Springer, 1934); Murray N. Rothbard, *Man, Economy, and State* (Los Angeles: Nash, 1970), vol. 2, chap. 12.

committed fraud. On the other hand, the bank cannot inflate its notes at such a pace that the public loses confidence in the notes' purchasing power, reduces its reservation demand for them and flees instead towards "real" values, including real money, and thereby drives the counterfeiter into bankruptcy. Under a system of free banking, however, with no legal tender laws and gold as money, an additional constraint on potential bank fraud arises, for then every bank is faced with the existence of nonclients or clients of different banks. If in this situation additional counterfeit money is brought into circulation by a bank, it must invariably reckon with the fact that the money may end up in nonclients' hands who demand immediate redemption, which the bank then would be unable to grant without at least a painful credit contraction. In fact, such a corrective contraction could only be avoided if the additional fiat money were to go exclusively into the cash reserves of the bank's own clients and were used by them exclusively for transactions with other clients. Yet since a bank would have no way of knowing whether or not such a specific outcome could be achieved, or how to achieve it, the threat of a following credit contraction would act as an inescapable economic deterrent to any bank fraud.[8]

---

[8]What about cartels? Could not the competing banks form a cartel and agree on a joint venture in counterfeiting? Again, under free banking this is most unlikely, because a system of free banking is characterized by the complete absence of any economic incentive for cartelization. With no restrictions of entry in existence, any such bank cartel would have to be classified as voluntary and would suffer from the same problems as any voluntary cartel: Faced with the threat of noncartelists and/or new entrants, and recognizing that like all cartel agreements, a banking cartel would favor the less efficient cartel members at the expense of the more efficient ones, there is simply no economic basis for successful action, and any attempt to cartelize would quickly break down as economically inefficient. Moreover, insofar as the counterfeit money would be employed to expand credit, banks acting in concert would set off a full-scale boom-bust cycle. This, too, would deter cartelization. See on the theory of free banking Mises, *Human Action*, pp. 434–48; Rothbard, *The Mystery of Banking*, chap. VIII.

II. THE STATE AND THE MONOPOLIZATION
OF MONEY AND BANKING

The present economic order is characterized by national monies instead of one universal money; by fiat money instead of a commodity such as gold; by monopolistic central banking instead of free banking; and by permanent bank fraud, and steadily repeated income and wealth redistribution, permanent inflation and recurring business cycles as its economic counterparts, rather than 100-percent-reserve banking with none of these consequences.

In complete contradiction, then, to man's self-interest of maximizing wealth through economic integration, different antieconomic interests prevailing over economic ones must be responsible for the emergence of the contemporary monetary order.

One can acquire and increase wealth either through homesteading, producing and contractual exchange, or by expropriating and exploiting homesteaders, producers, or contractual exchangers. There are no other ways. Both methods are natural to mankind. Alongside an interest in producing and contracting there has always been an interest in nonproductive and noncontractual property and wealth acquisitions. And in the course of economic development, just as the former interest can lead to the formation of productive enterprises firms and corporations, so can the latter lead to large-scale enterprises and bring about governments or states.[9]

---

[9]Contrary to the claim of the public choice school, states and private firms are not doing essentially the same sort of business, but instead are engaged in categorically different types of operations. Both types of institutions are the outcome of different, antagonistic interests. The "political" interest in exploitation and expropriation underlying the formation of states obviously requires and presupposes the existence of wealth, and hence an "economic" interest of at least one person in producing such wealth in the first place (while the reverse is not true). But at the same time, the more pronounced and successful political interests are, the more destructive of economic interests this will be. The public choice school is perfectly correct in pointing out that everyone—a government employee no less than an employee of an economic firm—normally prefers a higher to a lower income and that this interest explains why government should be expected to have no less of a tendency to grow than any other enterprise.

The size and growth of a productive enterprise is constrained on the one hand by voluntary consumer demand, and on the other hand by the competition of other producers that continuously forces each firm to operate with the lowest possible costs if it wishes to stay in business. For such an enterprise to grow in size, the most urgent consumer wants must be served in the most efficient ways. Nothing but voluntary consumer purchases support its size.

The constraints on the other type of institution—the state—are altogether different.[10] For one thing, it is obviously absurd to say that its emergence and growth is determined by demand in the same sense as an economic firm. One cannot say by any stretch of the imagination that the homesteaders, the producers and the contractual exchangers who must surrender (part of) their assets to a state have demanded such a service. Instead, they are coerced into accepting it, and this is conclusive proof of the fact that the service is not at all in

---

However, this discovery—that politicians and bureaucrats are no more altruistic or concerned about the public good than are people in other walks of life—is hardly new even if it has sometimes been overlooked. Yet what is in fact new with public choice is the inference drawn from this correct insight then, that all institutions should hence be regarded as an outgrowth of identical motivational forces and be treated analytically on a par with each other—is false to the point of being ridiculous. Regardless of a person's subjective beliefs, integrating one's actions into the institutional framework of either the state or a "normal" economic enterprise and pursuing one's wealth maximizing interests here or there will in fact produce categorically different outcomes. On a representative statement of the public choice school regarding the idea of the "state as a firm" and of "political exchange" as essentially the same as economic exchange, see James Buchanan and Gordon Tullock, *The Calculus of Consent* (Ann Arbor: University of Michigan Press, 1965), p. 19; for a critique of this view and the fundamental difference between economic and political means, see Franz Oppenheimer, *The State* (New York: Vanguard Press, 1914), pp. 24–27; Murray N. Rothbard, *Power and Market* (Kansas City: Sheed Andrews and McMeel, 1977), chap. 2.

[10]On the following theory of the state, see Murray N. Rothbard, *For a New Liberty* (New York: Macmillan, 1978); *The Ethics of Liberty* (Atlantic Highlands: Humanities Press, 1982); Hans-Hermann Hoppe, *Eigentum, Anarchie und Staat* (Opladen: Westdeutscher Verlag, 1987); *A Theory of Socialism and Capitalism* (Boston: Kluwer, 1989); Anthony de Jasay, *The State* (Oxford: Blackwell, 1985).

demand. On the other hand, the state is also not constrained in the same way by competition as is a productive firm. For unlike such a firm, the state must not keep its costs of operation at a minimum, but can operate at above-minimum costs, because it is able to shift its higher costs onto its competitors by taxing or regulating their behavior. Insofar as a state emerges, then, it does so in spite of the fact that it is neither in demand nor efficient.

Instead of by cost and demand conditions, the growth of an exploiting firm is constrained by public opinion: Nonproductive and noncontractual property acquisitions require coercion, and coercion creates victims. It is conceivable that resistance can be lastingly broken by force in the case of one man (or one group of men) exploiting one or maybe two or three others (or a group of roughly the same size). It is inconceivable, however, to imagine that force alone can account for the breaking down of resistance in the actually familiar case of small minorities expropriating and exploiting populations ten, hundreds, or thousands of times their size. For this to happen a firm must have public support in addition to coercive force. A majority of the population must accept its operations as legitimate. This acceptance can range from active enthusiasm to passive resignation. However, acceptance it must be in the sense that a majority must have given up the idea of actively or passively resisting any attempt to enforce nonproductive and noncontractual property acquisitions. Instead of displaying outrage over such actions, of showing contempt for everyone who engages in them, and of doing nothing to help make them successful (not to mention actively trying to obstruct them), a majority must actively or passively support them. State-supportive public opinion must counterbalance the resistance of victimized property owners such that active resistance appears futile. And the goal of the state, then, and of every state employee who wants to contribute toward securing and improving his own position within the state, is and must be that of maximizing exploitatively acquired wealth and income by producing favorable public opinion and creating legitimacy.

There are two complementary measures available to the state trying to accomplish this. On the one hand, there is ideological propaganda. Much time and effort is spent persuading the public that things are not really as they appear: Exploitation is really freedom;

taxes are really voluntary: noncontractual relations are really "conceptually" contractual ones;[11] no one is ruled by anyone but we all rule ourselves; without the state neither law nor security exists; and the poor would perish, etc.

On the other hand, there is redistribution. Instead of being a mere parasitic consumer of goods that others have produced, the state redistributes some of its coercively appropriated wealth to people outside the state apparatus and thereby attempts to corrupt them into assuming state-supportive roles.

But not just any redistribution will do. Just as ideologies must serve a—statist—purpose, so must redistribution. Redistribution requires cost-expenditures and thus needs a justification. It is not undertaken by the state simply in order to do something nice for some people, as, for instance, when someone gives someone else a present. Nor is it done simply to gain as high an income as possible from exchanges, as when an ordinary economic business engages in trade. It is undertaken in order to secure the further existence and expansion of exploitation and expropriation. Redistribution must serve this strategic purpose. Its costs must be justified in terms of increased state income and wealth. The political entrepreneurs in charge of the state apparatus can err in this task, as can ordinary businessmen, because their decisions about which redistributive measures best serve this purpose have to be made in anticipation of their actual results. And if entrepreneurial errors occur, the state's income may actually fall instead of rising, possibly even jeopardizing its own existence. It is the very purpose of state politics and the function of political entrepreneurship to avoid such situations and to choose instead a policy that increases state income.

While neither the particular forms of redistributive policies nor their particular outcomes can be predicted, but rather change with changing circumstances, the nature of the state still requires that its

---

[11]On the semantic confusion spread through the term "conceptual agreement" in particular by James Buchanan, see Hans-Hermann Hoppe, "The Fallacies of the Public Goods Theory and the Production of Security," *Journal of Libertarian Studies* 9, no. 1 (1989); supra, chap. 1.

redistributive policy must follow a certain order and display a certain structural regularity.[12]

As a firm engaged in the maximization of exploitatively appropriated wealth, the state's first and foremost area in which it applies redistributive measures is the production of security, i.e., of police, defense, and a judicial system. The state ultimately rests on coercion and thus cannot do without armed forces. Any competing armed forces—which would naturally emerge on the market in order to satisfy a genuine demand for security and protection services—are a threat to its existence and must be eliminated. To do this is to arrogate the job to itself and become the monopolistic supplier and redistributor of protection services for a defined territory. Similarly, a competing judicial system would pose an immediate threat to a state's claim to legitimacy. And again, for the sake of its own existence the judicial system must also be monopolized and legal services included in redistributive schemes.

The state's nature as an institution engaged in organized aggression also explains the importance of the next field of redistributive activities: that of traffic and communication. There can be no regular exploitation without monopolistic control of rivers, coasts, seaways, streets, railroads, airports, mail, and telecommunication systems. Thus, these things, too, must become the object of redistribution.

Of similar importance is the field of education. Depending as it does on public opinion and its acceptance of the state's actions as legitimate, it is essential for a state that unfavorable ideological competition be eliminated as far as possible and statist ideologies spread. The state attempts to accomplish this by providing educational services on a redistributive basis.

Furthered by a system of state education, the next crucial area for redistribution is that of redistributing state power itself, i.e., the right assumed by the state to expropriate, exploit and redistribute nonproductively appropriated assets. Instead of remaining an institution which restricts entry into itself and/or particular government positions, a state increasingly, and for obvious strategic reasons, adopts

---

[12]See Hoppe, *Eigentum, Anarchie, und Staat*, chap. 5.3; *A Theory of Socialism and Capitalism*, chap. 8.

an organizational structure which in principle opens up every position to everyone and grants equal and universal rights of participation and competition in the determination of state policy. Everyone—not just a privileged nobility—receives a legal stake in the state in order to reduce the resistance to state power.[13]

With the monopolization of law and security production, traffic, communication and education, as well as the democratization of state rule itself, all features of the modern state have been identified but one: the state's monopolization of money and banking. For all but this one it has been explained, albeit briefly, how they can and must be understood as performing strategic functions: why and how they are not normal productive contributions determined by demand and supply forces or simply good deeds, but redistributive activities which serve the purpose of stabilizing and, if possible, increasing a state's exploitatively appropriated income and wealth.

The monopolization of money and banking is the ultimate pillar on which the modern state rests. In fact, it has probably become the most cherished instrument for increasing state income. For nowhere else can the state make the connection between redistribution-expenditure and exploitation-return more directly, quickly and securely than by monopolizing money and banking. And nowhere else are the state's schemes less clearly understood than here.

Preferring, like everyone, a higher to a lower income, yet unlike others, being in the business of nonproductive and noncontractual property acquisitions, the state's position regarding money and banking is obvious: Its objectives are served best by a pure fiat money monopolistically controlled by the state. For only then are all barriers to counterfeiting removed (short of an entire breakdown of the monetary system through hyperinflation) and the state can increase its own income and wealth at another's expense practically without cost and without having to fear bankruptcy.[14]

---

[13]On democratization as a means of expanding state power, see Bertrand de Jouvenel, *On Power* (New York: Viking Press, 1949), pp. 9–10.

[14]On the state's inherent tendency toward achieving an unrestricted counterfeiting monopoly, see Murray N. Rothbard, *The Mystery of Banking;* idem, *What Has Government Done to Our Money?* (San Rafael, Calif.: Libertarian Publishers, 1985).

However, there are obstacles in the way of attaining this enviable state of affairs. On one hand, there is the inexorable fact that money can emerge only as a commodity. (It is impossible to start out with fiat money).[15] On the other hand, there is the problem that while enrichment through counterfeiting is no doubt less conspicuous than doing so by means of taxation, it is nonetheless a measure that is bound to be noticed, certainly by the banks, particularly if it occurs on a regular basis. And so it is also impossible for the state to get away with institutionalized counterfeiting unless it can be combined with redistributive measures which are capable of bringing about another favorable change in public opinion. This problem and the state's natural desire essentially determine the course of its actions.

As the result of free market processes, the state finds gold established as money and a system of free banking. Its goal is the destruction of this system and with it the removal of all obstacles to counterfeiting. Technically (ignoring for the moment all psychological difficulties involved in this), the sequence of steps that must be taken in order to accomplish this objective is then dictated: In a first step the minting of gold must be monopolized by the state. This serves the purpose of psychologically denationalizing gold by shifting the emphasis from gold as denominated in universal terms of weight to gold as denominated in terms of fiat labels. And it removes a first important obstacle toward counterfeiting because it gives the state the very institutional means of enriching itself through a systematic process of currency debasement.

Second, the use of money substitutes instead of actual gold must be systematically encouraged and such a tendency backed up by the enactment of legal tender laws. The counterfeiting process thereby becomes much less costly. Instead of having to remint gold, only paper tickets must be printed.

However, the problem already discussed earlier remains. As long as a system of free banking is in operation, the counterfeit notes

---

[15]On the impossibility of money originating as a fiat paper money, see the regression theorem: Mises, *The Theory of Money and Credit*, pp. 97–123; *Human Action*, pp. 408–10; Rothbard, *Man, Economy, and State*, vol. I, pp. 231–37.

cannot be prevented from returning to the new issuer with the request for redemption, and he then cannot—at least not without a contractive adjustment—fulfill his obligations. To overcome this obstacle, in the next step the state must monopolize the banking system or force the competing banks into a cartel under the tutelage of its own state-operated central bank. Once it is in command of a monopolized or cartelized banking system, the state can put the coordinated and joint counterfeiting process of the entire banking system into effect that avoids this risk.

In the next step gold must be nationalized, i.e., the state must require all banks to deposit their gold at the central bank and conduct their business exclusively with money substitutes instead of gold. This way gold disappears from the market as an actually used medium of exchange and instead everyday transactions become increasingly characterized by the use of central banknotes.

Finally, gold being already out of sight and in the state's sole possession, the state must cut the last tie to gold by reneging on its contractual obligations and declaring its notes irredeemable. Built on the ruins of gold, which as a commodity money standard initially made it possible that paper notes could actually acquire any purchasing power, a pure fiat money standard has been erected and can now be kept in operation, at long last handing the state the unlimited counterfeiting power that it had been vying for.

The goal of a complete counterfeiting autonomy likewise dictates the strategy that must be pursued on the psychological front. Obviously, in approaching its ultimate goal the state creates victims and thus it is also in need of favorable public opinion. Its rise to absolute counterfeiting power must be accompanied by redistributive measures that generate the support necessary to overcome all upcoming forces of resistance. It must look for allies.

Regarding the state's monopolization of law and order, traffic, communication and education, and the democratization of its organizational structure—while it is clear that they are all redistributive measures and as such imply favoring one person at the expense of another—it is difficult if not impossible to identify the gainers and the losers with definite social classes: there can be gainers (or losers) across different classes: within one social class there can be gainers and losers; and the pattern of redistribution can shift over time. In all of these cases the link between the state's redistributive expenditures and their payoffs is only indirect: whether or not certain education expenditures, for instance, pay off in terms of increased state income will only become visible at a later date; and even then it will be difficult to attribute such an outcome to a definite cause. In the case of the monopolization of money and banking, on the other hand, who outside the apparatus of the state itself will be the benefactors of its redistributive policies and who the losers will be is clear at once; and sociologically the benefactors can easily be identified with a specific social class. In this case the connection between the state's handing out redistributive favors and its own enrichment is direct and close-circuited; and the attribution of causes obvious: The state is compelled to make banks and the social class of bankers its accomplices by allowing them to participate in its counterfeiting operations and so enrich themselves along with the state's own enrichment.

Bankers would be the first ones to become aware of the state's attempts at counterfeiting. Without special incentives to the contrary they would have no reason to support such actions and every reason to uncover and stop them as quickly as possible. And the state would not run into just any opposition here: bankers, because of their exalted position in economic life and in particular because of their far-reaching interconnectedness as a professional group resulting from the nature of their business as facilitators of interspatial and intertemporal exchanges, would be the most formidable opposition one might encounter. The incentive necessary to turn such potential enemies into natural allies is the state's offer to cut them in on its own fraudulent machinations. Familiar with the ideas of counterfeiting and its great potential for one's own enrichment, but knowing, too, that there is no chance of engaging in it without running the immediate risk of bankruptcy under free, competitive banking and a gold standard, bankers are faced with an almost irresistible temptation. Going along with the state's policy of monopolizing money and banking also means fulfilling one's own dreams of getting rich fast. Not only the state comes into its own once a pure fiat money standard is established. Provided that they are accorded the privilege by the state to counterfeit in addition to its own counterfeited notes under a monetary regime of less than 100-percent-reserve banking, with the central bank functioning as a last resort counterfeiter banks can only too easily be persuaded to regard the establishment of such a monetary system as their ultimate goal and as a universal panacea.[16]

Economically, this coalition between the state—as the dominant partner—and the banking system—as its affiliate—leads to permanent inflation (constrained only by the imperative of not overdoing it and causing a breakdown of the entire monetary system), to credit expansion and steadily recurring boom-bust cycles, and to a smooth uninterrupted income and wealth redistribution in the state's and the banks' favor.

Still more important, however, are the sociological implications of this alliance: With its formation a ruling class whose interests are tied in closely with those of the state is established within civil society. Through its cooperation the state can now extend its coercive power to practically every area of society.

Before the establishment of the state-banking alliance, the sociological separation between state and society, i.e., between an exploitative ruling class and a class of exploited producers, is almost complete and clearly visible. Here is a civil society that produces all economic wealth; and there is the state and its representatives who draw parasitically on what others have produced. People are members either of civil society or the state and see their own interests connected with either the former or the latter. To be sure, there are then redistributive activities going on which favor parts of society at the expense of others and which help divert interests from the pursuit of economic integration to that of supporting exploitation. Yet social corruption is unsystematic at this stage. It is not corruption of social classes which are connected society-wide, but rather corruption of various disparate and dispersed individuals or groups. And these interests are only connected to those of the state rather tenuously through certain specific redistributive state activities, rather than through a direct cash-connection.

---

[16]On the enthusiastic participation of the banking elite in the creation of the Federal Reserve System, see Rothbard, *Mystery of Banking*, chaps. XV, XVI.

With the formation of a state-banking alliance all this becomes different. A cash-connection between parts of civil society and the state exists—and nothing ties people more closely together than joint financial interests. Moreover, this connection is established between the state and what can be identified not only as a closely interconnected social class, but as one of the most widely influential and powerful ones. In fact, it is not just the banks who join interests with the state and its policy of exploitation. The banks' major clients, the business establishment and the leaders of industry become deeply integrated in the state's counterfeiting schemes, too. For it is they who, apart from state and banks, are the earliest receivers of most of the regularly created counterfeit money. In receiving it before it gradually ripples through the economic system, and thereby changes relative prices as well as increases the overall price level, and in receiving credit at fraudulently lowered interest rates, they too enrich themselves at the expense of all savers and all later recipients or nonrecipients of this money.[17]

Moreover, this financial coalition between the industrial establishment, banks, and the state tends to be reinforced by each successive course of events. The credit expansion leads to increased investment and—since it is not covered by an increase in genuine savings—will inevitably result in a corrective contraction. In order to avoid losses or even bankruptcy the bank's clients will approach the banking system with an increased demand for liquidity (i.e., money). Naturally, to avoid losses of their own the banks are eager to help their clients out—and the more so the more established they are as clients. Unable to do this on their own, they turn to the state and its central bank. And the state, then, being offered another chance at its own enrichment, accepts and provides the banking system, and by extension the business establishment, with the needed liquidity by means of a

---

[17]On the formation of the state-banking-business coalition, see Gabriel Kolko, *The Triumph of Conservatism* (Chicago: Free Press, 1967); *Railroads and Regulations* (Princeton, N.J.: Princeton University Press, 1965); James Weinstein, *The Corporate Ideal in the Liberal State* (Boston: Beacon Press, 1968); Richard Radosh and Murray N. Rothbard, eds., *A New History of Leviathan* (New York: Dutton, 1972).

new round of counterfeiting. The alliance is renewed, and the state has reaffirmed its dominant role by having saved the established banking and the industrial elite from crumbling in the face of economic competition and allowing them instead to preserve the status quo or even further increase the wealth already concentrated in their hands. There is reason to be thankful and to reciprocate with invigorated public support for the state and its propaganda.

To be sure, this coalition between the state and the economic power elite by no means implies a complete identity of interests. The various established industrial enterprises may have different or even contrary interests; and the same is true for the banks. Similarly, the interests of banks and business clients may in many respects be different. Nor do the interests of the industrial elite or the banks coincide completely with those of the state. For after all, banks as well as industrial enterprises are also in the "normal" business of making money through production and productive exchanges—whatever other sources of income acquisition may be available to them. And in this function their interests may well clash with the state's desire for taxes, for instance. Nonetheless, the establishment of a system of monopolized money and banking still creates one interest common to all of them: an interest in the preservation of the state apparatus and the institution of political (i.e., exploitative) means of income appropriation as such. Not only could the state and its central bank destroy any commercial bank and, indirectly, practically any industrial enterprise; this threat is more severe the more established a business is. The state could also help any and all of them get richer, and more so if they are already rich. Hence, the more there is to lose from opposition and to gain from compliance, the more intensive will be the attempts by the economic power elite to infiltrate the state apparatus and have the state leaders assume financial interests in the business world. Bankers and industrialists become politicians; and politicians take positions in banking and industry. A social system emerges and is increasingly characteristic of the modern world in which the state and a closely associated class of banking and business leaders exploit everyone else.[18,19]

---

[18]In the Marxist tradition this stage of social development is termed "monopoly capitalism," "finance capitalism," or "state monopoly capitalism."

III. INTERNATIONAL POLITICS AND INTERNATIONAL MONETARY ORDER

Man's economic interests, i.e., his interests in improving his income and wealth by means of producing and exchanging, lead to the emergence of a universally used commodity money—gold—and a system of free banking.

The descriptive part of Marxist analyses is generally valuable. In unearthing the close personal and financial links between state and business, they usually paint a much more realistic picture of the present economic order than do the mostly starry-eyed "bourgeois economists." Analytically, however, they get almost everything wrong and turn the truth upside down.

The traditional, correct pre-Marxist view on exploitation was that of radical laissez-faire liberalism as espoused by, for instance, Charles Comte and Charles Dunoyer. According to them, antagonistic interests do not exist between capitalists as owners of factors of production and laborers, but between, on the one hand, the producers in society, i.e., homesteaders, producers and contractors, including businessmen as *well* as workers, and on the other hand, those who acquire wealth nonproductively and/or noncontractually, i.e., the state and state-privileged groups, such as feudal landlords. This distinction was first confused by Saint-Simon, who had at some time been influenced by Comte and Dunoyer, and who classified market businessmen along with feudal lords and other state-privileged groups as exploiters. Marx took up this confusion from Saint-Simon and compounded it by making only capitalists exploiters and all workers exploited, justifying this view through a Ricardian labor theory of value and his theory of surplus value. Essentially, this view on exploitation has remained typical for Marxism to this day despite Böhm-Bawerk's smashing refutation of Marx's exploitation theory and his explanation of the difference between factor prices and output prices through time preference (interest). To this day, whenever Marxist theorists talk about the exploitative character of monopoly capitalism, they see the root cause of this in the continued existence of the private ownership of means of production. Even if they admit a certain degree of independence of the state apparatus from the class of monopoly capitalists (as in the version of "state monopoly capitalism"), for them it is not the state that makes capitalist exploitation possible; rather it is the fact that the state is an agency of capitalism, an organization that transforms the narrow-minded interests of individual capitalists into the interest of an ideal universal capitalist (the *ideelle Gesamtkapitalist*), which explains the existence of exploitation.

In fact, as explained, the truth is precisely the opposite: It is the state that by its very nature is an exploitative organization, and capitalists can engage in

Man's political interests (i.e., his interests in improving his
income and wealth through exploitation at the expense of producers

---

exploitation only insofar as they stop being capitalists and instead join forces
with the state. Rather than speaking of state monopoly capitalism, then, it would
be more appropriate to call the present system "state financed monopoly socialism," or "bourgeois socialism."

For representative Marxist studies, see Rudolf Hilferding, *Finance Capital*
(London: Routledge and Kegan Paul, 1981); V.I. Lenin, *Imperialism Last Stage
of Capitalism* (Moscow: Foreign Languages Publishing House, 1947); Paul M.
Sweezy, *The Theory of Capitalist Development* (New York: Monthly Review
Press, 1942); Paul A. Baran and Paul M. Sweezy, *Monopoly Capital* (New York:
Monthly Review Press, 1966); Ernest Mandel, *Marxist Economic Theory*
(London: Merlin, 1962); *Late Capitalism* (London: New Left Books, 1975);
Herbert Meissner, ed., *Bürgerliche Ökonomie ohne Perspektive* (East Berlin:
Dietz, 1976); on the perversion of the classical liberal class analysis through
Marxism, see Murray N. Rothbard, "Left and Right" in *Egalitarianism As a
Revolt Against Nature and Other Essays* (Washington, D.C.: Libertarian Review
Press, 1974); on the refutation of the Marxist theory of exploitation, see Eugen
von Böhm-Bawerk, *Karl Marx and the Close of His System*, ed. Paul M. Sweezy,
(New York: Augustus M. Kelley, 1948).

[19]To recognize the far-reaching integration of state interests and those of the
economic power elite, which is brought about by the monopolization of money
and banking, is not to say that there cannot be conflicts arising within this coalition. As mentioned earlier, the state is also characterized, for instance, by the
necessity of democratizing its constitution. And the democratic process could
well bring egalitarian or populist sentiments to the surface which were opposed
to the state's favorable treatment of banks and big business. However, it is precisely the financial nature of the state-business connection that makes such an
occurrence unlikely. For not only would this pose an immediate threat to the
economic power elite; it would also imply severe financial losses in state income,
even if it did not threaten the stability of the state as such. Hence a powerful
incentive exists for both sides to join forces in filtering any such sentiment out of
the political process before it ever becomes widely heard and to ensure with all
resources at their command that the range of political alternatives admitted to
public discussion is so restricted as to systematically exclude any scrutinizing of
their joint counterfeiting racket.

See on this also such—in spite of their characteristic leftist misconceptions—
informative studies as C. Wright Mills, *The Power Elite* (New York: 1965); G.
William Domhoff, *Who Rules America?* (New York: 1967); E.E. Schattschneider,
The Semi-Sovereign People (New York: Holt 1960); Peter Bachrach and Morton
Baratz, *Power and Poverty* (New York: 1970); C. Offe, *Strukturprobleme des
Kapitalistischen Staates* (Frankfurt/M. Suhrkamp, 1972).

and contractors) lead to the formation of states, the destruction of the gold standard and the monopolization of money and banking.

Yet once a state is established as a monopolist of exploitation and counterfeiting new problems emerge. For even if its monopolistic position is secured within a given territory, competition between states operating in different territories still exists. It is this competition which imposes severe limits on any one government's exploitative powers. On one hand, it opens up the possibility that people will vote against a government with their feet and leave its territory if they perceive other territories as offering less exploitative living conditions. Or if other states are perceived as less oppressive, the likelihood increases of a state's subjects collaborating with such foreign competitors in their desire to "take over." Both of these possibilities pose a crucial problem for each state. For each literally lives off a population, and any population loss is thus a loss of potential state income. Similarly, any state's interest in another's internal affairs must be interpreted as a threat, in particular if it is supported by the latter's own subjects, because in the business of exploitation one can only prosper as long as there is something that can be exploited and, obviously, any support given to another state would reduce what remains left over for itself.

On the other hand, with several competing states each individual state's counterfeiting power becomes severely limited. In fact, on the international level a problem reemerges which is directly analogous to the obstacle to counterfeiting which was implied by a system of free banking, and which the states solved internally through the monopolization or cartelization of banking. The situation is characterized by different national paper monies with freely fluctuating exchange rates, If one state counterfeits more extensively than another, its currency is bound to depreciate in terms of the other, and for such a state this means (whatever different things it may mean for its various subjects) that its income has declined in relation to that of another state. With this its power vis-à-vis that of another state is decreased. It becomes more vulnerable to a competing state's attacks (military or economic). Naturally, it is in no state's interest to see this happen, and hence one's counterfeiting desire must be restrained accordingly. Counterfeiting still continues permanently, of course, because it is in every state's own interest; but no state is truly autonomous in its decision about how much to inflate and instead must at all times pay close attention to the inflationary policies of its competitors and flexibly adjust its own actions to theirs.

In order to maximize its exploitatively acquired income, it is in a state's natural interest to overcome both of these external restrictions on internal power. Cartelization would seem a possible solution. However, it must fail as such because—due to the lack of a monopolistic enforcement agency—interstate cartels could only be voluntary and would hence appear less attractive to a state the more powerful it already is and the less inflationary its counterfeiting policy. By joining any such cartel a state would harm itself to the advantage of less successful and more inflationary states. There is only one stable solution for the problem then: A state must aim to expand its territory, eliminate its competitors and, as its ultimate goal, establish itself as a world government. And parallel to this must be its attempts to make its paper currency used in wider territories and ultimately make it the world currency under the control of its own world central bank. Only if these goals are achieved will a state come into its own. There are many obstacles on this path, and these may prove so severe as to make it necessary to settle for less than such a perfect solution. However, as long as there is a state in existence, such an interest is operative and must be understood as such if one is to correctly interpret past developments as well as future tendencies (after all it also took the states several centuries to reach their present internal counterfeiting powers!).

The means for accomplishing the first of its two integrated goals is war. War and state are inextricably connected.[20] Not only is a state an exploitative firm and its leading representatives can thus have no principled objection to nonproductive and noncontractual property

---

[20]On the intimate relationship between state and war, see the important study by Ekkehart Krippendorff, *Staat and Krieg* (Frankfurt/M.: Suhrkamp, 1985); also Charles Tilly, "War Making and State Making as Organized Crime," in Peter Evans, et al. eds., *Bringing the State Back In* (Cambridge: Cambridge University Press, 1985); Robert Higgs, *Crisis and Leviathan* (New York: Oxford University Press, 1987).

acquisitions—otherwise they would not do what they do or the state would simply fall apart and dissolve. And it cannot be surprising then that they should also have no fundamental objection to a territorial expansion of exploitation by means of war. In fact, war is the logical prerequisite of a later cease-fire: and its own internal, institutionalized system of exploitation is nothing but a—legitimate—cease-fire, i.e., the result of previous conquests. In addition, as the representatives of the state they are also in command of the very means which make it increasingly likely that one's aggressive desires can actually be put into effect. In command of the instrument of taxation and, even better for this purpose, of absolute internal counterfeiting powers the state can let others pay for its wars. And naturally, if one does not have to pay for one's risky ventures oneself but can force others to do so, or if one can simply create the needed funds out of thin air, one tends to be a greater risk-taker and more trigger-happy than one would otherwise be.

While independent of demand and hence by nature a more aggressive institution than any normal business that would have to finance its wars with income gained exclusively through voluntary transactions and that would thus face immediate financial repercussions if only a single one of its clients reduced his purchases in response to his dissatisfaction with this business' war policy, the state is still not entirely free of all constraints in its pursuit of foreign aggression. Just as states emerge although there is no demand for them, so wars occur without having been demanded. But as the emergence and the growth of states is constrained by public opinion, so also are the state's war endeavors. For obviously, in order to come out of an interstate war successfully, a state must be in command of sufficient—in relative terms—economic resources which alone make its actions sustainable. However these resources can only be provided by a productive population. Thus, to secure the means necessary to win wars and to avoid being confronted with slackening productive outputs while at war, public opinion again turns out to be the decisive variable constraining a state's foreign policy. Only if popular support for the state's war exists can it be sustained and possibly won. The support from the banking and business establishment can be won easily, provided the foreign aggression promises a successful end and its cost can be established with a sufficient degree of accuracy. Not everyone of this class will be ready to join in, of course, because one may have vested interests in the to-be-conquered territory that will be damaged in the event of an interstate conflict; or one may wish that country C rather than B would be attacked; or one may even in principle be opposed to war. Generally, the expectation that along with one's own state's victory the business and banking elite would become established as a ruling class over a larger territory, with correspondingly expanded possibilities for financial exploitation, is a most powerful reason for the economic—in particular the banking—elite to pay close attention to the war option.

Yet their support is by no means sufficient. In a war even more so than during peacetime a state is dependent on every single person's willingness to work and produce (there can no longer be any loafers during wartime). To ensure widespread enthusiasm, all states must help create and support nationalistic ideologies. They have to wrap themselves up as nation states and pose as the banner carriers and protectors of the superior values of one's own nation as distinct from those of others, in order to generate the public identification with one specific state which is necessary in order to then turn around and wipe out the independence of more and more distinct nations and separate ethnic, linguistic and cultural groups.

However, something more substantial is required in order to keep the population working and producing the resources needed for a war: After all, the other states assumedly have the support of their business elite; and they, too, have created a spirit of nationalism in their territories. Assuming further that the antagonistic states initially control populations of comparable size and territories with similar natural endowments, the decisive variable determining victory or defeat becomes the relative economic wealth of the societies involved, their relative degree of economic development and capital accumulation. Those states tend to be victorious in interstate warfare that can parasitically draw on superior economic wealth. Clearly though, in order to be in this position conditions relatively favorable to wealth and capital formation in their respective territories must previously have existed. States do not positively contribute to this. On the contrary, as institutions engaged in nonproductive and noncontractual property acquisitions, their very existence is destructive of wealth and capital accumulation. However, they can make a negative contribution. Wealth and capital comes into existence only through homesteading, producing and contracting, and a relatively lower degree of exploitation of homesteaders, producers and contractors means a relative boost to capital formation, which in the next round of exploitation can give the state the additional resources needed to succeed militarily over its foreign competitors. Thus, what is also required in order to win wars is a relatively high degree of internal liberalism.

Paradoxical as it may first seem, the more liberal[21] a state is internally, the more likely it will engage in outward aggression. Internal liberalism makes a society richer; a richer society to extract from makes the state richer, and a richer state makes for more and more successful expansionist wars. And this tendency of richer states toward foreign intervention is still further strengthened, if they succeed in creating a "liberationist" nationalism among the public, i.e., the ideology that above all it is in the name and for the sake of the general public's own internal liberties and its own relatively higher standards of living that war must be waged or foreign expeditions undertaken.

In fact, something still more specific can be stated about internal liberalism as a requirement and means for successful imperialism. The need for a productive economy that a warring state must have also explains why it is that *ceteris paribus* those states tend to outstrip their competitors in the arena of international politics which have adjusted their internal redistributive policies so as to decrease the importance of economic regulations relative to that of taxation. Regulations through which states either compel or prohibit certain exchanges between two or more private persons as well as taxation imply a nonproductive and/or noncontractual income expropriation and thus both damage homesteaders, producers or contractors. However, while by no means less destructive of productive output than taxation, regulations have the peculiar characteristic of requiring the

---

[21]The term "liberal" is here and the following used in its traditional European sense and not in the present day U.S. sense as a synonym for "socialist" or "social-democratic."

state's control over economic resources in order to become enforceable without simultaneously increasing the resources at its disposal. In practice, this is to say that they require the state's command over taxes, yet they produce no monetary income for the state (instead, they satisfy pure power lust, as when A, for no material gain of his own, prohibits B and C from engaging in mutually beneficial trade). On the other hand, taxation and a redistribution of tax revenue according to the principle "from Peter to Paul," increases the economic means at the government's disposal at least by its own "handling charge" for the act of redistribution. Since a policy of taxation, and taxation without regulation, yields a higher monetary return to the state (and with this more resources expendable on the war effort!) than a policy of regulation, and regulation with taxation, states must move in the direction of a comparatively deregulated economy and a comparatively pure tax-state in order to avoid international defeat.[22]

With the backdrop of these theoretical considerations about the nature of the state and international politics, much of history falls into place. Lasting over centuries, practically uninterrupted series of interstate wars vividly confirm what has been stated about the inherently aggressive nature of states. Similarly, history dramatically illustrates the tendency towards increased relative concentration of states as the outcome of such wars: States' aggressive expansionism has led to the closing of all frontiers, and a steady decline in the number of states along with an equally steady increase in the territorial size of those states that managed to survive. No world state has yet been brought about, but a tendency in this direction is undeniably present. More specifically, history illuminates the central importance that internal liberalism has for imperial growth: First, the rise of the states of Western Europe to world prominence can be so explained. It is in Western Europe that, built on the older intellectual traditions of Greek and Stoic philosophy as well as Roman law, the ideology of

---

[22]A highly characteristic example of this connection between a policy of internal deregulation and increased external aggressiveness is provided by the Reagan administration.

natural rights and liberalism emerged.[23] It was here that—associated
with names such as St. Thomas Aquinas, Luis de Molina, Francisco
Suarez and the late sixteenth century Spanish Scholastics, Hugo
Grotius, Samuel Pufendorf, and John Locke—it increasingly gained
influence in public opinion; and where the various states' internal
powers of exploitation were then correspondingly weakened. And
their power was even further weakened by the fact that pre-modern
Europe was characterized by a highly competitive, almost anarchic
international system, with a multitude of rivaling small scale states
and feudal principalities. It was in this situation that capitalism originated.[24] Because the states were weak, homesteaders, producers and
contractors increasingly began to accumulate capital; previously
unheard of economic growth rates were registered; for the first time
a steadily increasing population could be sustained; and, in particular
with the population growth leveling off, gradually but continuously
the general standard of living began to rise, finally leading to what is
called the Industrial Revolution. Drawing on this superior wealth of
capitalist societies the weak, liberal states of Western Europe
became the richest states on earth. And this superior wealth in
their hands then led to an outburst of imperialist ventures which for
the first time in history established the European states as genuine
world powers, extending their hegemonic rule across all continents.

Similarly, England's outstanding role among the West European
states can be explained. The most liberal country of all, the British
government became the most successful imperialist.[25] And the relative decline of England (and Western Europe) and the rise of the
U.S. to the world's foremost imperialist power fits the theoretical picture as well. With no feudal past to speak of and British imperialism

[23]On the following see also Hans-Hermann Hoppe, "The Economics and
Sociology of Taxation," in *Journal des Economistes et des Etudes Humaines* 1, no.
2 (1990); supra chap. 2.

[24]On the importance of "political anarchy" for the origin of capitalism, see
Jean Baechler, *The Origins of Capitalism* (New York: St. Martin's, 1976), chap.
7.

[25]On British imperialism, see Lance E. Davis and Robert A. Huttenback,
*Mammon and the Pursuit of Empire: The Political Economy of British Imperialism
1860–1912* (Cambridge: Cambridge University Press, 1986).

defeated, liberalism was still more pronounced in the U.S. than anywhere in Europe. State power was at its weakest, hardly to be noticed in people's daily activities. Accordingly, economic growth was higher than in all other countries; standards of living went up; the population increased; and living standards and population size gradually surpassed those of all West European countries. At the same time, beginning in the late nineteenth century England and Western Europe suffered from reinvigorated internal statism brought about by the emergence of socialist ideologies on the European scene. It was this superior economic wealth—produced by a little exploited civil society—which allowed the internally weak U.S. government apparatus to slowly become the richest, most resourceful state, and turn these resources toward foreign aggression and in time establish itself as the dominant world power, with "home bases" all around the globe and direct or indirect military dominance and hegemonic control over a large part of the world (with the exception of the Soviet Union and China and their respective satellites).[26] The nineteenth century already displayed aggressive expansionism of the—liberal— U.S. government second to none. Since as early as 1801, when the U.S. Navy was sent on a punitive mission to the remote area around Tripolis, virtually no single year has passed without U.S. government intervention somewhere in the world.[27] Three major wars were waged: Against England (1812); against Mexico (1846–48), in which Mexico lost half its territory; and against Spain (1898), which resulted in the United States' occupation of Cuba and the Philippines. Contrary to popular myth, the Civil War, too, was essentially an expansionist war waged by the relatively more liberal North against the Confederate states. However, the great breakthrough to world dominance did not occur until the twentieth century, when the U.S. entered World Wars I and II. Both wars dramatically proved the superiority of U.S. might over the European states. The U.S. determined the victors as well as the losers, and both wars ended with a victory of the more liberal U.S. government—resting on a less taxed

---

[26]See on this and the following E. Krippendorff, *Staat and Krieg*, pp. 97–116.

[27]See the table in Ekkehart Krippendorff, *Die amerikanische Strategie* (Frankfurt/M. Suhrkamp, 1970), pp. 43ff.

and regulated economy—over all of the more socialist-authoritarian European states (including the Soviet Union) with their more heavily taxed and regulated economies. With the end of World War II the U.S. had reached hegemony over Europe and, as heir to the European states' foreign empires, over large territories all around the world. Since World War II the U.S. has continued and even intensified its unrivaled expansionism with smaller or larger military interventions in Greece, Iran, Korea, Guatemala, Indonesia, Lebanon, Laos, Cuba, the Congo, British Guiana, the Dominican Republic, Vietnam, Chile, Grenada, and Nicaragua.[28]

Finally, history also provides the most vivid illustration of the direct link between a state's internal powers of counterfeiting and its policy of external aggression, as well as the banking and business elite's conspiracy with the state in its expansionist desires. The watershed mark in the process leading to the rise of the U.S. as the world's premier power is World War I. The U.S. government could not have entered and successfully won this initially inner-European war without the absolute counterfeiting power that was achieved in 1913 with the establishment of the Federal Reserve System. It would have lacked the resources to do so. With a central banking system in place, a smooth transition to a war economy could be made and it became possible for the U.S. to get involved more deeply in the war and enlarge it to one of history's most devastating wars. And just as the prior establishment of the Federal Reserve System had been enthusiastically supported by the banking establishment (in particular by the houses of Rockefeller, Morgan, and Kuhn, Loeb and Co.), so the U.S. policy of entering the war on the Allied side found its most ardent supporters among the economic elite (notably in the firm of J.P. Morgan and Co. as the fiscal agent of the Bank of England and monopoly underwriter of British and French bonds as well as a major arms producer, and represented within the Wilson administration by such powerful forces as W.G. McAdoo, secretary of the Treasury and Wilson's son-in-law; Colonel P.M. House, Wilson's intimate foreign

---

[28]On twentieth-century U.S. foreign policy, see Leonard P. Liggio, "American Foreign Policy and National Security Management" in Radosh and Rothbard, *A New History of Leviathan*; Rothbard, *For a New Liberty*, chap. 14.

policy adviser; and B. Strong, governor of the Federal Reserve Bank of New York).[29]

There is only one important element still missing from a complete reconstruction of the present international order: money. It is in a state's natural interest to expand its territory militarily; and hence, one should expect a tendency toward a relative concentration of states. It is also in a state's interest to engage in "monetary imperialism" (i.e., to extend its counterfeiting power over larger territories); thus, a tendency toward a one-world paper currency should be expected. Both interests and tendencies complement each other. On the one hand, any step in the direction of an international counterfeiting cartel is bound to fail if it is not complemented by the establishment of military dominance and hierarchy. External and internal economic pressures would tend to burst the cartel. With military superiority, however, an inflation cartel becomes possible. On the other hand, once military dominance has made such a cartel possible, the dominant state can actually expand its exploitative power over other territories without further war and conquest. In fact, the international cartelization of counterfeiting allows the dominant state to pursue through more sophisticated (i.e., less visible) means what war and conquest alone might not be able to achieve.

In the first step a dominant state (a state, that is, which could crush another militarily and is perceived as capable of doing so, in particular by the dominated government) will use its superior power to enforce a policy of internationally coordinated inflation. Its own central bank sets the pace in the counterfeiting process, and the central banks of dominated states are ordered to inflate along with the dominating state. In practical terms, the dominating state's paper currency is imposed as a reserve currency on foreign central banks, and they are pressured to use it as a basis for their own inflationary actions.

Constrained not by actual demand but only by public opinion, it is relatively easy for a dominant state to accomplish this goal. Direct

---

[29]See on this Rothbard, *Mystery of Banking*, pp 230–47; on the role of the Morgans in pushing the Wilson administration into war, in particular see Charles Tansill, *America Goes to War* (Boston: Little, Brown, 1938), chaps. II–IV.

territorial conquest and the direct implementation of its own currency in foreign territories can be prohibitive because of the state of national or foreign public opinion. Yet with the power to destroy any specific foreign government—even thought it is not strong enough for a complete take-over—little is required in order for the dominant state to succeed in *monetary* imperialism.

Internally, it will most likely encounter no resistance whatsoever. The government itself will be satisfied with this solution. For once its own currency is employed as a reserve currency by foreign banks on which they then pyramid their various national paper monies, then it becomes possible for it to engage in an almost costless expropriation of foreign property owners and income producers without having to fear contractive consequences. Similarly, its own banking and business elite is ready to accept such an arrangement, because they, too, can thereby safely participate in foreign exploitation. Banks in particular are enthusiastic. And the public is largely ignorant of what is happening, or considers the exploitation of foreigners minor as compared to internal problems.

Externally, matters are only slightly more complicated. The dominated state loses resources to the dominating one as a consequence of monetary regime. But faced with the possibility of losing its internal control altogether, it naturally prefers acquiescing to a scheme which not only allows it to stay in power but to actually continue in its own fraudulent expropriations of its own population by inflating its currency on top of and in accordance with the dominating state's paper money creation. For essentially the same reason bank and business elites, as the first receivers of their respective state's counterfeit money, are willing to accept this solution. And the general public in the dominated territories, which through arrangement is subject to a double layer of exploitation of foreign states' elites on top of a national state and elite, is again largely unaware of all this and fails to identify it as one important cause of its own prolonged economic dependency and relative stagnation vis-à-vis the dominant nation.

This first step, however, does not provide a perfect solution. The international monetary system is characterized by a dominant paper currency, and a multitude of national paper monies pyramiding on top of it, and freely fluctuating exchange rates between such currencies.

On one hand, this is less than satisfactory for the dominant state, because under these circumstances ample room is left for the possibility of its own currency depreciating against others, and such a development would pose a threat to its own role as a dominant power. For exchange rates are not exclusively determined by the inflationary policies of various central banks. Ultimately and *ceteris paribus*, they are determined by purchasing power parity.[30] And even if a dominated central bank willingly inflates along with the dominating central bank, other factors (such as a lower level of taxation and regulation, for instance) can still make its currency appreciate against that of the dominant state.

On the other hand, the existence of a multitude of currencies freely fluctuating against each other is, as explained earlier, dysfunctional of the very purpose of money. It is a system of partial barter. It creates informational chaos, makes rational economic calculation impossible, accordingly leads to inefficiencies within the very system of production which the dominant state parasitically rests.

Thus, in order to assure its dominant position and maximize exploitatively appropriated income, in a second step a dominant state will invariably try to institute an international—and ultimately universal—currency monopolistically controlled and issued either directly by its own central bank or indirectly by an international or world bank dominated by its central bank.

There are some obstacles on the way to this goal. However, once the first step has been completed successfully, none of them would seem insurmountable. Naturally, the dominated state would lose some discretionary power under this arrangement. But this would be compensated for by the fact that its own economy would function more efficiently, too, if calculational chaos in international trade were reduced. Further, the banking and business elite in both countries would be adamantly in favor of such a monetary regime and would use their close ties to their respective state and international connections to promote its adoption. For, after all, banks and industrial firms are also in the business of making money through production and

---

[30]On the purchasing power parity theory, see Mises, *Human Action,* pp. 452–58; Rothbard, *Man, Economy, and State,* pp. 715–22.

exchanges. Freely fluctuating exchange rates are an artificial impediment in their pursuit of this economic interest. And they will be perceived as dysfunctional more intensively by larger businesses, because it is big business, in particular, for which foreign trade plays a more important role.

In fact, the most severe resistance to the adoption of an international currency is to be expected not from the states and the economic elites, but from the general public. Insofar as an international currency implies giving up an accustomed one, it runs against the very nationalism that all states eagerly bred for so long. This would be a problem especially if the public in the dominated countries were asked to adopt the dominant state's currency directly—name and all—because the underlying imperialist nature of such a monetary system would then become dangerously apparent. Yet with some degree of diplomacy and patient propaganda, this problem seems solvable, too. A new currency with a new name must be created and defined in terms of existing national monies in order not to arouse nationalistic or anti-imperialist sentiments. This new currency must only be somewhat overvalued against the various national monies (which in turn are defined in terms of the new currency) in order to drive all national monies out of circulation (in accordance with Gresham's law).[31] This must be accompanied by the states' and the economic elites' constant appeal to the general public's sound economic intuition that—regardless of all nationalistic feelings—freely fluctuating national monies are an anachronistic institution which cripples rational economic calculation, and that it is in everyone's best interest to have an internationally (and if possible universally) used money such as the international banking system under the leadership of the dominant state's central bank is willing to provide. Barring any drastic change in public opinion in the direction of a strengthened private property and sound money orientation and a correspondingly increased antistate vigilance, nothing will prevent the dominant state from achieving this complete international counterfeiting autonomy. And with a world money and world bank in place, and controlled by

---

[31]On Gresham's law see Mises, *Theory of Money and Credit*, pp. 75, 77; *Human Action*, pp. 781–83; Rothbard, *Power and Market*, pp. 29–31.

the dominant state's central bank, a decisive step is taken toward reaching its ultimate goal of establishing itself as a full-scale world government, with world-wide control not only over counterfeiting, but also over taxation and legal regulation.

In light of this explanation of monetary imperialism and its function as a "natural" (from a statist viewpoint, that is) complement of military expansionism, the remaining pieces from the history of international politics fall into place. Hand in hand with the rise of Great Britain to the rank of the foremost imperialist nation state went a sterling imperialism. Not entirely free at the time of all internal obstacles in the way of counterfeiting, British-dominated countries were compelled to keep their reserves in the form of sterling balances in London, where the Bank of England would redeem them in gold. This way, these countries would pyramid their national currencies on top of the pound, and Britain could inflate sterling notes on top of gold without having to fear an outflow of gold. With Britain's decline and the concurrent rise of the U.S. government to the position of the world's leading military power, sterling imperialism has gradually been replaced by a dollar imperialism. At the end of World War II, with U.S. domination extended over most of the globe, and essentially ratified in the Bretton Woods agreement, the dollar became the world reserve currency on top of which all other states have inflated their various national paper monies.[32] For a while, the U.S. officially still maintained the pretense of redeeming foreign central banks' dollars in gold, and this somewhat limited its own inflationary potential. However, it did not prevent steady dollar counterfeiting on top of gold from occurring. The position of the U.S. as a militarily dominant international power (in the meantime formalized through a number of military pacts, most notably the NATO) allowed it to compel foreign governments to exercise their right to ask for redemption only sparingly if at all, so that its own dollar inflation could take place without setting off contractive consequences. And when its counterfeiting policy had incited foreign governments to become all too

---

[32]On the dollar standard established with the Bretton Woods system, see Henry Hazlitt, *From Bretton Woods to World Inflation* (Chicago: Regnery, 1984).

daring in their attempts to obtain gold at bargain prices, it was the U.S. government's superior military might that finally allowed it to give up all pretense and declare its notes irredeemable. Since then the Federal Reserve System has acquired the position of an autonomous counterfeiter of last resort to the entire international banking system.[33]

The imperialist nature of this dollar standard takes effect in particular through such instruments as the International Monetary Fund (IMF), the International Bank for Reconstruction and Development (IBRD), and the Bank for International Settlement (BIS).[34] Money and credit, created by the strike of a pen, is passed from these U.S.-dominated institutions first to foreign governments which inflate their national currencies on top of it and in turn pass this money on to their own cartelized banking system which, adding a further dose of counterfeiting, then hand it on to the various states' favorite business establishments whence it ripples to the economic periphery. Parallel to this flow of money goes a reversed process of income and wealth redistribution from the periphery onto national business and banking elites and the various nation states as well as from the dominated territories to the U.S. government and the U.S. banking and business establishment as the ultimate center of world finance.

From a sociological point of view, the consequences are particularly interesting if these two integrated processes are superimposed on pre-modern, feudal societies. Such countries, primarily in Africa, Asia, Central and South America, are typically characterized by a class of feudal landlords, or feudal landlords-turned-financial-or-industrial-magnates controlling the state apparatus and mostly residing in the capital-city-and-seat-of-government; and by a class of largely landless, dependent peasants dispersed over the countryside

---

[33]Since 1971, at which time the gold standard was finally suspended, more money has been created than had previously been accumulated by all nations of the world since the beginning of time.

[34]On the imperialist nature of these institutions, see also Gabriel Kolko, *The Politics of War, the World and United States Foreign Policy 1943–1945* (New York: Random House, 1968), pp. 242–340.

and sustaining the state, the feudal elite, and the capital city through the payment of land rents.[35] Dollar imperialism here means upholding feudal rule, supporting and participating in the exploitation of an impoverished peasantry and the countryside by a parasitic feudal caste and the capital city, and contributing in the latter's suppression of any liberationist land reform movement. In fact, the typical Third World cycle of ruthless government oppression, revolutionary movements, civil war, renewed suppression, and prolonged economic dependency and mass poverty is to a significant extent caused and maintained by the U.S.-dominated international monetary system.

Since 1971, in particular, increased efforts have been undertaken in the direction of the second step in the process of monetary expansionism. Not all of the roughly 160 freely fluctuating currencies actually pose a problem, because most of them are in no danger for internal reasons of appreciating against the dollar and thereby strengthening the respective states' power vis-à-vis that of the U.S. government, or they play such a minor role in international trade that the calculational chaos which is introduced by their existence is largely insignificant. However, because of the relative strength of their currencies and their important role in international trade, the major West European states as well as Japan are a problem. Hence it is to these states and currencies in particular that U.S-led attempts to create a world currency that helps rationalize economic calculation and at the same time safeguard U.S. domination and further increase its own inflationary powers have been directed. The creation of Special Drawing Rights (SDRs), defined initially in terms of sixteen and later five leading export nations, and issued by the IMF, was a move toward a one-world currency and a one-world bank under U.S. domination.[36] Another important push toward this goal was provided through the activities of the Trilateral Commission (TC), founded in 1973 as an offshoot of David Rockefeller's Council on Foreign Relations. Composed of some 300 highly influential politicians, bankers,

---

[35]See Paul A. Baran, *Political Economy of Growth* (New York: Monthly Review Press, 1957), chaps. V–VI.

[36]See Hazlitt, *From Bretton Woods to World Inflation*.

businessmen, as well as intellectuals and journalists from North America, Western Europe and Japan, the TC has made the establishment of a world paper currency and a world central bank its primary concern.[37] Fervently supported by the TC as an intermediate step toward this ultimate goal as well as by several other politician-banker-industrialist associations with a substantial overlap of membership with the TC and devoted to the same ends, such as the Action Committee for Europe, the Association for the Monetary Union of Europe, the Banking Federation of the European Community, the ECU Banking Association, the Basel Committee and the Wilton Park Group, great advances have been made in aligning the European monetary front. In 1979, the newly created European Currency Unit (ECU), issued under the aegis of the European Economic Community, first appeared. Defined as a weighted average of ten European currencies, and assisted by organizations such as the European Monetary System, the European Investment Bank, the Society for Worldwide Interbank Financial Telecommunications, and the European Monetary Cooperation Fund, the ECU has assumed a more and more important rule. Since as an average it is less volatile than the various national currencies, multinational banks and corporations in

---

[37]A sample of prominent U.S. members of the Trilateral Commission includes David M. Abshire, counselor to the President; Frank C. Carlucci, national security advisor; J.C. Whitehead, Deputy Secretary of State; Alan Greenspan, Chairman of the Federal Reserve System; Winston Lord, Ambassador to China; George Bush, President; Paul A. Volcker, former Chairman of the Federal Reserve System; Alexander Haig, former Secretary of State; Jean Kirkpatrick, former Ambassador to the U.N.; David A. Stockman, former head of OMB; Caspar Weinberger, former Secretary of Defense; W. Michael Blumenthal, former Secretary of the Treasury; Zbigniew Brzezinski, former national security advisor; Harold Brown, former Secretary of Defense; James E. (Jimmy) Carter, former President; Richard N. Cooper, former Undersecretary of State for Economic and Monetary Affairs; Walter Mondale, former Vice President; Anthony M. Solomon, former Undersecretary of the Treasury for Monetary Affairs; Cyrus Vance, former Secretary of State; Andrew Young, former Ambassador to the U.N.; Lane E. Kirkland, head of AFL-CIO: Flora Lewis, *New York Times*; Thomas Johnson, *Los Angeles Times*; George Will, ABC television and *Newsweek*.

particular have found it increasingly attractive to use the ECU as a unit of account and a medium of settlement: economic calculation is less haphazard with only three currencies—the ECU, the yen, and the dollar—than with a dozen. In 1998, according to official inter-governmental agreements, the European Central Bank was established and the ECU became the all-European currency supplanting all national monies.[38]

---

[38]See on this also Jeffrey Tucker, "The Contributions of Menger and Mises to the Foundations of Austrian Monetary Theory Together With One Modern Application," (manuscript 1988), presented at the 13th annual conference of The Association for Private Enterprise Education, Cleveland, Ohio; and Ron Paul, "The Coming World Monetary Order," A Special Report from the *Ron Paul Investment Letter* (1988). Prominent Europeans explicitly supporting the idea of a European Central Bank, the ECU, and finally a one-world currency include: G. Agnelli, Chairman of FIAT, TC; J. Deflassieux, Chairman of the BIS, TC; G. FitzGerald, former Prime Minister of Ireland, TC; L. Solana, President of Compania Telefonica Nacional de Espana, TC; G. Thorn, President of the European Community and former Prime Minister of Luxembourg, TC; N. Thygesen, Professor of Economics, Copenhagen University, TC; U. Agnelli, Vice President of FIAT; E. Balladour, Financial Minister of France; N. Brady, Dillon Read Investments; J. Callaghan, former Prime Minister of Britain; K. Carstens, former President of West Germany; P. Coffey, Professor of Economics University of Amsterdam; E. Davignon, former European Commissioner; J. Delors, former President of the European Community; W. Dusenberg, President of BIS; L. Fabius, former Prime Minister of France; J.R. Fourtou, President of Rhone-Poulence; R. d. La Jemere, former Governor of the Banque de France; V. Giscard d'Estaing, former President of France; Ch. Goodhart, Professor of Banking, London School of Economics; P. Guimbretiere, Director of the European Community's ECU project; W. Guth, President of the Deutsche Bank; E. Heath, former British Prime Minister; M. Kohnstamm, former President of European University Institute, Florence; N. Lawson, British Chancellor of the Exchequer; L.M. Leveque, President of Credit Lyonnais; L. Lucchini, President of Confindustria Italy; F. Maude, British Minister for Corporate and Consumer Affairs; P. Mentre, Chairman of Credit National, France; H.L. Merkle, Chairman of Bosch Gmbh, West Germany; F. Mitterand, President of France; J. Monet, founder of the European Community; P.X. Ortoli, President of Total Oil and former Commissioner of the European Community; D. Rambure, Credit Lyonnais; H. Schmidt, former Chancellor of West Germany and Editor of die *ZEIT*; P. Sheehy, Chairman of BAT Industries; J. Solvay, Chairman of Solvay, Belgium; H.J. Vogel, Chairman of the German Social Democratic Party; J. Zijlstra, former President of the Nederlandse Bank.

With the European calculational chaos solved, then, and in particular with the European hard currency countries neutralized and weakened within a cartel that by its very nature favors more against less inflationary countries so as to protect and prolong U.S. hegemony over Europe, little indeed would remain to be done. With essentially only three central banks and currencies and U.S. dominance over Europe and Japan, the most likely candidates to be chosen as a U.S-dominated World Central Bank are the IMP or the BIS: and under its aegis then, initially defined as a basket of the dollar, the ECU, and the yen, the "phoenix" (or whatever else its name may be) will rise as a one-world paper currency—unless, that is, public opinion as the only constraint on government growth undergoes a substantial change and the public begins to understand the lesson explained in this book: that economic rationality as well as justice and morality demand a worldwide gold standard and free, 100-percent-reserve banking as well as free markets worldwide; and that world government, a world central bank and a world paper currency—contrary to the deceptive impression of representing universal values—actually means the universalization and intensification of exploitation, counterfeiting-fraud and economic destruction.[39]

---

[39]Jeffrey Tucker of the Ludwig von Mises Institute had an important influence on my understanding of the dynamics of the international monetary system—through frequent discussions as well as through granting me access to his own related research. Needless to say, all shortcomings are entirely my own.

4

Marxist and Austrian
Class Analysis

I will do the following in this chapter: First, I will present a series of theses that constitute the hard-core of the Marxist theory of history. I claim that all of them are essentially correct. Then I will show how these true theses are derived in Marxism from a false starting point. Finally, I want to demonstrate how Austrianism in the Mises-Rothbard tradition can give a correct but categorically different explanation of their validity.

Let me begin with the hard-core of the Marxist belief system:[1]

(1) "The history of mankind is the history of class struggles."[2] It is the history of struggles between a relatively small ruling class and a

---

[First printed in the *Journal of Libertarian Studies* 9, no. 2 (Fall, 1990). Also reprinted in *Requiem for Marx*, edited by Yuri N. Maltsev (Auburn, Ala.: Ludwig von Mises Institute, 1993).]

[1]See on the following Karl Marx and Frederic Engels, *The Communist Manifesto* (1848); Karl Marx, *Das Kapital*, 3 vols. (1867; 1885; 1894); as contemporary Marxists, Ernest Mandel, *Marx's Economic Theory* (London: Merlin, 1962); idem, *Late Capitalism* (London: New Left Books, 1975); Paul Baran and Paul Sweezy, *Monopoly Capital* (New York: Monthly Review Press, 1966); from a non-Marxist perspective, Leszek Kolakowski, *Main Currents of Marxism* (Oxford: Clarendon Press, 1995); G. Wetter, *Sovietideologie heute* (Frankfurt/M.: Fischer, 1962), vol. 1; W. Leonhard, *Sovietideologie heute* (Frankfurt/M.: Fischer, 1962), vol. 2.

[2]Marx and Engels, *The Communist Manifesto* (section 1).

larger class of the exploited. The primary form of exploitation is economic: The ruling class expropriates part of the productive output of the exploited or, as Marxists say, "it appropriates a social surplus product and uses it for its own consumptive purposes."

(2) The ruling class is unified by its common interest in upholding its exploitative position and maximizing its exploitatively appropriated surplus product. It never deliberately gives up power or exploitation income. Instead, any loss in power or income must be wrestled away from it through struggles, whose outcome ultimately depends on the class consciousness of the exploited, i.e., on whether or not and to what extent the exploited are aware of their own status and are consciously united with other class members in common opposition to exploitation.

(3) Class rule manifests itself primarily in specific arrangements regarding the assignment of property rights or, in Marxist terminology, in specific "relations of production." In order to protect these arrangements or production relations, the ruling class forms and is in command of the state as the apparatus of compulsion and coercion. The state enforces and helps reproduce a given class structure through the administration of a system of "class justice," and it assists in the creation and the support of an ideological superstructure designed to lend legitimacy to the existence of class rule.

(4) Internally, the process of competition within the ruling class generates a tendency toward increasing concentration and centralization. A multipolar system of exploitation is gradually supplanted by an oligarchic or monopolistic one. Fewer and fewer exploitation centers remain in operation, and those that do are increasingly integrated into a hierarchical order. Externally (i.e., as regards the international system), this centralization process will (and all the more intensively the more advanced it is) lead to imperialist interstate wars and the territorial expansion of exploitative rule.

(5) Finally, with the centralization and expansion of exploitative rule gradually approaching its ultimate limit of world domination, class rule will increasingly become incompatible with the further development and improvement of "productive forces." Economic stagnation and crises become more and more characteristic and create the "objective conditions" for the emergence of a revolutionary class consciousness of the exploited. The situation becomes ripe for

the establishment of a classless society, the "withering away of the state," the replacement of government of men over men by the administration of things[3] and, as its result, unheard-of economic prosperity.

All of these theses can be given a perfectly good justification, as I will show. Unfortunately, however, it is Marxism, which subscribes to all of them, that has done more than any other ideological system to discredit their validity in deriving them from a patently absurd exploitation theory.

What is this Marxist theory of exploitation? According to Marx, such precapitalist social systems as slavery and feudalism are characterized by exploitation. There is no quarrel with this. For after all, the slave is not a free laborer, and he cannot be said to gain from his being enslaved. Rather, in being enslaved his utility is reduced at the expense of an increase in wealth appropriated by the slave master. The interest of the slave and that of the slave owner are indeed antagonistic. The same is true as regards the interests of the feudal lord who extracts a land rent from a peasant who works on land homesteaded by himself (i.e., the peasant). The lord's gains are the peasant's losses. It is also undisputed that slavery as well as feudalism indeed hamper the development of productive forces. Neither slave nor serf will be as productive as they would be without slavery or serfdom.

The genuinely new Marxist idea is that essentially nothing is changed as regards exploitation under capitalism (if the slave becomes a free laborer), or if the peasant decides to farm land homesteaded by someone else and pays rent in exchange for doing so. To be sure, Marx, in the famous chapter 24 of the first volume of his *Kapital*, titled "The So-called Original Accumulation," gives a historical account of the emergence of capitalism which makes the point that much or even most of the initial capitalist property is the result of plunder, enclosure, and conquest. Similarly, in chapter 25, on the "Modern Theory of Colonialism," the role of force and violence in

---

[3]*The Communist Manifesto* (section 2, last 2 paragraphs); Frederic Engels, *Von tier Autorität*, in Karl Marx and Frederic Engels, *Ausgewählte Schriften*, 2 vols. (East Berlin: Dietz, 1953), vol. I, p. 606; idem, *Die Entwicklung des Sozialismus von der Utopie zur Wissenschaft*, ibid., vol. 2, p. 139.

exporting capitalism to the, as we would nowadays say, Third World is heavily emphasized. Admittedly, all this is generally correct, and insofar as it is there can be no quarrel with labeling such capitalism exploitative. Yet one should be aware of the fact that here Marx is engaged in a trick. In engaging in historical investigations and arousing the reader's indignation regarding the brutalities underlying the formation of many capitalist fortunes, he actually side-steps the issue at hand. He distracts from the fact that his thesis is really an entirely different one: namely, that even if one were to have "clean" capitalism so to speak (one in which the original appropriation of capital were the result of nothing else but homesteading), work and savings, the capitalist who hired labor to be employed with this capital would nonetheless be engaged in exploitation. Indeed, Marx considered the proof of this thesis his most important contribution to economic analysis.

What, then, is his proof of the exploitative character of a clean capitalism?

It consists in the observation that the factor prices, in particular the wages paid to laborers by the capitalist, are lower than the output prices. The laborer, for instance, is paid a wage that represents consumption goods which can be produced in three days, but he actually works five days for his wage and produces an output of consumption goods that exceeds what he receives as remuneration. The output of the two extra days, the surplus value in Marxist terminology, is appropriated by the capitalist. Hence, according to Marx, there is exploitation.[4]

---

[4]See Marx, *Das Kapital*, vol. I; the shortest presentation is his *Lohn, Preis, Profit* (1865). Actually, in order to prove the more specific Marxist thesis that exclusively the owner of labor services is exploited (but not the owner of the other originary factor of production: land), yet another argument would be needed. For if it were true that the discrepancy between factor and output prices constitutes an exploitative relation, this would only show that the capitalist who rents labor services from an owner of labor, and land services from an owner of land would exploit either labor, or land, or labor and land simultaneously. It is the labor theory of value, of course, which is supposed to provide the missing link here by trying to establish labor as the sole source of value. I will spare myself the task of refuting this theory. Few enough remain today, even among

What is wrong with this analysis?[5] The answer becomes obvious, once it is asked why the laborer would possibly agree to such a deal! He agrees because his wage payment represents present goods— while his own labor services represent only future goods—and he values present goods more highly. After all, he could also decide not to sell his labor services to the capitalist and then map the full value of his output himself. But this would of course imply that he would have to wait longer for any consumption goods to become available to him. In selling his labor services he demonstrates that he prefers a smaller amount of consumption goods now over a possibly larger one at some future date. On the other hand, why would the capitalist want to strike a deal with the laborer? Why would he want to advance present goods (money) to the laborer in exchange for services that bear fruit only later? Obviously, he would not want to pay out, for instance, $100 now if he were to receive the same amount in one year's time. In that case, why not simply hold on to it for one year and receive the extra benefit of having actual command over it during the entire time? Instead, he must expect to receive a larger sum than $100 in the future in order to give up $100 now in the form of wages paid to the laborer. He must expect to be able to earn a profit, or

---

those claiming to be Marxists, who do not recognize the faultiness of the labor theory of value. Rather, I will accept for the sake of argument the suggestion made, for instance, by the self-proclaimed "analytical Marxist" John Roemer (*A General Theory of Exploitation and Class* [Cambridge, Mass.: Harvard University Press, 1982]; idem, *Value, Exploitation and Class* [London: Harwood Academic Publishers, 1985]) that the theory of exploitation can be separated analytically from the labor theory of value; and that a "generalized commodity exploitation theory" can be formulated which can be justified regardless of whether or not the labor theory of value is true. I want to demonstrate that the Marxist theory of exploitation is nonsensical even if one were to absolve its proponents from having to prove the labor theory of value and, indeed, even if the labor theory of value were true. Even a generalized commodity exploitation theory provides no escape from the conclusion that the Marxist theory of exploitation is dead wrong.

[5]See on the following Eugen von Böhm-Bawerk, *The Exploitation Theory of Socialism-Communism* (South Holland, Ill.: Libertarian Press, 1975); idem, *Shorter Classics of Böhm-Bawerk* (South Holland, Ill.: Libertarian Press, 1962).

more correctly an interest return. He is also constrained by time preference, i.e., the fact that an actor invariably prefers earlier over later
goods, in yet another way. For if one can obtain a larger sum in the
future by sacrificing a smaller one in the present, why then is the capitalist not engaged in more saving than he actually is? Why does he
not hire more laborers than he does, if each one of them promises an
additional interest return? The answer again should be obvious:
because the capitalist is a consumer, as well, and cannot help being
one. The amount of his savings and investing is restricted by the
necessity that he, too, like the laborer, requires a supply of present
goods "large enough to secure the satisfaction of all those wants the
satisfaction of which during the waiting time is considered more
urgent than the advantages which a still greater lengthening of the
period of production would provide."[6]

What is wrong with Marx's theory of exploitation, then, is that he
does not understand the phenomenon of time preference as a universal category of human action.[7] That the laborer does not receive
his "full worth" has nothing to do with exploitation but merely
reflects the fact that it is impossible for man to exchange future goods
against present ones except at a discount. Contrary to the case of
slave and slave master where the latter benefits at the expense of the
former, the relationship between the free laborer and the capitalist is
a mutually beneficial one. The laborer enters the agreement because,
given his time preference, he prefers a smaller amount of present
goods over a larger future one; and the capitalist enters it because,
given his time preference, he has a reverse preference order and
ranks a larger future amount of goods more highly than a smaller
present one. Their interests are not antagonistic but harmonious.
Without the capitalist's expectation of an interest return, the laborer
would be worse off having to wait longer than he wishes to wait; and

---

[6]Ludwig von Mises, *Human Action* (Chicago: Regnery, 1966), p. 407; see also
Murray N. Rothbard, *Man, Economy, and State* (Los Angeles: Nash, 1970), pp.
300–01.

[7]See on the time preference theory of interest in addition to the works cited
in notes 5 and 6; also Frank Fetter, *Capital, Interest and Rent* (Kansas City: Sheed
Andrews and McMeel, 1977).

without the laborer's preference for present goods the capitalist would be worse off having to resort to less roundabout and less efficient production methods than those which he desires to adopt. Nor can the capitalist wage system be regarded as an impediment to the further development of the forces of production, as Marx claims. If the laborer were not permitted to sell his labor services and the capitalist to buy them, output would not be higher but lower, because production would have to take place with relatively reduced levels of capital accumulation.

Under a system of socialized production, quite contrary to Marx's proclamations, the development of productive forces would not reach new heights but would instead sink dramatically.[8] For obviously, capital accumulation must be brought about by definite individuals at definite points in time and space through homesteading, producing and/or saving. In each case it is brought about with the expectation that it will lead to an increase in the output of future goods. The value an actor attaches to his capital reflects the value he attaches to all expected future incomes attributable to its cooperation and discounted by his rate of time preference. If, as in the case of collectively owned factors of production, an actor is no longer granted exclusive control over his accumulated capital and hence over the future income to be derived from its employment, but partial control instead is assigned to nonhomesteaders, nonproducers, and nonsavers, the value for him of the expected income and hence that of the capital goods is reduced. His effective rate of time preference will rise and there will be less homesteading of scarce resources, and less saving for the maintenance of existing resources and the production of new capital goods. The period of production, the roundaboutness of the production structure, will be shortened, and relative impoverishment will result.

If Marx's theory of capitalist exploitation and his ideas on how to end exploitation and establish universal prosperity are false to the

---

[8]See on the following Hans-Hermann Hoppe, *A Theory of Socialism and Capitalism* (Boston: Kluwer Academic Publishers, 1989); idem, "Why Socialism Must Fail," *Free Market* (July 1988); idem, "The Economics and Sociology of Taxation," *Journal des Economistes et des Etudes Humaines* (1990); supra chap. 2.

point of being ridiculous, it is clear that any theory of history which can be derived from it must be false, too. Or if it should be correct, it must have been derived incorrectly. Instead of going through the lengthier task of explaining all of the flaws in the Marxist argument as it sets out from its theory of capitalist exploitation and ends with the theory of history which I presented earlier, I will take a shortcut here. I will now outline in the briefest possible way the correct—Austrian, Misesian-Rothbardian—theory of exploitation; give an explanatory sketch of how this theory makes sense out of the class theory of history; and highlight along the way some key differences between this class theory and the Marxist one and also point out some intellectual affinities between Austrianism and Marxism stemming from their common conviction that there does indeed exist something like exploitation and a ruling class.[9]

---

[9]Mises's contributions to the theory of exploitation and class are unsystematic. However, throughout his writings he presents sociological and historical interpretations that are class analyses, if only implicitly. Noteworthy here is in particular his acute analysis of the collaboration between government and banking elite in destroying the gold standard in order to increase their inflationary powers as a means of fraudulent, exploitative income and wealth redistribution in their own favor. See for instance his *Monetary Stabilization and Cyclical Policy* (1928) in idem, *On the Manipulation of Money and Credit,* ed. Percy Greaves (Dobbs Ferry, N.Y.: Free Market Books 1978); idem, *Socialism* (Indianapolis: Liberty Fund, 1981), chap. 20; idem, *The Clash of Group Interests and Other Essays* (New York: Center for Libertarian Studies, Occasional Paper Series No. 7, 1978). Yet Mises does not give systematic status to class analysis and exploitation theory because he ultimately misconceives of exploitation as merely an intellectual error which correct economic reasoning can dispel. He fails to fully recognize that exploitation is also and probably even more so a moral-motivational problem that exists regardless of all economic reasoning. Rothbard adds his insight to the Misesian structure of Austrian economics and makes the analysis of power and power elites an integral part of economic theory and historical-sociological explanations; and he systematically expands the Austrian case against exploitation to include ethics in addition to economic theory, i.e., a theory of justice next to a theory of efficiency, such that the ruling class can also be attacked as immoral. For Rothbard's theory of power, class and exploitation, see in particular his *Power and Market* (Kansas City: Sheed Andrews and McMeel, 1977); idem, *For a New Liberty* (New York: Macmillan, 1978); idem, *The Mystery of Banking* (New York: Richardson and Snyder, 1983); idem, *America's Great Depression* (Kansas City:

The starting point for the Austrian exploitation theory is plain and simple, as it should be. Actually, it has already been established through the analysis of the Marxist theory: Exploitation characterized the relationship between slave and slave master and serf and feudal lord. But no exploitation was found possible under a clean capitalism. What is the principle difference between these two cases? The answer is: the recognition or nonrecognition of the homesteading principle. The peasant under feudalism is exploited because he does not have exclusive control over land that he homesteaded, and the slave because he has no exclusive control over his own homesteaded body. If, contrary to this, everyone has exclusive control over his own body (is a free laborer, that is) and acts in accordance with the homesteading principle, there can be no exploitation. It is logically absurd to claim that a person who homesteads goods not previously homesteaded by anybody else, or who employs such goods in the production of future goods, or who saves presently homesteaded or produced goods in order to increase the future supply of goods, could thereby exploit anybody. Nothing has been taken away from anybody in this process and additional goods have actually been created. And it would be equally absurd to claim that an agreement between different homesteaders, savers and producers regarding their nonexploitatively appropriated goods or services could possibly contain any foul play, then. Instead, exploitation takes place whenever any *deviation* from the homesteading principle occurs. It is exploitation whenever a person successfully claims partial or full control over scarce resources which he has not homesteaded, saved or produced, and which he has not acquired contractually from a previous producer-owner. Exploitation is the expropriation of homesteaders, producers and

---

Sheed and Ward, 1975). On important nineteenth-century forerunners of Austrian class analysis, see Leonard Liggio, "Charles Dunoyer and French Classical Liberalism," *Journal of Libertarian Studies* 1, no. 3 (1977); Ralph Raico, "Classical Liberal Exploitation Theory," *Journal of L ibertarian Studies* 1, no. 3 (1977); Mark Weinburg, "The Social Analysis of Three Early 19th Century French Liberals: Say, Comte, and Dunoyer," *Journal of Libertarian Studies* 2, no. 1 (1978); Joseph T. Salerno, "Comment on the French Liberal School," *Journal of Libertarian Studies* 2, no. 1 (1978); David M. Hart, "Gustave de Molinari and the Anti-Statist Liberal Tradition," 2 parts, *Journal of Libertarian Studies* 5, nos. 3 and 4 (1981).

savers by late-coming nonhomesteaders, nonproducers, nonsavers and noncontractors; it is the expropriation of people whose property claims are grounded in work and contract by people whose claims are derived from thin air and who disregard others' work and contracts.[10]

Needless to say, exploitation thus defined is in fact an integral part of human history. One can acquire and increase wealth either through homesteading, producing, saving, or contracting, or by expropriating homesteaders, producers, savers or contractors. There are no other ways. Both methods are natural to mankind. Alongside homesteading, producing and contracting, there have always been nonproductive and noncontractual property acquisitions. And in the course of economic development, just as producers and contractors can form firms, enterprises and corporations, so can exploiters combine to large-scale exploitation enterprises, governments and states. The ruling class (which may again be internally stratified) is initially composed of the members of such an exploitation firm. And with a ruling class established over a given territory and engaged in the expropriation of economic resources from a class of exploited producers, the center of all history indeed becomes the struggle between exploiters and the exploited. History, then, correctly told, is essentially the history of the victories and defeats of the rulers in their attempt to maximize exploitatively appropriated income and of the ruled in their attempts to resist and reverse this tendency. It is in this assessment of history that Austrians and Marxists agree, and it is why a notable intellectual affinity between Austrian and Marxist historical investigations exists. Both oppose a historiography which recognizes only action or interaction, economically and morally all on a par; and both oppose a historiography that instead of adopting such a value-neutral stand thinks that one's own arbitrarily introduced subjective value judgments have to provide the foil for one's historical narratives. Rather, history must be told in terms of freedom and exploitation,

---

[10]See on this also Hoppe, *A Theory of Socialism and Capitalism*; idem, "The Justice of Economic Efficiency," *Austrian Economics Newsletter* 1 (1988); infra chap. 9; idem, "The Ultimate Justification of the Private Property Ethics," *Liberty* (September 1988): infra chap. 10.

parasitism and economic impoverishment, private property and its destruction—otherwise it is told false.[11]

While productive enterprises come into or go out of existence because of voluntary support or its absence, a ruling class never comes to power because there is a demand for it, nor does it abdicate when abdication is demonstrably demanded. One cannot say by any stretch of the imagination that homesteaders, producers, savers and contractors have demanded their expropriation. They must be coerced into accepting it, and this proves conclusively that the exploitation firm is not in demand at all. Nor can one say that a ruling class can be brought down by abstaining from transactions with it in the same way as one can bring down a productive enterprise. For the ruling class acquires its income through nonproductive and noncontractual transactions and thus is unaffected by boycotts. Rather, what makes the rise of an exploitation firm possible, and what alone can in turn bring it down is a specific state of public opinion or, in Marxist terminology, a specific state of class consciousness.

An exploiter creates victims, and victims are potential enemies. It is possible that this resistance can be lastingly broken down by force in the case of a group of men exploiting another group of roughly the same size. However, more than force is needed to expand exploitation over a population many times its own size. For this to happen, a firm must also have public support. A majority of the population must accept the exploitative actions as legitimate. This acceptance can range from active enthusiasm to passive resignation. But it must be acceptance in the sense that a majority must have given up the idea of actively or passively resisting any attempt to enforce nonproductive and noncontractual property acquisitions. The class consciousness must be low, undeveloped and fuzzy. Only as long as this state of affairs lasts is there still room for an exploitative firm to prosper even if no actual demand for it exists. Only if and insofar as the

---

[11]See on this theme also Lord (John) Acton, *Essays in the History of Liberty* (Indianapolis: Liberty Fund, 1985); Franz Oppenheimer, *System der Soziologie*, vol. II: *Der Staat* (Stuttgart: G. Fischer, 1964); Alexander Rüstow, *Freedom and Domination* (Princeton, N.J.: Princeton University Press, 1986).

exploited and expropriated develop a clear idea of their own situation and are united with other members of their class through an ideological movement which gives expression to the idea of a classless society where all exploitation is abolished, can the power of the ruling class be broken. Only if, and insofar as, a majority of the exploited public becomes consciously integrated into such a movement and accordingly displays a common outrage over all nonproductive or noncontractual property acquisitions, shows a contempt for everyone who engages in such acts, and deliberately contributes nothing to help make them successful (not to mention actively trying to obstruct them), can its power be brought to crumble.

The gradual abolition of feudal and absolutist rule and the rise of increasingly capitalist societies in Western Europe and the U.S., and along with this unheard-of economic growth and rising population numbers were the result of an increasing class consciousness among the exploited, who were ideologically molded together through the doctrines of natural rights and liberalism. In this Austrians and Marxists agree.[12] They disagree, however, on the next assessment: The reversal of this liberalization process and steadily increased levels of exploitation in these societies since the last third of the nineteenth century, and particularly pronounced since WW I, are the result of a loss in class consciousness. In fact, in the Austrian view Marxism must accept much of the blame for this development by misdirecting attention from the correct exploitation model of the homesteader-producer-saver-contractor vs. the non-homesteader-producer-saver-contractor to the fallacious model of the wage earner vs. the capitalist, thus muddling things up.[13]

---

[12]See on this Murray N. Rothbard, "Left and Right: The Prospects for Liberty," in idem, *Egalitarianism As a Revolt Against Nature and Other Essays* (Washington, D.C.: Libertarian Review Press, 1974).

[13]All socialist propaganda to the contrary notwithstanding, the falsehood of the Marxist description of capitalists and laborers as antagonistic classes also comes to bear in certain empirical observations: Logically speaking, people can be grouped into classes in infinitely different ways. According to orthodox positivist methodology (which I consider false but am willing to accept here for the sake of argument), that classification system is better which helps us predict

The establishment of a ruling class over an exploited one many times its size by coercion and the manipulation of public opinion (i.e., a low degree of class consciousness among the exploited), finds its most basic institutional expression in the creation of a system of public law superimposed on private law. The ruling class sets itself apart and protects its position as a ruling class by adopting a constitution for their firm's operations. On the one hand, by formalizing the internal operations within the state apparatus as well as its relations vis-à-vis the exploited population, a constitution creates some degree of legal stability. The more familiar and popular private law notions are incorporated into constitutional and public law, the more conducive this will be to the creation of favorable public opinion. On the other hand, any constitution and public law also formalizes the exemplary status of the ruling class as regards the homesteading principle. It formalizes the right of the state's representatives to engage in nonproductive and noncontractual property acquisitions and the ultimate subordination of private to public law.

Class justice, i.e., a dualism of one set of laws for the rulers and another for the ruled, comes to bear in this dualism of public and private law and in the domination and infiltration of public law over and into private law. It is not because private-property rights are recognized by law, as Marxists think, that class justice is established. Rather, class justice comes into being precisely whenever a legal

---

better. Yet the classification of people as capitalists or laborers (or as representatives of varying degrees of capitalist- or laborer-ness) is practically useless in predicting what stand a person will take on fundamental political, social and economic issues. Contrary to this, the correct classification of people as tax producers and the regulated vs. tax consumers and the regulators (or as representatives of varying degrees of tax producer- or consumer-ness) is indeed also a powerful predictor. Sociologists have largely overlooked this because of almost universally shared Marxist preconceptions. But everyday experience overwhelmingly corroborates my thesis: Find out whether or not somebody is a public employee (and his rank and salary), and whether or not and to what extent the income and wealth of a person outside of the public sector is determined by public sector purchases and/or regulatory actions; people will systematically differ in their response to fundamental political issues depending on whether they are classified as direct or indirect tax consumers or as tax producers!

distinction exists between a class of persons acting under and being protected by public law and another class acting under and being protected instead by some subordinate private law. More specifically then, the basic proposition of the Marxist theory of the state in particular is false. The state is not exploitative because it protects the capitalists' property rights, but because it itself is exempt from the restriction of having to acquire property productively and contractually.[14]

In spite of this fundamental misconception, however, Marxism, because it correctly interprets the state as exploitative (contrary, for

---

[14]Franz Oppenheimer, *System der Soziologie*, vol. II. pp. 322–23, presents the matter thus:

> The basic norm of the state is power. That is, seen from the side of its origin: violence transformed into might. Violence is one of the most powerful forces shaping society, but is not itself a form of social interaction. It must become law in the positive sense of this term, that is, sociologically speaking, it must permit the development of a system of "subjective reciprocity," and this is only possible through a system of self-imposed restrictions on the use of violence and the assumption of certain obligations in exchange for its arrogated rights; in this way violence is turned into might, and a relationship of domination emerges which is accepted not only by the rulers, but under not too severely oppressive circumstances by their subjects as well, as expressing a "just reciprocity." Out of this basic norm secondary and tertiary norms now emerge as implied in it: norms of private law, of inheritance, criminal, obligational and constitutional law, which all bear the mark of the basic norm of power and domination, and which are all designed to influence the structure of the state in such a way as to increase economic exploitation to the maximum level which is compatible with the continuation of legally regulated domination.

The insight is fundamental that "law grows out of two essentially different roots." On the one hand, out of the law of the association of equals, which can be called a "natural right," even if it is no natural right, and on the other hand, out of the law of violence transformed into regulated might, the law of unequals.

On the relation between private and public law, see also F.A. Hayek, *Law, Legislation and Liberty*, 3 vols. (Chicago: University of Chicago Press, 1973–79), esp. vol. I, chap. 6 and vol. II, pp. 85–88.

instance, to the Public Choice School, which sees it as a normal firm among others),[15] is on to some important insights regarding the logic of state operations. For one thing, it recognizes the strategic function of redistributionist state policies. As an exploitative firm, the state must at all times be interested in a low degree of class consciousness among the ruled. The redistribution of property and income—a policy of *divide et impera*—is the state's means with which it can create divisiveness among the public and destroy the formation of a unifying class consciousness of the exploited. Furthermore, the redistribution of state power itself through democratizing the state constitution and opening up every ruling position to everyone and granting everyone the right to participate in the determination of state personnel and policy is a means for reducing the resistance against exploitation as such. Second, the state is indeed, as Marxists see it, the great center of ideological propaganda and mystification: Exploitation is really freedom; taxes are really voluntary contributions; noncontractual relations are really "conceptually" contractual ones; no one is ruled by anyone but we all rule ourselves; without the state neither law nor security would exist; and the poor would perish, etc. All of this is part of the ideological superstructure designed to legitimize an underlying basis of economic exploitation.[16] And finally, Marxists are also correct in noticing the close association between the state and business, especially the banking elite—even though their explanation for it is faulty. The reason is not that the bourgeois establishment sees and supports the state as the guarantor of private property rights and contractualism. On the contrary, the establishment correctly perceives the state as the very antithesis to private property that it is and takes a close interest in it for this reason. The more successful a business, the larger the potential danger of governmental exploitation, but the larger also the potential gains that can be achieved if it can come under government's special protection and is exempt from the full

---

[15]See James Buchanan and Gordon Tullock, *The Calculus of Consent* (Ann Arbor: University of Michigan Press, 1962), p. 19.

[16]See Hans-Hermann Hoppe, *Eigentum, Anarchie, und Staat* (Opladen: Westdeutscher Verlag, 1987); idem, *A Theory of Socialism and Capitalism.*

weight of capitalist competition. This is why the business establishment is interested in the state and its infiltration. The ruling elite in
turn is interested in close cooperation with the business establishment because of its financial powers. In particular, the banking elite
is of interest because as an exploitative firm the state naturally wishes
to possess complete autonomy for counterfeiting.

By offering to cut the banking elite in on its own counterfeiting
machinations and allowing them to counterfeit on top of its own
counterfeited notes under a regime of fractional reserve banking, the
state can easily reach this goal and establish a system of state monopolized money and cartelized banking controlled by the central bank.
And through this direct counterfeiting connection with the banking
system and by extension the banks' major clients, the ruling class in
fact extends far beyond the state apparatus to the very nerve centers
of civil society—not that much different, at least in appearance, from
the picture that Marxists like to paint of the cooperation between
banking, business elites and the state.[17]

Competition within the ruling class and among different ruling
classes brings about a tendency toward increasing concentration.
Marxism is right in this. However, its faulty theory of exploitation
again leads it to locate the cause for this tendency in the wrong place.
Marxism sees such a tendency as inherent in capitalist competition.
Yet it is precisely so long as people are engaged in a clean capitalism
that competition is *not* a form of zero-sum interaction. The homesteader, the producer, saver and contractor do not gain at another's
expense. Their gains either leave another's physical possessions completely unaffected or they actually imply mutual gains (as in the case
of all contractual exchanges). Capitalism thus can account for
increases in absolute wealth. But under its regime no systematic tendency toward relative concentration can be said to exist.[18] Instead,

---

[17]See Hans-Hermann Hoppe, "Banking, Nation States and International
Politics," *Review of Austrian Economics* 4 (1990); supra chap. 3; Rothbard, *The
Mystery of Banking*, chaps. 15–16.

[18]See on this in particular Rothbard, *Man, Economy, and State*, chap. 10, esp.
the section "The Problem of One Big Cartel"; also Mises, *Socialism*, chaps.
22–26.

zero-sum interactions characterize not only the relationship between the ruler and the ruled, but also between competing rulers. Exploitation defined as nonproductive and noncontractual property acquisitions is only possible as long as there is anything that can be appropriated. Yet if there were free competition in the business of exploitation, there would obviously be nothing left to expropriate. Thus, exploitation requires monopoly over some given territory and population; and the competition between exploiters is by its very nature eliminative and must bring about a tendency toward relative concentration of exploitative firms as well as a tendency toward centralization within each exploitative firm. The development of *states* rather than capitalist firms provides the foremost illustration of this tendency: There are now a significantly smaller number of states with exploitative control over much larger territories than in previous centuries. And within each state apparatus there has in fact been a constant tendency toward increasing the powers of the central government at the expense of its regional and local subdivisions. Yet outside the state apparatus a tendency toward relative concentration has also become apparent for the same reason. Not, as should be clear by now, because of any trait inherent in capitalism, but because the ruling class has expanded its rule into the midst of civil society through the creation of a state-banking-business alliance and in particular the establishment of a system of central banking. If a concentration and centralization of state power then takes place, it is only natural that this be accompanied by a parallel process of relative concentration and cartelization of banking and industry. Along with increased state powers, the associated banking and business establishment's powers of eliminating or putting economic competitors at a disadvantage by means of nonproductive and/or noncontractual expropriations increases. Business concentration is the reflection of a "state-ization" of economic life.[19]

---

[19]See on this Gabriel Kolko, *The Triumph of Conservatism* (Chicago: Free Press, 1967); James Weinstein, *The Corporate Ideal in the Liberal State* (Boston: Beacon Press, 1968); Ronald Radosh and Murray N. Rothbard, eds., *A New History of Leviathan* (New York: Dutton, 1972); Leonard Liggio and James J. Martin, eds., *Watershed of Empire* (Colorado Springs, Colo.: Ralph Myles, 1976).

The primary means for the expansion of state power and the elimination of rival exploitation centers is war and military domination. Interstate competition implies a tendency toward war and imperialism. As centers of exploitation their interests are by nature antagonistic. Moreover, with each of them—internally—in command of the instrument of taxation and absolute counterfeiting powers, it is possible for the ruling classes to let others pay for their wars. Naturally, if one does not have to pay for one's risky ventures oneself, but can force others to do so, one tends to be a greater risk taker and more trigger happy than one would otherwise be.[20] Marxism, contrary to much of the so-called bourgeois social sciences, gets the facts right: there is indeed a tendency toward imperialism operative in history; and the foremost imperialist powers are indeed the most advanced capitalist nations. Yet the explanation is once again faulty. It is the *state* as an institution exempt from the capitalist rules of property acquisitions that is by nature aggressive. And the historical evidence of a close correlation between capitalism and imperialism only seemingly contradicts this. It finds its explanation, easily enough, in the fact that in order to come out successfully from interstate wars, a state must be in command of sufficient (in relative terms) economic resources. *Ceteris paribus*, the state with more ample resources will win. As an exploitative firm, a state is by nature destructive of wealth and capital accumulation. Wealth is produced exclusively by civil society; and the weaker the state's exploitative powers, the more wealth and capital society accumulates. Thus, paradoxical as it may sound at first, the weaker or the more liberal a state is internally, the further developed capitalism is; a developed capitalist economy to extract from makes the state richer; and a richer state then makes for more and more successful expansionist wars. It is this relationship that explains why initially the states of Western Europe, and in particular

---

[20]On the relationship between state and war see Ekkehart Krippendorff, *Staat Und Krieg* (Frankfurt/M.: Suhrkamp, 1985); Charles Tilly, "War Making and State Making as Organized Crime," in Peter Evans et al., eds., *Bringing the State Back In* (Cambridge: Cambridge University Press, 1985); also Robert Higgs, *Crisis and Leviathan* (New York: Oxford University Press, 1987).

Great Britain, were the leading imperialist powers, and why in the 20th century this role has been assumed by the U.S.

And a similarly straightforward yet once again entirely non-Marxist explanation exists for the observation always pointed out by Marxists, that the banking and business establishment is usually among the most ardent supporters of military strength and imperial expansionism. It is not because the expansion of capitalist markets requires exploitation, but because the expansion of state protected and privileged business requires that such protection be extended also to foreign countries and that foreign competitors be hampered through non-contractual and nonproductive property acquisitions in the same way or more so than internal competition. Specifically, it supports imperialism if this promises to lead to a position of military domination of one's own allied state over another. For then, from a position of military strength, it becomes possible to establish a system of—as one may call it—*monetary imperialism.* The dominating state will use its superior power to enforce a policy of internationally coordinated inflation. Its own central bank sets the pace in the process of counterfeiting, and the central banks of the dominated states are ordered to use its currency as their own reserves and inflate on top of them. This way, along with the dominating state and as the earliest receivers of the counterfeit reserve currency its associated banking and business establishment can engage in an almost costless expropriation of foreign property owners and income producers. A double layer of exploitation of a foreign state and a foreign elite on top of a national state and elite is imposed on the exploited class in the dominated territories, causing prolonged economic dependency and relative economic stagnation vis-à-vis the dominant nation. It is this—very uncapitalist—situation that characterizes the status of the United States and the U.S. dollar and that gives rise to the—correct—charge of U.S. economic exploitation and dollar imperialism?[21]

---

[21]On a further elaborated version of this theory of military and monetary imperialism see Hoppe, *Banking, Nation States and International Politics* (supra chap. 3).

Finally, the increasing concentration and centralization of exploitative powers leads to economic stagnation and thereby creates the objective conditions for their ultimate demise and the establishment of a classless society capable of producing unheard-of economic prosperity.

Contrary to Marxist claims, this is not the result of any historical laws, however. In fact, no such things as inexorable historical laws as Marxists conceive of them exist.[22] Nor is it the result of a tendency for the rate of profit to fall with an increased organic composition of capital (an increase in the proportion of constant to variable capital, that is), as Marx thinks. Just as the labor theory of value is false beyond repair, so is the law of the tendential fall of the profit rate, which is based on it. The source of value, interest and profit is not the expenditure of labor but of acting, i.e., the employment of scarce means in the pursuit of goals by agents who are constrained by time preference and uncertainty (imperfect knowledge). There is no reason to suppose, then, that changes in the organic composition of capital should have any systematic relation to changes in interest and profit.

Instead, the likelihood of crises which stimulate the development of a higher degree of class consciousness (i.e., the subjective conditions for the overthrow of the ruling class) increases because—to use one of Marx's favorite terms—of the dialectics of exploitation which I have already touched on earlier: Exploitation is destructive of wealth formation. Hence, in the competition of exploitative firms (of states), less exploitative or more liberal ones tend to outcompete more exploitative ones because they are in command of more ample resources. The process of imperialism initially has a relatively liberating effect on societies coming under its control. A relatively more capitalist social model is exported to relatively less capitalist (more exploitative) societies. The development of productive forces is stimulated: economic integration is furthered, division of labor extended, and a genuine world market established. Population

---

[22]See on this in particular Ludwig von Mises, *Theory and History* (Auburn, Ala.: Ludwig von Mises institute, 1985), esp. part 2.

figures go up in response, and expectations as regards the economic future rise to unprecedented heights.[23] With exploitative domination taking hold, and interstate competition reduced or even eliminated in a process of imperialist expansionism, however, the external constraints on the dominating state's power of internal exploitation and expropriation gradually disappear. Internal exploitation, taxation and regulation begin to increase the closer the ruling class comes to its ultimate goal of world domination. Economic stagnation sets in and the—worldwide—higher expectations become frustrated. And this— high expectations and an economic reality increasingly falling behind these expectations—is the classical situation for the emergence of a revolutionary potential.[24] A desperate need for ideological solutions to the emerging crises arises, along with a more widespread recognition of the fact that state rule, taxation and regulation—far from offering such a solution—actually constitute the very problem that must be overcome. If in this situation of economic stagnation, crises,

---

[23]It may be noted here that Marx and Engels, foremost in their *Communist Manifesto*, championed the historically progressive character of capitalism and were full of praise for its unprecedented accomplishments. Indeed, reviewing the relevant passages of the *Manifesto* concludes Joseph A. Schumpeter,

> Never, I repeat, and in particular by no modern defender of the bourgeois civilization has anything like this been penned, never has a brief been composed on behalf of the business class from so profound and so wide a comprehension of what its achievement is and what it means to humanity. ("The Communist Manifesto in Sociology and Economics," in idem, *Essays of Joseph A. Schumpeter*, ed. Richard Clemence [Port Washington, N.Y.: Kennikat Press, 1951], p. 293)

Given this view of capitalism, Marx went so far as to defend the British conquest of India, for example, as a historically progressive development. See Marx's contributions to the *New York Daily Tribune*, of June 25, 1853, July 11, 1853, August 8, 1853 (Marx and Engels, *Werke* [East Berlin: Dietz, 1960], vol. 9). As a contemporary Marxist taking a similar stand on imperialism see Bill Warren, *Imperialism: Pioneer of Capitalism* (London: New Left Books, 1981).

[24]See on the theory of revolution in particular Charles Tilly, *From Mobilization to Revolution* (Reading, Mass.: Addison-Wesley, 1978); idem, *As Sociology Meets History* (New York: Academic Press, 1981).

and ideological disillusion[25] a positive solution is offered in the form of a systematic and comprehensive libertarian philosophy coupled with its economic counterpart: Austrian economics; and if this ideology is propagated by an activist movement, then the prospects of igniting the revolutionary potential to activism become overwhelmingly positive and promising. Antistatist pressures will mount and bring about an irresistible tendency toward dismantling the power of the ruling class and the state as its instrument of exploitation.[26]

If and insofar as this occurs, however, this will not mean social ownership of means of production, contrary to the Marxist model. In fact, social ownership is not only economically inefficient as has already been explained; it is incompatible with the idea that the state is "withering away."[27] For if means of production are owned collectively, and if it is realistically assumed that not everyone's ideas as to how to employ these means of production happen to coincide (as if by miracle), then it is precisely socially owned factors of production which require continued state actions, i.e., an institution coercively imposing one person's will on another disagreeing one's. Instead, the withering away of the state, and with this the end of exploitation and the beginning of liberty and unheard-of economic prosperity, means the establishment of a pure private property society regulated by nothing but private law.

---

[25]For a neo-Marxist assessment of the present era of "late capitalism" as characterized by "a new ideological disorientation" born out of permanent economic stagnation and the exhaustion of the legitimatory powers of conservatism and social-democratism, (i.e., "liberalism" in American terminology) see Jürgen Habermas, *Die Neue Unübersichtlichkeit* (Frankfurt/M.: Suhrkamp, 1985); also idem, *Legitimation Crisis* (Boston: Beacon Press, 1975); C. Offe, *Strukurprobleme des kapitalistischen Staates* (Frankfurt/M.: Suhrkamp, 1972).

[26]For an Austrian-libertarian assessment of the crisis-character of late capitalism and on the prospects for the rise of a revolutionary libertarian class consciousness see Rothbard, "Left and Right"; idem, *For a New Liberty,* chap. 15; idem, *The Ethics of Liberty* (Atlantic Highlands, N.J.: Humanities Press, 1982), part V.

[27]On the internal inconsistencies of the Marxist theory of the state see also Hans Kelsen, *Sozialismus und Staat* (Vienna, 1965).

5

Theory of Employment, Money, Interest, and the Capitalist Process: The Misesian Case Against Keynes

I t is my goal to reconstruct some basic truths regarding the process of economic development and the role played in it by employment, money, and interest. These truths neither originated with the Austrian School of economics, nor are they an integral part of this tradition of economic thinking alone. In fact, most of them were part and parcel of what is now called classical economics, and it was the recognition of their validity that uniquely distinguished the economist from the crackpot. Yet the Austrian School, in particular Ludwig von Mises and, later, Murray N. Rothbard, has given the clearest and most complete presentation of these truths.[1] Moreover, they have also presented their most rigorous defense by showing them to be ultimately deducible from basic, incontestable propositions (such as that man acts and knows what it means to act) so as to establish them as truths whose denial would not only be factually incorrect but,

---

[A slightly different version appears in *Dissent on Keynes: A Critical Appraisal of Keynesian Economics*, edited by Mark Skousen (New York: Praeger, 1992).]

[1]See in particular Ludwig von Mises, *Human Action* (Chicago: Regnery, 1966); Murray N. Rothbard, *Man, Economy, and State* (Los Angeles: Nash, 1970).

much more decisively, would amount to logical-praxeological contradictions and absurdities.[2]

First, I will systematically reconstruct this Austrian theory of economic development. Then I will turn to the "new" theory of Keynes,
which belongs, as he himself cannot help but acknowledge, to the tradition of "underworld" economics (like Mercantilism) and of economic cranks (like Silvio Gesell).[3] I will show that Keynes's new economics, too, is cranky: a tissue of logical-praxeological falsehoods
reached by means of obscure jargon, shifting definitions, and logical
inconsistencies, intent to create an anticapitalist, anti-private-prop-
erty, and antibourgeois mentality.

I.

1. EMPLOYMENT

"Unemployment in the unhampered market is always voluntary."[4]
Man works, because he prefers its anticipated result to the disutility
of labor and the psychic income to be derived from leisure. He "stops
working at that point, at which he begins to value leisure, the absence
of labor's disutility, more highly than the increment in satisfaction

---

[2]See on the foundations of economics Ludwig von Mises, *Epistemological
Problems of Economics* (New York: New York University Press, 1981); idem,
Theory and History (Auburn, Ala.: Ludwig von Mises Institute, 1985); idem, *The
Ultimate Foundation of Economic Science* (Kansas City: Sheed Andrews and
McMeel, 1978); Murray N. Rothbard, *Individualism and the Philosophy of the
Social Sciences* (San Francisco: Cato Institute, 1979); Hans-Hermann Hoppe,
*Kritik der kausalwissenschaftlichen Sozialforschung. Untersuchugen zur Grundlegung
von Soziologie und Ökonomie* (Opladen: Westdeutscher Verlag, 1983); idem,
Praxeology and Economic Science (Auburn, Ala.: Ludwig von Mises Institute,
1988).

On the competing, positivist view of economics, according to which economic laws are hypotheses subject to empirical confirmation and falsification
(much like the laws of physics), see Milton Friedman, "The Methodology of
Positive Economics," in idem, *Essays in Positive Economics* (Chicago: University
of Chicago Press, 1953).

[3]John Maynard Keynes, *The General Theory of Employment, Interest, and
Money* (New York: Harcourt, Brace and World, 1964), esp. chap. 23.

[4]Mises, *Human Action*, p. 599.

expected from working more."[5] Obviously, then, Robinson Crusoe, the self-sufficient producer, can only be unemployed voluntarily (because he prefers to remain idle and consume present values instead of expending additional labor in the production of future ones).

The result is not different when Friday enters and a private property economy is established based on a initial recognition of each person's rights of exclusive ownership over those resources which he had recognized as scarce and appropriated (homesteaded) by mixing his labor with them before anyone else had done so, and of all goods produced with their help. In this situation not only exchange ratios—prices—for the purchase or rental of material goods become possible, but also prices (wages) for the rental of labor services. Employment will ensue whenever the offered wage is valued more highly by the laborer than the satisfaction to be derived from self sufficiently working with and/or consuming his own resources (or of appropriating previously submarginal resources). Employment will increase, and wages rise, so long as entrepreneurs perceive existing wages as lower than the marginal value product (discounted by time preference)[6] which a corresponding increment in the employment of labor can be expected to bring about. On the other hand, unemployment will result, and increase, so long as a person values the marginal value product attained through self-employment more highly than a wage that reflects his labor services' marginal productivity.

In this construction there is no logical room for such a thing as involuntary unemployment. As employment is always voluntary, so is unemployment (self-employment).[7]

---

[5]Ibid., p. 611.

[6]On time preference, see the following section 1.3.

[7]The claim that involuntary unemployment is possible in the framework of a private property economy as characterized above is due to an elementary logical-conceptual confusion: It ignores the fact that employment is a two-party affair; i.e., an exchange which, like any voluntary exchange, can only take place if it is deemed *mutually, bilaterally* beneficial. It makes no more sense to classify someone as involuntarily unemployed if he cannot find anybody willing to meet his unilaterally fixed demands for employment, than to call a person in search of a wife, a house, or a Mercedes involuntarily wifeless, homeless, or Mercedesless

Involuntary unemployment is only logically possible once the situation is fundamentally changed and a person or institution is introduced which can successfully exercise control over resources which he has not homesteaded, or acquired through voluntary exchange from homesteaders. Such an extra-market institution, by imposing, for instance, a minimum wage higher than the marginal productivity of labor, can effectively prohibit an exchange between a supplier of labor service and a capitalist which would be preferred by both, if both had unrestricted control over their homesteaded property. The would-be laborer then becomes involuntarily unemployed, and the would-be employer is forced to dislocate complementary factors of production from more into less value productive usages. As a matter of fact, an extra-market institution can in principle create any desired amount of involuntary unemployment. A minimum wage of say, $1 million per hour would, if enforced, involuntarily disemploy practically everyone and would, along this way toward forced self-employment, condemn most of today's population to death by starvation.

In the absence of an institution exempt from the rules of the market involuntary unemployment is logically impossible, and prosperity instead of impoverishment will result.

---

because no one wants to marry him or supply him with a house or a Mercedes *at terms which this person has unilaterally determined as agreeable to him.* Absurdity and contradiction would result if one were to do so. For then one would not only have to accept, as the other side of the same coin, that the boycotting employer, woman, or owner of a house or a Mercedes in turn would have to be regarded as an involuntary *non*employer, *non*wife, or *non*trader of a house or a Mercedes *because his/her unilateral demands had not been met by the would-be employee, would-be husband, or would-be house or Mercedes owner just as much as they had not met his.* Moreover, with both the would-be employee as well as the would-be employer classified as involuntarily being what they are because no mutual agreement had been reached between them, to create "voluntary employment" would imply coercing either one or both parties to accept an exchange whose terms one or both of them regard as unacceptable. Hence, to say involuntary unemployment is possible on the unhampered market is to say coercion means voluntariness and voluntariness coercion, which is nonsense.

2. MONEY

Man participates in an exchange economy (instead of remaining in self-sufficient isolation) insofar as he is capable of recognizing the higher productivity of a system of the division of labor and he prefers more goods over less. Out of his market participation arises in turn his desire for a medium of exchange (money). Indeed, only if one were to assume the humanly impossible (that man had perfect foresight regarding the future), would there be no purpose for him to have money. For with all uncertainties removed, in the never-never land of equilibrium one would know precisely the terms, times, and locations of all future exchanges, and everything could be prearranged accordingly and would take on the form of direct rather than indirect exchanges.[8] Under the inescapable human condition of uncertainty, however, when all this is not known and action must by nature be speculative, man will begin to demand goods no longer exclusively because of their use-value, but also because of their value as media of exchange.

Faced with a situation where his reservation demand for some supplied goods or services is low or nonexistent, and where a directly satisfying exchange, due to the absence of double coincidences of wants, is out of the question, he will also consider trading whenever the goods to be acquired are more marketable than those to be surrendered, such that their possession would then facilitate the acquisition of directly serviceable goods and services at not yet known future dates.

Moreover, since it is the very function of a medium of exchange to facilitate future purchases of directly serviceable goods, man will naturally prefer the acquisition of a more marketable and, at the limit,

---

[8]See Mises, *Human Action*, pp. 244–50.

  In a system without change in which there is no uncertainty whatever about the future, nobody needs to hold cash. Every individual knows precisely what amount of money he will need at any future date. He is therefore in a position to lend all the funds he receives in such a way that the loans fall due on the date he will need them. (p. 249)

See also Rothbard, *Man, Economy, and State*, p. 280.

universally marketable medium of exchange to that of a less or non-universally marketable one so that

> there would be an inevitable tendency for the less marketable of the series of goods used as media of exchange to be one by one rejected until at last only a single commodity remained, which was universally employed as a medium of exchange; in a word, money.[9]

On the way toward this ultimate goal, by selecting monies that are increasingly more widely used, the division of labor is extended and productivity increased.

However, once a commodity has been established as a universal medium of exchange, and the prices of all directly serviceable exchange goods are expressed in terms of units of this money (while the price of the money unit is its power to purchase an array of non-money goods), money no longer exercises any systematic influence on the division of labor, employment, and produced income. Once established, any amount of money is compatible with any amount of employment and income.[10] Indeed, as explained above, in the never-never land of equilibrium there would be no money, but there would still be employment and income. This demonstrates that money on the one hand and employment and income on the other must be regarded as logically-praxeologically independent and unrelated

---

[9]Ludwig von Mises, *The Theory of Money and Credit* (Irvington, N.Y.: Foundation for Economic Education, 1971), pp. 32–33; see also Carl Menger, *Principles of Economics* (New York: New York University Press, 1981); idem, *Geld*, in Carl Menger, *Gesammelte Werke*, ed. F.A. Hayek (Tübingen: Mohr, 1970), vol. 4.

[10]See Rothbard, *Man, Economy, and State*, pp. 669–71.

> Goods are useful and scarce, and any increment in goods is a social benefit. But money is useful not directly, but only in exchanges. . . . When there is less money, the exchange-value of the monetary unit rises; when there is more money, the exchange-value of the monetary unit falls. We conclude that there is no such thing as "too little" or "too much" money, *that, whatever the social money stock, the benefits of money are always utilized to the maximum extent.* (p. 670)

See also Murray N. Rothbard, *The Mystery of Banking* (New York: Richardson and Snyder, 1983).

concepts. For instance, should the supply of money increase, other things being equal, this would surely have redistributive effects, depending on where and how the additional money entered the economy; but it would just as surely have no systematic effect on the amount of employment and the size of the social product. Prices and wages generally would go up, and the purchasing power of the money unit would go down. However, nothing would follow with regard to employment and social product. They may be different, or they may be the same. The same is true of changes in the demand for money. An increase in the demand for money (i.e., a higher relative value attached to additional cash as compared to additional nonmoney), would certainly change relative prices; yet it would not imply anything as far as employment and social product is concerned. In equilibrating an increased demand for money with a given stock of money, the general level of prices and wages must fall, and the purchasing power of the money unit must rise, *mutatis mutandis*. But there is no reason to suppose that this should have any impact on employment or income. Money wages fall, but simultaneously the purchasing power of money increases, leaving real wages and real social product entirely unaffected.

The result is no different if changes on the nonmoney side are considered. Other things being equal, an increase in the supply of goods and services, for instance, brings about an increase in the purchasing power of money; money prices fall. This reduces the quantity of money demanded (the demand schedule for money being given), because the cost of holding onto money instead of spending it on non-money has risen; and this lowered demand for cash implies in turn a reverse tendency toward rising prices and a reduced purchasing power of money. Nothing concerning employment and social product follows. Nor does the picture change when expectations are explicitly taken into account. Inflationary (deflationary) expectations reduce (increase) the demand for money immediately and thus speed up the adjustment toward whatever has been anticipated; and if something wrong has been anticipated (i.e., something out of line with the underlying reality), then the process of self-corrective adjustments is sped up through the workings of expectations. But none of these monetary phenomena has any systematic praxeological connection with employment and social product, which may well remain the same throughout all monetary changes.

Invariably, money is "neutral" to employment and social product.

3. INTEREST

Money is "neutral" also to interest. However, interest, unlike money, is praxeologically related to employment and social product.

As money is the result of uncertainty, so interest results from time preference, which is as essential to action as uncertainty (and in a sense to be explained shortly even more so). In acting, an actor not only invariably aims to substitute a more for a less satisfactory state of affairs and so demonstrates a preference for more rather than less goods; he must invariably also consider when in the future his goals will be reached (i.e., the time necessary to accomplish them) as well as a good's duration of serviceability, and every action thus also demonstrates a universal preference for earlier over later goods and of more over less durable ones. Every action requires some time to attain its goal; since man must consume something sometimes and cannot stop consuming entirely, time is always scarce. Thus, *ceteris paribus*, present or earlier goods are, and must invariably be, valued more highly than future or later ones.[11] In fact, if man were not constrained by time preference and the only constraint operating were that of preferring more over less, he would invariably choose those production processes that would yield the largest output per input,

---

[11]On the time preference theory of interest see William Stanley Jevons, *Theory of Political Economy* (New York: Augustus M. Kelley, 1965); Eugen von Böhm-Bawerk, *Capital and Interest*, 3 vols. (South Holland, Ill.: Libertarian Press, 1959); Richard von Strigl, *Kapital und Produktion* (Vienna: Julius Springer, 1934 [Engl. trans., Ludwig von Mises Institute, 1988]); Frank Fetter, *Capital, Interest, and Rent* (Kansas City: Sheed Andrews and McMeel, 1971); Roger Garrison, "In Defense of the Misesian Theory of Interest," *Journal of Libertarian Studies* 3, no. 2 (1979); idem, "Professor Rothbard and the Theory of Interest," in Walter Block and Llewellyn H. Rockwell, Jr., eds., *Man, Economy, and Liberty: Essays in Honor of Murray N. Rothbard* (Auburn, Ala.: Ludwig von Mises Institute, 1988).

regardless of the length of time needed for these methods to bear fruit. For instance, instead of building a fishing net first, Crusoe would immediately begin constructing a fishing trawler, as the economically most efficient method for catching fish. That no one, including Crusoe, acts in this way makes it evident that man cannot but "value fractions of time of the same length in a different way according as they are nearer or remoter from the instant of the actor's decision."[12]

Thus, constrained by time preference, man will only exchange a present good against a future one if he anticipates thereby increasing his amount of future goods. The rate of time preference, which can be different from person to person and from one point in time to the next, but which can never be anything but positive for everyone, simultaneously determines the height of the premium which present goods command over future ones as well as the amount of savings and investment. The market rate of interest is the aggregate sum of all individual time preference rates, reflecting, so to say, the social rate of time preference, and equilibrating social savings (i.e., the supply of present goods offered for exchange against future goods) and social investment (i.e., the demand for present goods capable of yielding future returns).

No supply of loanable funds could exist without previous savings, i.e., without the abstention from some possible consumption of present goods. Furthermore, no demand for loanable funds would exist if no one were to perceive any opportunity to employ present goods productively (i.e., to invest them so as to produce a future output that would exceed current input). Indeed, if all present goods were consumed and none invested in time-consuming production processes, there would be no interest or time preference rate, or rather, the interest rate would be infinitely high, which outside of the Garden of Eden, would be tantamount to eking out a primitive subsistence living by encountering reality with nothing but one's bare hands and with nothing but a desire for instantaneous gratification.

---

[12]Mises, *Human Action,* p. 483.

A supply of and a demand for loanable funds only arises—and this is the human condition—once it is recognized that indirect, more roundabout, lengthier production processes can yield a larger or better output per input than direct and short ones;[13] and it is possible, by means of savings, to accumulate the amount of present goods needed to provide for all those wants whose satisfaction during the prolonged waiting time is deemed more urgent than the increment in future well-being expected from the adoption of a more time-consuming production process.[14]

So long as this is the case, capital formation and accumulation will set in and continue. Instead of being supported by and engaged in instantaneously gratifying production processes, the originary factors of production, land and labor, are supported by an excess of production over consumption and employed in the production of capital goods. These have no value except as intermediate products in the process of turning out final (consumer) goods. In other words, their value lies in the fact that whoever possesses them can use them to produce other capital goods more efficiently. The excess in value (price) of a capital good over the sum expended on the complementary originary factors required for its production is due to this time difference and the universal fact of time preference. It is the price paid for buying time; for moving closer to the completion of one's ultimate goal rather than having to start at the very beginning. Because of time preference, the value of the final output must exceed the sum spent on its factors of production (the price paid for the capital good and all complementary labor services).

The lower the time preference rate, then, the earlier the process of capital formation will set in, and the faster it will lengthen the

---

[13]To be sure, not all lengthier production processes are more productive than shorter ones; but under the assumption that man, constrained by time-preference, will invariably and at all times select the shortest conceivable methods of producing some given output, any increase in output then can—praxeologically—only be achieved if the production structure is lengthened.

[14]Mises, *Human Action*, pp. 490ff.

roundabout structure of production. Any increase in the accumulation of capital goods and in the roundaboutness of the production structure in turn raises the marginal productivity of labor. This leads to either increased employment and/or wage rates, and, in any case (even if the labor supply curve should become backward sloping with increased wages), to a higher wage total.[15] Supplied with an increased amount of capital goods then, a better paid population of wage earners will produce an overall increased—future—social product, raising at last, after that of the employees, also the real incomes of the owners of capital and land. While interest (time preference) thus has a direct praxeological relation to employment and social income, it has nothing whatsoever to do with money. To be sure, in a money economy there also exists a monetary expression for the social rate of time preference. Yet this does not change the fact that interest and money are systematically independent and unrelated, and interest is a "real," not a monetary phenomenon. In fact, in the never-never land of equilibrium there would be no place for money because the future by definition would be certain and with all uncertainty removed no one would have any need for cash holdings (whose sole purpose it is, cash being neither productive nor consumable, to have one prepared for not yet known purchases at not yet known dates). Time preference and interest, however, cannot be conceived of as disappearing even then. For even in equilibrium the existing capital structure needs to be constantly maintained over time (so as to prevent it from gradually becoming consumed in the even course of an endlessly repeated pattern of productive operations). There can be no such maintenance, however, without ongoing savings and reinvestments: and there can be no such things as these without the expectation of a positive rate of interest. (Indeed, if the rate of interest paid were zero, capital consumption would result, and one would move out of equilibrium.)[16]

---

[15]See also Rothbard, *Man, Economy, and State*, pp. 663f.

[16]See also Mises, *Human Action*, pp. 530–32; Rothbard, *Man, Economy, and State*, pp. 385–86.

Matters become somewhat more complex under conditions of uncertainty, with money actually in use, but the praxeological independence of money and interest remains fully intact. Under these conditions, man invariably has three instead of two alternatives as to how to allocate his current income. He must not only decide how much to allocate to the purchase of present goods and how much to future goods (i.e., how much to consume and how much to invest), but also how much to keep in cash. There are no other alternatives. Yet while man must at all times make adjustments concerning three margins at once, invariably the outcome is determined by two distinct and praxeologically unrelated factors. The consumption/investment proportion is determined by time preference. The source of the demand for cash, on the other hand, is the utility attached to money (i.e., its usefulness in allowing immediate purchases of directly serviceable goods at uncertain future dates). Both factors can vary, independent of one another.

If the supply of money changes, or if the demand for money changes with a given social stock of money, the purchasing power of money will also change. However, aside from causing changes in relative incomes, no such changes in a money unit's purchasing power would have any effect on overall real income. Incomes in terms of money increase or decrease, yet the purchasing power of money correspondingly falls or rises, leaving real income unchanged. Or, with money incomes unchanged, more or less of it will be held in cash (hoarded), but then the purchasing power of money correspondingly rises or falls, once again leaving the real income purchased with a smaller or larger sum of money unaltered. It is this real income, however, not money as such, to which a man's time preference schedule is related, and in light of which his effective rate of time preference is determined. Since real income does not change through all these monetary changes, there is no reason to suppose that the rate of time preference will. If, for instance, the Keynesian nightmare of increased hoarding becomes reality and prices generally fall while the purchasing power of money correspondingly rises, this will leave the real investment/consumption proportion entirely unaffected. Unless the time preference schedule is assumed to have changed at the same time, the additional hoards will be drawn from funds that formerly were spent on consumption and from funds that formerly went into investment in the same pre-established proportion, so as to leave real consumption and real investment at precisely their old levels. However, if time-preference is assumed to change concomitantly, then everything is possible. Indeed, if the additional hoards come exclusively from previous consumption spending, an increased demand for money can go hand in hand even with a fall in the rate of interest and increased investment. Yet this is due not to changes in the demand for money but exclusively to a change (a fall) in the time preference schedule.[17]

4. THE CAPITALIST PROCESS

With the division of labor established and extended to its ultimate limit via the development of a universal medium of exchange, the process of economic development is essentially determined by time preference.

To be sure, there are other factors that are important: the quality and quantity of the population, the endowment with nature-given resources, and the state of technology. Yet of these, the quality of a people is largely beyond anyone's control and must be taken as a given: the quantity of a population may or may not advance economic development, depending on whether the population is below or above its optimum size for a given-sized territory: and nature-given resources or technological know-how can only have an economic impact if discovered and utilized. To do this, though, there must be prior savings and investment. It is not the availability of resources and technical or scientific knowledge that imposes limits on economic advancement: rather, it is time preference that imposes limits on the exploitation of actually available resources as well as on the utilization of existing knowledge (and also on scientific progress for that matter, insofar as research activities, too, must be supported by saved-up funds).

---

[17]See also Murray N. Rothbard, *America's Great Depression* (Kansas City: Sheed and Ward, 1975), pp. 39–41.

Thus, the only viable path toward economic growth is through savings and investment, governed as they are by time preference. Ultimately there is no way toward prosperity except through an increase in the per capita quota of invested capital. This is the only way to increase the marginal productivity of labor and only if this is done can future income rise in turn. With real incomes rising, the effective rate of time preference falls (without, however, ever reaching zero or even becoming negative), adding still further increased doses of investment, and setting in motion an upward spiraling process of economic development.

There is no reason to suppose that this process should come to a halt short of reaching the Garden of Eden where all scarcity has disappeared—unless people deliberately choose otherwise and begin to value additional leisure more highly than any further increase in real incomes. Nor is there any reason to suppose that the process of capitalist development would be anything but smooth and that the economy would flexibly adjust not only to all monetary changes but to all changes in the social rate of time preference as well. Of course, so long as the future is uncertain, there will be entrepreneurial errors, losses, and bankruptcies. But no systematic reason exists why this should cause more than temporary disruptions, or why these disruptions should exceed, or drastically fluctuate around, a "natural rate" of business failures.[18]

Matters become different only if an extra-market institution such as government is introduced. It not only makes involuntary unemployment possible, as explained above: the very existence of an agency that can effectively claim ownership over resources which it has neither homesteaded, produced, nor contractually acquired, also raises the social rate of time preference for homesteaders, producers, and contractors, and hence creates involuntary impoverishment, stagnation, or even regression. It is only through government that mankind can be stopped on its natural course toward a gradual emancipation from scarcity long before ever reaching the point of a

---

[18]See also Rothbard, *America's Great Depression*, pp. 12–17.

voluntarily chosen zero-growth.[19] And it is in the presence alone of a government, that the capitalist process can possibly take on a cyclical (rather than a smooth) pattern, with busts following booms. Exempt from the rules of private property acquisition and transfer, government naturally desires a monopoly over money and banking and wants nothing better than to engage in fractional reserve (deposit) banking—in nontechnical terms: monopolistic counterfeiting—so as to enrich itself at the expense of others through the much less conspicuous means of fraud rather than through outright confiscation.[20] Boom and bust cycles are the outcome of fraudulent fractional reserve banking. If and insofar as the newly created counterfeit money enters the economy as additional supplies on the credit market, the rate of interest will have to fall below what it otherwise would have been. Credit must become cheaper. Yet at a lower price more credit is taken, and more resources then are invested in the production of future goods (instead of being used for present consumption) than otherwise would have been. The roundaboutness of the entire production structure is lengthened. In order to complete all investment projects that now are underway, more time is needed than that required to complete those begun before the credit expansion. All the goods which would have been created without credit expansion must be produced; plus those that are newly added. For this to be possible, however, more capital is required. The larger amount of future goods can only be produced successfully if additional savings provide for a fund of means of sustenance sufficiently large to bridge, and carry workers through, the longer waiting time. But, by assumption, no

----

[19]On the role of government as destructive of wealth formation, see in particular Murray N. Rothbard, *Power and Market* (Kansas City: Sheed Andrews and McMeel, 1977); Hans-Hermann Hoppe, *A Theory of Socialism and Capitalism* (Boston: Kluwer Academic Publishers, 1989); idem, "The Economics of Sociology and Taxation," *Journal des Economistes et des Etudes Humaines* (1990); supra chap. 2.

[20]See in particular Rothbard, *The Mystery of Banking*; Hans-Hermann Hoppe, "Banking, Nation States, and International Politics," *Review of Austrian Economics* 4 (1990); supra chap. 3; idem, "Marxist and Austrian Class Analysis," *Journal of Libertarian Studies* 9, no. 2 (1990); supra chap. 4; idem, "European Economic Integration and the ECU," *Austrian Economics Newsletter* (1989).

such increase in savings has taken place. The lower interest rate is not the result of a larger supply of capital goods. The social rate of time preference has not changed at all. It is solely the result of counterfeit money entering the economy through the credit market. It follows logically that it must be considered impossible to successfully complete all investment projects underway after a credit expansion due to a systematic lack of real capital. Projects will have to be liquidated so as to shorten the overall production structure and to readjust it to an unchanged rate of social time preference and the corresponding real investment-consumption proportion.[21]

These cyclical movements can neither be avoided by expecting them (according to the motto "a cycle anticipated is a cycle avoided"): They are the praxeologically necessary consequence of additional counterfeit credit being successfully placed. Once this is

------

[21]On the theory of the business cycle see Mises's original contribution in his *Theory of Money and Credit*, part III, chap. 5; his first elaborate version is *Geldwertstabilisierung und Konjunkturpolitik* (Jena: Gustav Fischer, 1928), the English translation of which did not appear until 1978 in Ludwig von Mises, *On the Manipulation of Money and Credit* (Dobbs Ferry, N.Y.: Free Market Books, 1978); F.A. Hayek, *Monetary Theory and the Trade Cycle* (New York: A.M. Kelley, 1966); idem, *Prices and Production* (New York: Augustus M. Kelley, 1967); Hayek's works were first published in 1929, resp. 1931; it is interesting to note that Hayek, who received the Nobel prize in 1974, the year after Mises's death, for his contributions to the Mises-Hayek theory of the business cycle, obviously misrepresents Mises's achievements as regards the development of this theory: In his *Prices and Production* of 1931, the first presentation of the Austrian business cycle theory to appear in English, he acknowledges Mises's prior claim to fame. Yet even though he cites Mises's above mentioned 1928 work, he falsely claims that Mises's contributions to the theory were essentially confined to a few remarks in his original work of 1912; see chap. 3 fn. 1 in *Prices and Production*; Strigl, *Kapital und Produktion*; Lionel Robbins, *The Great Depression* (Freeport, N.Y.: Books for Libraries Press, 1971); Rothbard, *America's Great Depression*; Ludwig von Mises, et al., *The Austrian Theory of the Trade Cycle and Other Essays* (Auburn, Ala.: Ludwig von Mises Institute, 1983); Hoppe, *Kritik der kausalwissenschaftlichen Sozialforschung*, chap. 3; Roger Garrison, "Hayekian Trade Cycle Theory: A Reappraisal," *Cato Journal* 6, no. 2 (1986); idem, "The Austrian Theory of the Business Cycle in the Light of Modern Macroeconomics," *Review of Austrian Economics* 3 (1988).

the case, a boom-bust cycle is inevitable, regardless of what actors correctly or incorrectly believe or expect. The cycle is induced by a monetary change, but it takes effect in the realm of "real" phenomena and will be a "real" cycle no matter what beliefs people happen to hold.[22]

Nor can it be realistically expected that the inevitable cyclical movements resulting from an expansion of credit will ever come to a halt: So long as an extra-market institution like government is in control of money, a permanent series of cyclical movements will mark the process of economic development. For through the creation of fraudulent credit, a government can engender a smooth and highly inconspicuous income and wealth redistribution in its own favor. There is no reason (short of angelic assumptions) to suppose that it would ever deliberately stop using this magic wand merely because credit expansion has the "unfortunate" side-effect of business cycles.

II.

After this reconstruction of the classical, and especially the Austrian theory of employment, money, interest, and the capitalist process, I will now turn to Keynes and his "new" theory. Before the backdrop of our explanation of the old one it shall be easy to recognize Keynes's "new" *General Theory of Employment, Interest, and Money* as fundamentally flawed and the Keynesian revolution as one of the twentieth century's foremost intellectual scandals.[23]

---

[22]See also Roger Garrison, "'Rational Expectations' Offers Nothing That's Both New and True," *Austrian Economics Newsletter* 6, no. 1 (1985); idem, "The Austrian Theory of the Business Cycle in Light of Modern Macroeconomics" esp. pp. 19–23. See also the critique of psychological—as opposed to praxeological—business cycle theories below.

[23]For pro-Keynesian literature see in particular Seymour P. Harris, ed., *The New Economics* (New York: Alfred Knopf, 1947); Alvin Hansen, *A Guide to Keynes* (New York: McGraw-Hill, 1953); for anti-Keynesian literature see in particular Henry Hazlitt, *The Failure of the "New Economics"* (Princeton, N.J.: D. Van Nostrand, 1959); idem, ed., *The Critics of Keynesian Economics* (Lanham, Md.: University Press of America, 1983).

1. EMPLOYMENT

Keynes sets out with a false theory of employment. Contrary to the classical view, he claims that there can be involuntary unemployment on the free market; and, further, that a market can reach a stable equilibrium with persistent involuntary unemployment. And in claiming such market failures to be possible he contends to have uncovered the ultimate economic rationale for interfering in the operations of markets by extra-market forces.

Since the free market is defined in terms of homesteaded or produced private property and the voluntariness of all interactions between private property owners, it should be clear that what Keynes claims to show is roughly equivalent to a squaring of the circle.

Keynes begins with the false statement that the classical theory assumed "that there is no such thing as involuntary unemployment in the strict sense."[24] In fact, it assumed no such thing. Classical theory assumed that involuntary unemployment is logically-praxeologically impossible so long as a free market is in operation. That involuntary unemployment, indeed any amount of it, can exist in the presence of an extra-market institution, minimum wage laws, etc., has never been seriously doubted.

After this falsehood, Keynes then proceeds to give his definition of involuntary unemployment:

> Men are involuntarily unemployed if, in the event of a small rise in the price of wage-goods [i.e., consumer goods] relative to the money wage, both the aggregate supply of labor willing to work for the current money-wage and the aggregate demand for it at that wage would be greater than the existing volume of employment.[25]

Translated into plain English, what Keynes is saying in his typical obfuscating way is that men are involuntarily unemployed if an

---

[24]Keynes, *The General Theory*, p. 21; also pp. 6, 15.

[25]Ibid., p. 15. Keynes at this point promises an alternative definition to be given on p. 26; revealingly, no such definition appears there or anywhere else in the book!

increase in prices relative to wage rates leads to more employment.[26] Yet such a change in relative prices is logically equivalent to a fall in real wage rates; and a fall in real wages can be brought about on the unhampered market by wage earners at any time they so desire, simply by accepting lower nominal wage rates with commodity prices remaining where they are. If laborers decide not to do this, there is nothing involuntary in all this. Given their reservation demand for labor, they choose to supply that amount of labor which is actually supplied. Nor would the classification of this as voluntary unemployment-employment change a bit, if at another point in time with lower real wage rates the amount of employment were to increase. By virtue of logic, such an outcome can only be brought about if in the meantime laborers have increased their relative evaluation of a given wage rate versus their labor reservation demand (otherwise, if no such change had occurred, employment would decrease instead of increasing). The fact, however, that one can change one's mind from one point in time to the next hardly implies that one's earlier choice was involuntary, as Keynes would have it. Of course, one can define one's terms any way one wishes, and in a truly Orwellian fashion one may even choose to call voluntary involuntary and involuntary voluntary. Yet through this method anything under the sun can be "proven," while in fact nothing of substance whatsoever is shown. Keynes's way of demonstrating the possibility of involuntary unemployment is a verbal nonsense proof which leaves entirely unaffected the fact that no such thing as involuntary employment, in the usual sense of this term, can ever exist on the unhampered market.

As if this were not enough, Keynes tops it off by claiming that involuntary unemployment is conceivable even in the never-never land of equilibrium. Indeed, he criticizes his earlier *Treatise on Money* by saying, "I had not then understood that, in certain conditions, the system could be in equilibrium with less than full employment."[27] Yet equilibrium is *defined* as a situation in which changes in values, technology, and resources no longer occur where all actions are completely adjusted to a final constellation of data; and where all factors

---

[26]See also Hazlitt, *The Failure of the "New Economics,"* p. 30.

[27]Keynes, *The General Theory*, pp. 242–43; also p. 28.

of production then, including labor, are employed to the fullest
extent possible (given these unchanging data) and are repeatedly and
endlessly employed in the same constant production pattern. Hence,
as H. Hazlitt has remarked, the discovery of an unemployment equilibrium by Keynes, in his *General Theory*, is like the discovery of a tri-
angular circle—a contradiction in terms.[28]

2. MONEY

Having thrown out logic in his treatment of employment and
unemployment, Keynes, in his discussion of money, then throws out
economic reasoning by advancing the claim that money and monetary changes (can) have a systematic effect on employment income,
and interest.

Given the fact that "money" appears in the title of the *General
Theory,* Keynes's positive theory of money is amazingly brief and
undeveloped. Brevity, of course, can be a virtue. In the case of
Keynes, it offers the opportunity to pinpoint rather easily his elementary mistakes. For Keynes, *"the importance of money essentially
flows from its being a link between the present and the future."*[29]
"Money in its significant attributes is, above all, a subtle device for
linking the present and the future."[30] That this is false follows from
the fact that in the never-never land of equilibrium no money would
exist,[31] yet even under equilibrium conditions there would still be a

---

[28]See also Hazlitt, *The Failure of the "New Economics,"* p. 52.

[29]Keynes, *General Theory*, p. 293.

[30]Ibid., p. 294.

[31]Mises explains:

Let us assume that there is only gold money and only one central
bank. With the successive progress toward the state of an evenly
rotating economy all individuals and firms restrict step by step their
holding of cash and the quantities of gold thus released flow into nonmonetary—industrial—employment. When the equilibrium of the
evenly rotating economy is finally reached, there are no more cash
holdings; no more gold is used for monetary purposes. The individuals and firms own claims against the central bank, the maturity of

present and a future, and both would still be linked. Rather than functioning as a link to the future, money serves as a medium of exchange; a role that is inextricably tied to the uncertainty of the future.[32] Action, which invariably begins in the present and is aimed at some future goal, more or less distant in time from the point of beginning, constitutes the real link between the present and the future. And it is time preference as a universal category of action that gives this link between the present and the future its specific shape. Money, contrary to interest, no more relates the present to the future than do other economic phenomena, such as nonmonetary goods. Their present value, too, reflects anticipations regarding the future, no more and no less so than does money.

From this first misconception regarding the nature of money, all other misconceptions flow automatically. Being defined as a subtle link between present and future, the demand for money (its supply being given), which Keynes, in line with his general inclination of misinterpreting logical-praxeological categories as psychological ones, terms "liquidity preference" or "propensity to hoard,"[33] is said to be

---

each part of which precisely corresponds to the amount they will need on the respective dates for the settlement of their obligations. The central bank does not need any reserves as the total sum of the daily payments of its customers exactly equals the total sum of withdrawals. All transactions can in fact be effected through transfer in the bank's books without any recourse to cash. Thus the "money" of this system is not a medium of exchange; it is not money at all; it is merely a *numéraire*, an ethereal and undetermined unit of accounting of that vague and indefinable character which the fancy of some economists and the errors of many laymen mistakenly have attributed to money. (*Human Action*, p. 249)

[32]Keynes recognizes that money also has something to do with uncertainty. The fundamental mistake in his theory of money pointed out here, however, surfaces again when he relates money not to uncertainty as such, but, more specifically, to uncertainty of interest rates. "The necessary condition" [for the existence of money] he writes, "is the existence of uncertainty as to the future rate of interest" (*General Theory*, p. 168; also p. 169). See also the following discussion.

[33]Ibid., p. 174.

functionally related to the rate of interest (and vice versa).[34] "Interest," writes Keynes, "is the reward of not-hoarding,"[35] "the reward for parting with liquidity,"[36] which makes liquidity preference in turn the unwillingness to invest in interest-bearing assets. That this is false becomes obvious as soon as one asks the question "What, then, about prices?" The quantity of beer, for instance, that can be bought for a definite sum of money is obviously no less a reward for parting with liquidity than is the interest rate, which would make the demand for money then the unwillingness to buy beer as much as it is an unwillingness to invest.[37] Formulated in general terms, the demand for money is the unwillingness to buy or rent nonmoney, including interest-bearing assets (land, labor, and/or capital goods, or future goods) *and* non-interest-bearing assets (consumer or present goods). To recognize this is to recognize that the demand for money has nothing to do with investment or with consumption; nor has it anything to do with the ratio of investment-to-consumption expenditures, or the spread between input and output prices (the discount of higher order or future goods versus lower order or present goods). Increases or decreases in the demand for money, other things being equal, lower or raise the overall level of money prices, but real consumption and investment, as well as the real consumption-investment proportion remain unaffected; and such being the case, employment and social income remain unchanged as well. The demand for money determines the spending/cash balance proportion. The investment/consumption proportion, pace Keynes, is an entirely different and unrelated matter. It is solely determined by time-preference.[38]

The same conclusion is reached if changes in the supply of money (liquidity preference being given) are considered. Keynes claims that

---

[34]On the absurd implications of the assumption of functional—rather than causal—relations, see the discussion below.

[35]Keynes, *The General Theory*, p. 174.

[36]Ibid., p. 167.

[37]See also Hazlitt, *The Failure of the "New Economics,"* pp. 188f.

[38]See also Rothbard, *America's Great Depression*, pp. 40–41; Mises, *Human Action*, pp. 521–23.

an increase in the supply of money, other things being equal, can have a positive effect on employment. He writes, "so long as there is unemployment, employment will change in the same proportion as the quantity of money."[39] Yet this is not only a highly curious pronouncement because it *assumes* the existence of unemployed resources instead of *explaining* why such a thing should possibly occur—for, obviously, a resource can be unemployed only because it is either not recognized as scarce at all and thus has no value whatsoever, or because its owner voluntarily prices it out of the market and its unemployment then is no problem that would call for a solution.[40]

Even if one were to waive this criticism, the statement would still be fallacious. For if other things were indeed equal, then the additional supply of money would simply lead to increased overall prices and simultaneous and proportional increased wage rates, and nothing would change at all. If, contrary to this, employment should increase, this is only possible if wage rates do not rise along with, and to the same extent as, other prices. However, other things then can no longer be said to be equal, because real wage rates would be lowered, and employment can only rise while real wages fall if the relative evaluation of employment versus self-employment (i.e., unemployment) is assumed to have changed. Yet if this is assumed, no increase in the money supply would have been required. The same result (increased employment) could also have been brought about by laborers accepting lower nominal wage rates.

3. INTEREST

With logic and economic theory thrown out of the window, in his discussion of the interest phenomenon Keynes abandons reason and common sense entirely.

---

[39]Keynes, *The General Theory*, p. 296.

[40]See also W.H. Hutt, *The Theory of Idle Resources* (Indianapolis: Liberty Fund, 1977).

According to Keynes, since money has a systematic impact on employment, income, and interest, interest, in turn—quite consistently, for that matter—must be conceived of as a purely monetary phenomenon.[41] I need not explain the elementary fallacy of this view. Suffice it to say here again that money would disappear in equilibrium, but interest would not, which demonstrates that interest must be considered a real, not a monetary phenomenon.

Moreover, Keynes, in talking about "functional relationships" and "mutual determination" of variables instead of causal, unidirectional relations, becomes entangled in inescapable contradictions as regards his theory of interest.[42] As has been explained above, on the one hand Keynes thinks of liquidity preference (and the supply of money) as *determining* the interest rate, such that an increased demand for money, for instance, would raise the interest rate (and an increased supply of money would lower it) and that this then will reduce investment "whilst a decline in the rate of interest may be expected, *ceteris paribus*, to increase the volume of investment."[43] On the other hand, characterizing the interest rate as "the reward for parting with liquidity," he contends that the demand for money is *determined* by the interest rate, such that a fall in the interest rate, for instance, would increase one's demand for cash (and also, one should add, one's propensity to consume) and hence lead to *reduced* investment. Obviously, however, a lower interest rate can hardly both increase and decrease investment at the same time. Something must be wrong here.

Keynes, however, combines falsehood and contradiction into one of the most fantastic conspiracy theories ever heard of.

Since interest, according to Keynes, is a purely monetary phenomenon, it is only natural to assume that it can be manipulated at will through monetary policy (provided, of course, one is not restricted in this by the existence of a 100-percent-reserve commodity

---

[41]Keynes, *The General Theory*, p. 173; see also his laudatory remarks on mercantilist economics, and in particular, Silvio Gesell, as precursors of this view on pp. 341, 355.

[42]See on this also Rothbard, *Man, Economy, and State*, pp. 687–89.

[43]Keynes, *The General Theory*, p. 173.

money standard such as the gold standard).[44] "There is," writes Keynes, "no special virtue in the pre-existing rate of interest."[45] In fact, if the supply of money is sufficiently increased, the interest rate supposedly can be brought down to zero. Keynes recognizes that this would imply a superabundance of capital goods, and one would think that this realization should have given him cause to reconsider. Not so! On the contrary, in all seriousness he tells us

> that a properly run community equipped with modern technical resources, of which the population is not increasing rapidly, ought to be able to bring down the marginal efficiency of capital in equilibrium approximately to zero within a single generation.[46]

It is "comparatively easy to make capital goods so abundant that the marginal efficiency of capital is zero (and) this may be the most sensible way of gradually getting rid of many of the objectional features of capitalism."[47] "There are no intrinsic reasons for the scarcity of capital."[48] Rather, it is "possible for communal saving through the agency of the State to be maintained at a level where it ceases to be scarce."[49]

Don't worry that this would imply that no maintenance or replacement of capital would be needed any longer (for, if this were the case, capital goods would still be scarce and hence command a price), and capital goods instead would have to be "free goods" in the same sense in which air is usually "free." Don't worry that if capital goods were no longer scarce, then consumer goods could no longer be scarce either (for, if they were, the means employed to produce them would have to be scarce, too). And don't worry that in this Garden of Eden, which Keynes promises to establish within one generation (why so long?!), there would no longer be any use for money. For, as he informs us, "I am myself impressed by the great

---

[44]See also below.

[45]Keynes, *The General Theory*, p. 328.

[46]Ibid., p. 220.

[47]Ibid., p. 221.

[48]Ibid., p. 376.

[49]Ibid., p. 376.

social advantages of increasing the stock of capital until it ceases to be scarce."[50] Who would dare disagree with this![51]

Yet more is to come. Because, as Keynes sees it, there are some obstacles on the path toward paradise. For one thing, the gold standard stands in the way, because it makes the expansion of credit impossible (or difficult at least, in that a credit expansion would lead to an outflow of gold and a subsequent economic contraction). Hence Keynes's repeated polemics against this institution.[52] Furthermore, there is the just explained problem of his own making: that a lower interest rate supposedly increases and decreases investment simultaneously. And it is to get out of this logical mess that Keynes comes up with a conspiracy theory: For, while the interest rate must be reduced to zero so as to eliminate scarcity, as we were just told, the

---

[50]Keynes, *The General Theory*, p. 325.

[51]See also Hazlitt, *The Failure of the "New Economics,"* pp. 231–35. What about the seemingly obvious objection, that the expansion of monetary credit through which Keynes wants to bring about the reduction of the interest rate to zero is nothing but an expansion of paper, and that the problem of scarcity is a matter of "real" goods, which can only be overcome through "genuine savings"? To this he has the following funny answer in *The General Theory*:

> The notion that the creation of credit by the banking system allows investment to take place to which "no genuine saving" corresponds, i.e., the idea that saving and investment . . . can differ from one another, is to be explained, I think, by an optical illusion. (p. 81)

> [T]he savings which result from this decision are just as genuine as any other savings. No one can be compelled to own the additional money corresponding to the new bank-credit unless he deliberately prefers to hold more money rather than some other form of wealth. (p. 83)

> The new money is not "forced" on anyone. (p. 328)

As Henry Hazlitt remarks,

> [o]n the same reasoning we can create any amount of new "savings" we wish overnight, simply by printing that amount of new paper money, because *somebody* will necessarily hold that new paper money! (*The Failure of the "New Economics,"* p. 227)

[52]See Keynes, *The General Theory*, pp. 129ff., 336ff., 348f. On Keynes's role in the actual destruction of the gold standard see Henry Hazlitt, *From Bretton Woods to World Inflation* (Chicago: Regnery, 1984).

lower the interest rate the lower also the reward for parting with liquidity. The lower the interest rate, that is to say, the lower the incentive for capitalists to invest, because their profits will be reduced accordingly. Thus, they will try to undermine, and conspire against, any attempt to resurrect the Garden of Eden.

Driven by "animal spirits,"[53] "gambling instincts,"[54] and "addicted to the money-making passion,"[55] they will conspire so "that capital has to be kept scarce enough."[56] "The acuteness and peculiarity of our contemporary problem arises, therefore," writes Keynes,

> out of the possibility that the average rate of interest which will allow a reasonable average level of employment [and of social income] is one so unacceptable to wealth owners that it cannot be readily established merely by manipulating the quantity of money.[57]

In fact,

> the most stable, and least easily shifted, element in our contemporary economy has been hitherto, and may prove to be in the future, the minimum rate of interest acceptable to the generality of wealth owners.[58]

Fortunately, we are informed, there is a way out of this predicament; through "the euthanasia of the rentier, and, consequently, the euthanasia of the cumulative oppressive power of the capitalist to exploit the scarcity-value of capital."[59] And surely they deserve such

---

[53]Keynes, *The General Theory*, p. 161.

[54]Ibid., p. 157.

[55]Ibid., p. 374.

[56]Ibid., p. 217.

[57]Keynes, *The General Theory*, pp. 308–09.

[58]Ibid., p. 309, and he adds, in a footnote, "The nineteenth-century saying, quoted by Bagehot, that 'John Bull' can stand many things, but he cannot stand 2 per cent." On Keynes's conspiracy theory see also Hazlitt, *The Failure of the "New Economics,"* pp. 3, 16–18.

[59]Keynes, *The General Theory*, p. 376, also p. 221.

a fate. For "the business world" is ruled by an "uncontrollable and disobedient psychology,"[60] and private investment markets are

> under the influence of purchasers largely ignorant of what they are buying and of speculators who are more concerned with forecasting the next shift of market sentiment than with a reasonable estimate of the future yield of capital assets.[61]

As a matter of fact, don't we all know that "there is no clear evidence from experience that the investment policy which is socially advantageous coincides with that which is most profitable;"[62] indeed, that the decisions of private investors depend largely on "the nerves and hysteria and even the digestions and reactions to the weather,"[63] rather than on rational calculation?! Thus, concludes Keynes, "the duty of ordering the current volume of investment cannot safely be left in private hands."[64] Instead, to turn the present misery into a land of milk and honey, "a somewhat comprehensive socialization of investment will prove the only means."[65]

> The State, which is in a position to calculate the marginal efficiency of capital-goods on long views and on the basis of the general social advantage [must take] an ever greater responsibility for directly organizing investment.[66]

I trust that none of this requires further comment. It is too obvious that these are the outpourings of someone who deserves to be called anything, except an economist.

4. THE CAPITALIST PROCESS

Such a verdict finds still more support when Keynes's theory of the capitalist process is finally considered. That Keynes is no friend of

---

[60]Ibid., p. 317.
[61]Ibid., p. 316.
[62]Ibid., p. 157.
[63]Ibid., p. 162.
[64]Ibid., p. 320.
[65]Ibid., p. 378.
[66]Ibid., p. 164.

capitalism and capitalists should be obvious from the above quotations. In fact, by advocating "a socialization of investment" he comes out openly as a socialist.[67] For Keynes, capitalism *means* crisis.

He identifies essentially two reasons for this, the first one, to which Keynes attributes the cyclical nature of the capitalist process, has already been touched upon. Surely, so long as the course of the economy is largely determined by capitalists who, as we have heard, "are largely ignorant of what they are purchasing," and who conspire "to keep things scarce," it cannot be a smooth and even one. Depending mostly on people who base their decisions on their "digestion and the weather," the capitalist process must be erratic. Moved by the "waxing and waning" of entrepreneurial optimism and pessimism, which in turn is determined by the "uncontrollable and disobedient psychology of the business world," booms and busts are inevitable. Business cycles—so the central message of chapter 22 of Keynes's *General Theory*, the "Notes on the Trade Cycle"—are *psychologically* determined phenomena. This is surely incorrect. A psychological explanation of the business cycle is strictly impossible, and to think of it as an explanation involves a category mistake: Business cycles are obviously real events, experienced by individuals, but experienced by them as occurring outside of them in the world of real goods and real wealth. Beliefs, sentiments, expectations, optimism, and pessimism on the other side are *psychological* phenomena. One can think of one psychological phenomenon as affecting or influencing another one, but it is impossible to conceive of a psychological phenomenon as having any direct impact on outcomes in the outside world of real

---

[67]Keynes's socialism, however, is not the egalitarian-proletarian version as espoused by the Bolsheviks. For this Keynes has nothing but contempt. His socialism is of the fascist or Nazi variety. In the preface to the German edition of his *General Theory* (which appeared in late 1936) he wrote:

> The theory of aggregate production that is the goal of the following book can be much more easily applied to the conditions of a totalitarian state than the theory of the production and distribution of a given output turned out under the conditions of free competition and of a considerable degree of *laissez-faire*. (quoted from Hazlitt, *The Failure of the "New Economics,"* p. 277)

things and goods. Only through *actions* can the course of real events be influenced; and any explanation of the business cycle then must necessarily be a *praxeological* (as opposed to a psychological) one. Keynes's psychological business cycle theory in fact *cannot explain that anything real happens at all.* However, as real things are made to happen people must act, and allocate and reallocate scarce resources to valued goals. One cannot act as arbitrarily, though, as Keynes would have it, because in acting one is invariably constrained by real scarcity which cannot be affected by our psychology at all. Nor does Keynes explain with his theory why entrepreneurial mood-swings would result in any *particular* pattern of business fluctuations—such as the boom-bust cycle, that he supposedly wants to explain—instead of any other conceivable pattern of fluctuations.

The second reason for the instability of capitalism, and the desirability of a socialist solution, according to Keynes, is capitalism's inherent stagnationist tendencies. His stagnation theory centers around the notion which he takes from Hobson and Mummery, and endorses, "that in the normal state of modern industrial communities, consumption limits production and not production consumption."[68] With this as one of his axioms only nonsense can follow.

Stagnation is due to a lack of consumption. "Up to the point where full employment prevails," he writes, "the growth of capital depends not at all on a low propensity to consume but is, on the contrary, held back by it."[69] Combined with this underconsumptionist thesis is a "fundamental psychological law, upon which we are entitled to depend with great confidence both a priori from our knowledge of human nature and from the detailed facts of experience, that men are disposed, as a rule and on the average, to increase

---

[68]Keynes, *The General Theory*, p. 368. On the Keynesian theory of stagnation see also Alvin H. Hanson, *Fiscal Policy and Business Cycles* (New York: Norton, 1941); for a critique see George Terborgh, *The Bogey of Economic Maturity* (Chicago: Machinery and Allied Products Institute, 1945); also Murray N. Rothbard, "Breaking Out of the Walrasian Box: The Cases of Schumpeter and Hansen," *Review of Austrian Economics* 1 (1987).

[69]Keynes, *The General Theory*, pp. 372–73.

their consumption as their income rises, but not by as much as the increase in their income."[70] "As a rule . . . a greater proportion of income [will be] saved as real income increases."[71]

On its own, this second law, which is accepted as plausible here for the sake of argument (except for adding that consumption can, of course, never fall to zero), would not seem to indicate any trouble. So what? If savings overproportionally increase with increasing incomes, so much the better for the social product.[72] But Keynes, in his characteristic logic-carefree way of thinking joins this law to the thesis that production is limited by consumption, and he has then no difficulty proving whatever he wishes.

If consumption limits production, and if nonconsumption rises with rising incomes, then it indeed seems to follow that increasing incomes imply their own undoing by increasing nonconsumption, which in turn limits production, etc. And if this is so, it also seems to follow that wealthier societies, which non-consume more, should be plagued particularly hard by this "stagnitis"; and that in any given society it should be the rich, who nonconsume more, who contribute most to economic stagnation (except for the "minor" problem that one cannot explain, according to this theory, why individuals or societies could be wealthier than others in the first place!). In any case, Keynes accepts these conclusions as true.[73] Accordingly, he presents

---

[70]Ibid., p. 96.

[71]Ibid., p. 97; also pp. 27f.

[72]In fact, Keynes informs us that *savings is by definition identical to investment* (p. 63), "that the excess of income over consumption, which we call saving, cannot differ from the addition to capital equipment which we call investment" (p. 64). Then, however, a reduced proportion of consumption expenditures must by definition go hand in hand with accordingly increased investments, and this would lead to a higher future income, to still more absolute consumption and still more absolute and relative saving and investment. Where, indeed, is the problem here?

[73]Keynes writes,

> If in a potentially wealthy community the inducement to invest is weak, then, in spite of its potential wealth, the working of the principle of effective demand will compel it to reduce its actual output, until, in spite of its potential wealth, it has become so poor that its

his recommendations on how to get out of stagnation. In addition to a "comprehensive socialization of investment," Keynes suggests measures to stimulate consumption, in particular an income redistribution from the rich (people with a low propensity to consume) to the poor (those with a high propensity to consume).

> Whilst aiming at a socially controlled rate of investment with a view to a progressive decline in the marginal efficiency of capital I should support at the same time all sorts of policies for increasing the propensity to consume. For it is unlikely that full employment can be maintained, whatever we may do about investment, with the existing propensity to consume. There is room, therefore, for both policies to operate together;—to promote investment and, at the same time, to promote consumption, not merely to the level which with the existing propensity to consume would correspond to the increased investment, but to a higher level still.[74]

How is such a thing as simultaneously promoting investment and consumption in order to increase income conceivably possible? In fact, Keynes gives us his own formal definitions of the terms involved:

> surplus over its consumption is sufficiently diminished to correspond to the weakness of the inducement to invest. (*The General Theory*, p. 31)

Or:

> The greater, moreover, the consumption for which we have provided in advance, the more difficult it is to find something further to provide for in advance, and the greater our dependence on present consumption as a source of demand. Yet the larger our incomes, the greater, unfortunately, is the margin between our incomes and our consumption. So, failing some novel expedient, there is, as we shall see, no answer to the riddle, except that there must be sufficient unemployment to keep us so poor that our consumption falls short of our income by no more than the equivalent of the physical provision for future consumption which it pays to produce to-day. (p. 105)

[74]Ibid., p. 325; or "the remedy would lie in various measures designed to increase the propensity to consume by the redistribution of incomes or otherwise" (p. 324).

"income = consumption + investment; saving = income - consumption; therefore, saving = investment."[75] Under these definitions, a simultaneous increase in consumption and investment out of a given income is conceptually impossible!

Keynes is not terribly disturbed over "details" such as these. In order to get what he wants, he simply shifts, completely unnoted, the meanings of his terms. He drops the just quoted formal definitions, which would render such a result impossible, and he adopts a new meaning for the term saving. Instead of unconsumed income, saving quietly comes to mean hoarding (i.e., the act of not-spending money on *either* consumer *or* capital goods).[76] Thereby the results can be easily made to come out right. For then savings are no longer equal to investment; and saving, being defined as the act of *not*-spending, automatically acquires a negative connotation, while investment and consumption take on a positive one. Moreover, now one must almost naturally be worried about savings exceeding investment, or so it seems, for this would seem to imply that something is leaking out of the economy, and that income (defined as investment + consumption) must be somehow reduced. Keynes certainly worries about this possibility. He calls it "a chronic tendency throughout human history for the propensity to save to be stronger than the inducement to invest."[77] And this chronic tendency must surely be particularly pronounced if incomes are high, for then, as we have been told, savings reach a particularly high proportion of income. But do not despair. Where something can leak out, something also can leak in. If savings is unspent money, then savings can be brought into existence, simple enough, by means of governmental money creation, so as to compensate for the outward leakage which tends to increase with increasing incomes. There is the danger, of course, that these compensatory "community savings" immediately leak out again by being added to

---

[75]Ibid., p. 63. It is typical of Keynes's philosophy of abundance that he gets things upside down here as well. For the correct definitions are: product produced = income; income - consumption = saving; saving = investment. Where does Keynes's income come from?

[76]See on this also Hazlitt, *The Failure of the "New Economics,"* pp. 120–23.

[77]Keynes, *The General Theory*, p. 347.

the private sector's cash hoardings (because, according to Keynes, the newly created savings would lower the interest rate, and this in turn would increase the capitalists' liquidity preference so as to counteract such a tendency and to artificially "keep capital scarce"). But this can be taken care of by the "socialization of investment" as we know, and by some Gesellian stamped money schemes ("The idea behind stamped money is sound").[78] And once saving and investing is done publicly—through the agency of the State, as Keynes would say—and all money is spent, and no keep-things-scarce motive is in the way any longer, there is indeed no longer any problem with increasing consumption and investment simultaneously. Since savings is unspent money, and newly created money and credit is just as genuine as any other because it is not "forced" on anyone, savings can be created by the stroke of a pen.[79] And since the State, contrary to the scarcity-exploiting capitalists, can make sure that these additional genuine savings are indeed being spent (instead of wandering into hoards), any increase in the supply of money and credit through governmental counterfeiting increases consumption and investment at the same time and so promotes income twice. Permanent inflation is Keynes's cure-all. It helps overcome stagnation; and more of it overcomes the more severe stagnation crises of the more advanced societies. And once stagnation is defeated, still more inflation will abolish scarcity within one generation.[80]

Yet the wonders do not cease. What is this leakage, this surplus of savings over investment, that constitutes all such dangers? Something must leak from somewhere to someplace else, and it must play some role here and some there. Keynes tries to disperse such thoughts by asking us once again not to apply logic to economics. "Contemporary thought," he writes, "is still deeply steeped in the notion that

---

[78]Ibid., p. 357.

[79]See on this note 51.

[80]On his program of permanent inflation see also this remark on the trade cycle: "The right remedy for the trade cycle is not to be found in abolishing booms and keeping us permanently in a semi-slump; but in abolishing slumps and thus keeping us permanently in a quasi-boom" (p. 322). The answer to credit expansion, that is, is still more credit expansion.

if people do not spend their money in one way they will spend it in another."[81] It would seem hard to imagine how this contemporary thought could possibly be wrong, but Keynes believes it false. For him there exists a third alternative. Something, an economic good one would think, simply drops out of existence, and this means trouble.

> An act of individual saving means—so to speak—a decision not to have dinner to-day. But it does *not* necessitate a decision to have dinner or buy a pair of boots a week hence or a year hence or to consume any specified thing at any specified date. Thus it depresses the business of preparing to-day's dinner without stimulating the business of making ready for some future act of consumption. It is not a substitution of future consumption-demand for present consumption-demand—it is a net *diminution* of such demand.[82]

Still, the strictures of a two-valued logic do not quite crumble yet. How can there be any net diminution of something? What is not spent on consumer goods or capital goods must still be spent on something else—namely on cash. *This exhausts all possibilities.* Income and wealth can be and must be allocated to consumption, investment, or cash. Keynes's diminution, the leakage, the excess of savings over investment, is income spent on, or added to, cash hoardings. But such an increase in the demand for cash has no effect on income, consumption, and investment whatever, as has already been explained. With the social money stock being given, a general increase in the demand for cash can only be brought about by bidding down the money prices of nonmoney goods. But so what?[83] Nominal income (i.e., income in terms of money) will fall; but real income and the real consumption-investment proportion will be entirely unchanged. And people along the way get what they want: an

---

[81]Ibid., p. 20.

[82]Ibid., p. 210; second emphasis added.

[83]Contrary to Keynes's fanciful fears, the demand for money can never be infinite, because everyone must obviously consume sometimes (and cannot delay consumption further); and at such points liquidity preference is definitely finite.

increase in the real value of their cash balances, and of the purchasing power of the money unit. There is nothing stagnating here, or draining, or leaking, and Keynes has offered *no theory of stagnation at all* (and with this, of course, also no theory of how to get out of stagnation). He merely has given a perfectly normal phenomenon such as falling prices (caused by an increased demand for money, or by an expanding productive economy) a bad name in calling it stagnation, or depression, or the result of a lacking effective demand, so as to find just another excuse for his own inflationary schemes.[84]

Here we have Keynes in his entire greatness: the twentieth century's most famous "economist." Out of false theories of employment, money, and interest, he has distilled a fantastically wrong theory of capitalism and of a socialist paradise erected out of paper money.

---

[84]The second element of Keynes's stagnation theory is equally false. It may be that that saving in the definition of equaling investment increases overproportionally with increasing incomes—while it can never reach 100 percent. Yet this situation certainly should give no one concern regarding the social income produced. It is, however, *not* true that savings in the sense of hoarding increases with increasing incomes, and that the greatest leakage then occurs among the rich and in wealthy societies. The opposite is true. If real income increases because the economy, supported by additional savings, is expanding, the purchasing power of money increases (the money stock being given). But at a higher purchasing power of the money unit, the amount of cash demanded actually falls (the demand for money schedule being given). Thus, if anything, the leak-stagnation nonproblem should actually diminish rather than increase with increasing wealth.

6

How is Fiat Money Possible?
—or, The Devolution of
Money and Credit

Fiat money is the term for a medium of exchange which is neither a commercial commodity, a consumer, a producer good,
nor title to any such commodity. It is irredeemable paper
money. In contrast, *commodity* money refers to a medium of
exchange which is either a commercial commodity or a title thereto.

There is no doubt that fiat money is *possible*. Its theoretical possibility was recognized long ago, and since 1971, when the last remnants of a former international gold (commodity) standard were
abolished, all monies have in fact been nothing but irredeemable
pieces of paper.

The question to be addressed in this paper is *how* is a fiat money
possible? More specifically, can fiat money arise as the natural outcome of the interactions between self-interested individuals; or, is it
possible to introduce it without violating either principles of justice or
economic efficiency?

It will be argued that the answer to the latter question must be
negative, and that no fiat money can ever arise "innocently" or
"immaculately." The arguments advancing this thesis will be largely
constructive and systematic. However, given the fact that the thesis
has frequently been disputed, along the way various prominent

[Reprinted from the *Review of Austrian Economics* 7, no. 2 (1994).]

counterarguments will be criticized. Specifically, the arguments of the *monetarists*, especially Irving Fisher and Milton Friedman, and of some *Austrian* "free bankers," especially Lawrence White and George Selgin, in ethical and/or economic support of either a total or a fractional fiat money will be refuted.

THE ORIGIN OF MONEY

Man participates in an exchange economy (instead of remaining in self-sufficient isolation) insofar as he prefers more goods over less and is capable of recognizing the higher productivity of a system of division of labor. The same narrow intelligence and self-interest is sufficient to explain the emergence of a—and ultimately only one—commodity money and a—and ultimately only one, worldwide—monetary economy.[1] Finding their markets as buyers and sellers of goods restricted to instances of double coincidence of wants (A wants what B has and B wants what A has), each person may still expand his own market and thus profit more fully from the advantages of extended division of labor if he is willing to accept not only directly useful goods in exchange, but also goods with a higher degree of marketability than those surrendered. For even if they have no direct use-value to an actor, the ownership of relatively more marketable goods implies by definition that such goods may in turn be more easily resold for other, directly useful goods in later exchanges, and hence that their owner has come closer to reaching an ultimate goal unattainable through direct exchange.

Motivated only by self-interest and based on the observation that directly traded goods possess different degrees of marketability, some individuals begin to demand specific goods not for their own sake but for the sake of employing them as a medium of exchange. By adding a new component to the pre-existing (barter) demand for

---

[1]See on the following, in particular Carl Menger, *Principles of Economics* (New York: New York University Press, 1981); idem, *Geld*, in Carl Menger, *Gesammelte Werke*, F.A. Hayek, ed. (Tübingen: Mohr, 1970), vol. 4; Ludwig von Mises, *The Theory of Money and Credit* (Irvington-on-Hudson, N.Y.: Foundation for Economic Education, 1971); idem, *Human Action: A Treatise on Economics* (Chicago: Regnery, 1966).

these goods, their marketability is still further enhanced. Based on their perception of this fact, other market participants increasingly choose the same goods for their inventory of exchange media, as it is in their own interest to select such commodities as media of exchange that are already employed by others for the same purpose. Initially, a variety of goods may be in demand as common media of exchange. However, since a good is demanded as a medium of exchange— rather than for consumption or production purposes—in order to facilitate future purchases of directly serviceable goods (i.e., to help one buy more cheaply) and simultaneously widen one's market as a seller of directly useful goods and services (i.e., help one sell more dearly), the more widely a commodity is used as a medium of exchange, the better it will perform its function. Because each market participant naturally prefers the acquisition of a more marketable and, in the end, universally marketable medium of exchange to that of a less or non-universally marketable one,

> there would be an inevitable tendency for the less marketable of the series of goods used as media of exchange to be one by one rejected until at last only a single commodity remained, which was universally employed as a medium of exchange; in a word, money.[2]

With this, and historically with the establishment of the international gold standard in the course of the nineteenth century (until 1914), the end desired through any one market participant's demand for media of exchange is fully accomplished. With the prices of all consumer and capital goods expressed in terms of a single commodity, demand and supply can take effect on a worldwide scale, unrestricted by absences of double coincidence of wants. Because of its universal acceptability, accounting in terms of such money contains the most complete and accurate expression of any producers' opportunity costs. At the same time, with only one universal money in use—rather than several ones of limited acceptability—the market participants' expenditures (of directly serviceable goods) on holdings of only indirectly useful media of exchange are optimally economized; and with expenditures on indirectly useful goods so economized, real

---

[2]Mises, *The Theory of Money and Credit*, pp. 32–33.

wealth (wealth in the form of stocks of producer and consumer goods) is optimized as well.

According to a long—Spanish-French-Austrian-American—tradition of monetary theory,[3] a money's originary function—arising out of the existence of uncertainty—is that of a *medium of exchange*. Money *must* emerge as a *commodity* money because something can be demanded as a medium of exchange only if it has a pre-existing barter demand (indeed, it must have been a highly marketable barter commodity), and the competition between monies *qua* media of exchange inevitably leads to a tendency of converging toward a *single* money—as the most easily resold and readily accepted commodity.

In light of this, several popular notions of monetary theory are immediately revealed as misguided or fallacious.

What about the idea of a commodity reserve currency? Can bundles (baskets) of goods or titles thereto be money?[4] No, because bundles of different goods are by definition less easily salable than the most easily salable of its various components, and hence commodity baskets are uniquely *unsuited* to perform the function of a medium of exchange (and it thus is no mere accident that no historical examples for such money exist).

What about the—Friedmanite—idea of freely fluctuating "national monies" or of "optimal currency areas?"[5] It must be regarded

---

[3]See Murray N. Rothbard, "New Light on the Prehistory of the Austrian School," in *The Foundations of Modern Austrian Economics*, Edwin G. Dolan, ed. (Kansas City: Sheed and Ward, 1976); Joseph T. Salerno, "Two Traditions in Modern Monetary Theory," *Journal des Economistes et des Etudes Humaines* 2, nos. 2–3 (1991).

[4]On commodity reserve proposals see Benjamin Graham, *Storage and Stability* (New York: McGraw Hill, 1937); Frank D. Graham, *Social Goals and Economic Institutions* (Princeton, N.J.: Princeton University Press, 1942); also F.A. Hayek, "A Commodity Reserve Currency," *Economic Journal* 210 (1943); Milton Friedman, "Commodity-Reserve Currency," *Journal of Political Economy* (1951).

[5]See Milton Friedman, "The Case for Flexible Exchange Rates," in Friedman, *Essays in Positive Economics* (Chicago: University of Chicago Press, 1953); idem, *A Program for Monetary Stability* (New York: Fordham University Press, 1959); also *Policy Implications of Trade and Currency Zones: A Symposium* (Kansas City: Federal Reserve Bank of Kansas City, 1991).

as absurd, except as an intermediate step in the development of an inter-national money. Strictly speaking, a monetary system with rival monies of freely fluctuating exchange rates is still a system of partial barter, riddled with the problem of requiring double coincidence of wants in order for exchanges to take place. The lasting existence of such a system is dysfunctional of the very purpose of money: of facilitating exchange (instead of making it more difficult) and of expanding one's market (rather than restricting it). There are no more "optimal"—local, regional, national or multinational monies or currency areas than there are "optimal trading areas." Instead, as long as more wealth is preferred to less and under conditions of uncertainty, just as the only "optimal" trading area is the whole world market, so the only "optimal" money is *one* money and the only "optimal" currency area the entire globe.

What about the idea, central to monetarist thought since Irving Fisher, that money is a "measure of value" and of the notion of monetary "stabilization?"[6] It represents a tangle of confusion and falsehood. First and foremost, while there exists a motive, a purpose for actors wanting to own media of exchange, no motive, purpose or need can be discovered for wanting to possess a measure of value. Action and exchange are expressive of *preferences*—each person values what he acquires more highly than what he surrenders—*not* of identity or equivalency. No one ever needs to *measure* value. It is easily explained why actors would use cardinal numbers—to count—and construct measurement instruments—to measure space, weight, mass and time: In a world of quantitative determinateness, where means can only produce limited effects, counting and measuring are the prerequisite for successful action. But what imaginable technical or economic need could there possibly be for a measure of *value*?

---

[6]See Irving Fisher, *The Purchasing Power of Money* (New York: Augustus M. Kelley, 1963); idem, *Stabilizing the Dollar* (New York: Macmillan, 1920); idem, *The Money Illusion* (New York: Adelphi, 1929); Milton Friedman, "A Monetary and Fiscal Framework for Economic Stability," *American Economic Review* 38 (1948).

Second, setting these difficulties aside for a moment and assuming that money indeed measures value (such that the money price paid for a good represents a cardinal measure of this good's value) in the same way as a ruler measures space, another insurmountable problem results. Then the question arises "what is the value of this measure of value?" Surely it must have value just as a ruler must have value, otherwise no one would want to own either one. Yet it would obviously be absurd to answer that the value of a unit of money—one dollar—is one. One what? Such a reply would be as nonsensical as answering a question concerning the value of a yardstick by saying "one yard." The value of a cardinal measure cannot be expressed in terms of this measure itself. Rather, *its* value must be expressed in ordinal terms: It is better to have cardinal numbers and measures of length or weight than merely to have ordinal measures at one's disposal. Likewise it is better if, because of the existence of a medium of exchange, one is able to resort to cardinal numbers in one's cost-accounting, rather than having to rely solely on ordinal accounting procedures, as would be the case in a barter economy. But it is impossible to express in cardinal terms *how much* more valuable the former techniques are as compared with the latter. Only ordinal judgments are possible. It is precisely in this sense, then, that ordinal numbers—ranking, preferring—must be regarded as more fundamental than cardinal ones and value be considered an irreducibly subjective, non-quantifiable magnitude.

Moreover, if it were indeed the function of money to serve as a measure of value, one must wonder why the demand for such a thing should ever systematically exceed one per person. The demand for rulers, scales, and clocks, for instance, exceeds one per person only because of differences in location (handiness) or the possibility of their breaking or failing. Apart from this, at any given point in time and space, no one would want to hold more than one measurement instrument of homogeneous quality, because a *single* measurement instrument can render *all* possible measurement services. A second instrument of its kind would be useless.

Third, in any case, whatever the *characteristicum specificum* of money may be, money is a *good*. Yet if it is a good, then it falls under the law of marginal utility, and this law *contradicts* any notion of a stable- or constant-valued good. The law follows from the proposition that every actor, at any given point in time, acts in accordance with his subjective preference scale and chooses to do what he expects—rightly or wrongly—to satisfy him more rather than less, and that in so doing he must invariably employ quantitatively definite (limited) units of qualitatively distinct goods as means and thus, by implication, must be capable of recognizing unit-additions and -subtractions to and from his supply of means. From this incontestably true proposition it follows that an actor always prefers a larger supply of a good over a smaller one (he ranks the marginal utility of a larger sized unit of a good higher than that of a smaller sized unit of the same good) and that any increment to the supply of a good by an additional unit—of any unit-size that an actor considers and distinguishes as relevant—will be ranked lower (valued less) than any same-sized unit of this good *already* in one's possession, for it can only be employed as a means for the removal of an uneasiness deemed less urgent than the least urgent one *up-to-now* satisfied by the same sized unit of this good. In other words, the marginal utility of a given-sized unit of a good decreases or increases as the supply of such units increases or decreases. Each change in the supply of a good therefore leads to a change in this good's marginal utility. Any change in the supply of a good A, as perceived by an actor X, leads to X's *re*-evaluation of A. X attaches a *different* value-rank to A now. Hence, the search for a stable or constant-valued good is obviously illusory from the outset, on a par with wanting to square the circle, for every action involves exchange, and every exchange alters the supply of some good. It either results in a diminution of the supply of a good (as in pure consumption), or it leads to a diminution of one and an incrementation of another (as in production or interpersonal exchange). In either case, as supplies are changed in the course of any action, so are the values of the goods involved. To act is to purposefully *alter* the value of goods. Hence, a stable-valued good—money or anything else—must be considered a constructive or praxeological impossibility.

Finally, as regards the idea of a money—a dollar—of constant purchasing power, there is the fundamental problem that the purchasing power of money *cannot be measured* and that the construction of price indices—any index—is scientifically arbitrary. (What goods are to be included? What relative weight should be attached to each of them? What about the problem that individual actors value the same things differently and are concerned about different commodity baskets, or that the same individual evaluates the same basket differently at different times? What is one to do with changes in the quality of goods or with entirely new products?)[7] Moreover, what is so great about "stable" purchasing power anyway (however that term maybe arbitrarily defined)? To be sure, it is obviously preferable to have a "stable" money rather than an "inflationary" one. Yet surely a money whose purchasing power per unit *increased*—"deflationary" money—would be preferable to a "stable" one.

What about the thesis that in the absence of any legal restrictions money—non-interest-bearing cash—would be completely replaced by interest-bearing securities?[8] Such displacement is conceivable only in equilibrium, where there is no uncertainty and hence no one could gain any satisfaction from being prepared for future contingencies as these are per assumption ruled out of existence. Under the omnipresent human condition of uncertainty, however, even if all legal restrictions on free entry were removed, a demand for non-interest-bearing cash—as distinct from a demand for equity or debt claims (stocks, bonds or mutual fund shares)—would necessarily remain in effect, for whatever the specific nature of these claims may be, they represent titles to *producer* goods, otherwise they *cannot* yield interest. Yet even the most easily convertible production factor must be less salable than the most salable one of its final products, and hence, even the most liquid security can never perform the same service of preparing its owner for future contingencies as can be provided by the most marketable *final* non-interest-bearing product: money. All of this could be different only if it were assumed—as Wallace in accordance with the Chicago School's egalitarian predispositions tacitly does—that all goods are equally marketable. Then, by definition

---

[7]Mises, *The Theory of Money and Credit*, pp. 187–94; idem, *Human Action*, pp. 219–23.

[8]See Neil Wallace, "A Legal Restrictions Theory of the Demand for 'Money'," *Federal Reserve Bank of Minneapolis Quarterly Review* (1983); Eugene Fama, "Financial Intermediation and Price Level Control," *Journal of Monetary Economics* 9, no. 1 (1983); for a critique see Lawrence White, "Accounting for Non-Interest-Bearing Currency" *Journal of Money, Credit, and Banking* 19, no. 4 (1987).

there is no difference between the salability of cash and securities. However, then all goods must be assumed to be identical to each other, and if this were the case neither division of labor nor markets would exist.

From Commodity Money to Fiat Money: The Devolution of Money

If money must arise as a commodity money, how can it become fiat money? It does so via the development of money substitutes (paper titles to commodity money)—but only fraudulently and only at the price of economic inefficiencies.

Under a commodity money standard such as the gold standard until 1914, money "circulated" on the one hand in the form of standardized bars of bullion and gold coins of various denominations trading against each other at essentially fixed ratios according to their weight and fineness. On the other hand, to economize on the cost of storing (safekeeping) and transacting (clearing) money, in a development similar to that of transferable property titles—including stock and bond certificates—as means of facilitating the spatial and temporal exchange of *non*money goods, side by side with money proper also gold certificates—property titles (claims) to specified amounts of gold deposited at specified institutions (banks)—served as a medium of exchange. This coexistence of money proper (gold) and money substitutes (claims to money) affects neither the total supply of money—for any certificate put into circulation an equivalent amount of gold is taken out of circulation (deposited)—nor the interpersonal income and wealth distribution. Yet without a doubt the coexistence of money and money substitutes and the possibility of holding money in either form and in variable combinations of such forms constitutes an added convenience to individual market participants. This is how intrinsically worthless pieces of paper can acquire purchasing power. If and insofar as they represent an unconditional claim to money and if and insofar as no doubt exists that they are valid and may indeed be redeemed at any time, paper tickets are bought and sold *as if* they are genuine money—they are traded against money at par. Once they have thus acquired purchasing

power and are then deprived of their character as claims to money
(by somehow suspending redeemability), they may continue functioning as money. As Mises writes:

> Before an economic good begins to function as money it must
> already possess exchange-value based on some other cause than
> its monetary function. But money that already functions as such
> may remain valuable even when the original source of its
> exchange-value has ceased to exist.[9]

However, would self-interested individuals *want* to deprive paper
tickets of their character as titles to money? Would they *want* to suspend redeemability and adopt intrinsically worthless pieces of paper
as money? Paper money champions like Milton Friedman claim this
to be the case, and they typically cite a savings-motive as the reason
for the substitution of fiat for commodity money: A gold standard
involves social waste in requiring the mining and minting of gold.
Considerable resources have to be devoted to the production of
money.[10] With essentially costless paper money instead of gold, such
waste would disappear, and resources would be freed up for the production of directly useful producer or consumer goods. It is thus a fiat
money's higher economic efficiency which explains the present world's
universal abandonment of commodity money. But is it so? Is the triumph of fiat money indeed the outcome of some innocuous saving? Is
it even conceivable that it could be? Can self-interested individuals
really *want* to save as fiat money champions assume that they do?

Somewhat closer scrutiny reveals that this is impossible, and that
the institution of fiat money requires the assumption of a very different—not innocuous but sinister—motive: Assume a monetary economy with (at least) one bank and money proper ("outside money" in
modern jargon) as well as money substitutes ("inside money") in circulation. If market participants indeed wanted to save on the
resource costs of a commodity money (with the ultimate goal of
demonetizing gold and monetizing paper), one would expect that

---

[9]Mises, *The Theory of Money and Credit*, p. 111.

[10]See Friedman, "Essays in Positive Economics, p. 210; idem, *A Program for
Monetary Stability*, pp. 4–8; idem, *Capitalism and Freedom* (Chicago: University
of Chicago Press, 1962), p. 40.

first—as an approximation to this goal—they would want to give up using any outside money (gold). All transactions would have to be carried out with inside money (paper), and all outside money would have to be deposited in a bank and thus taken out of circulation entirely (Otherwise, as long as genuine money was still in circulation, those individuals making use of gold coins would demonstrate unmistakably—through their very actions—that they did *not* want to save on the associated resource costs.)

However, is it possible that money substitutes can thus outcompete and displace genuine money as a medium of exchange? Even many hard money theoreticians have been too quick to admit such a possibility. The reason is that money substitutes are *substitutes* and have one permanent and decisive disadvantage as compared to money proper. Paper notes (claims to money) are redeemable at par only to the extent that a deposit fee has been paid to the depositing institution. Providing safeguarding and clearing services is a costly business, and a deposit fee is the price paid for guarded money. If paper notes are presented for redemption after the date up to which safeguarding fees were paid by the original or previous depositor, the depositing institution would have to impose a redemption charge and such notes would then trade at a discount against genuine money. The disadvantage of money substitutes is that they must be continuously re-deposited and re-issued in order to maintain their character as money—their salability at par—and thus that they function as money only temporarily and discontinuously. Only money proper (gold coins) is permanently suited to perform the function as a medium of exchange. Accordingly, far from inside money ever displacing outside money, the use of money substitutes should be expected to be forever severely limited—restricted essentially to the transaction of very large sums of money and the dealings between regular commercial traders—while the overwhelming bulk of the population would employ money proper for most of their purchases or sales, thus demonstrating their preference for *not* wanting to save in the way fancied by Friedman.[11]

---

[11]Indeed, historically this has been the case: Traditionally, notes have always been widely distrusted, and their acceptability—as compared to that of genuine money such as gold or silver coins—was severely limited.

Moreover, even if one assumed for the sake of argument that only inside money is in circulation while all genuine money is stored in a bank, the difficulties for fiat money proponents do not end here. To be sure, in their view matters appear simple enough: All commodity money sits idle in the bank. Wouldn't it be more efficient if all of this idle gold were used instead for purposes of consumption or production—for dentistry or jewelry—while the function of a medium of exchange were assumed by a less expensive—indeed, practically costless—fiat money? Not at all.

First, the envisioned demonetization of gold certainly cannot mean that a bank thereby assumes ownership of the entire money stock, while the public gets to keep the notes. No one except the bank owner would agree to that! No one would want *such* savings. In fact, this would not be savings at all but an expropriation of the public by and to the sole advantage of the bank. No one could possibly *want* to be expropriated by somebody else. (Yet the expropriation of privately owned commodity money through governments and their central banks is the only method by which commodity money has ever been replaced by fiat money.) Instead, each depositor would want to retain ownership of his deposits and get his gold back.

Then, however, an insurmountable problem arises: Regardless who—the bank or the public—now owns the notes, they represent nothing but irredeemable paper. Formerly, the cost associated with the production of such paper was by no means only that of printing

---

In order to increase the popularity of money substitutes two complementary measures were actually required: First, the note-issuing depositing institution had to overvalue deposit notes against genuine money by either charging no depositing fee or by even paying interest on deposits. Secondly, because the guarding of money is actually *not* costless and deposited money *cannot* possibly generate an interest return, the bank, in order to cover its otherwise unavoidable losses, had to engage in fractional reserve banking, i.e, it had to issue and bring into circulation new, additional deposit tickets that, while physically indistinguishable from any other notes, were actually not covered by genuine money.

On the ethical and economic status of the practice of fractional-reserve banking see the section, "From Deposit and Loan Banking to Fractional-Reserve Banking: The Devolution of Credit," below.

paper tickets, but more importantly that of attracting gold depositors through the provision of safeguarding and clearing services. Now, with irredeemable paper there is nothing worth guarding anymore. The cost of money production falls close to zero, to mere printing costs. Previously, with paper representing claims to gold, the notes had acquired purchasing power. But how can the bank or the public get anyone to accept them now? Would they be bought and sold for nonmoney goods at the formerly established exchange ratios? Obviously not. At least not as long as no legal barriers to entry into the note-production business existed; for under competitive conditions of free entry, if the (nonmoney) price paid for paper notes exceeded their production costs, the production of notes would immediately be expanded to the point at which the price of money approached its cost of production. The result would be hyperinflation. No one would accept paper money anymore, and a flight into *real values* would set in. The monetary economy would break down completely and society would revert back to a primitive, highly inefficient barter economy. Out of barter then, once again a new (most likely a gold) commodity money would emerge (and the note producers once again, so as to gain acceptability for their notes, would begin backing them by this money). What a way of achieving savings!

If one is to succeed in replacing commodity money by fiat money, then, an additional requirement must be fulfilled: Free entry into the note-production business must be restricted, and a money *monopoly* must be established. A single paper money producer is also capable of causing hyperinflation and a monetary breakdown. However, insofar as he is legally shielded from competition, a monopolist can safely and knowingly restrict the production of his notes and thus assure that they retain their purchasing power. He then presumably would assume the task of *redeeming* old notes at par for new ones, as well as that of again providing safeguarding and clearing services in accepting note deposits in exchange for his issuance of substitutes of notes—demand deposit accounts and checkbook money—against a depositing fee.

Regarding this scenario, several related questions arise. Formerly, with commodity money every person was permitted to enter the gold mining and coining business freely—in accordance with the assumption of self-interested, wealth-maximizing actors. In contrast, in order for Friedman's "fiat money dividend" to come into existence, competition in the field of money production would have to be outlawed and a monopoly erected. Yet how can the existence of a legal monopoly be reconciled with the assumption of self-interest? Is it conceivable that self-interested actors could agree on establishing a fiat money monopoly in the same way as they can naturally agree on participating in the division of labor and on using one and the same commodity as a medium of exchange? If not, does this not demonstrate that the cost associated with such a monopoly must be considered higher than all attending resource cost savings?

To raise these questions is to answer them. Monopoly and the pursuit of self-interest are incompatible. To be sure, a reason why someone might want to become the money monopolist exists. After all, by not having to store, guard and redeem a precious commodity, the production costs would be dramatically reduced and the monopolist could thus reap an extra profit. By being legally protected from all future competition, this monopoly profit would immediately become "capitalized" (reflected permanently in an upward valuation of his assets), and on top of his inflated asset values he then would be guaranteed a normal rate of return in the form of interest. Yet to say that such an arrangement would be advantageous to the monopolist is not to say that it would be advantageous to anybody else, and hence that it could arise naturally. In fact, there is no motive for anyone wanting *anyone but himself* to be this monopolist, and accordingly no agreement on the selection of any particular monopolist would be possible. The position of a monopolist can only be arrogated—enforced against the will of all excluded nonmonopolists. By definition, a monopoly creates a distinction between two classes of individuals of different legal quality: between those—privileged—individuals who are permitted to produce money, and those—subordinate—ones who, to the exclusive advantage of the former, are prohibited from doing the same. Such an institution *cannot* be supported in the same voluntary way as the institutions of the division of labor and a commodity money. It is *not*, as they are, the "natural" result of mutually advantageous interactions, but that of an unilaterally advantageous act of expropriation (abrogation). Accordingly, instead of relying for its continued existence on voluntary support and cooperation, a monopoly requires the threat of physical violence.[12]

Moreover, the incompatibility of self-interest and monopoly does not end once the monopoly has been established but continues as long as the monopoly remains in operation. It cannot but operate inefficiently and at the expense of the excluded nonmonopolists. First, under a regime of free competition (free entry), every single producer is under constant pressure to produce whatever he produces at minimum costs, for if he does *not* do so, he invites the risk of being outcompeted by new entrants who produce the product in question at lower costs. In contrast, a monopolist, shielded from competition, is under no such pressure. In fact, since the cost of money

---

[12]It might be argued that a monopoly agreement would be possible (conceivable), if the monopolistic bank of issue were owned by—and its profits distributed to—everyone. Wouldn't everyone, then, not just the monopolist, profit from the savings of substituting paper for gold?

In fact, such an agreement is illusionary. Joint ownership of the monopoly bank would imply that tradeable stock certificates must be issued and distributed. But who should get how much stock? Bank clients, according to their deposit size? Yet all private holders of notes help save on gold and would want to be included among the bank owners according to the size of their note holdings. What about the owners and sellers of nonmoney goods? In showing themselves willing to accept paper instead of gold, they, too, play their part in the resource cost savings. But how in the world is one to determine how many shares to award *them* when their contribution consists, as it does, of various quantities of heterogeneous consumer and producer goods? Here, at the very latest it would become impossible to reach agreement.

Moreover, why would any new market participant—any later deposit, note and/or nonmoney good owner *not* initially endowed with bank stock—want to consent to and support this arrangement? Why should he *pay* for banking stock, while it was distributed to the initial wealth owners free of charge, even though he is now involved in resource cost savings just as much as they were then? Such an arrangement would involve a systematic redistribution of income and wealth in favor of all initial wealth owners and at the expense of all later ones. Yet if new additional bank stock were issued for each new deposit, note, or nonmoney good owner, such stock would be worthless from the outset and any bank offering it would be a nonstarter.

In addition, as will be explained below, regardless of how the ownership problem is resolved, the very operation of the bank will—indeed *must*—have effects on the interpersonal income and wealth distribution.

production includes the monopolist's own salary as well as all of his nonmonetary rewards, a monopolist's "natural" interest is to *raise* his costs. Hence, it should be expected that the cost of a monopolistically provided paper money would very soon, if not from the very outset, *exceed* those associated with a competitively provided commodity money.

Furthermore, it can be predicted that the price of monopolistically provided paper money will steadily increase and the purchasing power per unit money, and its quality will continuously fall. Protected from new entrants, every monopolist is always tempted to raise price and lower quality. Yet this is particularly true of a money monopolist. While other monopolists must consider the possibility that price increases (or quality decreases) due to an elastic demand for their product may actually lead to reduced revenues, a money monopolist can rest assured that the demand for his particular product—the common medium of exchange—will be highly inelastic. Indeed, short of a hyperinflation, when the demand for money disappears entirely, a money monopolist is practically always in a position in which he may assume that his revenue from the sale of money will increase even as he raises the price of money (reduces its purchasing power). Equipped with the exclusive right to produce money and under the assumption of self-interest the monopoly bank should be expected to engage in a steady increase of the money supply, for while an increased supply of paper money does not add anything to social wealth—the amount of directly useful consumer and producer goods in existence—but merely causes inflation (lowers the purchasing power of money), with each additional note brought into circulation the monopolist can increase *his* real income (at the expense of lowering that of the non-monopolistic public). He can print notes at practically zero cost and then turn around and purchase *real* assets (consumer or producer goods) or use them for the repayment of *real* debts. The real wealth of the non-bank public will be reduced—they own less goods and more money of lower purchasing power. However, the monopolist's real wealth will increase—he owns more non-money goods (and he always has as much money as he wants). Who, in this situation, except angels, would *not* engage in a steady expansion of the money supply and hence in a continuous depreciation of the currency?

It may be instructive to contrast the theory of fiat money as outlined above to the views of Milton Friedman, as the outstanding modern champion of fiat money.

While the younger Friedman paid no systematic attention to the question of the origin of money the older Friedman recognizes that, as a matter of historical fact, all monies originated as commodity monies (and all money substitutes as warehouse claims to commodity money), and he is justly skeptical of the older Friedrich A. Hayek's proposal of competitively issued fiat currencies.[13] However, misled by his positivist methodology Friedman fails to grasp that money (and money substitutes) *cannot* originate in any other way and accordingly that Hayek's proposal must fail.

In contrast to the views developed here, throughout his entire work Friedman maintains that a commodity money in turn would be "naturally" replaced by a—more efficient, resource cost saving—fiat money regime. Amazingly, however, he offers no argumentative support for this thesis, evades all theoretical problems, and whatever argument or empirical observation he does offer *contradicts* his very claim. There is, first off, no indication that Friedman is aware of the fundamental limitations of replacing outside money by inside money. Yet if outside money cannot disappear from circulation, how, except through an act of expropriation, can the link between paper and a money commodity be severed? The continued use of outside money in circulation demonstrates that it is *not* regarded as an inferior money; and the fact that expropriation is needed for the decommoditization of money would demonstrate that fiat money is *not* a natural phenomenon!

Interestingly, after evading the problem of explaining how the suspension of redeemability can possibly be considered natural or efficient, Friedman quite correctly recognizes that fiat money cannot, for the reasons given above, be provided competitively but requires a monopoly. From there he proceeds to assert that "the production of

---

[13]See Milton Friedman and Anna Schwartz, "Has Government Any Role in Money?" *Journal of Monetary Economics* (1986); for Hayek's proposal see his *Denationalization of Money* (London: Institute of Economic Affairs, 1976).

fiat currency is, as it were, a natural monopoly."[14] However, from the fact that fiat money requires a monopoly, it does not follow that there is anything "natural" about such a monopoly and Friedman provides no argument whatsoever as to how any monopoly can possibly be considered the natural outcome of the interactions of self-interested individuals. Moreover, the younger Friedman in particular appears to be almost completely ignorant of classical political economy and its antimonopolistic arguments: the axiom that if you give someone a privilege he will make use of it, and hence the conclusion that every monopolistic producer will be inefficient (in terms of costs as well as of price and quality). In light of these arguments it has to be regarded as breathtakingly naive on Friedman's part first to advocate the establishment of a governmental money monopoly and then to expect this monopolist *not* to use its power, but to operate at the lowest possible costs and to inflate the money supply only gently (at a rate of 3–5 percent per year). This would assume that, along with becoming a monopolist, a fundamental transformation in the self-interested nature of mankind would take place.

Having had extensive experience with his own ideal of a world of pure fiat currencies as it came into existence after 1971 and looking back on his own central resource cost savings argument for a monopolistically provided fiat money of nearly four decades earlier, it is not surprising that the older Friedman cannot but acknowledge that his predictions turned out blatantly false.[15] Since abolishing the last remnants of the gold commodity money standard, he realizes, inflationary tendencies have dramatically increased on a worldwide scale; the predictability of future price movements has sharply decreased; the market for long-term bonds (such as consols) has been largely wiped out; the number of investment and "hard money" advisors and the resources bound up in such businesses have drastically increased; money market funds and currency futures markets have developed and absorbed significant amounts of real resources which otherwise—

---

[14]See Friedman, *Essays in Positive Economics*, p. 216; also Friedman and Schwartz, "Has Government Any Role in Money?"

[15]Milton Friedman, "The Resource Cost of Irredeemable Paper Money," *Journal of Political Economy* (1986).

without the increased inflation and unpredictability—would not have come into existence at all or at least would never have assumed the same importance that they now have; and finally it appears that even the direct resource costs devoted to the production of gold accumulated in private hoards as a hedge against inflation have increased.[16] But what conclusion does Friedman draw from this empirical evidence? In accordance with his own positivist methodology according to which science is prediction and false predictions falsify one's theory, one should expect that Friedman would finally discard his theory as hopelessly wrong and advocate a return to commodity money. Not so. Rather, in a remarkable display of continued ignorance (or arrogance), he emphatically concludes that none of this evidence should be interpreted as "a plea for a return to a gold standard. On the contrary I regard a return to a gold standard as neither desirable nor feasible."[17] Now as then he holds onto the view that the appeal of the gold standard is merely "nonrational, emotional," and that only a fiat money is "technically efficient."[18] According to Friedman, what needs to be done to overcome the obvious shortcomings of the current fiat money regime is find

> some anchor to provide long-term price predictability, some substitute for convertibility into a commodity or, alternatively some device that would make predictability unnecessary. Many possible anchors and devices have been suggested, from monetary growth rules to tabular standards to the separation of the medium of exchange from the unit of account. As yet, no consensus has been reached among them.[19]

---

[16]Monetarists had predicted that, as the result of the demonetization of gold and the transition to a pure fiat money system, the price of gold would fall—from the then official rate of $35 per ounce to an estimated nonmonetary value of gold of around $6. In fact, the price of gold rose. At one point it reached $850 per ounce, and for most of the time it has lingered between $300 and $400. As of this writing the price is $375.

[17]Friedman, "The Resource Cost of Irredeemable Paper Money," p. 648.

[18]Friedman, *Essays in Positive Economics*, p. 250.

[19]Friedman, "The Resource Cost of Irredeemable Paper Money," p. 646; also idem, *Money Mischief Episodes in Monetary History* (New York: Harcourt Brace Jovanovich, 1992), chap. 10.

FROM DEPOSIT AND LOAN BANKING TO FRACTIONAL
RESERVE BANKING: THE DEVOLUTION OF CREDIT

Banks perform two strictly separate tasks, only one of which has
been considered so far.[20] On the one hand, they serve as depositing

---

Among the suggestions for an alternative fiat money "anchor" recently considered by Friedman, the "frozen monetary base rule" deserves a brief comment
(see Friedman, "Monetary Policy for the 1980s" in *To Promote Prosperity*, John
H. Moore, ed. [Stanford: Hoover Institution, 1984]). In one respect this rule represents an advance over his earlier 3 to 5 percent monetary growth rule. His
advocacy of the latter rule was based essentially on the erroneous proto-
Keynesian notion that money constitutes part of social capital, such that an economy cannot grow by 5 percent unless it is accommodated to do so by a proportional increase in the money supply. In contrast, the frozen monetary base rule
indicates a recognition of the old Humean insight that any supply of money is
equally optimal or, in Friedman's own words, that money's "usefulness to the
community as a whole does not depend on how much money there is (Friedman,
Money Mischief, p. 28). Otherwise, the proposal represents no advance at all, for
how in the world can a monopolist be expected to follow a frozen monetary base
rule any more than a less stringent 3 to 5 percent growth rule?

Moreover, even if this problem were solved miraculously, this would still not
alter the monopoly's character as an instrument of unilateral expropriation and
income and wealth redistribution. The monopolist, apart from offering depositing and clearing services (for which his customers would pay him a fee), would
also have to perform the function, for customers and noncustomers alike, of
replacing old, worn-out notes—one-to-one and free of charge—with new, identical ones (otherwise, who would want to replace a permanent commodity
money by a perishable fiat money?). However, while the costs associated with
this task may be low, they are definitely not zero. Accordingly, in order to avoid
losses and recoup his expenses, the monopolist cannot but *increase* the monetary
base—and hence one would essentially be back at the older monetary growth
rule.

[20]On the following see in particular Murray N. Rothbard, *The Mystery of
Banking* (New York: Richardson and Synder, 1983); idem, *The Case for a 100
Percent Gold Dollar* (Auburn, Ala.: Ludwig von Mises Institute, 1991); Mises,
The Theory of Money and Credit; idem, *Human Action*; also Walter Block,
"Fractional Reserve Banking: An Interdisciplinary Perspective," in *Man,
Economy, and Liberty: Essays in Honor of Murray N. Rothbard*, Walter Block and
Llewellyn H. Rockwell, Jr., eds. (Auburn, Ala.: Ludwig von Mises Institute,
1988); S. Koch, *Fractional Reserve Banking: A Practical Critique* (Master's thesis,
University of Nevada, Las Vegas, 1992).

institutions, offering safekeeping and clearing services. They accept deposits of (commodity) money and issue claims to money (warehouse receipts; money substitutes) to their depositors, redeemable at par and on demand. For every claim to money issued by them they hold an equivalent amount of genuine money on hand, ready for redemption (100 percent reserve banking). No interest is paid on deposits. Rather, depositors pay a fee to the bank for providing safekeeping and clearing services. Under conditions of free competition—free entry into the banking industry—the deposit fee, which constitutes a bank's revenue and possible source of profit, tends to be a minimum fee; and the profits—or rather, the interest returns—earned in banking tend to be the same as in any other, nonbanking industry.

On the other hand, originally entirely separate institutionally from deposit institutions, banks also serve as intermediaries between savers and investors—as loan banks. In this function they first offer and enter into time-contracts with savers. Savers loan money to the bank for a specified—shorter or longer—period of time in exchange for the banks' contractual obligation of future repayment plus some additional interest return. From the point of view of savers, they exchange present money for a promise of future money: the interest return constituting their reward for performing the function of waiting. Having thus acquired temporary ownership of savings from savers, the bank then reloans the same money to investors (including itself) in exchange for the latters' obligation of future repayment and interest. The interest differential—the difference between the interest paid to savers and that charged to borrowers—represents the price for intermediating between savers and investors and constitutes the loan bank's income. As for deposit banking and deposit fees, under competitive conditions the costs of intermediation also tend to be minimum costs, and the profits from loan banking likewise tend to be the same as those that can be earned elsewhere.

Neither deposit banking nor loan banking as characterized here involve an increase in the money supply or a unilateral income or wealth redistribution. For every newly issued deposit note an equivalent amount of money is taken out of circulation (only the form of money changes, not its quantity), and in the course of loan banking the same sum of money simply changes hands repeatedly. All exchanges—

between depositors and depositing institution as well as between savers, the intermediating bank and investors—are mutually advantageous.

In contrast, fractional reserve banking involves a deliberate confusion between the deposit and the loan function. It implies an increase in the money supply, and it leads to a unilateral income redistribution in the bank's favor as well as to economic inefficiencies in the form of boom-bust business cycles.

The confusion of both banking functions comes to light in the fact that under fractional reserve banking, either depositors are being paid interest (rather than having to pay a fee), and/or savers are granted the right of instant withdrawal (rather than having to wait with their request for redemption until a specified future date). Technically, the possibility of a bank's engaging in such practices arises out of the fact that the holders of demand deposits (claims to money redeemable on demand, instantly, at par) typically do *not* exercise their right simultaneously, such that all of them approach the bank with the request for redemption at the same time. Accordingly, a deposit bank will typically hold an amount of reserves (of money proper) in excess of actual daily withdrawals. It becomes thus feasible for the bank to loan these "excess" reserves to borrowers, thus earning the bank an interest return (which the bank then may partially pass on to its depositors in the form of interest paying deposit accounts).

Proponents of fractional reserve banking usually claim that this practice of holding less than 100 percent reserves represents merely an innocuous money "economizing," and they are fond of pointing out that not only the bank, but depositors (receiving interest) and savers (receiving instant withdrawal rights) profit from the practice as well. In fact, fractional reserve banking suffers from two interrelated fatal flaws and is anything but innocuous and all-around beneficial. First off, it should be noted that anything less than 100 percent reserve deposit banking involves what one might call a legal impossibility, for in employing its excess reserves for the granting of credit, the bank actually transfers temporary ownership of them to some borrower, while the depositors, entitled as they are to instant redemption, retain their ownership over the same funds. However, it is impossible that for some time depositor *and* borrower are entitled to exclusive control over the same resources. Two individuals *cannot be* the exclusive owner of one and the same thing at the same time. Accordingly any bank pretending otherwise—in assuming demand liabilities in excess of actual reserves—must be considered as acting fraudulently. Its contractual obligations *cannot be* fulfilled. From the outset, the bank must be regarded as inherently bankrupt—as revealed by the fact that it could not, contrary to its own presumption, withstand a possible bank run.

Second, in lending its excess reserves to borrowers, the bank increases the money supply, regardless whether the borrowers receive these reserves in the form of money proper or in that of demand deposits (checking accounts). If the loan takes the form of genuine money, then the amount of money proper in circulation is increased without withdrawing an equivalent amount of money substitutes from circulation; and if it takes the form of a checking account, then the amount of money substitutes is increased without taking a corresponding amount of genuine money out of circulation. In either case, there will be more money in existence now than before, leading to a reduction in the purchasing power of money (inflation) and, in its course, to a systematic redistribution of real income in favor of the bank and its borrower clients and at the expense of the nonbank public and all other bank clients. The bank receives additional interest income while it makes no additional contribution whatsoever to the real wealth of the nonbank public (as would be the case if the interest return were the result of reduced bank spending, i.e., savings); and the borrowers acquire real, nonmonetary assets with their funds, thereby reducing the real wealth of the rest of the public by the same amount.

Moreover, insofar as the bank does not simply spend the excess reserves on its own consumption but instead loans them out against interest charges, invariably a business cycle is set in motion.[21] The

---

[21]On the theory of the business cycle see in particular Ludwig von Mises, *Geldwertstabilisierung und Konjunkturpolitik* (Jena: Gustav Fischer, 1928); idem, *Human Action*, chap. 20; F.A. Hayek, *Prices and Production* (London: Routledge and Kegan Paul, 1931); Murray N. Rothbard, *America's Great Depression* (Kansas City: Sheed and Ward, 1975).

quantity of credit offered is larger than before. As a consequence, the price of credit—the interest charged for loans—will fall below what it otherwise would have been. At a lower price, more credit is taken. Since money cannot breed more money, in order to be able to earn an interest return and a pure profit on top of it, the borrowers will have to convert their borrowed funds into investments. That is, they will have to purchase or rent factors of production—land, labor, and possibly capital goods (produced factors of production)—capable of producing a future output of goods whose value (price) exceeds that of the input. Accordingly with an expanded volume of credit, more presently available resources will be bound up in the production of *future* goods (instead of being used for present consumption) than otherwise would have been; and in order to complete all investment projects now under way, more time will be needed than that required to complete only those that would have been begun without the credit expansion. All the future goods which would have been created without the expansion plus those that are newly added on account of the credit expansion must be produced.

However, in distinct contrast to the situation in which the interest rate falls due to a fall in the rate of time preference (the degree to which present goods are preferred over future goods), and hence where the public has in fact saved more so as to make a larger fund of present goods available to investors in exchange for their promise of a return of future goods, no such change in time preference and savings has taken place in the case under consideration. The public has *not* saved more, and accordingly, the additional amount of credit granted by the bank does not represent *commodity credit* (credit covered by nonmoney goods which the public has abstained from consuming), but it is *fiduciary* or *circulation credit* (credit that has been literally created out of thin air—without any corresponding sacrifice, in the form of nonconsumed nonmoney goods, on the part of the creditor).[22] Had the additional credit been commodity credit, an expanded volume of investment activities would have been warranted. There would have been a sufficiently large supply of present

---

[22]On the fundamental distinction between commodity credit and circulation credit, see Mises, *The Theory of Money and Credit*, pp. 263ff.

goods that could be devoted to the production of future goods such that all—the old as well as the newly begun—investment projects could be successfully completed and a higher level of future consumption attained. If the credit expansion is due to the granting of circulation credit, however, the ensuing volume of investment must actually prove overambitious. Misled by a lower interest rate, investors act *as if* savings had increased. They withdraw more of the presently available resources for investment projects, to be converted into future capital goods, than is warranted in light of actual savings. Consequently, capital goods prices will increase initially relative to consumer goods prices, but once the public's underlying time preference rate begins to reassert itself, a systematic shortage of consumer goods will arise. Accordingly, the interest rate will adjust upward, and it is now consumer goods prices which rise relative to capital goods prices, requiring the liquidation of part of the investment as unsustainable malinvestment. The earlier boom will turn bust, reducing the future standard of living below the level that otherwise could have been reached.

Among recent proponents of fractional reserve banking the cases of Lawrence White and George Selgin[23] deserve a few critical comments, if for no other reason than that both are critics of Friedmanite monetarism who hark back, instead, to the tradition of Austrian and in particular Misesian monetary theory.[24] Their monetary ideal is a universal commodity money such as an international gold standard and, based on this, a system of competitive banking which, they claim, would—and should be permitted to do so for reasons of economic efficiency as well as justice—engage in fractional reserve banking and the granting of fiduciary credit.

---

[23]See Lawrence White, *Competition and Currency* (New York: New York University Press, 1989); George Selgin, *The Theory of Free Banking* (Totowa, N.J.: Rowman and Littlefield, 1988).

[24]For a critique of White and Selgin as misinterpreting the fundamental thrust of Mises's theory of money and banking see Joseph Salerno, "The Concept of Coordination in Austrian Macroeconomics," in *Austrian Economics: Perspectives on the Past and Prospects for the Future*, Richard Ebeling, ed. (Hillsdale, Mich.: Hillsdale College Press, 1991); idem, "Mises and Hayek Dehomogenized," *Review of Austrian Economics* 6, no. 2 (1993): 113–46.

As to the question of justice, White and Selgin offer but one argument destined to show the allegedly nonfraudulent character of fractional reserves: that outlawing such a practice would involve a violation of the principle of freedom of contract by preventing "banks and their customers from making whatever sorts of contractual arrangements are mutually agreeable."[25] Yet this is surely a silly argument. First off, as a matter of historical fact fractional reserve banks never informed their depositors that some or all of their deposits would actually be loaned out and hence could not possibly be ready for redemption at any time. (Even if the bank were to pay interest on deposit accounts, and hence it *should* have been clear that the bank *must* loan out deposits, this does not imply that any of the depositors actually understand this fact. Indeed, it is safe to say that few if any do, even among those who are not economic illiterates.) Nor did fractional reserve banks inform their borrowers that some or all of the credit granted to them had been created out of thin air and was subject to being recalled at any time. How, then, can their practice be called anything but fraud and embezzlement!

Second, and more decisive, to believe that fractional reserve banking should be regarded as falling under and protected by the principle of freedom of contract involves a complete misunderstanding of the very meaning of this principle. Freedom of contract does not imply that *every* mutually advantageous contract should be permitted. Clearly, if A and B contractually agree to rob C, this would not be in accordance with the principle. Freedom of contract means instead that A and B should be allowed to make any contract whatsoever *regarding their own properties*, yet fractional reserve banking involves the making of contracts regarding the property of third parties. Whenever the bank loans its "excess" reserves to a borrower, such a bilateral contract affects the property of third parties in a threefold way. First, by thereby increasing the money supply, the purchasing power of all other money owners is reduced; second, all depositors are harmed because the likelihood of their successfully recovering

---

[25]White, *Competition and Currency*, p. 156, also pp. 55–56; George Selgin, "Short-Changed in Chile: The Truth about the Free-Banking Episode," *Austrian Economics Newsletter* (Winter/Spring, 1990): 5.

their own possessions is lowered; and third, all other borrowers—borrowers of commodity credit—are harmed because the injection of fiduciary credit impairs the safety of the entire credit structure and increases the risk of a business failure for every investor of commodity credit.

In order to overcome these objections to the claim that fractional reserve banking accords with the principle of freedom of contract, White and Selgin then, as their last line of defense, withdraw to the position that banks may attach an "option clause" to their notes, informing depositors that the bank may at any time suspend or defer redemption, and letting borrowers know that their loans may be instantly recalled.[26] While such a practice would indeed dispose of the charge of fraud, it is subject to another fundamental criticism, for such notes would no longer be *money* but a peculiar form of *lottery tickets*.[27] It is the function of money to serve as the most easily resalable and most widely acceptable good, so as to prepare its owner for instant purchases of directly or indirectly serviceable consumer or producer goods at not yet known future dates; hence, whatever may serve as money so as to be instantly resalable at any future point in time, it must be something that bestows an *absolute* and *unconditional* property right on its owner. In sharp contrast, the owner of a note to which an option clause is attached does *not* possess an unconditional property title. Rather, similar to the holder of a "fractional reserve parking ticket" (where more tickets are sold than there are parking places on hand, and lots are allocated according to a "first-come-first-served" rule), he is merely entitled to participate in the drawing of certain prizes, consisting of ownership or time-rental services to specified goods according to specified rules. But as drawing rights—and not unconditional ownership titles—they only possess *temporally conditional* value until the time of the drawing, and they become worthless as soon as the prizes have been allocated to the ticket holders;

---

[26]White, *Currency and Competition,* p. 157; Selgin, *The Theory of Free Banking*, p. 137.

[27]See Block, "Fractional Reserve Banking: An Interdisciplinary Perspective," p. 30.

thus, they would be uniquely *un*suited to serve as a medium of exchange.

As regards the second contention: that fractional reserve banking is economically efficient, it is noteworthy to point out that White, although he is undoubtedly familiar with the Austrian-Misesian claim that *any* injection of fiduciary credit must result in a boom-bust cycle, nowhere even mentions the problem of business cycles. Only Selgin addresses the problem. In his attempt to show that fractional reserve banking does not cause business cycles, however, Selgin then falls headlong into the fundamental Keynesian error of confusing the demand for money (determined by the utility of money) and savings (determined by time preference).[28]

According to Selgin, "to hold inside money is to engage in voluntary saving"; and accordingly "an increase in the demand for money warrants an increase in bank loans and investments" because

> [w]henever a bank expands its liabilities in the process of making new loans and investments, it is the holders of the liabilities who are the ultimate lenders of credit, and what they lend are the real resources they could acquire if, instead of holding money, they spent it.[29]

Based on this view of the holding of money as representing saving and an increased demand for money as being the same thing as increased saving, then, Selgin goes on to criticize Mises's claim that *any* issuance of fiduciary media, in lowering the interest rate below its "natural" level, must cause a business cycle as "confused." "No ill consequences result from the issue of fiduciary media in response to a greater demand for balances of inside money."[30]

Yet the confusion is all Selgin's. First off, it is false to say that the holding of money (the act of not spending it), is equivalent to saving.

---

[28]For a critique of this error see Rothbard, *America's Great Depression*, pp. 39–43; Hans-Hermann Hoppe, "Theory of Employment, Money Interest, and the Capitalist Process: The Misesian Case Against Keynes," in *The Economics and Ethics of Private Property*, Hoppe, ed. (Boston: Kluwer, 1993), pp. 119–20, 137–38.

[29]Selgin, *The Theory of Free Banking*, p. 55.

[30]Ibid., pp. 61–62.

One might as well say—and this would be equally wrong—that the not-spending of money is equivalent to *not* saving. In fact, saving is not-consuming, and the demand for money has nothing to do with saving or not-saving. The demand for money is the unwillingness to buy or rent nonmoney goods, and these include consumer goods (present goods) *and* capital goods (future goods). Not-spending money is to purchase, *neither* consumer goods *nor* investment goods. Contrary to Selgin, then, matters are as follows: Individuals may employ their monetary assets in one of three ways. They can spend them on consumer goods; they can spend them on investment; or they can keep them in the form of cash. There are no other alternatives. While a person must at all times make decisions regarding three margins at once, invariably the outcome is determined by two distinct and praxeologically unrelated factors. The consumption/investment proportion (the decision of how much of one's money to spend on consumption and how much on investment) is determined by a person's time preference (the degree to which he prefers present consumption over future consumption). On the other hand, the source of his demand for cash is the utility attached to money (the personal satisfaction derived from money in allowing him immediate purchases of directly or indirectly serviceable consumer or producer goods at uncertain future dates).

Accordingly, if the demand for money increases while the social stock of money is given, this additional demand can only be satisfied by bidding down the money prices of nonmoney goods. The purchasing power of money will increase, the *real* value of individual cash balances will be raised, and at a higher purchasing power per unit money, the demand for and the supply of money will once again be equilibrated. The relative price of money versus nonmoney will have changed. But unless time preference is assumed to have changed at the same time, *real* consumption and *real* investment will remain the same as before: the additional money demand is satisfied by reducing nominal consumption *and* investment spending in accordance with the same pre-existing consumption/investment proportion, driving the money prices of both consumer as well as producer goods down and leaving real consumption and investment at precisely their old levels. If time preference is assumed to change concomitantly with an increased demand for money, however, then everything is possible.

Indeed, if spending were reduced exclusively on investment goods, an increased demand for money could even go hand in hand with an increase in the rate of interest and reduced saving and investment. However, this, or the equally possible opposite outcome, would not be due to a change in the demand for money but exclusively to a change (a rise, or a fall) in the time preference schedule. In any case, if the banking system were to follow Selgin's advice and accommodate an increased demand for cash by issuing fiduciary credit, the social rate of time preference would be falsified, excessive investment would result, and a boom-bust cycle would be set in motion, rendering the practice of fractional reserve banking fraudulent *as well as* economically inefficient.

White's and Selgin's proposal of a commodity money based system of competitive fractional reserve banking—of partial fiat money—is neither just (and hence the term "free banking" is inappropriate), nor does it produce economic stability. It is no fundamental improvement as compared to the monetarist reality of monopolistically issued pure fiat currencies. Indeed, in one respect Friedman's pure fiat money proposal contains a more realistic and correct analysis than White's and Selgin's because Friedman recognizes "what used to be called 'the inherent instability' of fractional reserve banking," and he understands that this inherent instability of competitive fractional reserve banking will sooner or later collapse in a "liquidity crisis" and then lead to his favored regime—a governmentally provided pure fiat currency—anyway.[31]

Only a system of universal commodity money (gold), competitive banks, *and* 100-percent-reserve deposit banking with a strict functional separation of loan and deposit banking constitutes a just monetary system that can assure economic stability and present a genuine answer to the current monetarist fiasco.

---

[31]See Friedman and Schwartz, "Has Government Any Role in Money?"

7

Against Fiduciary Media

Almost all contemporary Austrian economists are united in their opposition to central banking and in their advocacy of a system of free competitive banking. However, a vigorous debate has arisen over the precise meaning of "free competitive banking." Does "free banking" require 100-percent-reserve-deposit banking, or does it allow or even require fractional reserve banking? In a recent article that appeared in the *Review of Austrian Economics*, George A. Selgin and Lawrence White, the two most prominent contemporary Austrian proponents of "free banking" as fractional reserve banking, have undertaken a systematic attempt to answer their numerous Austrian critics and defenders of 100-percent-reserve-deposit banking.[1]

[This article was written with the assistance of Jörg Guido Hülsmann and Walter Block and is reprinted from the *Quarterly Journal of Austrian Economics* 1, no. 1 (Spring, 1998).]

[1]George Selgin and Lawrence White, "In Defense of Fiduciary Media—or, We are Not Devo(lutionists), We are Misesians!" *Review of Austrian Economics* 9 no. 2 (1996): 83–107.

Curiously, in the reply to their various critics, Selgin and White selected as their central target an article by Hans-Hermann Hoppe ("How is Fiat Money

Against the charges made by their critics, Selgin and White try to establish two theses. First, they claim to show that the practice of fractional reserve banking, that is, the issue of fiduciary media, does not constitute fraud but is justified by the principle of freedom of contract, and in particular they contend that fractional reserve banking is in accordance with the title-transfer theory of contract as developed by Murray N. Rothbard (such that Rothbard, who holds that fractional reserve banking is fraudulent, must have failed to grasp his own theory). Second, they attempt to show that the creation of fiduciary media does not of necessity lead to economic inefficiencies and discoordination but may actually help prevent an otherwise unavoidable crisis and thus improve economic performance. In the following,

---

Possible?—or, The Devolution of Money and Credit," *Review of Austrian Economics* 7, no. 2 (1994): 49–74, that deals only cursorily with their position. Other Austrian critics of fractional reserve banking explicitly dealt with in Selgin and White's article including Walter Block, "Fractional Reserve Banking: An Interdisciplinary Perspective," in *Man, Economy, and Liberty: Essays in Honor of Murray N. Rothbard*, Walter Block and Llewellyn H. Rockwell, Jr., eds. (Auburn, Ala.: Ludwig von Mises Institute, 1988) and Jesús Huerta de Soto, "A Critical Analysis of Central Banks and Fractional-Reserve Free Banking from the Austrian Perspective," *Review of Austrian Economics* 8, no. 2 (1995): 25–36. Murray N. Rothbard, the most prominent critic of fractional reserve banking, is targeted only indirectly; and although several of his works are mentioned in their bibliography, Rothbard's later writings on the subject ("The Myth of Free Banking in Scotland," *Review of Austrian Economics* 2 [1988]: 229–57; idem, "Aurophobia: or, Free Banking on What Standard?" *Review of Austrian Economics*, 6, no. 1 [1992]: 97–108; idem, "The Present State of Austrian Economics," *Journal des Economistes et des Etudes Humaines* 6, no. 2 [1995]) are not mentioned. Likewise ignored entirely are the criticisms by Joseph T. Salerno ("Two Traditions in Modern Monetary Theory: John Law and A.R.J. Turgot," *Journal des Economistes et des Etudes Humaines* 2, no. 2/3 [1991]; idem, "The Concept of Coordination in Austrian Macroeconomics," in *Austrian Economics: Perspectives on the Past and Prospects for the Future*, Richard Ebeling, ed. [Hillsdale, Mich.: Hillsdale College Press, 1991]; and idem, "Mises and Hayek Dehomogenized," *Review of Austrian Economics* 6, no. 2 [1993]: 113–46). Selgin and White also do not address, and in this case could not have done so, the most recent and most extensive criticism of their work by Jörg Guido Hülsmann ("Free Banking and the Free Bankers," *Review of Austrian Economics* 9, no. 1 [1996]: 3–53).

we will demonstrate that neither the central normative claim nor the secondary positive claim is established.[2]

THE ISSUE OF FRAUD I:
MONEY, MONEY SUBSTITUTES, FIDUCIARY MEDIA, AND THE TITLE-TRANSFER THEORY OF CONTRACT

In order to resolve the question of whether or not fractional reserve banking constitutes fraud, from the outset a few factual assumptions and terminological issues will have to be clarified. Fortunately almost complete agreement on these matters exists on both sides of the debate, and thus we can be extremely brief. Money cannot but originate as a commodity, such as gold. Gold, then, as money is defined as "the generally acceptable medium of exchange," and as such is uniquely characterized by its "supreme salability in comparison with

---

[2]As a doctrinal matter, Selgin and White also suggest that their view of fractional reserve banking coincides with Ludwig von Mises's view; hence, they call themselves Misesians and claim it is the defenders of 100-percent-reserve banking who are deviationists. This claim can be rejected. In fact, Selgin (*The Theory of Free Banking: Money Supply under Competitive Note Issue* [Totowa, N.J.: Rowman and Littlefield, 1988], pp. 60–63) has frankly acknowledged that Mises's and his own views concerning fiduciary media are contradictory and White's attempt to claim Mises as a proponent of fractional reserve free banking has been addressed by Salerno ("Mises and Hayek Dehomogenized," *Review of Austrian Economics* 6, no. 2 [1993]: 113–46). Here it suffices to provide a quotation from Mises:

The main thing is that the government should no longer be in a position to increase the quantity of money in circulation and the amount of cheque-book money not fully—i.e., 100 percent—covered by deposits paid in by the public. . . . No bank must be permitted to expand the total amount of its deposits subject to cheque or the balance of such deposits of any individual customer . . . otherwise than by receiving cash deposits . . . or by receiving a cheque payable by another domestic bank subject to the same limitations. This means a rigid 100 per cent reserve for all future deposits; i.e., all deposits not already in existence on the first day of the reform. (*The Theory of Money and Credit* [Irvington-on-Hudson, N.Y.: Foundation for Economic Education, 1978], pp. 438 and 48)

See also notes 11, 25, 37, 47, and 48 below.

all other assets" (such that its "possession puts one in the position of being able to make any potential purchase with minimum inconvenience").[3] Money substitutes, in turn, are defined as claims or titles to specified amounts of money gold. If money substitutes (paper notes) are fully covered by reserves of money (gold), Mises denotes them "money certificates," and we will refer to them here simply as money substitutes. If money substitutes (paper notes) are uncovered by money (gold), they will be referred to as fiduciary media instead.[4]

---

[3]Lawrence H. White, *Competition and Currency* (New York: New York University Press, 1989).

[4]See Salerno, "Ludwig von Mises's Monetary Theory in Light of Modern Monetary Thought," *Review of Austrian Economics* 8, no. 1 (1994): 71–115. Selgin and White highlight the fact that Hoppe referred to them as proponents of "partial fiat money," but then are ultimately compelled to admit that he did in fact not misrepresent their position as advocates of fractional reserve banking based on an underlying gold standard. Their complaint amounts to no more than a dispute over semantics. We will treat it as such here, too, and will concentrate instead exclusively on substantive disagreements.

There is actually more to the charge of Selgin and White being fiat money advocates in the article under scrutiny. For, in "the mature free-banking system," according to Selgin and White (but in contrast to the analysis of the operation of such a system given by Mises), a situation is supposed to emerge in which

> At the limit, if inter-clearinghouse settlements were made entirely with other assets (perhaps claims on a super-clearinghouse which itself holds negligible commodity money), and if the public were completely weaned from holding commodity money, the active demand for the old-fashioned money commodity would be wholly nonmonetary. (Lawrence White, *Competition and Currency* [New York: New York University Press, 1989], p. 235)

Thus, notes Salerno ("Ludwig von Mises's Monetary Theory in Light of Modern Monetary Thought," *Review of Austrian Economics* 8, no. 1 [1994]: 71–115, p. 76, n. 7) regarding Selgin and White's ultimate objective, "the public would presumably finally be freed from its shackles of gold to enjoy the virtues of an invisible-hand-generated private fiat money." Moreover, as far as semantic innovations and deviations from orthodox Misesian terminology, and hence potential sources of confusion are concerned, we have to consider Selgin and White's own writings. For in referring to money and money substitutes as "outside and "inside" money respectively, in talking of "base money," "basic

Based on these assumptions and definitions, we can now turn to the question of whether or not the issue of fiduciary media constitutes fraud. Fortunately the discussion of this issue is facilitated by the fact that Selgin and White explicitly accept the Rothbardian title-transfer theory of contract. That the issue of fiduciary media is inherently fraudulent, as Rothbard and Hoppe claim, Selgin and White find

> impossible to reconcile with Rothbard's . . . title-transfer-theory of contract which we accept, and which Rothbard otherwise uses to defend the freedom of mutually consenting individuals to engage in capitalist acts with their (justly owned) property. Rothbard defines fraud as "failure to fulfill a voluntarily-agreed-upon transfer of property." Fractional-reserve arrangements cannot then be *inherently* or *inescapably* fraudulent. Whether a particular bank is committing fraud by holding fractional reserves must depend on the terms of the title-transfer agreements between the bank and its customers.[5] . . .
>
> Whether it is fraudulent to hold fractional reserves against a bank liability does not depend *per se* on whether it is a demand or time liability, but only on whether the bank has misrepresented itself as holding 100 percent reserves. The demandability of a particular claim issued by a bank, i.e., the holder's contractual option to redeem it at any time, is not *per se* a representation that the bank is holding 100 percent reserves against the total of its demandable claims. Rothbard argues otherwise, based on the view that a bank's demand deposits and notes are necessarily "warehouse receipts" and not debts. We do not see why bank and customer cannot contractually agree to make them debts and not warehouse receipts, and we believe that historically they have so agreed.[6]

---

money," "bank money," "high-powered" and "low-powered" money, and, yes, the gold dollar "as a substitute for bank deposits," they display an unusual degree of semantic creativity. Moreover, in suggesting, by their selection of terms, that all of these things are somehow equally "money," their writings actually have become a source of obfuscation. See on this Hülsmann, "Free Banking and the Free Bankers," pp. 5ff.

[5]Selgin and White, "In Defense of Fiduciary Media," pp. 86–87.

[6]Ibid., p. 87, n. 8.

While this may sound plausible at first glance, it does not withstand serious scrutiny. In fact, the quoted passage reveals that the most basic lesson concerning property and contract has been overlooked. As Hoppe formulated it, "two individuals cannot be the exclusive owner of one and the same thing at the same time."[7] This is an immutable principle; it is a law of action and nature that no contract can change or invalidate. Rather, any contractual agreement that involves presenting two different individuals as simultaneous owners of the same thing (or alternatively, the same thing as simultaneously owned by more than one person) is objectively false and thus fraudulent.[8] Yet this is precisely what a fractional-reserve agreement between bank and customer involves.

In issuing and accepting a fiduciary note (at a necessarily discounted price), both bank and customer have *in fact*, regardless of whatever they may believe or think about the transaction, agreed to represent themselves—fraudulently—as the owner of one and the same object at the same time. They have in fact contracted to create additional titles and claims to the same existing quantity of property. In issuing fiduciary notes, they do not—and cannot—bring more property into existence. Indeed, no contract whatsoever can possibly increase the existing quantity of property, but can only transfer (redistribute) existing property from one person to another. The quantity of existing property can only be increased through additional appropriation and production (and a thus enlarged quantity of property can in turn lead to a correspondingly increased number of titles to property). But fractional reserve banking and the issue of fiduciary media, while it does not and cannot increase the amount of property in existence, also does not involve (as all other contracts do) a transfer of

---

[7]It is also "impossible that some time depositor and borrower are entitled to exclusive control over the same resources" (Hoppe, "How is Fiat Money Possible?", p. 67).

[8]Even partners cannot simultaneously own the *same* thing. A and B can each own half of a household, or half the shares in it but they each own a *different* 50 percent. It is as logically impossible for them to own the same half as for two people to occupy the same space. Yes, A and B can both be in New York City at the same time, but only in different parts of it.

existing property or titles to existing property from one hand to another. Neither does the issue and acceptance of a fiduciary note signify a transfer of property from bank to client or vice versa. To be sure, as the result of a fiduciary issue, the distribution of assets and liabilities in the accounts of bank and client is altered. But no existing quantity of property is actually transferred from bank to client, or vice versa, and the total quantity of property in existence has remained unchanged. Rather, fiduciary media represent new and additional titles to or claims on an existing and unchanged stock of property. They are not the result and documented outcome of an additional supply of property on the part of the bank or its client. Instead, they represent an additional supply of property titles, while the supply of *property* has remained constant. It is precisely in this sense that it can be said of fiduciary media that they are created out of thin air. They are property-less titles in search of property. This, in and of itself, constitutes fraud, whether according to Rothbard's definition of the term as "a failure to fulfill a voluntarily-agreed-upon transfer of property" or according to Selgin and White's own definition of it as "a *willful* or *deliberate* deception for purposes of gain." Each issuer and buyer of a fiduciary note (a title to money uncovered by money), regardless of what he may believe, is in fact—objectively—engaged in a misrepresentation for the purpose of personal gain. The bank and its client have consented to misrepresent themselves as the owners of a quantity of property that they do not own and that plainly does not exist; and whenever they buy an existing quantity of property in exchange for titles to a nonexisting quantity of property, they have become invariably and inescapably guilty of an act of fraudulent appropriation.[9]

---

[9]Jesús Huerta de Soto ("A Critical Analysis of Central Banks," p. 33) correctly likens the effect of fractional reserve banking to that of the so-called tragedy of the commons. Selgin and White ("In Defense of Fiduciary Media," pp. 92–93, n. 12) object to de Soto's analogy on the ground that the tragedy of the commons refers "to a particular sort of technological externality," according to Selgin and White, involves "a physical or otherwise direct interference with someone's consumption or production" and represents "interaction outside the market." In contrast, write Selgin and White, the "externality from fiduciary

Selgin and White's failure to recognize this, and their belief in the ethical innocence of fractional reserve banking, is due to two confusions. On the one hand, as has already been indicated, they do not recognize that no object—and no quantity of money (gold)—can be owned by more than one party at a time and that no contract can possibly increase the quantity of property in existence, and thus that any pretension to the contrary is inherently fraudulent. On the other hand, and intimately related, Selgin and White do not recognize the fundamental praxeological difference between property and property titles. Rather, in subsuming money (gold) and money substitutes (banknotes) under the same heading of "money" they continually obfuscate this very distinction. For if money (gold) and titles to money (banknotes) are both defined as "money," then it indeed seems to follow that it does not make any difference whether the supply of money or that of banknotes increases. Both are "money" and hence, by definition, in both cases the same event—an increase in the supply of money—has taken place. But this does not alter the facts; it only defines them out of existence.

---

media" is a harmless pecuniary "effect on someone's wealth transmitted via the price system," that is, through changes in the system of relative prices, and represents "an interdependence through the market." Selgin and White err: an object and a title to an object are not the same thing.

In lumping money and money substitutes together under the joint title of "money," as if they were somehow the same thing, Selgin and White fail to grasp that the issue of fiduciary media—an increase of property titles—is not the same thing as a larger supply of property and that relative price changes effected through the issue of fiduciary media are an entirely different "externality" matter than price changes effected through an increase in the supply of property. With this the fundamental distinction between property and a property title in mind, de Soto's analogy between fractional reserve banking and the tragedy of the commons makes perfect sense. As under the scenario of a tragedy of the commons, every issue of fiduciary media—to titles in search of property—sets in motion a rush, always starting with the bank and its client, to fill these empty tickets with existing property; and in the course of this rush, invariably the first-comers will physically enrich themselves (through the appropriation of existing quantities of property) at the expense of a corresponding impoverishment of later-comers, whose quantity of existing property is physically diminished while they have been left with a larger number of property tickets.

Of course, as Selgin and White correctly note, everyone is free to adopt any definition and make any distinction that he wishes. Yet definitions do not create real distinctions; they can, though, make them disappear. They can only either reflect such distinctions or else ignore and confuse them; and clearly, to refer to both money and money substitutes indiscriminately as money is to obscure the difference between two categorically—praxeologically—distinct phenomena and states of affairs. A title to money and an increase of titles is not the same thing as money and an increase of money. Rather, unlike an increase in the quantity of money (gold) or an increase of titles backed by a corresponding increase of money, any increase in the quantity of titles to money unaccompanied by an increased quantity of money necessarily implies that one and the same quantity of money is owned by more than one person at the same time; and since such a thing is physically impossible—the quantity of money is unchanged and all existing money must be presently owned by someone—every redemption of a fiduciary title, then, be it into money or any other form of real property, involves an act of illicit appropriation.

Assume there exists both property itself and property titles (notes). Besides property in consumer goods, producer goods, and money, titles to consumer goods, titles to producer goods, and titles to money are assumed to exist. The origin of property titles in addition to the existence of property itself promotes legal certainty and reduces and facilitates legal disputes, and hence undoubtedly represents a beneficial (natural) development. Moreover, it allows for two innovations. On the one hand, it becomes possible to separate the act of transferring ownership in property from the act of transferring its possession. That is, it becomes possible to surrender or acquire ownership in objects without simultaneously surrendering or acquiring possession, disposition, and control of the very same objects. Applied to money it becomes possible that, all the while the ownership of existing quantities of money (gold) can change constantly from one person to another, the entire quantity of money may remain—unchangingly—in the hands of one and the same bank (as the manager of money owned by others). On the other hand, with the development of property titles, intertemporal exchanges will be systematically facilitated. Existing (present) property or titles thereto may be transferred in exchange against titles to future property (debt claims); and hence it will be also assumed that next to titles to existing property (consumer goods, producer goods, and money), titles (debt claims) to future consumer goods, future producer goods, and future money exist and are traded as well.

In light of these developments, the following transactions (contracts) between any two parties A (bank client) and B (bank) are possible. A may transfer his money (gold) into B's disposition and thereby either (1) *not* give up his ownership in it, or (2) give up his ownership. There is no third *possibility*. If (1), then A keeps the title to the sum of money transferred to B; B does not have title to it, but acts as a money warehouser (a bailee) for A (as a money bailor). *There is no third possibility*. If (2), then B acquires the title to the quantity of money put into its disposition by A; A receives from B in exchange either (a) a present-existing-quantity of consumer and/or producer goods previously possessed and owned by B; or (b) a title to a present-existing-quantity of consumer and/or producer goods in B's possession (but owned now by A) (an equity claim); or (c) a title to a quantity of future consumer and/or producer goods and/or money (a debt claim). Again, *there is no third possibility*. That is, A cannot both retain ownership of this property and transfer it to B.

Among all possible transactions, not one would result in the issue of a fiduciary note. Fiduciary media, according to Selgin and White's own definition, are "that portion of redeemable money substitutes backed by assets other than base money."[10] There are money (gold) and money substitutes (titles to money) in existence, and there are titles to non-money goods (equity titles), and titles to not-yet-existing future goods (debt claims). Apparently, however, no such thing as "money substitutes backed by assets other than base money" would arise out of any of these transactions. Selgin and White *assume* the existence of fiduciary media (and they simply *assume* that the absence of fiduciary media must be the result of legal restrictions), but they do not provide a praxeological explanation and reconstruction of the origin of such a peculiar entity and state of affairs. Rather, they only

---

[10]Selgin and White, "In Defense of Fiduciary Media," p. 85.

ask, why not? "We do not see why bank and customer cannot contractually agree to make them [that is, demand deposits and banknotes]
debts and not warehouse receipts." *Why* is it that there can—and
should—be no money substitutes backed by assets other than money?
For the same reason that there can and should be no car or house
titles backed by assets other than cars or houses, that there can and
should be no equity titles backed by assets other than equity, and that
there can and should be no assets—money, equity, or debt—owned
(backed) by more than one person at a time. Titles to money are—
and should be—backed by money in the same way and for the same
reason as titles to cars are and should be backed by cars. This is what
defines them as property titles. It is in accordance with and a reflection of the nature of property and property titles. In distinct contrast,
a title to money backed by assets other than money is a contradiction
in terms, and its issue and use involves the same sort of objective misrepresentation as the issue of a title to a car backed by assets other
than a car (parts of planes and bikes, for instance).[11]

---

[11]Similar logic-semantic confusions are at work when Selgin and White try
to reduce the difference between demand and time liabilities to one of degree
rather than kind ("In Defense of Fiduciary Media," p. 90). Explains Selgin:

> Holders of demand liabilities are granters of credit just as are holders
> of time liabilities. The only difference is that in the former case the
> duration of individual loans is unspecified; they are "call loans" that
> may mature at any time;

and "Mises," who holds the opposite view, "confuses a difference of degree with
one of substance" (Selgin, *The Theory of Free Banking*, p. 62). In fact, it is Selgin
who is confused.

To be sure, one might say that it is only a matter of degree whether a loan (of
a car or of money) matures in an hour, a day, a week, or a month. Just as surely,
however, this does not change the categorical distinction between present—
existing—goods and not (yet) existing future goods. At any point in time, a car
or a sum of money (gold) either exists or it does not exist. Nor does it alter the
praxeological datum that no one, at any time, can act with anything except present goods. Future goods are the goal of actions, but in order to attain them,
every actor must first invariably employ present means goods. Nor does Selgin's
observation concerning degrees of time affect in the slightest the fundamental
human condition of scarcity. The supply of present goods is at all times limited,

The answer to why fractional reserve agreements are ethically impermissible, and why there can be no contracts to make warehouse receipts debt, is that such agreements and contracts contradict (deny) the nature of things. Any such contract is from the outset—a priori—invalid. Selgin and White try to get around this inescapable conclusion by adopting, wittingly or not, an ultra-subjectivist view of contracts and agreements. According to this view, the very fact that a voluntary agreement is reached and/or a contract is concluded demonstrates that it must be a valid—true or permissible—agreement and contract. Yet this view is not only false, it is also incompatible with Rothbard's title-transfer theory of contract that these authors claim to have accepted. Agreements and contracts per se do not imply anything regarding their validity for the fundamental reason that agreements and contracts do not create reality, but rather presuppose it. More specifically, contracts do not bring property into existence, but

---

and the limited quantity of present goods limits in turn the quantity of possible future goods.

Whereas Mises recognizes the distinction between present goods and future goods as a universal praxeological category, Selgin's attempt to conflate demand and time deposits (thus distinguish himself fundamentally from Mises) implies a denial that there is no such fundamental difference between present (existing) goods and future (not-existing) goods (or that their existence differs only in degrees). Contrary to Selgin, it is not a matter of degree but rather one of substance whether a car or a sum of money presently exists or not, and whether one person or someone else owns them. Either they exist or they don't exist, and either A owns them or someone else does. Accordingly if a property title (demand deposit note) then states that one person is the owner of a present car or present money and no car or money exists, or the car or money is presently owned by someone else, this does not represent a degree of truth but a falsehood. Explains Mises:

> A depositor of a sum of money who acquires in exchange for it a claim convertible into money at any time which will perform exactly the same service for him as the sum it refers to has exchanged no present good for a future good. The claim that he has acquired by his deposit is also a present good for him. The depositing of money in no way means that he has renounced immediate disposal over the utility that it commands. (*The Theory of Money and Credit*, p. 268)

See also the two following notes.

rather recognize and transfer existing property. Hence, as in Rothbard's ethical system, the theory of property must precede the treatment of contracts. Contracts and contract theory presuppose and are constrained by property and property theory. That is, the range of possible (valid) contracts is limited and restricted by the existing quantity (stock) of property and the nature of things, rather than the other way around. Thus, agreements regarding flying elephants, centaurs, squared circles, of *perpetui mobile*, for instance, are invalid contracts. They cannot—by virtue of biological, physical, or mathematical law—be fulfilled, and are from the outset false and fraudulent.

While Selgin and White may acknowledge this, they fail to recognize that a fractional reserve banking agreement implies no lesser an impossibility and fraud than that involved in the trade of flying elephants or squared circles. In fact, the impossibility involved in fractional reserve banking is even greater. For, whereas the impossibility of contracts regarding flying elephants, for instance, is merely a contingent and empirical one (it is not inconceivable that in another possible world, somewhere and sometime, flying elephants may actually exist, thus making such contracts possible), the impossibility of fractional reserve banking contracts is a necessary and categorical one. That is, it is inconceivable—praxeologically impossible—that a bank and a customer can agree to make money substitutes (banknotes, demand deposit accounts) debts instead of warehouse receipts. They may say or certify otherwise, of course, just as one may say that triangles are squares. But what they say would be objectively false. As triangles would remain triangles and be different from squares, so money substitutes would still be money substitutes (titles to present money) and be distinct from debt claims (titles to not yet existing future goods) and equity claims (titles to existing property other than money). To say otherwise does not change reality but objectively misrepresents it.

In doing what Selgin and White believe clients and banks to have done—to agree to make warehouse receipts debt—the money depositor A receives from the bank B a claim to present money, rather than a debtor equity title. That is, A does not in fact give up ownership of the deposited money (as would have been the case if he had received a debtor equity claim from B). While A retains title to the money deposit, however, B does not treat A's deposit as a bailment, but rather as a loan, and enters it as an asset onto its own (B's) balance sheet (offset by an equal sum of outstanding demand liabilities). While this may appear initially to be merely a harmless accounting practice, it involves from the outset a misrepresentation of the real state of affairs.[12] Since both, B as well as A, count the same quantity of money simultaneously among their own assets, they have in effect conspired to represent themselves in their financial accounts as owning a larger quantity of property than they actually own: that is, they have become financial impostors.[13] Though fraudulent, this would

---

[12]See on this point Rothbard. "How," asks Rothbard,

> do these warehouse receipt transactions relate to the T-account balance sheets of the deposit banks? In simple justice, not at all. When I store a piece of furniture worth $5,000 in warehouse, in law and in justice the furniture does *not* show up as an asset of the warehouse during the time that I keep it there. The warehouse does not add $5,000 to both its assets and liabilities because it in no sense *owns* the furniture; neither can we say that I have *loaned* the warehouse the furniture for some indefinite time period. The furniture is mine and remains mine; I am only keeping it there for safekeeping and therefore I am legally and morally entitled to redeem it any time I please. I am not therefore the bank's "creditor"; it doesn't *owe* me money which I may some day collect. Hence, there is no debt to show up on the Equity + Liability side of the ledger. Legally, the entire transaction is not a loan but a *bailment*. (*The Mystery of Banking* [New York: Richardson and Snyder, 1983], pp. 88–89)

Interestingly, while Selgin and White manifest a strong positivistic tendency (fractional reserve banking is recognized by the courts, so it must be all right; on this tendency see "The Issue of Fraud III" below), they do not come to terms with legal reality. For if money deposits are debt, why, then, don't the courts apply the same reasoning to all other fungible commodities such as wheat? Why are wheat warehouse receipts not considered a debt but a bailment by the courts? Why is this treatment peculiar to money and the banking business? Moreover, why is it that the courts, even if they falsely consider money deposits as debts, still insist that they are more than an ordinary debt, and the depositor's relation to the bank is not identical with that of an ordinary creditor? See Rothbard, *Mystery of Banking*, p. 275.

[13]See also William Stanley Jevons (*Money and the Mechanism of Exchange* [London: Kegan Paul, 1905], pp. 206–12, 221), who lamented the existence of

not matter so much if everything were left at this. However, as soon as B acts as if things were the way he represents them on his balance sheet to be—as if the bank owned the deposited money and only had the obligation to redeem outstanding warehouse receipts on demand—mere misrepresentation is turned into misappropriation. If B, in accordance with this misrepresentation, lends out money, or more likely, issues additional warehouse receipts for money and lends these out to some third party C, in the expectation of eventually being repaid principal and interest, the bank becomes engaged in undue appropriation, because what it lends out to C—whether money or titles to money—is in fact not its (B's) own property but that of someone else (A). It is this fact—that the title transferred from B to C concerns property B does not own—that makes fractional reserve banking from the outset fraudulent.

It is not the case, as is claimed, that fraud (breach of contract) is committed only if B, the fractional reserve bank, is actually unable to fulfill all requests for redemption as they arise. Rather, fraud is also committed each time B does fulfill its redemption obligations. Because whenever B redeems a fractionally covered banknote into money (gold) (whenever a note holder takes possession of his property), it does so with someone else's money: if B redeems C's note, it does so with money owned by A, and if A wants his money too, B pays him with money owned by D, and so on. Qua defenders of fiduciary media and fractional reserve banking, Selgin and White would have to maintain that there is no breach of contract as long as B is able to fulfill its contractual obligations with *someone else's* property (money).

Yet this is patently wrong, and it stands in clear contradiction to Rothbard's title transfer theory of contract that Selgin and White

---

general deposits since it has "become possible to create a fictitious supply of a commodity, that is, to make people believe that a supply exists which does not exist." On the other hand, special deposits, such as "bills of lading, pawn-tickets, dock-warrants, or certificates which establish ownership to a definite object," are superior because "they cannot possibly be issued in excess of the good actually deposited, unless by distinct fraud." And Jevons concluded that "it used to be held as a general rule of law, that a present grantor assignment of goods not in existence is without operation."

claim to have accepted. In accordance with Rothbard's contract theory, individuals are only entitled to make contracts regarding the transfer of *their own property*. In contrast, fractional reserve banking, by its very nature (even if it is practiced successfully), involves contracts concerning the transfer of *other people's property*. Hence this practice—the issue of fiduciary media—is in principle (inherently) incompatible with the title-transfer theory of contract—and it turns out, not surprisingly, that it is Rothbard, and not his two interpreters, who ultimately demonstrates a better grasp of his own contract theory.

THE ISSUE OF FRAUD II: FRACTIONAL RESERVE BANKING AND FREEDOM OF CONTRACT

Murray Rothbard's classification of fractional reserve banking as fraud was the result of long and intensive study of ethics and property-rights theory in particular. Selgin and White rightly regard economics as intellectually independent and separate from ethics. It may be studied without any prior knowledge of property and property-rights theory. Yet they do not hesitate to make sweeping ethical pronouncements. In their moral defense of fractional reserve banking Selgin and White rarely mention property, let alone outline a theory of property. This results in a series of fundamental errors and problems: confusion regarding the distinction between property and property titles; confusion as to the (im-)possibility of something (property) being owned simultaneously by more than one owner; confusion concerning the logical priority of property and property theory vis-à-vis contract and contract theory; and confusion concerning the necessity of fulfilling one's contractual obligations with one's own property (not just anyone's).

These difficulties enter into the authors' discussion of the issue of "freedom of contract." Their argument is straightforward.

> If a bank does not represent or expressly oblige itself to hold 100 percent reserves, then fractional reserves do not violate the contractual agreement between the bank and its customer. . . . Outlawing voluntary contractual arrangements that permit fractional reserve-holding is thus an intervention into the market, a restriction

on the freedom of contract which is an essential aspect of private property rights.[14]

This passage reveals again Selgin and White's already noted ultra-subjectivism. According to this view, it is voluntary agreements that make for—constitute and define—a valid contract. However, valid contracts are agreements regarding the transfer of real property; hence, the range of valid contracts is in fact first and foremost constrained by the nature of things and property (and only then by agreement). It was thus that Hoppe (p. 70) explained that

> Freedom of contract does not imply that *every* mutually advantageous contract should be permitted. . . . Freedom of contract means instead that A and B should be allowed to make any contract whatsoever *regarding their own properties*, yet fractional reserve banking involves the making of contracts regarding the property of third parties.[15]

Selgin and White refer to this charge somewhat misleadingly as "third-party effects" and counter it by charging Hoppe in turn with elementary confusion as regards the nature of property and property rights. They state first, that

> spill-overs from others' actions to the *value* of C's property . . . are an inescapable free-market phenomenon and not a violation of C's private-property rights, [whereas] *physical invasions* of C's property . . . are of course inconsistent with the protection of C's property rights. It should be obvious that if A and B are to be barred from any transaction that merely affects the *market value* of C's possessions, without any physical aggression or threat against C or C's rightful property, then the principles of private property, freedom of contract, and free-market competition are completely obliterated. Is B to be barred from offering to sell compact disc recordings to A, merely because doing so reduces the market value of C's inventory of vinyl records?[16]

---

[14]Selgin and White, "In Defense of Fiduciary Media," p. 87.

[15]Hoppe, "How is Fiat Money Possible?", p. 70.

[16]Selgin and White, "In Defense of Fiduciary Media," pp. 92–93.

Second, they state that the reduction of the purchasing power of money, which they admit must result from every issue of fiduciary media, is as such a harmless value-effect and thus "provides no justification for legally barring the bank's action." Hence they conclude that Hoppe's argument is "invalid" (and incompatible with Rothbard's theory of property).

Selgin and White's counterargument contains two errors. First, while the major premise is correct, it is false that Hoppe is mistaken about it. Hoppe has written extensively on the theory of property rights, and is not only aware of the distinction mentioned by Selgin and White but even provides a praxeological defense of it; hence, in this regard no difference of judgment whatsoever between Rothbard and Hoppe exists.[17]

Second, the minor premise is demonstrably false (and hence, so is the conclusion). Selgin and White claim that the fall in the purchasing power of money resulting from the issue of fiduciary media is the same sort of harmless event as a fall in the price of anything else (caused by changes in supply and/or demand). That money owners lose purchasing power as a result of fractional reserve banking, they claim, is not different from the situation in which the owners of potatoes or cars suffer a value-loss due to a larger supply of or a reduced demand for potatoes and cars.

Here again, Selgin and White conflate money (gold)—that is, property—and money substitutes (banknotes)—that is, property titles. To be sure, the issue of fiduciary media does not lead to physical damage to real property. After all, a banknote is just a piece of paper, and paper does not exert any relevant physical effect on the external world. But the same can be said also about the issue of fiduciary titles to potatoes or cars (titles backed by assets other than potatoes

---

[17]For instance, Hans-Hermann Hoppe ("From the Economics of Laissez-Faire to the Ethics of Libertarianism," in *Man, Economy, and Liberty: Essays in Honor of Murray N. Rothbard*, Walter Block and Llewellyn H. Rockwell, Jr., eds. [Auburn, Ala.: Ludwig von Mises Institute, 1988], pp. 69ff.); and White's review of Hoppe (Lawrence White, "Review of *Man, Economy, and Liberty: Essays in Honor of Murray N. Rothbard,*" *Journal of Economic Literature* [June 1990]: 664–65).

or cars). They, too, are merely pieces of paper, and as such have no impact on the real world. Yet there exists an important difference between changes in a potato or car owner's wealth position due to changes in the supply or demand for potatoes or cars on the one hand, and changes brought about by changes in the supply or demand for titles to nonexisting (unchanged) quantities of potatoes or cars on the other hand. Surely, the owners of potatoes or cars are affected differently in both cases. In the first case, if the price of potatoes or cars falls due to a larger potato or car supply, all current potato or car owners remain (unchangingly) in possession of the same quantity of property (potatoes or cars). No one's physical property is diminished. Likewise, if the price falls because potato or car buyers are willing to offer only lesser quantities of other goods in exchange for potatoes or cars, this by itself has no effect on any current potato or car owner's physical quantity of potatoes or cars. In distinct contrast in the second case, the issue and sale of an additional title to an unchanged quantity of potatoes or cars *does* lead to a quantitative diminution of some current potato or car owner's physical property. It does not merely have a value-effect: the purchasing power of potato or car titles will fall. It does have a physical effect: the issuer and seller of fiduciary potato or car titles misappropriates other people's potatoes or cars. He appropriates other people's property without relinquishing any property of his own (in exchange for an empty property title).[18]

THE ISSUE OF FRAUD III: THE "PROOF FROM EXISTENCE" FRACTIONAL RESERVE BANKING AND STATE FORMATION

Neither the title-transfer theory of contract nor the principle of freedom of contract supports the claim that the issue of fiduciary media and fractional reserve banking is ethically justified. To the contrary,

---

[18]Also see note 7 above. We will also show that these authors' meaning of demand for (and supply of) money is misconceived. An increased demand for money (or potatoes or cars) is not just a wish to have more money (or potatoes), but greater *effective* demand.

only one other argument remains in support of the claim that fractional reserve banking represents a legitimate form of business.

The argument boils down to a proof from existence: X, Y, or Z exists; it would not exist if it were not beneficial; hence, it should exist (and outlawing it would be detrimental and morally wrong).

Thus, write Selgin and White:

> the group [of people] whose freedom of contract we are concerned with here is not a small eccentric bunch, but is the great mass of people who have demonstrated that they do prefer banks that operate on fractional reserves. . . . Depositors continue to patronize these banks, demonstrating their preference, for them. [19]

> . . . By the principle of demonstrated preference depositors must be presumed to benefit from the package they have agreed to accept, risk and all.[20]

> [Consequently,] [if] *any* person knowingly prefers to put money into an (interest-bearing) fractional-reserve account, rather than into a (storage-fee-charging) 100 percent reserve account, then a blanket prohibition on fractional-reserve banking by force of law is a binding legal restriction on freedom of contact in the market for banking services.[21]

> [Moreover,] . . . [b]enefits accrue to bank depositors and noteholders, who receive interest and services paid for by the extra bank revenue generated from lending out a portion of its liabilities. Benefits accrue to bank borrowers who enjoy a more ample supply of intermediated credit, and to everyone who works with the economy's consequently larger stock of capital equipment. And benefits must accrue to bank shareholders, who could choose to have the bank not issue demand liabilities if they found the risks not worth bearing.[22]

Selgin and White have here put the cart before the horse. The existence of a practice, however widespread, has no bearing on the

---

[19]Selgin and White, "In Defense of Fiduciary Media," p. 95.
[20]Ibid., p. 93.
[21]Ibid., p. 88.
[22]Ibid., p. 94.

question of whether it is justifiable or not. Consider first, for illustrative purposes, the following analogy concerning the ethical permissibility of a state, that is, of a territorial monopolist of law and order (or of justice and protection).[23]

In the words of Selgin and White (applied here in a different context and paraphrased), the group of people whose freedom of contract we are concerned with is not a small eccentric bunch, but is the great mass of people who have demonstrated that they do prefer states (judges and protectors) that operate on a monopolistic basis. Territorial inhabitants continue to patronize these states, demonstrating their preference for them. By the principle of demonstrated preference, territorial inhabitants must be presumed to benefit from the package they have agreed to accept, risk and all. Consequently, if any person knowingly prefers to put money into a tax-bearing state account, rather than into a protection-fee-charging account in non-taxing justice and protection agencies, then a blanket prohibition on state-formation by force of law is a binding legal restriction on freedom of contract in the market for justice and protection services. Moreover, benefits accrue to state depositors and noteholders, who receive interest and services paid for by the extra state revenue generated from employing parts of the deposits for extra tax collections. Benefits accrue to state borrowers who enjoy a more ample supply of intermediated credit, and to everyone who works with the economy's consequently larger stock of capital equipment. And benefits must accrue to state shareholders, who could choose to have the state not engage in taxation if they found the risks not worth taking.

Given their own libertarian credentials, Selgin and White would presumably reject this analogy as false and inappropriate. But if so, why? What is it that invalidates the second *proof*, but not the first? What if anything, makes a blanket prohibition (or permission) of

---

[23]To avoid any misunderstanding, the term monopoly is employed here in its Rothbardian definition as an exclusive privilege (or the absence of free entry). A monopoly of law and order means that one may turn for justice and protection only to one party—the state—and that it is exclusively this party that determines the content of justice and protection.

fractional reserve banking categorically different from a blanket prohibition (or permission) of state formation and operation?

The answer—that no such difference exists and that both proofs
are equally invalid—is to be found in the Rothbardian principle of
demonstrated preference. While Selgin and White invoke this principle in support of their conclusion regarding the ethical permissibility
of fractional reserve banking, they miss its implication. The principle
of demonstrated preference, as explained by Rothbard in his celebrated "Toward a Reconstruction of Utility and Welfare Economics,"
presupposes property rights. Not all demonstrated preferences are
ethically permissible or socially beneficial. Instead, the only such
preferences that are permissible and welfare enhancing are these that
are expressed by means of one's own property and nothing but one's
own property. Every preference demonstration by means of property
other than one's own—with other people's property—is impermissible and nonbeneficial.

As for the demonstrated preference for states, it runs afoul of
Rothbard's principle. In Rothbard's analysis, which is presumably
accepted by the participants on both sides of the current debate, the
violation can be quickly pinpointed. Private property, as the result of
acts of (original) appropriation and/or production, implies the
owner's right to exclusive jurisdiction regarding his property, including the right to employ this property in defense against possible invasions and invaders. Indeed, there can be no property without an
owner's right to physical defense, and it is the very purpose of private
property to establish separate domains of exclusive jurisdiction. No
private-property owner can possibly surrender his right to ultimate
jurisdiction over and defense of his property to someone else—unless
he sells or otherwise transfers his property (in which case someone
else would have exclusive jurisdiction over it). That is, so long as
something (a good) has not been abandoned, its owner must be presumed as retaining these rights; and as far as his relations to others
are concerned, every property owner may then only partake in the
advantages of the division of labor and seek better and improved protection of his unalterable property rights through cooperation with
other owners of property. Every property owner can buy from, sell to,
or otherwise contract with everyone else concerning supplemental
property protection and security services. Yet each owner also may at

any time unilaterally discontinue any such cooperation with others. In distinct contrast, a territorial monopoly of protection and jurisdiction—a state—implies that every property owner is prohibited from discontinuing his cooperation with his protector, and that no one (except the monopolist) may exercise ultimate jurisdiction over his own property. Rather, everyone except the monopolist has lost his right to defense and is thus rendered defenseless vis-à-vis his own protector. Obviously, such an institution stands in contradiction to every owner's demonstrated preference of not giving up his property. Contrary to their demonstrated preference, the monopolist prohibits the people from using their property in physical defense against possible invasions by himself and his agents. A monopoly of protection and jurisdiction rests thus from the outset on an impermissible act of expropriation (taxation) and provides the monopolist and his agents with a license to further expropriation and taxation. Every owner's range of permissible actions regarding his own property, and hence the value of his property, is diminished, whereas the monopolist's range of action and control is correspondingly enlarged and his exclusive privilege is reflected in an increase in the value of his property (capitalization of monopoly profit).

Presently, states exist everywhere, and almost everyone resides under state *protection*. Regardless of this preference demonstration, however, there is nothing wrong, ethically or economically, with blanket protection against state formation. No one may form a state, for the same reason that no one may expropriate or rob anyone else. In a court of law, it would be sufficient that a single property owner objected to the monopoly's existence, and the monopolist would have to cease in his current operation as a tax-yielding protection agency and be repaired to the legal status of a nontaxing but fee-charging law-and-security agency (a normal specialized firm). A tax-yielding protection agency is a contradiction in terms—an invasive protector—and must be forbidden, irrespective of any benefits accruing to state depositors, state borrowers, and state owners. To do so is not a legal restriction on freedom of contract in the market for justice and protection services, but the very presupposition of freedom of contract and justice. Everyone putting money or any other resources into a tax-yielding protection account is engaged in unlawful action and subject to punishment.

Just as states exist everywhere, so do fractional reserve banks, and nowadays practically everyone is banking with fractional reserve banks. What, if anything, is the difference between the status of a state and that of a fractional reserve bank? Why should fractional reserve banks not be outlaw banks just as states outlaw protection agencies? To be sure, just as there can be no doubt concerning a demand for protection services, there can also be no doubt as to a demand for banking services. Yet the demand for protection services that private property owners may properly demonstrate does not include a demand for tax-yielding protection services, as we have seen. It exclusively permits a demand for fee-charging protection agencies. Why should an analogous distinction not be true also for banking services? Why should a demand for interest-yielding demand deposit accounts not be just as impermissible as the demand for tax-yielding protection accounts, on the ground that both interest-yielding deposit accounts and tax-yielding property protection are contradictions in terms? Why should the functions of a money warehouser and clearing institution (100-percent-reserve-deposit banking) and as an intermediary of credit (savings-and-loan banking) not be the only just forms of banking (just as fee-charging protection agencies are the only legitimate form of protection)?

The answer depends on whether or not the demonstrated preference for fractional reserve banking services, that is, the issue and acceptance of fiduciary media, involves solely and exclusively the property of the two contracting parties. At any given point in time, the quantity of property (appropriated goods)—whether consumer goods, producer goods, or money—is given. Fractional reserve banking does not increase the quantity of existing property (money or otherwise), nor does it transfer existing property from one party to another. Rather, it involves the production and sale of an increased quantity of titles to an unchanged stock of money property (gold); that is, the supply of and the demand for counterfeit money and illegitimate appropriation. As in every other case of counterfeiting (forgery)—of stock and commodity certificates, banknotes, land titles, original art, etc.—the issue and sale of money copies (banknotes) uncovered by originals (gold) will physically diminish or despoil the original money—stock, commodity, land, or art—owners' property.

But a counterfeiter of money is particularly dangerous and invasive because of money's defining characteristic as the most easily salable and widely acceptable of all goods; that is, because *money*-counterfeits open to their seller the widest possible range of objects for undue appropriation (from money to almost every other form of real property).

Thus, it is no wonder that of all forms of forgery, the counterfeiting of money has always held the greatest attraction. So long as money exists there will also exist a persistent demand for counterfeit money. Regardless of this attraction and demand, however, there is nothing wrong with a blanket prohibition against fractional reserve banking. No one may operate a fractional reserve bank for the same reason that no one, in any other line of business, may engage in counterfeiting, that is, the production and sale of titles or copies to non-existing property or originals. In a court of law, it would be sufficient that a single money or other property owner brought suit against a fractional reserve bank as a manufacturer of counterfeit money, and the bank immediately would have to cease its current operation and be reduced to its two original functions: deposits and loans. An interest-yielding (rather than fee-charging) deposit bank is a contradiction in terms: it is a counterfeiting money warehouser, and must be outlawed, irrespective of any benefits accruing to bank depositors, borrowers, and owners. To do so is not a restriction on freedom of contract in the market for banking services, but the requirement of lawful money and banking. Everyone putting money or other resources into interest-yielding deposit accounts is engaged in undue and unlawful appropriation.[24]

---

[24]Explains Rothbard:

The champions of free competition in counterfeiting retort that this is simply the market at work, that the market registers a "demand" for more expanded credit, and that the private bankers, those Kirznerian entrepreneurs, are simply "alert" to such market demands. Well, of course, there is always a "demand" for fraud, and embezzlement, on the market, and there will always be plenty of "alert" swindlers who are eager and willing to furnish a supply of these items. But if we define the "market" not simply as a supply of

The relationship between states and fractional reserve banks is even more intimate, and in any case quite different from that suggested by Selgin and White. They claim that it would be an illegitimate interference with the operation of free markets if the state were to prohibit fractional reserve banking. In fact, fractional reserve banking is the result of an illegitimate state interference with the market, and prohibiting it would only repair this earlier intervention. Selgin and White recognize that in the evolution of a free banking system, 100-percent-reserve-deposit banking and, functionally separated, loan banking, must (praxeologically) precede fractional reserve banking. In their view, fractional reserve banking is the natural outgrowth of an earlier 100-percent-reserve system. However, they do not offer an explanation for this transition as a natural solution to a problem that cannot be solved under the prior system of 100-percent banking (in the way that Austrians conceive of money as the natural solution to the problem of lacking coincidences of wants under a preceding barter system). They merely affirm that the transition actually occurred.

While one can easily see why and how a banker might want to take advantage of the possibilities of counterfeiting, it is just as clear that any such attempt would not go by without quickly and continually being challenged. Surely the current writers and thousands of earlier legal and economic theorists would have accused fractional reserve banks of counterfeiting and would have brought suit against them. The further course of banking evolution would then depend on a court decision. If the court decided that the issue of fiduciary media *qua* titles to money uncovered by money constitutes counterfeiting, fractional reserve banks would not come into existence; and only if it decided otherwise would they ever actually appear. Nothing in this evolution is natural; everything appears rather deliberate. Nor would the outcome of such trials naturally be to Selgin and White's liking.

---

desired goods and services, but as a supply of such goods *within a* framework of inviolate property rights, then we see a very different picture. ("The Present State of Austrian Economics," *Journal des Economistes et des Etudes Humaines* 6, no. 2, [1995]: 77)

On the contrary, if one were to assume that fractional reserve bankers would be tried on counterfeiting charges before a jury of their own peers (of other businessmen), we dare say that, empirically, the overwhelming number of such cases would end in conviction (the testimony of Selgin and White notwithstanding). Why, then, the almost complete dominance of fractional reserve banking?

The answer is that the courts deciding these matters everywhere are state courts. Only if a single court possesses a territorial monopoly of jurisdiction is it possible that the dispute at hand could be settled once and for all. And that it has been uniformly settled in the way it was, that is, by permitting rather than prohibiting fractional reserve banking, follows from the interest of every court and judge *qua* state court and state judge. The owners and agents of the state recognize fully as much as bankers the potentials of money counterfeiting as a source of income. In permitting bankers to issue fiduciary media (rather than prohibiting the practice as counterfeiting), banks are made existentially dependent on the state. They can only operate because the state, due to its territorial monopoly of jurisdiction, shields them from counterfeiting suits; and the state does so only under the provision that banks will share with it in the extra revenue and credit derived from legalized counterfeiting. Hence, by permitting fractional reserve free banking the state actually creates the first and preliminary form of a joint-bank-state-counterfeiting cartel under its own ultimate control.

Once fractional reserve banking receives blanket protection from the state, it follows naturally that fractional reserve banks will outcompete 100 percent reserve banks. Not, as Selgin and White[25] assert, because they are better or more efficient banks, but for the reason that, once money counterfeiting is permitted, banks that engage in it tend to outcompete banks that do not. That is, for the same reason that, once industrial air pollution is permitted a polluting steel producer will tend to outcompete a steel producer who does not pollute, and for the same reason that a protection agency with taxing powers, a state, will tend to outcompete protectors without taxing power. Put differently, it is not always the case that good drives

---

[25]Selgin and White, "In Defense of Fiduciary Media," pp. 97–98.

out bad. This is the case only so long as private property rights are inviolate. If they are not, and there exist privileged agents or agencies, who are exempt from the universal rules regarding the appropriation, production and transfer of property, then these will tend to outcompete other normal agents. In this case, bad drives out good. Thus, it is completely mistaken to interpret the empirical success of fractional reserve banking as proof of its greater economic efficiency. The success of fractional over 100 percent deposit banking is no more a market phenomenon than is the success of tax-yielding protectors, states, over competitive and nontaxing security producers. It is false to suggest, as Selgin and White do, that fractional reserve banking has stood the market test and represents the outcome of voluntary consumer choices. After all, 100-percent-reserve-deposit banking is not outlawed and consumers are free to bank with them instead of fractional banks if they so prefer. Or would they likewise argue that the polluting steel producer had stood the test of the market because, after all, consumers are free to buy their steel from nonpolluting steel producers, or that states have proven themselves in the market because, after all, consumers are free to buy their security also from agencies without any tax and jurisdictional powers?[26]

---

[26]A similar confusion characterizes Selgin and White's view on the relationship between money proper (gold) and banknotes. They criticize Hoppe for claiming that, in a genuine free-market order, most people would use money proper rather than banknotes (without mentioning Hoppe's theoretical reason). "The facts," they claim, "are otherwise" ("In Defense of Fiduciary Media," p. 99). Yet these facts—the historical success of the banknote over genuine money—are *the result of an earlier state interference* with private-property rights (the legalization of fractional reserve banking). As Ludwig von Mises noted,

> [t]he truth is that, except for small groups of businessmen who were able to distinguish between good and bad banks, bank notes were always looked upon with distrust. It was the special charters which governments granted to privileged banks that slowly made these suspicions disappear. (p. 438)

> In [governments'] eyes the foremost task of the banks was to lend money to the treasury. The money-substitutes were favorably considered as pace-makers for government-issued paper money. The convertible banknote was merely a first step on the way to the nonredeemable

Moreover, whereas 100-percent-reserve banking is crisis-proof, fractional reserve banking, as even Selgin and White admit, is not in fact, as we can only briefly indicate here. A system of free fractional reserve banking will, in accordance with Mises's theory of interventionism, lead to further state interventions and the successive devolution of money. Free fractional reserve banking *qua* state-protected competition in counterfeiting will lead to a steady contest among banks of testing the viability of increasingly lower reserve ratios. This is bound to lead to banking crises, and these will be used by governments for the introduction of central banking. Central banking leads to still more counterfeiting, and to the abolition of commodity money and adoption of national fiat currencies. Lastly, international—inter-central bank—competition in fiat money counterfeiting will lead to state bankruptcies, and their financial default will be used by the most powerful among the surviving states for the establishment of a one-world government, central bank, and fiat currency.

---

banknote. With the progress of statolatry and the policy of interventionism these ideas have become general and are no longer questioned by anybody. (p. 442)

Governments did not foster the use of bank notes in order to avoid inconvenience to ladies shopping. Their idea was to lower the rate of interest and to open a source of cheap credit to their treasuries. In their eyes the increase in the quantity of fiduciary media was a means of promoting welfare. Banknotes are not indispensable. All the economic achievements of capitalism would have been accomplished if they had never existed. (*Human Action: A Treatise on Economics*, 3rd rev. ed. [Chicago: Contemporary Books, 1966], p. 447)

Accordingly, Mises's view regarding sound money is completely different from Selgin and White's. Whereas the latter believe that gold would—and should—ultimately disappear from circulation altogether (see note 3 above), Mises considered it a requirement of a sound monetary system that

[g]old must be in the cash holdings of everybody. Everybody must see gold coins changing hands, must be used to having gold coins in his pockets, to receiving gold coins when he cashes his pay check, and to spending gold coins when he buys in a store. (*The Theory of Money and Credit*, pp. 450–51)

Hence, the solution proposed by Selgin and White to the current monetary disorder, that is, a gold-based free—fractional reserve—banking system, is in fact the initial interventionist cause of virtually all contemporary monetary problems.[27]

---

[27]On the relationship between state money and banking and political centralization see Hans-Hermann Hoppe, "Banking, Nation States, and International Politics," *Review of Austrian Economics* 4 (1990): 55–87; and Jörg Guido Hülsmann, "Banking and Political Centralization," *Journal of Libertarian Studies* 13, no. 1 (1997). Selgin and White argue:

> We also reject the notion . . . that *competitive* banks issuing redeemable liabilities can create credit "out of thin air." By the nature of the balance sheet, all bank loans must be funded by liabilities or equity. Neither source of funds can be conjured out of thin air. No one is forced to hold a competitive bank's redeemable liabilities or to buy its shares; anyone can hold claims on other banks instead, or on no bank. A competitive bank must therefore *expend real resources to attract a clientele* by the provision of interest and services. The notion that a bank can extend credit . . . gratuitously is valid only with respect to the inframarginal credits of a monopoly bank, or to [the] issuer of a forced tender; it does not apply to a bank in a competitive system. (p. 94, n. 13)

> Thus competition will beat down the returns to capital invested in fractional-reserve banking until the marginal bank is earning only the normal rate of return. ("In Defense of Fiduciary Media," p. 97)

While we have no difficulty accepting the distinction drawn here between competitive and monopolistic banking, none of this has any bearing on the issue at hand, that is, the validity of the analogy between states and fractional reserve banks as outlaw organizations. For one, states have to compete for clients (residents). Indeed, competition between states (or banks) for clients only comes to a complete halt with the establishment of a single world state (or central bank). And the intra-state competition between fractional reserve banks is, as explained, competition within a state-privileged industry; that is, monopolistic competition (just as inter-state competition is an example of monopolistic competition). Second and more importantly, the difference between competitive and monopolistic banks (or states), interesting as it may otherwise be, does not affect in the slightest their common characteristic as fractional reserve banks (or states). Counterfeiting and taxation do not change their nature because they are undertaken competitively.

The error can be revealed by analogy. Selgin and White are paraphrased here: We also reject the notion that competitive states issuing tax liabilities can

THE POSITIVE ECONOMICS OF FIDUCIARY MEDIA: MONEY BALANCE, PRICE, ADJUSTMENT, SAVING, AND INVESTMENT

From the nature of fiduciary media—as titles to nonexisting quantities of money property (gold), titles to money covered by things other than money, or plain counterfeit money—it would seem to follow that fractional reserve banking cannot possibly effect anything but a continual wealth and income redistribution. As the uncovered money substitutes ripple from the issuing bank and its borrower clientele outward through the economy, and thereby successively raise the price of increasingly more goods, real wealth (property) is transferred and redistributed in favor of the issuing bank and the initial and early recipients and sellers of this money, and at the expense of its late or never receivers and sellers. Explains Rothbard,

> the first receivers of the new money gain the most, the next gain slightly less, etc., until the midpoint is reached, and then each receiver loses more and more as he waits for the new money. For the first individuals' selling prices soar while buying prices remain almost the same; but later, buying prices have risen while selling prices remain unchanged.[28]

---

create taxes out of thin air. By the nature of state budgets all expenditures must be funded by conquest, robbery, or theft. Neither source of funds can be conjured out of thin air. No one is forced to hold any particular state's tax liabilities or buy its shares; anyone can move and pay taxes to another state, or to no state. A competitive state must therefore *expend real resources* to attract a clientele by the provision of protection and services. The notion that a state can increase taxes gratuitously is valid only with respect to the inframarginal taxes of a monopoly state; it does not apply to a state in a competitive system. Thus, competition will beat down the returns to capital invested in states until the marginal state is earning only the normal rate of return.

According to Selgin and White, it would seem to follow that taxation (like money counterfeiting) is not to be considered a problem until the arrival of a single world monopoly bank. Up until then, under competitive conditions, taxes represent nothing but a normal market income.

[28]Murray N. Rothbard, *Man, Economy, and State* (Auburn, Ala.: Ludwig von Mises Institute, 1993), p. 851.

According to Selgin and White, however, fiduciary media can accomplish far more. Rather than only redistributing existing property, the issue of fiduciary media can, under certain conditions, lead to an increase in real wealth (property). We have already quoted them stating that "benefits accrue to bank borrowers who enjoy a more ample supply of intermediate credit, and to everyone who works with the economy's consequently larger stock of capital equipment." They refrain from putting it this bluntly, yet what they claim is that, under specific circumstances, an increase of titles to an unchanged fund of goods will somehow make this fund grow or prevent it from shrinking.

When and how can such a miracle be accomplished? According to Selgin and White, (unanticipated) changes in the demand for money lead to "temporary" or "short-run monetary disequilibrium" involving "serious misallocations of resources"—that is, *unless* such changes are accommodated by fractional reserve banking practices. They write:

> In the long run, nominal prices will adjust to equate supply and demand for money balances, whatever the nominal quantity of money. It does not follow, however, that each and every *change* in the supply of or demand for money will lead *at once* to a new long-run equilibrium, because the required price adjustments take time. They take time because not all agents are instantly and perfectly aware of changes in the money stock or money demand, and because some prices are costly to adjust and therefore "sticky." It follows that, in the short run (empirically, think "for a number of months"), less than fully anticipated changes to the supply of or demand for money can give rise to monetary disequilibrium. . . . It is therefore an attractive feature of free banking with fractional reserves that the nominal quantity of bank-issued money tends to adjust so as to offset changes in the velocity of money.[29]

> If the banking system fails to increase the quantity of bank-issued money and the price level does not promptly drop, an excess demand for money arises (assuming also that the quantity of base

---

[29]Selgin and White, "In Defense of Fiduciary Media," pp. 100–01.

money does not immediately increase). A corresponding excess supply of goods arises: unsold consumer goods pile up on sellers' shelves (this is of course what proximately puts downward pressure on prices, until at last goods prices have fallen sufficiently). Business is depressed until the purchasing power of money gets back to equilibrium.[30]

From the outset, one must wonder about the very existence of the problem of monetary disequilibrium (not to speak yet about the solution). In the just-given quote, one can substitute any other good for money: televisions, steel, beer, or pretzels. The quantities of goods such as these are also rigidly fixed (as is the quantity of gold), and yet (unanticipated) changes in the demand for televisions, steel, beer, or pretzels do not lead to temporary disequilibria involving serious misallocations of resources. Or, in any case, they do not cause problems that would require the invention of a special new device (such as fractional television or beer production).

Nor is it clear why we are supposed to believe that "it is important to distinguish between short-run and long-run implications of

---

[30]Ibid., p. 105. As Roger Garrison, another fractional reserve free banker, has put it, "in terms of the equation of exchange [$MV=PQ$], we can say that free banking adjusts M so as to offset changes in V; but allows changes in Q to be accommodated by changes in P." Garrison describes the short-run "monetary disequilibrium" in almost identical form:

An increase in the demand for money puts downward pressure on product and factor prices in general. If there were no money-supply response, a general decline in economic activity would follow, since prices and wages could not fully and instantaneously adjust themselves to the new market conditions. Goods in general would go unsold; production would be cut; workers would be laid off. . . . With a less-than-perfectly flexible price system, general deflationary pressures can push the economy below its potential during the period in which prices are adjusting to the higher monetary demand. And the fact that some prices and some wages are more flexible than others means that the adjustment period will involve changes in relative prices that reflect no changes in relative scarcities. These are precisely the kinds of problems . . . avoided by free banking's responsiveness to increases in money demand. ("Central Banking, Free Banking, and Financial Crises," *Review of Austrian Economics* 9, no. 2 [1996]: 117)

changes in the demand schedule for money or in the stock of money,"[31] or, in any case, why this distinction should be of different importance or significance in the case of money from that of everything else. To be sure, it takes time before an unexpected increase in the demand for televisions and beer, for instance, will have exhausted all of its effects on the system of relative prices and a new adjusted production structure will have been established. But this does not mean that price adjustments take any time (meanwhile causing short-run problems). On the contrary, price adjustments occur immediately and without any delay. Every change in the supply of or demand for anything affects prices instantly. This fact is overlooked because of an un-Austrian concern for macroeconomic artifacts such as the general price level, long-run equilibrium, and the velocity of money. However, viewed from the proper individualist perspective, there can be no doubt about the immediacy of price adjustments and the praxeological integration of the short and the long run.

In individualistic terms, an increased demand for money is the result of the purposeful actions of individuals; that is, people intent upon increasing their individual cash balances. To do so, a person must restrict his purchases and/or increase his sales. In either case, the outcome is an immediate fall of some prices. As the result of restricting one's purchases of x, y, or z, the money price of x, y, or z will be lowered immediately (as compared with what it would have been otherwise), and likewise, by increasing one's sales of a, b, or c, their prices will fall instantly. No one is concerned about the general price level or the generalized purchasing power of money. Instead, everyone is always concerned about specific prices and the purchasing power of money regarding specific items (and everyone is interested in his very own and different specific array of prices and purchasing power). In restricting his specific purchases and/or increasing his specific sales, each actor accomplishes exactly and immediately what he wants: certain prices that he deems too high are lowered, the purchasing power of a unit of money increases, the real

---

[31]Selgin and White, "In Defense of Fiduciary Media," p. 100.

value of his cash balance rises, and his demand for and supply of money is immediately brought back into equilibrium (and he wishes to hold neither more nor less money than he actually does).[32]

The adjustment of the praxeologically meaningless general price level necessitated by an increased demand for money is nothing but the summation of a series of countless immediate and purposeful individual cash-balance adjustments. If the increased demand for money is accommodated by the issue of fiduciary media, as Selgin and White advocate this adjustment process will not be facilitated but delayed.[33] The speed of the adjustment of prices depends on the

---

[32]Thus writes Mises:

Buyers and sellers on the market never concern themselves with the elements in the equation of exchange, of which two—velocity of circulation and the price level—do not even exist before market parties act and the other two—the quantity of money (in the whole economy) and the sum of transactions—could not possibly be known to the parties in the market. Only the importance which the various actors in the market attach, on the one hand, to the maintenance of a cash balance of a certain magnitude and, on the other hand, to the ownership of the various goods in question determines the formation of the exchange relationship between money and goods. ("The Position of Money Among Economic Goods," in *Money, Method, and the Market Process*, Richard Ebeling, ed. [Boston: Kluwer, 1990], p. 61)

[33]Moreover, from an individualist perspective, the increased demand for money occurs with specific actors at specific times and places. It is not sufficient for banks to accommodate some abstract higher money demand by more money; rather, but the accommodation would have to occur precisely with the correct people and locations. If this is not the case, one can hardly speak of an accommodation but of an additional distortion. This difficulty was recognized by the early Hayek:

in order to eliminate all monetary influences on the formation of prices, and the structure of production, it would not be sufficient merely quantitatively to adapt the supply of money to these changes in demand, it would be necessary also to see that it came into the hands of those who actually require it; that is, to that part of the system where that change in business organization or the habits of payment had taken place. (*Prices and Production* [London: Routledge, 1935], p. 124)

market-participants' expectations concerning the given quantity of money. If it is reasonable to assume that fractional reserve banks will increase their fiduciary issues in response to an unanticipated increase in the demand for money, then the adjustment will take *more* time. Production would adjust and begin *earlier* without the additional influence of inflation.[34]

Moreover, the proposed solution to the alleged problem of short-run monetary disequilibrium displays a fundamental confusion regarding the concept of demand (and supply), and the relationship between the demand for money, saving, and investment in particular. First, an increased demand for money (as for televisions, beer, or pretzels) is not just a wish to have more money (or televisions, beer, etc.), but *effective* demand. That is, an increased demand for money (as for anything else) can be satisfied only if the demander is willing to increase his market-supply of and/or reduce his demand for something else. Likewise, the supplier (seller) of money can only increase his supply of money if he reduces simultaneously the supply of (or his reservation demand for) something else. The authors have overlooked Say's law: all goods (property) are bought with other goods, no one can demand anything without supplying something else, and no one can demand or supply more of anything unless he demands or supplies less of something else. But this is here *not* the case whenever a fiduciary note is supplied and demanded. The increased demand for money is satisfied without the demander demanding, and without

---

With the later Hayek, one wonders how banks could possibly have the requisite knowledge of performing this task.

[34]As regards the stickiness of prices, and the redistributive consequences of an increased demand for money vis-à-vis an array of prices of varying degrees of stickiness, which Selgin and White as well as Garrison raise as matters of concern, it is of utmost importance to recognize that prices are the outcome of purposive action—and so is their stickiness. That is, the flexibility or inflexibility of various product and service prices is not accidental to, but a deliberate part of, these products and services. Contrary to Garrison's claim, the stickiness of prices does affect and is related to, real relative scarcities. If more sticky prices suffer more, so to speak, so be it; that will teach them to be less sticky in the future—if the owners of the property in question act in a manner compatible with this end.

the supplier supplying, less of anything else. Through the issue and sale of fiduciary media, wishes are accommodated, not effective demand. Property is appropriated (effectively demanded) without supplying other property in exchange. Hence, this is not a market exchange—which is governed by Say's law—but an act of undue appropriation. Or would it be an efficient solution to the problem of unanticipated short-run television, beer, or pretzel-shortages if television, beer, and pretzel producers were to accommodate such increased demand "temporarily" by issuing and selling additional titles to televisions, beer, and pretzels but not these goods themselves?

Second, Selgin and White further misconstrue the nature of money and demand for money held in making the extraordinary claim that the issue of fiduciary media *"matched by an increased demand to hold fiduciary media"* is not only not disequilibrating, but will actually afford the economy a "larger stock of capital equipment," because

> [t]he act of holding fractional-reserve *bank-issued* money not only (like holding base money) defers consumption for a longer or shorter period, but also *temporarily lends funds* to the bank of issue in doing so. The period of the loan is unspecified . . . but if the bank can estimate with a fair degree of accuracy the lengths of time for which its demand claims will remain in circulation . . . it can safely make investments of corresponding length.[35]

Following the lead of Rothbard, Hoppe criticized this essentially Keynesian view concerning the relationship between the demand for money and savings (loanable funds)[36] by pointing out that

---

[35]Selgin and White, "In Defense of Fiduciary Media," p. 103. The error of confusing property and titles lies also at the bottom of Selgin and White's attempts to separate analytically the demand for outside money from the demand for inside money, as if these were somehow two different kinds of money with two different and independent demands.

[36]Selgin stated the same thesis thus:

> Whenever a bank expands its liabilities in the process of making new loans and investments, it is the holders of the liabilities who are the ultimate lenders of credit, and what they lend are the real resources they could acquire if, instead of holding money, they spent it. When the expansion or contraction of bank liabilities proceeds in such a way

[n]ot-spending money is to purchase *neither* consumer goods *nor* investment goods. . . . Individuals may employ their monetary assets in one of three ways. They can spend them on consumer goods; they can spend them on investment; or they can keep them in the form of cash. There are no other alternatives. . . . The consumption/investment proportion, i.e., the decision of how much . . . to spend on consumption and how much on investment, is determined by a person's time preference; i.e., the degree to which he prefers present consumption over future consumption. On the other hand, the source of his demand for cash is the utility attached to money; i.e., the personal satisfaction derived from

---

as to be at all times in agreement with changing demands for inside money, the quantity of real capital funds supplied to borrowers by the banks is equal to the quantity voluntarily offered to the banks by the public. Under these conditions, banks are simply intermediaries of loanable funds. (*The Theory of Free Banking: Money Supply under Competitive Note Issue*, p. 55)

As for John Maynard Keynes (*The General Theory of Employment, Interest, and Money* [New York: Harcourt, Brace, 1936], p. 82), he had written that the notion that the creation of credit by banking systems allows investment to take place to which "no genuine saving" corresponds; that is, "the idea that saving and investment . . . can differ from one another, is to be explained, I think, by an optical illusion" (p. 81).

[T]he savings which result from this decision are just as genuine as any other savings. No one can be compelled to own the additional money corresponding to the new bank-credit, unless he deliberately prefers to hold more money rather than some other form of wealth. (p. 83)

Indeed, Selgin acknowledges that

many Keynesians might accept the prescription for monetary equilibrium offered [by him]. Those who do not regard the liquidity trap as an important factual possibility would probably accept it as entirely adequate. (*The Theory of Free Banking*, p. 59)

Henry Hazlitt remarked on this Keynesian idea that

[o]n the same reasoning we can create any amount of new "savings" we wish overnight, simply by printing that amount of new paper money, because *somebody* will necessarily hold that new paper money! (*The Failure of the "New Economics": An Analysis of the Keynesian Fallacies* [Lanham, Maryland: University Press of America, 1983], p. 227)

money in allowing him immediate purchases of directly or indirectly serviceable consumer or producer goods at uncertain future dates.

Accordingly, if the demand for money increases while the social stock of money is given, this additional demand can only be satisfied by bidding down the money prices of non money goods. The purchasing power of money will increase, the *real* value of individual cash balances will be raised, and at a higher purchasing power per unit money, the demand for and the supply of money will once again be equilibrated. The relative price of money versus non-money will have changed. But *unless* time preference is assumed to have changed at the same time, *real* consumption and *real* investment will remain the same as before: the additional money demand is satisfied by reducing nominal consumption *and* investment spending in accordance with the same pre-existing consumption/investment proportion, driving the money prices of both consumer as well as producer goods down and leaving real consumption and investment at precisely their old levels.[37]

Accordingly, Hoppe concluded, it is *never* warranted to accommodate an increased demand for money by issuing fiduciary credit.[38] In fact, to do so will either—insofar as the accommodating

---

[37]Hoppe, "How is Fiat Money Possible?," pp. 72–73.

[38]See also Hoppe, "The Theory of Employment, Money, Interest, and the Capitalist Process: The Misesian Case against Keynes," in *The Economics and Ethics of Private Property* (Norwell, Mass.: Kluwer, 1993), and Rothbard, *Man, Economy, and State* (Auburn, Ala.: Ludwig von Mises Institute, 1993), pp. 167ff., 667ff.; idem, *America's Great Depression* (New York: Richardson and Snyder, 1983), pp. 39ff.

As for Selgin and White's claim of being Misesians, it is worthwhile to quote Mises on

the role cash holding plays in the process of saving and capital accumulation. . . . [i]f an individual employs a sum of money not for consumption but for the purchase of factors of production, saving is directly turned into capital accumulation. If the individual saver employs his additional savings for increasing his cash holding because this is in his eyes the most advantageous mode of using them, he brings about a tendency toward a fall in commodity prices and a rise

increase of fiduciary media is unanticipated and the market rate of interest falls temporarily below the natural rate of interest—lead to a boom-bust cycle; or else—insofar as the monetary change arising from the banking system is anticipated and the market rate of interest is bid up (in the expectation of higher selling prices) in accordance with the height of the natural rate—it will accomplish no more than a plain wealth and income redistribution among various members of society. It is praxeologically impossible, however, that the issue of fiduciary media can lead to an "enlarged stock of capital equipment."

In their attempt to rebut this argument, Selgin and White first concede the central theoretical point: "We agree that time preference and money demand are distinct, and that a change in one does not imply a change in the other."[39] Likewise:

> [t]hat holding money is one form of saving does not imply that an increase in the demand for money is identically an increase in

in the monetary unit's purchasing power. If we assume that the supply of money in the market system does not change, this conduct on the part of the saver will not directly influence the accumulation of capital and its employment for an expansion of production. The effect of our saver's saving, i.e., the surplus of goods produced over goods consumed, does not disappear on account of his hoarding. The prices of capital goods do not rise to the height they would have attained in the absence of such hoarding. But the fact that more capital goods are available is not affected by the striving of a number of people to increase their cash holdings. If nobody employs the goods—the nonconsumption of which brought about the additional saving—for an expansion of his consumptive spending, they remain as an increment in the amount of capital goods available, whatever their prices may be. The two processes—increased cash holding of some people and increased capital accumulation—take place side by side. A drop in commodity prices, other things being equal, causes a drop in the money equivalent of the various individuals' capital. But this is not tantamount to a reduction in the supply of capital goods and does not require an adjustment of production activities to an alleged impoverishment. It merely alters the money items to be applied in monetary calculation. (Mises, *Human Action*, pp. 521–22)

[39]Selgin and White, "In Defense of Fiduciary Media," p. 102.

total saving. An increased demand for money may accompany a reduced demand for holding other assets, and not a reduction in consumption; hence it may be part of a change in the manner of saving with no change in total savings.[40]

However, if an increased demand for money is not identically an increase in total savings, then it is impossible to maintain that it provides for a larger pool of loanable funds and increased capital formation (a lengthening of the structure of production). Hence, to rescue their economic-growth thesis, immediately following this concession Selgin and White try to take it back again by arguing that:

> Nonetheless [the nonidentity of time preference and money demand notwithstanding] to hold money *is* to hold it for *later* spending, even though *how much later* is not signalled (and typically has not yet been decided by the money-holder). Holding money for later spending, rather than spending it on consumption now, does defer consumption to the future. As Hoppe himself points out, the demand for cash stems from the convenience it allows one in purchasing "consumer or producer goods at uncertain *future* dates." So perhaps our disagreement here is merely over words.[41]

Unfortunately, this suggestion is unfounded. Rather than a verbal quibble, the disagreement is a substantive one concerning the nature of money.

It is difficult not to interpret the two previous pronouncements as contradictory. Selgin and White try to escape from this conclusion by an *ad hoc* semantic shift, that is, in characterizing money as a future good. Essentially, their argument is that while increased money demand does not imply increased savings, it provides nonetheless for a larger loan fund, because money is held only to be spent "at uncertain *future* dates" (their emphasis), such that an increased demand for money is always and at the same time an increase in the demand for future goods.[42] Yet money is demonstrably *not* a future good. In

---

[40]Ibid., p. 103.

[41]Ibid., p. 102.

[42]Selgin and White's view here is quite similar to that of Keynes (*The General Theory*, pp. 293–94), when he emphasized that "the importance of

fact, when the money is spent—in the future—it loses all its utility for the present owner. It has utility only while and insofar as it is not spent, and its character as a present good stems from the omnipresent human condition of *uncertainty*.[43]

The error in classifying money as a future good can be revealed in a twofold manner. On the one hand, negatively, it can be shown that this assumption still leads to contradiction. In support of their thesis, Selgin and White claim that "holding money for later spending, rather than spending it on consumption now, does defer consumption to the future," implying that the holding of money involves the exchange of a future good (satisfaction) for a present one. In the next sentence they admit that money held is spent neither on consumer goods nor or producer goods. Yet they fail to notice that this implies also, as a further consequence, that holding money for later spending, rather than spending it on production now, does defer production (and hence future consumption) to the future. If the holding of money defers consumption and production, however, then it becomes impossible to maintain that the holder of money has thereby invested in a future good, because there are no future goods— whether consumer or producer goods—which result from the act of holding money and to which its holder could thus be entitled. Yet as claims to no future goods whatsoever, money would be worthless. By implication, if money is not worthless (and no one would hold money if it had no value), then its value must be that of a present good.

On the other hand, positively, the nature of money as a paradigmatically present good can be established by praxeological proof. As Mises and Rothbard have explained, in general equilibrium or, more appropriately, within the imaginary construction of an evenly rotating economy, no money exists. With all uncertainties by assumption

---

money essentially flows from its being a link between the present and the future," and characterized money as "above all, a subtle device for linking the present and the future."

[43]Put differently: rather than, as Selgin and White ("In Defense of Fiduciary Media," p. 102) say, that "the demand for cash stems from the convenience it allows one in purchasing . . . goods at uncertain *future* dates," the demand for money stems from the convenience it allows one in purchasing goods at *uncertain* future dates.

removed, everyone would know precisely the terms, times, and locations of all future exchanges, and all exchanges could be prearranged accordingly and take the form of direct rather than indirect exchanges.

> In a system without change in which there is no uncertainty whatever about the future, nobody needs to hold cash. Every individual knows precisely what amount of money he will need at any future date. He is therefore in a position to lend all the funds he receives in such a way that the loans fall due on the date he will need them.[44]

While there is no place for money in the construction of an evenly rotating economy, however, there exists within its framework a present and a future, now and later, the beginning of an action and its later completion, immediately serviceable consumer goods (present goods) and indirectly serviceable producer goods (future goods), a structure of production, and savings and investment, that is, exchange of present against future goods governed by time preference. If anything, this proves again that money and the demand for money are systematically unrelated to consumption, production, and time preference, and that the source of the utility of money must be a categorically different one from that of consumer goods and producer goods. The source of the utility of a consumer good is its direct and present serviceability, and the source of the utility of a producer good is its indirect future serviceability. Money, by contrast, is neither consumed nor employed in production. It is neither directly serviceable (as consumer goods are) nor indirectly useful as a way station to future consumer goods (as producer goods are). Rather, the utility of money must be that of an *indirectly yet presently* serviceable good.

Outside the imaginary construction of an evenly rotating economy, under the inescapable human condition of uncertainty, when the terms, times, and locations of all future exchanges cannot be predicted with certitude, and when action is by nature speculative and subject to error, man can conceivably demand goods no longer exclusively on account of their use-value (present or future), but also

---

[44]Mises, *Human Action*, p. 249.

because of their value as *media of exchange* (for resale purposes). Faced with situations where, due to the absence of double coincidences of wants, a direct exchange is impossible, man can evaluate goods also on account of their degree of marketability, and can consider trading whenever a good to be acquired is more marketable than that to be surrendered, such that its possession would facilitate the acquisition of directly or indirectly serviceable goods and services. Moreover, because it is the sole function of a medium of exchange to facilitate purchases of directly or indirectly serviceable goods, man will naturally prefer the acquisition of a more marketable and, at the limit, universally marketable medium of exchange to that of a less or nonuniversally marketable one, such that

> [T]here would be an inevitable tendency for the less marketable of a series of goods used as media of exchange to be one by one rejected until at last only a single commodity remained, which was universally employed as a medium of exchange; in a word, money.[45]

Selgin and White are familiar with this Mengerian-Misesian reconstruction of monetary evolution, of course. They apparently fail to recognize, however, that this feature of money as the most easily and widely salable commodity far from rendering it a future good, qualifies money at the same time as the good best suited to alleviate presently felt uncertainty and, as such, the most universally present good of all.[46] Although only indirectly useful—in this regard like producer goods, and unlike any consumer good—money is precisely on account of its supreme saleability a uniquely present good—in this regard like consumer goods, and unlike any producer good. Because money can be employed for the instant removal of the widest range of possible needs (or the satisfaction of the widest range of possible desires), it provides its owner with the best humanly possible protection

---

[45]Mises, *The Theory of Money and Credit*, pp. 32–33.

[46]In fact, one can only wonder how Selgin and White could have possibly overlooked money's character as a uniquely present good. After all, the interest rate as the most visible manifestation of the phenomenon of time preference is expressed in terms of *money*.

(insurance) against uncertainty; that is, against his uneasiness of *not* being able to predict—of *not* being certain about—all of his future needs and desires. In holding money, its owner gains in the satisfaction of being able instantly to meet, as they arise unpredictably, the widest possible range of future contingencies.

> The keeping of cash holding requires sacrifices. To the extent that a man keeps money in his pockets or in his balance with a bank, he forsakes the instantaneous acquisition of goods he could consume or employ for production.[47]

Accordingly, to the extent that he feels certain regarding his future, a man will want to invest in consumer and producer goods. Only to the extent that he feels uncertain about his future will he want to make the sacrifice referred to by Mises; that is, will he possibly want to invest in relief from any uneasiness felt concerning the uncertainty

---

[47]Mises, *Human Action*, p. 430. The term uncertainty is employed here in its technical meaning as defined by Frank H. Knight (*Risk, Uncertainty, and Profit* [Chicago: University of Chicago Press, 1971], esp. chap. 7) and Mises (*Human Action*, esp. chap. 6); that is, as categorically distinct from risk instances of class probability; also Hoppe ("On Certainty and Uncertainty, Or: How Rational Can Our Expectations Be?" *Review of Austrian Economics* 10, no. 1 [1979]: 49–78). Insofar as man faces a risky future, he does not need to hold cash. In order to satisfy his desire to be protected against risks, he can instead buy (or produce) insurance. A buyer of insurance demonstrates by his purchase that he is in fact *certain* about some future events. Hence, in paying a premium, he sacrifices a present good in exchange for a future one (payment in the event of actual risk-damage) and so contributes to and invests in a physical structure of production. Specifically, his premium becomes embodied in the production structure maintained by his insurance agency. In distinct contrast: insofar as man faces uncertainty he is, quite literally *not certain* concerning his future, that is, as to what will happen to him and when. Hence, in order to be protected against uncertainty, he cannot possibly invest in any future good. Only present goods can insure against instantly arising—unpredictable—events. Nor can he invest in (present) consumer goods (for this would mean that he actually felt certain as to the specific nature of his future contingencies). Only a medium of exchange, on account of its supreme saleability, can insure him against contingencies of an uncertain nature. Hence, just as insurance is the price that must be paid for protection against risks, so cash holdings are the price that must be paid for protection against uncertainty. See also the following final note below.

of his future consumption—production (income—expenditure) pattern. Hence, rather than indicating his increased willingness to sacrifice present satisfaction in exchange for future satisfaction, an increased demand for money demonstrates a man's more intensely felt uncertainty regarding his future; and rather than being an investment in the future, an addition to his cash balance represents an investment in present certainty (protection) vis-à-vis a future perceived as less certain.[48]

In light of this praxeological reconstruction of money as a singularly present good, Selgin and White's entire positive case for fractional reserve banking is revealed as mistaken. If banks indeed accommodate an (unanticipated) increased demand for money through the temporary issue of additional fiduciary media (credit), as Selgin and White propose, this can have only disruptive and disequilibrating effects. If and insofar as the accommodating response on the part of the banks is unanticipated, the interest rate will be reduced temporarily below its natural height, investment will increase, and the structure of production will be lengthened. Yet this result is fundamentally at odds with the public's demonstrated preference. The

---

[48]Selgin and White never raise the question of *why* changes in the demand for money occur, and thus never penetrate to their ultimate—microeconomic—sources; that is, changes in individuals' subjective evaluations of presently perceived personal uncertainty. In contrast, whereas they portray changes in the demand for money as seemingly unmotivated and inexplicable events, Mises is explicit and emphatic about the irrational character:

> The advantages and disadvantages derived from cash holding are not objective factors which could directly influence the size of cash holdings. They are put on the scales by each individual and weighed against one another. The result is a subjective judgment of value, colored by the individual's personality. Different people and the same people at different times value the same objective facts in a different way. Just as knowledge of a man's wealth and his physical condition does not tell us how much he would be prepared to spend for food of a certain nutritive power, so knowledge about data concerning a man's material situation does not enable us to make definite assertions with regard to the size of his cash holding. (Mises, *Human Action*, p. 430)

public perceives the future as more (increasingly) uncertain and, accordingly, in striving to increase the size of its cash holdings and thereby bidding the prices of nonmoney goods down and correspondingly increasing the purchasing power per unit money, is intent upon providing for more (increased) present protection against uncertainty. To commit additional resources to the future is the expression of *less* public uncertainty (rather than more), and thus stands at cross-purpose to the public's actual wishes and implies a systematic misallocation of resources (to be revealed in a boom-bust cycle). And in any case, even if the banks' accommodating money supply increase could be fully anticipated and the structure of production were not unduly lengthened, any such accommodation would still be disruptive, because—even apart from its inescapable redistributionist consequences—it can only *delay* the arrival of the desired goal. In order to be better protected against perceived uncertainty, prices must fall and the purchasing power of money must rise. With an additional influx of money, it cannot but take *longer* before this goal is accomplished.[49]

----

[49]Mises summarizes:

> The services money renders are conditioned by the height of its purchasing power. Nobody wants to have in his cash holding a definite number of pieces of money or a definite weight of money; he wants to keep a cash holding of a definite amount of purchasing power. As the operation of the market tends to determine the final state of money's purchasing power at a height at which the supply of and the demand for money coincide, there can never be an excess or a deficiency of money. Each individual and all individuals together always enjoy fully the advantages which they can desire from indirect exchange and the use of money, no matter whether the total quantity of money is great or small. Changes in money's purchasing power generate changes in the disposition of wealth among the various members of society. From the point of view of people eager to be enriched by such changes, the supply of money may be called insufficient or excessive, and the appetite for such gains may result in policies designed to bring about cash-induced alterations in purchasing power. However, the services which money renders can be neither improved nor repaired by changing the supply of money. There may

A FINAL NOTE:
SOME MISTAKEN ANALOGIES

In light of the fundamental distinction between property (money) and property titles (money substitutes) explained in earlier sections of this article and the foregoing elucidation of money as a uniquely present good, several analogies popularly employed in the attempted justification of fractional reserve banking can be finally disposed of as mistaken. Even if they correctly distinguish between property titles (tickets) and property, all proposed analogies—between fractional reserve banking on the one hand and airline overbooking, fractional reserve parking lots, lotteries, and insurance on the other hand—fail to recognize properly the fundamental distinction between present and future goods.

The owner of a title to money owns a present good (money property)—an indirectly yet immediately serviceable good. The fractional reserve banker is found guilty of fraud; he issued and sold additional titles to an unchanged quantity of money property. In distinct contrast; the owner of an airline ticket owns a future good. Hence, in overbooking *now* (today) a flight at a future date (tomorrow), an airline cannot possibly have committed fraud already now (today). Fraud cannot occur until tomorrow, when the tickets must be actually redeemed, and only if the airline is then unable to satisfy each and every ticket holder's claim. In fact, airlines typically fulfill their contractual obligation: each ticket holder is assured a seat on the scheduled flight, because the airline is prepared to pay every excess ticket holder off, that is, to repurchase his ticket at a price (by exchange of another good) that the holder considers more valuable than his

---

appear an excess or a deficiency of money in an individual's cash holding. But such a condition can be remedied by increasing or decreasing consumption or investment. (Of course, one must not fall prey to the popular confusion between the demand for money for cash holding and the appetite for more wealth.) The quantity of money available in the whole economy is always sufficient to secure for everybody all that money does and can do. (Mises, *Human Action*, p. 421)

present airline seat. And certainly, no airline typically oversells spot-tickets (titles to seats right now, that is, present goods) and assigns two people to occupy the same seat, which is essentially what fractional reserve banking amounts to.

Similarly, the owner of a fractionally covered parking permit (with more permit holders than parking spaces) does not own a present good. He owns the right to participate for a specified period of time in repeated search for parking space. The owner of the parking facility cannot possibly commit any fraud in selling his permits, unless he then refused entry to a valid permit holder when there was empty space available, or if he changed the contractually agreed upon rules of the game; that is, if he had agreed to print up to a maximum of 200 permits, for instance, but actually printed 300. It is only the owner of a spot parking ticket, or the owner of a reserved parking space, who are owners of a present good; and there is, of course, characteristically no overselling of spot spaces or of reserved parking.

The same reasoning applies to the case of lotteries. The holder of a lottery ticket does not own any present good. He owns the right to participate in the drawing of specified prizes, whereby it is self-understood among buyer and seller—as inherent in the nature of a lottery—that there are—and must be—more tickets than prizes. The lottery operator cannot possibly have committed any crime, unless he failed to redeem the winning tickets into the promised prizes or surreptitiously changed the preannounced rules of the game. If this is rarely the case, it is practically unheard of that a lottery would print more than one winning ticket for one and the same prize (present good), which would be likewise fraudulent, of course, and which is essentially what fractional reserve bankers do.

Finally, the proposed analogy between fractional reserve banking and insurance has already been refuted implicitly in note 46 above, concerning the relationship between risk and insurance on the one hand and uncertainty and money on the other. Unlike the owner of money, the owner of an insurance policy does not own a present but a future good. An insurance company may be unable to meet its contractually assumed obligations at some future point in time, and one may then come to the conclusion that it had engaged in an overselling of tickets. However, it is impossible to say that a crime has been already committed now, at the moment when the insurance policy is sold, because the good sold by the insurance agency is a future one. In distinct contrast, the owner of a money ticket is the owner of a present good, and every overissue of tickets to present goods is from the very outset—instantly and immediately—fraudulent, and accordingly is contrary to market ethics.

8

Socialism: A Property or Knowledge Problem?

I

In a series of recent articles in the *Review of Austrian Economics*, Joseph Salerno began to de-homogenize the often conflated economic and social theories of Ludwig von Mises and Friedrich A. Hayek. In particular, he has shown that their views on socialism are distinctly different, and he has argued in effect that Mises's original argument in the so-called socialist calculation debate was correct all along and was also the final word, whereas Hayek's distinct contribution to the debate was fallacious from the outset and merely added confusion. The following note will provide additional support to Salerno's thesis.

Mises's well-known calculation argument states this: If there is no private property in land and other production factors, then there can also be no market prices for them. Hence, economic calculation, i.e., the comparison of anticipated revenue and expected cost expressed in terms of a common medium of exchange (which permits *cardinal* accounting operations), is literally impossible. Socialism's fatal error is the absence of private property in land and production factors, and by implication, the absence of economic calculation.

[Reprinted from the *Review of Austrian Economics* 9, no. 1 (1992).]

For Hayek, socialism's problem is not a lack of property but a lack of knowledge. His distinctive thesis is altogether different from Mises's.[1] For Hayek, the ultimate flaw of socialism is the fact that knowledge, in particular "the knowledge of the particular circumstances of time and place," exists only in a widely dispersed form as the personal possession of various individuals; hence, it is *practically* impossible to assemble and process all the actually existing knowledge within the mind of a single socialist central planner. Hayek's solution is not private property, but the decentralization of the use of knowledge.

Yet this is surely an absurd thesis. First, if the centralized use of knowledge is the problem, then it is difficult to explain why there are families, clubs, and firms, and why they do not face the very same problems as socialism. Families and firms also involve central planning. The family head and the owner of the firm also make plans which bind the use other people can make of their private knowledge, yet families and firms are not known to share the problems of socialism. For Mises, this observation poses no difficulty: under socialism private property is *absent*, whereas individual families and private firms are *based* on the very *institution* of private property. However, for Hayek the smooth operation of families and firms is puzzling because his idea of a fully decentralized society is one in which each person makes his own decisions based on his own unique knowledge of the circumstances, unconstrained by any central plan or supraindividual (social) norm (such as the institution of private property).

Second, if the *desideratum* is merely the decentralized use of knowledge in society, then it is difficult to explain why the problems of socialism are fundamentally different from those encountered by any other form of social organization. *Every* human organization, composed as it is of distinct individuals, constantly and unavoidably makes use of decentralized knowledge. In socialism, decentralized knowledge is utilized no less than in private firms or households. As

---

[1]See in particular the widely acclaimed 1945 article, "The Use of Knowledge in Society," reprinted in F.A. Hayek, *Individualism and Economic Order* (Chicago: University of Chicago Press, 1948).

in a firm, a central plan exists under socialism, and within the constraints of this plan, the socialist workers and the firm's employees utilize their own decentralized knowledge of circumstances of time and place to implement and execute the plan. For Mises, all of this is completely beside the point. Within Hayek's analytical framework, no difference between socialism and a private corporation exists. Hence, there can be no more wrong with socialism than with a private firm.

Clearly, Hayek's thesis regarding the central problem of socialism is nonsensical. What categorically distinguishes socialism from firms and families is *not* the existence of centralized knowledge or the lack of the use of decentralized knowledge, but rather the absence of private property, and hence, of prices. In fact, in occasional references to Mises and his original calculation argument, Hayek at times appears to realize this, too. But his attempt to integrate his very own thesis with Mises's and thereby provide a new and higher theoretical synthesis fails.

The Hayekian synthesis consists of the following propositional conjunction: "Fundamentally, in a system in which the knowledge of the relevant facts is dispersed among many people, prices can act to coordinate the separate actions of different people" and "the price system" can serve as "a mechanism for communicating information."[2] While the second part of this proposition strikes one as vaguely Misesian, it is anything but clear how it is logically related to the first, except through Hayek's elusive association of "prices" with "information" and "knowledge." However, this association is more of a semantic trick than rigorous argumentation. On one hand, it is harmless to speak of prices as conveying information. They inform about past exchange ratios, but it is a non-sequitur to conclude that socialism's central problem is a lack of *knowledge*. This would only follow if prices actually *were* information. However, this is not the case. Prices convey knowledge, but they are the exchange ratios of various goods, which result from the voluntary interactions of distinct individuals *based on the institution of private property*. Without the institution of private property, the information conveyed by prices

---

[2]Ibid., pp. 85–86.

The Economics and Ethics of Private Property

simply does not exist. Private property is the necessary condition—*die Bedingung der Möglichkeit*—of the knowledge communicated through prices. Yet then it is only correct to conclude, as Mises does, that it is the absence of the institution of private property which constitutes socialism's problem. To claim that the problem is a lack of knowledge, as Hayek does, is to confuse cause and effect, or premise and consequence.

On the other hand, Hayek's identification of "prices" and "knowledge" involves a deceptive equivocation. Not only does Hayek fail to distinguish between what one might call institutional knowledge—information that requires for its existence an institution (such as the knowledge of prices requires private property)—and *raw or extra-institutional knowledge*—such as this is an oak tree, I like peanuts, or birds can fly. Moreover, Hayek fails to notice that the knowledge of prices is not at all the same sort of knowledge whose existence he believes to be responsible for the "practical impossibility" of socialism and central planning. What makes central planning impossible, according to Hayek, is the fact that part of human knowledge exists only as essentially *private* information:

> practically every individual has some advantage over all others because he possesses unique information of which beneficial use might be made, but of which use can be made only if the decisions depending on it are left to him or are made with his active co-operation.[3]

While it is certainly true that such knowledge exists, and while it is also true that uniquely private knowledge can never be centralized (without information losses), it is just as certainly *not* true that the knowledge of prices falls into this category of uniquely *private* information. To be sure, prices are "prices paid at specific times and places," but this does not make them private information in the Hayekian sense. To the contrary, the information conveyed by *prices* is *public* information, because prices—*qua* objective exchange ratios—are *real* events. It may be *difficult* to know all of the prices paid at a specified date and location, just as it may be difficult to

---

[3]Ibid., p. 80.

know every person's physical location at any given time. Yet it is hardly *impossible* to know either one, and with current computer technology it is probably easy. In any case, while I may never know everything that you know, and *vice versa*, it is no more problematic to assume that both of us can simultaneously possess the same *price* information than that we can both simultaneously know the same baseball results. Hence, the knowledge conveyed by prices actually *can be centralized*. However, if price information is public information and thus can be centralized, then, according to Hayek's thesis that socialism's problem stems from the inefficiency of trying to centralize genuinely uncentralizable private knowledge, it would follow that the absence of prices, and hence of private property has *nothing to do* with the plight of socialism. Otherwise, if one insists with Mises that the absence of private property, and prices *does* have something to do with the plight of socialism, Hayek's contribution to the socialism debate must be discarded as false, confusing, and irrelevant.

Hayek's misconception of the nature of socialism is symptomatic of a fundamental flaw in his thinking, pervading not only his economics but in particular also his political philosophy: his ultra-subjectivism. Hayek, as noted and quoted *ad nauseam* by his numerous followers, was convinced that "it is probably no exaggeration to say that every important advance in economic theory during the last hundred years was a further step in the consistent application of subjectivism."[4] While this may well be true, it does not logically follow that every further advance toward subjectivism must also lead to an advance in economic theory. However, Hayek seems to have drawn this conclusion and has thus become a prime example illustrating its falsehood.

Mises, and in his steps even more clearly Murray N. Rothbard, conceives of economics as the science of human *action*. Action has two inseparable aspects: a subjective aspect (action is rational, intelligible action) and an objective aspect (acting is always acting with real things and physical stuff). Accordingly, Mises's and Rothbard's

---

[4]F.A. Hayek, *The Counterrevolution of Science* (New York: Free Press, 1955), p. 21.

economics and political philosophy is never anything but robust, and their categories and theories invariably possess real, operational meaning: private property, division of labor based on private property, production, direct and indirect exchange, and compulsory interference with private property and production and exchange such as taxation, counterfeiting, legislation, and regulation.

In distinct contrast, Hayek—and misled by him to different degrees also Israel Kirzner and Ludwig Lachmann—views economics as some sort of science of human *knowledge*. Accordingly, Hayek's categories and theories refer to purely subjective phenomena and are invariably elusive or even illusory. He is not concerned about acting with things but about knowledge and ignorance, the division, dispersion, and diffusion of knowledge, alertness, discovery, learning, and the coordination and divergence of plans and expectations. The external (physical) world and real (material) events have almost completely disappeared from his view. Hayek's categories refer to *mental* states of affairs and relationships, completely detached from and compatible with *any* real physical state of affairs and events.

Most notable and disturbing is the ultra-subjectivist turn in Hayek's political philosophy. According to a long-standing tradition of political philosophy shared by Mises and Rothbard, freedom is defined as the freedom to privately own and control real property, and coercion is the initiation of physical damage upon the private property of others. In distinct contrast, Hayek defines freedom as "a state in which each can use his own *knowledge* and for his own *purposes*,"[5] and coercion means "such control of the environment or circumstances of a person by another that, in order to avoid greater evil, he is forced to act not according to a coherent plan of his own but to serve the *ends* of another,"[6] or alternatively, "coercion occurs when one man's actions are made to serve another man's will, not for his

---

[5]F.A. Hayek, *Law, Legislation, and Liberty* (Chicago: University of Chicago Press, 1973), vol. 1, pp. 55–56.

[6]F.A. Hayek, *The Constitution of Liberty* (Chicago: University of Chicago Press, 1960), pp. 20–21.

own but for the other's *purpose*"[7] (all emphases mine). Clearly, Hayek's definition contains no reference to scarce goods and real tangible property, and provides no *physical* criterion or indicator whatsoever for the existence or nonexistence of either state of affairs. Rather coercion and freedom refer to specific configurations of subjective wills, plans, thoughts, or expectations. As *mental* predicates, Hayek's definitions of freedom and coercion are compatible with every *real*, physical state of affairs.[8]

It is beyond the scope of this note to offer a detailed critique and refutation of Hayek's ultra-subjectivism. However, in addition to the fundamental question whether a science of knowledge as envisioned by Hayek is even possible (i.e., whether there can be any other science of knowledge apart from logic and epistemology on the one hand and the history of ideas on the other),[9] two conclusions are painfully clear. Even if Hayek's science of knowledge is possible, it appears at best irrelevant because it is praxeologically meaningless. At worst it is intellectually pernicious in promoting relativism.

As for the real world of acting with physical property, of production and exchange, of money and markets, of profits and losses, of capital accumulation and of bankruptcies, there can be no lasting doubt about the existence of *laws* and the ceaseless operation of a *tendency* toward general equilibrium (action-coordination). Likewise, there can be no doubt about the existence of laws and the constant operation of dis-equilibrating tendencies within the world of actual taxation, counterfeiting, legislation, and regulation. Indeed, it would be extremely costly, even prohibitive, to not recognize such laws and tendencies and to adopt relativistic views. In contrast, in surreptitiously shifting attention from the tangible world of action and property to the ethereal world of knowledge, ideas, plans and expectations, relativistic views become attractive and cheap. There are no

---

[7]Ibid., p. 133.

[8]See also Hans-Hermann Hoppe, "Hayek on Government and Social Evolution," *Review of Austrian Economics* 7, no. 1 (1994): esp. 70ff.

[9]For some serious doubts on this see Hans-Hermann Hoppe, *Kritik der kausalwissenschaftlichen Sozialforschung* (Opladen: Westdeutscher Verlag, 1983).

apparent regularities and tendencies in Hayek's knowledge world. In fact, it is difficult to even imagine what "law" and "equilibrium" could possibly mean in the context of purely subjective phenomena. Instead there appears to exist nothing but constant kaleidoscopic change.

It is hardly surprising then that Hayek and his followers could proclaim such relativistic slogans as that we cannot do anything to improve our condition except rely on spontaneous evolution, that our future is completely unknowable, or that we cannot but participate in an endless and open-ended stream of conversation. As far as the realm of purely subjective phenomena is concerned and as addressed to a purely spiritual disembodied being, this may well be good advice. However, why would anyone with a bodily existence even care? As applied to the world of bodily action and property, such advice is self-destructive nonsense.

Part Two

PHILOSOPHY

9

On Praxeology and the
Praxeological Foundation
of Epistemology

I.

As have most great and innovative economists, Ludwig von Mises intensively and repeatedly analyzed the problem of the logical status of economic propositions (i.e., how we come to know them and how we validate them). Indeed, Mises ranks foremost among those who hold that such a concern is indispensable in order to achieve systematic progress in economics, for any misconception regarding the answer to such fundamental questions of one's intellectual enterprise would lead to intellectual disaster, i.e., to false economic doctrines. Accordingly, three of Mises's books are devoted to clarifying the logical foundations of economics: His early *Epistemological Problems of Economics*, published in German in 1933; his *Theory and History* in 1957; and his *Ultimate Foundation of Economic Science* in 1962, Mises's last book, which appeared when he was already well past his eightieth birthday. His works in the field of economics proper invariably display the importance which Mises attached to the

[First printed in the *Meaning of Ludwig von Mises: Contributions in Economics, Epistemology, Sociology, and Political Philosophy*, edited by Jeffrey M. Herbener (Auburn, Ala.: Ludwig von Mises Institute, 1993). Also reprinted in Hans-Hermann Hoppe, *Economic Science and the Austrian Method* (Auburn, Ala.: Ludwig von Mises Institute, 1995).]

analysis of epistemological problems. Most characteristically, *Human Action*, his masterpiece, deals in its first hundred odd pages exclusively with such problems, and the remaining nearly 800 pages of the book are permeated with epistemological considerations.

Quite in line with the tradition of Mises, the foundations of economics are also the subject of this chapter. I have set myself a twofold goal. First, I will explain the solution which Mises advances regarding the problem of the ultimate foundation of economic science (i.e., his idea of a pure theory of action, or praxeology, as he himself terms it). Second, I will demonstrate why Mises's solution is much more than just an incontestable insight into the nature of economics and economic propositions.

Mises provides an insight that also enables us to understand the foundation on which epistemology ultimately rests. In fact, as the title of the chapter suggests, I will show that it is praxeology which must be regarded as the very foundation of epistemology, and that Mises, in addition to his great achievements as an economist, also contributed pathbreaking insights regarding the justification of the entire enterprise of rationalist philosophy.[1]

II.

Let me begin with Mises's solution. What is the logical status of a typical economic proposition such as the law of marginal utility (that whenever the supply of a good whose units are regarded as of equal serviceability by a person increases by one additional unit, the value attached to this unit must decrease as it can only be employed as a means for the attainment of a goal that is considered less valuable than

---

[1]See on the following also Hans-Hermann Hoppe, *Kritik der kausalwissenschnftlichen Sozialforschung. Untersuchungen zur Grundlegung von Soziologie und Ökonomie* (Opladen: Westdeutscher Verlag, 1983); idem, "Is Research Based on Causal Scientific Principles Possible in the Social Sciences?" *Ratio* (1983): infra chap. 7; idem, *Praxeology and Economic Science* (Auburn, Ala.: Ludwig von Mises Institute, 1988); idem, in "Defense of Extreme Rationalism," *Review of Austrian Economics* 3 (1988).

the least valuable goal previously satisfied by a unit of this good) or of the quantity theory of money (that whenever the quantity of money is increased while the demand for money to be held in cash reserve on hand is unchanged, the purchasing power of money will fall)?

In formulating his answer, Mises faced a double challenge. On one hand, there was the answer offered by modern empiricism. The Vienna Ludwig von Mises knew was in fact one of the early centers of the empiricist movement: a movement which was on the verge of establishing itself as the dominant academic philosophy of the Western world for several decades, and which to this very day shapes the image that an overwhelming majority of economists have of their own discipline.[2]

Empiricism considers nature and the natural sciences to be its model. According to empiricism, the just mentioned examples of economic propositions have the same logical status as laws of nature. Like laws of nature, they state hypothetical relationships between two or more events, essentially in the form of if-then statements. And like hypotheses of the natural sciences, the propositions of economics require continual testing vis-à-vis experience. A proposition regarding the relationship between economic events can never be validated once and for all with certainty. Instead, it is forever subject to the

---

[2]On the Vienna Circle see Viktor Kraft, *Der Wiener Kreis* (Wien: Springer, 1968); for empiricist-positivist interpretations of economics see such representative works as Terrence W. Hutchison, *The Significance and Basic Postulates of Economic Theory* (London: Macmillan, 1938). Hutchison, an adherent of the Popperian variant of empiricism, has since become much less enthusiastic about the prospects of a Popperized economics—see, for instance, his *Knowledge and Ignorance in Economics* (Chicago: University of Chicago Press, 1977)—yet he still sees no alternative but to cling to Popper's falsificationism. See also Milton Friedman, "The Methodology of Positive Economics" in idem, *Essays in Positive Economics* (Chicago: University of Chicago Press, 1953); Mark Blaug, *The Methodology of Economics* (Cambridge: Cambridge University Press, 1980); a positivist account by a participant in Mises's Privat-Seminar in Vienna is Felix Kaufmann, *Methodology of the Social Sciences* (New York: Humanities Press, 1958); the dominance of empiricism in economics is documented by the fact that there is probably not a single textbook which does not explicitly classify economics as—what else?—an empirical (a posteriori) science.

outcome of contingent, future experiences. Such experience might confirm the hypothesis. But this would not prove the hypothesis to be true, since the economic proposition would use general terms (in philosophical terminology, universals) in its description of the related events and thus would apply to an indefinite number of cases or instances, thereby always leaving room for possibly falsifying future experiences. All that a confirmation would prove is that the hypothesis had not yet turned out wrong. On the other hand, the experience might falsify the hypothesis. This would surely prove that something was wrong with the hypothesis as it stood, but it would not prove that the hypothesized relationship between the specified events could never be observed. It would merely show that considering and controlling in one's observations only what up to now had been actually accounted for and controlled, the relationship had not yet shown up. It could not be ruled out, however, that it might show up as soon as some other circumstances are controlled.

The attitude that this philosophy fuels and that has indeed become characteristic of most contemporary economists and their way of conducting their business is one of skepticism with the motto being "nothing can be known with certainty to be impossible in the realm of economic phenomena." Even more precisely, since empiricism conceives of economic phenomena as objective data, extending in space and subject to quantifiable measurement—in strict analogy to the phenomena of the natural sciences—the peculiar skepticism of the empiricist economist may be described as that of a social engineer who will not guarantee anything.[3]

The other challenge came from the side of the Historicist School. Indeed, during Mises's life in Austria and Switzerland, the historicist philosophy was the prevailing ideology of the German speaking universities and their establishment. With the upsurge of empiricism its former prominence has been reduced considerably. However, over

---

[3]On the relativistic consequences of empiricism-positivism see also Hans-Hermann Hoppe, *A Theory of Socialism and Capitalism* (Boston: Kluwer Academic Publishers, 1989), chap. 6; idem, "The Intellectual Cover for Socialism," *Free Market* (February 1988); see also infra chap. 11.

roughly the last decade historicism has regained momentum among the Western world's academia. Today it is pervasive under the names of hermeneutics, rhetoric, deconstructivism, and epistemological anarchism.[4]

For historicism, and most conspicuously for its contemporary versions, the model is not nature but a literary text. According to the historicist doctrine, economic phenomena are not objective magnitudes that can be measured. Instead, they are subjective expressions and interpretations unfolding in history to be understood and interpreted by the economist just as a literary text unfolds before and is interpreted by its reader. As subjective creations, the sequence of their events follows no objective law. Nothing in the literary text and nothing in the sequence of historical expressions and interpretations is governed by constant relations. Of course, certain literary texts actually exist, and so do certain sequences of historical events. But this by no means implies that anything had to happen in the order it did. It simply occurred. In the same way as one can always invent different literary stories, history and the sequence of historical events might also have happened in an entirely different way. Moreover, according to historicism, and particularly visible in its modern hermeneutical version, the formation of these always contingently related human expressions and their interpretations are also not constrained by any objective law. In literary production anything can be expressed or interpreted in any way, and along the same line, historical and

---

[4]See Ludwig von Mises, *The Historical Setting of the Austrian School of Economics* (Auburn, Ala.: Ludwig von Mises Institute, 1984); idem, *Erinnerungen* (Stuttgart: Gustav Fischer, 1978); idem, *Theory and History: An Interpretation of Social and Economic Evolution* (Auburn, Ala.: Ludwig von Mises Institute, 1985), chap. 10; Murray N. Rothbard, *Ludwig von Mises: Scholar, Creator, Hero* (Auburn, Ala.: Ludwig von Mises Institute, 1988); for a critical survey of historicist ideas see also Karl R. Popper, *The Poverty of Historicism* (London: Routledge and Kegan Paul, 1957); for a representative of the older version of a historicist interpretation of economics see Werner Sombart, *Die drei Nationalökonomien* (Munich: Duncker and Humblot, 1930); for the modern, hermeneutical twist Donald McCloskey, *The Rhetoric of Economics* (Madison: University of Wisconsin Press, 1985); Ludwig Lachmann, "From Mises to Shackle: An Essay on Austrian Economics and the Kaleidic Society," *Journal of Economic Literature* 14, no. 1 (1976).

economic events are whatever someone expresses or interprets them to be, and their description by the historian and economist is then whatever he expresses or interprets these past subjective events to have been.

The attitude that historicist philosophy generates is one of relativism. Its motto is "everything is possible." Unconstrained by any objective law, history, economics, and literary criticism are matters of esthetics for the historicist-hermeneutician. Accordingly, his output takes on the form of disquisitions on what someone feels about what he feels was felt by someone else. This is a literary form with which we are only too familiar, in particular in such fields as sociology and political science.[5]

One senses intuitively that something is seriously amiss in both the empiricist as well as the historicist philosophies. Their epistemological accounts do not even seem to fit their own chosen models: nature on the one hand and literary texts on the other. In any case, with regard to economic propositions such as the law of marginal utility or the quantity theory of money, their accounts seem to be simply wrong. The law of marginal utility certainly does not strike one as a hypothetical law forever subject for its validation to confirming or disconfirming experiences popping up here or there. And to conceive of the phenomena referred to in the law as quantifiable magnitudes seems to be nothing short of ridiculous. Nor does the historicist interpretation seem to be any better. To think that the relationship between the events referred to in the quantity theory of money can be undone if one only wishes to do so seems absurd. The idea appears no

---

[5]On the extreme relativism of historicism-hermeneutics see Hans-Hermann Hoppe, "In Defense of Extreme Rationalism"; Murray N. Rothbard, "The Hermeneutical Invasion of Philosophy and Economics," *Review of Austrian Economics* 3 (1988); Henry Veatch, "Deconstruction in Philosophy: Has Rorty Made it the Denouement of Contemporary Analytical Philosophy," *Review of Metaphysics* (1985); Steven Horwitz and Peter Boettke, "Misesian Integrity: A Comment on Barnes," *Austrian Economics Newsletter* (Fall, 1987); David Gordon, *Hermeneutics vs. Austrian Economics* (Auburn, Ala.: Ludwig von Mises Institute, Occasional Paper Series, 1987); for a brilliant critique of contemporary sociology see Stanislav Andreski, *Social Science as Sorcery* (New York: St. Martin's Press, 1973).

less absurd that concepts such as money, demand for money, and pur-chasing power are formed without any objective constraints and refer merely to whimsical subjective creations. Instead, contrary to the empiricist doctrine, both examples of economic propositions appear to be logically true and to refer to events which are subjective in nature. Contrary to historicism, it would seem that what they state could not possibly be undone in all of history and contain conceptual distinctions which, while they refer to subjective events, are nonetheless objectively constrained and incorporate universally valid knowledge.

Like most of the better known economists before him, Mises shares these intuitions.[6] Yet in his quest of the foundation of eco-nomics, Mises goes beyond intuition. He takes on the challenge posed by empiricism and historicism in order to reconstruct the basis on which these intuitions can be understood as correct and justified systematically. He does not want thereby to bring about a new disci-pline of economics, but in explaining what formerly had only been grasped intuitively, Mises goes far beyond what had ever been done before. In reconstructing the rational foundations of the economists' intuitions, he assures us of the proper path for any future develop-ment in economics and safeguards us against systematic intellectual error.

Empiricism and historicism, Mises notes at the outset of his recon-struction, are self-contradictory doctrines.[7] The empiricist notion

---

[6]Regarding the epistemological views of such predecessors as Jean Baptiste Say, Nassau W. Senior, John E. Cairnes, John Stuart Mill, Carl Menger, and Friedrich Wieser, see Ludwig von Mises, *Epistemological Problems of Economics* (New York: New York University Press, 1981), pp. 17–23; also Murray N. Roth-bard, "Praxeology: The Methodology of Austrian Economics," in Edwin Dolan, ed., *The Foundations of Modern Austrian Economics* (Kansas City: Sheed and Ward, 1976); Hoppe, *Praxeology and Economic Science*.

[7]In addition to Mises's works cited at the outset of this chapter and the lit-erature mentioned in note 1, see Murray N. Rothbard, *Individualism and the Philosophy of the Social Sciences* (San Francisco: Cato Institute, 1979); for a splendid philosophical critique of empiricist economics see Martin Hollis and Edward Nell, *Rational Economic Man* (Cambridge: Cambridge University Press, 1975); for particularly valuable defenses of rationalism against empiricism and

that all events, natural or economic, are only hypothetically related is contradicted by the message of this very basic empiricist proposition itself, for if this proposition were regarded as itself being merely hypothetically true (i.e., a hypothetically true proposition regarding hypothetically true propositions), it would not even qualify as an epistemological pronouncement. It would provide no justification whatsoever for the claim that economic propositions are not and cannot be categorically, or a priori, true as our intuition informs us they are. If, however, the basic empiricist premise were assumed to be categorically true (i.e., if we assume that one could say something a priori true about the way events are related), then this would belie its very own thesis that empirical knowledge must invariably be hypothetical knowledge, thus making room for a discipline such as economics claiming to produce a priori valid empirical knowledge. Further, the empiricist thesis that economic phenomena must be conceived of as observable and measurable magnitudes—analogous to those of the natural sciences—is rendered inconclusive on its own account, for empiricism provides us with meaningful empirical knowledge when it informs us that our economic concepts are grounded in observations. However, the concepts of observation and measurement, which empiricism must employ in claiming what it does, are themselves obviously not derived from observational experience in the sense that concepts such as hens and eggs or apples and pears are. One cannot observe someone making an observation or measurement. Rather, one must first understand what observations and measurements are in order to be able to interpret certain observable phenomena as the making of an observation or the taking of a measurement. Thus, contrary to its own doctrine, empiricism is compelled to admit that there is empirical knowledge which is based on understanding—just as according to our intuitions economic

---

relativism—without reference to economics—see Brand Blanshard, *Reason and Analysis* (La Salle, Ill.: Open Court, 1964); Friedrich Kambartel, *Erfahrung und Struktur. Bausteine zu einer Kritik des Empirismus und Formalismus* (Frankfurt/M.: Suhrkamp, 1968).

propositions claim to be based on understanding rather than on observations.[8]

Regarding historicism, its self-contradictions are no less manifest. If, as historicism claims, historical and economic events, which it conceives of as sequences of subjectively understood rather than observed events, are not governed by constant, time-invariant relations, then this very proposition also cannot claim to say anything constantly true about history and economics. Instead, it would be a proposition with a fleeting truth value: it may be true now, if we wish, yet possibly false in a moment, in case we do not, and no one would ever know whether we do or do not. However, if this were the status of the basic historicist premise, it too would obviously not qualify as epistemology. Historicism would not have given us any reason why we should believe any of it. If, however, the basic proposition of historicism were assumed to be invariantly true, then such a proposition about the constant nature of historical and economic phenomena would contradict its own doctrine denying any such constants. Furthermore, the historicist's (and even more so its modern heir, the hermeneutician's) claim that historical and economic events are mere subjective creations, unconstrained by any objective factors, is proven false by the very statement making it. Evidently, a historicist must assume this very statement to be meaningful and true; he must presume to say something specific about something, rather than merely to utter meaningless sounds such as abracadabra. However, if this is the case, clearly his statement must be assumed to be constrained by something outside the realm of arbitrary subjective creations. Of course, I can say what the historicist says in English, German, Chinese, or any other language I wish, and in so far historic and economic expressions and interpretations may well be regarded as mere subjective creations. But whatever I say in whatever language I choose must be assumed to be constrained by some underlying propositional meaning of my statement, which is the same for any

---

[8]For an elaborate defense of epistemological dualism see also K.O. Apel, *Transformation der Philosophie*, 2 vols. (Frankfurt/M: Suhrkamp, 1973); Jürgen Habermas, *Zur Logik der Sozialwissenschaften* (Frankfurt/M.: Suhrkamp, 1970).

language, and exists completely independent of whatever the peculiar linguistic form may be in which it is expressed. Contrary to historicist belief, the existence of such a constraint is not such that one could possibly dispose of it at will. Rather, it is objective in that we can understand it to be the logically necessary presupposition for saying anything meaningful at all, as opposed to merely producing meaningless sounds. The historicist could not claim to say anything if it were not for the fact that his expressions and interpretations are actually constrained by laws of logic as the very presupposition of meaningful statements as such.[9]

With such a refutation of empiricism and historicism, Mises notices, the claims of rationalist philosophy are successfully reestablished, and the case is made for the possibility of a priori true statements, as those of economics seem to be. Indeed, Mises explicitly regards his own epistemological investigations as the continuation of the work of western rationalist philosophy. With Leibniz and Kant he stands opposite the tradition of Locke and Hume.[10] He takes Leibniz's side when he answers Locke's famous dictum "nothing is in the intellect that has not previously been in the senses" with his equally famous one "except the intellect itself." And he recognizes his task as a philosopher of economics as strictly analogous to that of Kant's as a philosopher of pure reason   (i.e., of epistemology). Like Kant, Mises wants to demonstrate the existence of true a priori synthetic propositions, or propositions whose truth values can be definitely established, even though for such an undertaking the means of formal logic are insufficient and observations are unnecessary.

This criticism of empiricism and historicism has proved the general rationalist claim. It has proved that we indeed do possess knowledge which is not derived from observation yet is constrained by objective laws. In fact, our refutation of empiricism and historicism contains such a priori synthetic knowledge. Yet what about the

---

[9]See on this in particular Hoppe, "In Defense of Extreme Rationalism."

[10]See Ludwig von Mises, *The Ultimate Foundation of Economic Science* (Kansas City: Sheed Andrews and McMeel, 1978), p. 12.

constructive task of showing that the propositions of economics—such as the law of marginal utility and the quantity theory of money—qualify as this type of knowledge? In order to do so, Mises notices in accordance with the strictures traditionally formulated by rationalist philosophers, economic propositions must fulfill two requirements. First, it must be possible to demonstrate that they are not derived from observational evidence, for observational evidence can only reveal things as they happen to be: there is nothing in it that would indicate why things must be the way they are. Instead, economic propositions must be shown to be grounded in reflective cognition, in our understanding of ourselves as knowing subjects. Second, this reflective understanding must yield certain propositions as self-evident material axioms, not in the sense that such axioms would have to be self-evident in a psychological sense, that is, that one would have to be immediately aware of them or that their truth depends on a psychological feeling of conviction. On the contrary, like Kant before him, Mises stresses the fact that it is usually much more painstaking to discover such axioms than it is to discover some observational truth such as that the leaves of trees are green or that I am 6 foot 2 inches.[11] Rather, what makes them self-evident material axioms is the fact that no one can deny their validity without self-contradiction, for in attempting to deny them one already presupposes their validity.

Mises points out that both requirements are fulfilled by what he terms the axiom of action (i.e., the proposition that humans act, that they display intentional behavior).[12] Obviously, this axiom is not derived from observation—there are only bodily movements to be observed but no such thing as actions—but stems instead from reflective understanding. And this understanding concerns a self-evident proposition, for its truth cannot be denied, since the denial would

---

[11]See Immanuel Kant, *Kritik der reinin Vernunft*, in idem, *Werke*, 12 vols., ed. W. Weischedel (Frankfurt/M.: Suhrkamp, 1968), vol. 3, p. 45; Ludwig von Mises, *Human Action: A Treatise on Economics* (Chicago: Regnery, 1966), p. 38.

[12]On the following see in particular Mises, *Human Action*, chap. IV; Murray N. Rothbard, *Man, Economy, and State* (Los Angeles: Nash, 1962), chap. 1.

itself have to be categorized as an action. But is this not just trivial? And what has economics got to do with this? Of course, it was previously recognized that economic concepts such as prices, costs, production, money, and credit had something to do with the fact that there were acting people. But that and how all of economics could be grounded in and reconstructed based on such a trivial proposition, is anything but clear. It is one of Mises's greatest achievements to have shown precisely that there are insights implied in this psychologically speaking trivial axiom of action that were not themselves psychologically self-evident as well; and that it is these insights which provide the foundation for the theorems of economics as true a priori synthetic propositions.

It is certainly not psychologically evident that with every action an actor pursues a goal, and that whatever the goal may be, the fact that it was pursued by an actor reveals that he must have placed a relatively higher value on it than on any other goal of action that he could have thought of at the start of his action. It is not evident that in order to achieve his most highly valued goal an actor must interfere or decide not to interfere (which is also an intentional interference) at an earlier point in time in order to produce a later result, nor is it obvious that such interferences invariably imply the employment of some scarce means—at least those of the actor's body, its standing room, and the time absorbed by the action. It is not self-evident that these means must also have value for an actor—a value derived from that of the goal—because the actor must regard their employment as necessary in order to effectively achieve the goal; and that actions can only be performed sequentially and always involve the choice of taking up that one course of action which at some given time promises the most highly valued results to the actor and excluding at the same time the pursual of other, less highly valued goals. It is not automatically clear that as a consequence of having to choose and give preference to one goal over another—of not being able to realize all goals simultaneously—each and every action implies the incurrence of costs (forsaking the value attached to the most highly ranking alternative goal that cannot be realized or whose realization must be deferred) because the means necessary to attain it are bound up in the production of another, even more highly valued goal. Finally, it is not evident that at its starting point every goal of action must be considered worth more to the actor than its cost and capable of yielding a profit (a result whose value is ranked higher than that of the foregone opportunity), and that every action is also invariably threatened by the possibility of a loss if an actor finds in retrospect that contrary to his expectations the actually achieved result has a lower value than the relinquished alternative would have had.

All of these categories which we know to be the very heart of economics—values, ends, means, choice, preference, cost, profit and loss—are implied in the axiom of action. Like the axiom itself, they are not derived from observation. Rather, that one is able to interpret observations in terms of such categories requires that one already knows what it means to act. No one who is not an actor could ever understand them, as they are not "given," ready to be observed, but observational experience is cast in these terms as it is construed by an actor. Further, while they and their interrelations are not obviously implied in the action axiom, once it has been made explicit that and how they are implied, one no longer has any difficulty recognizing them as being a priori true in the same sense as the axiom itself is. Any attempt to disprove the validity of what Mises has reconstructed as implied in the very concept of action would have to be aimed at a goal, requiring means, excluding other courses of action, incurring costs, subjecting the actor to the possibility of achieving or not achieving the desired goal, and leading to a profit or a loss. Thus, it is manifestly impossible to dispute or falsify the validity of Mises's insights. In fact, a situation in which the categories of action would cease to have a real existence could itself never be observed or spoken of, as making an observation or speaking are also actions.

All true economic propositions, and this is what praxeology is all about and what Mises's great insight consists of, can be deduced by means of formal logic from this incontestably true material knowledge regarding the meaning of action and its categories. More precisely, all true economic theorems consist of (a) an understanding of the meaning of action, (b) a situation or situational change—assumed to be given or identified as being given—and described in terms of action-categories, and (c) a logical deduction of the consequences—

again in terms of such categories—which are to result for an actor from this situation or situational change. For instance, the law of marginal utility[13] follows from our indisputable knowledge of the fact that every actor always prefers what satisfies him more over what satisfies him less, plus the assumption that he is faced with an increase in the supply of a good (a scarce mean) whose units he regards as of equal serviceability by one additional unit. From this it follows with logical necessity that this additional unit can only be employed as a means for the removal of an uneasiness that is deemed less urgent than the least valuable goal previously satisfied by a unit of such a good. Provided there is no flaw in the process of deduction, the conclusions which economic theorizing yields must be valid a priori. These propositions' validity ultimately goes back to the indisputable axiom of action. To think, as empiricism does, that these propositions require continual empirical testing for their validation is absurd and a sign of outright intellectual confusion. And it is no less absurd and confused to believe, as does historicism, that economics has nothing to say about constant and invariable relations but merely deals with historically accidental events. To say so is to prove such a statement wrong, as saying anything meaningful at all already presupposes acting and a knowledge of the meaning of the categories of action.

III.

This will suffice as an explanation of Mises's answer regarding the quest for the foundations of economics. I shall now turn to my second goal: the explanation of why and how praxeology also provides the foundation for epistemology. Mises had been aware of this and was convinced of the great importance of this insight for rationalist philosophy. Yet he did not treat the matter in a systematic fashion. There are no more than a few brief remarks concerning this problem

---

[13]On the law of marginal utility see Mises, *Human Action*, pp. 119–27; Rothbard, *Man, Economy, and State*, pp. 268–71.

interspersed throughout his massive body of writing.[14] Thus, in the following I must try to break new ground.

I shall begin my explanation by introducing a second a priori axiom and clarifying its relation to the axiom of action. Such an understanding is the key to solving our problem. The second axiom is the so-called "a priori of argumentation," which states that humans are capable of argumentation and hence know the meaning of truth and validity.[15] As in the case of the action axiom, this knowledge is not derived from observation: there is only verbal behavior to be observed and prior reflective cognition is required in order to interpret such behavior as meaningful arguments. The validity of the axiom, like that of the action axiom, is indisputable. It is impossible to deny that one can argue, as the very denial would itself be an argument. In fact, one could not even silently say to oneself "I cannot argue" without thereby contradicting oneself. One cannot argue that one cannot argue. Nor can one dispute knowing what it means to make a truth or validity claim without implicitly claiming the negation of this proposition to be true.

---

[14]Mises writes:

> [K]nowledge is a tool of action. Its function is to advise man how to proceed in his endeavors to remove uneasiness. . . . The category of action is the fundamental category of human knowledge. It implies all the categories of logic and the category of regularity and causality. It implies the category of time and that of value. . . . In acting, the mind of the individual sees itself as different from its environment, the external world, and tries to study this environment in order to influence the course of events happening in it. (*The Ultimate Foundation of Economic Science*, pp. 35–36)

Or:

> Both, a priori thinking and reasoning on the one hand and human action on the other, are manifestations of the mind. Reason and action are congeneric and homogeneous, two aspects of the same phenomenon. (Ibid., p. 42)

Yet he leaves the matter more or less at this and concludes that "it is not the scope of praxeology to investigate the relation of thinking and action" (*Human Action*, p. 25).

[15]On the a priori of argumentation see also Apel, *Transformation der Philosophie*, vol. 2.

It is not difficult to detect that both a priori axioms—of action and argumentation—are intimately related. On one hand, actions are more fundamental than argumentation with whose existence the idea of validity emerges, as argumentation is only a subclass of action. On the other hand, to recognize this regarding action and argumentation and their relation to each other requires argumentation. Thus, in this sense, argumentation must be considered more fundamental than action, for without argumentation nothing can be said to be known about action. However, argumentation itself reveals the possibility that argumentation presupposes action because validity claims can only be explicitly discussed in the course of an argumentation if the individuals doing so already know what it means to act and have knowledge implied in action. Thus, both the meaning of action in general and argumentation in particular must be thought of as logically necessary interwoven strands of a priori knowledge.

What this insight into the interrelation between the a priori of action and the a priori of argumentation suggests is the following: Traditionally, the task of epistemology has been conceived of as that of formulating what can be known to be true a priori and what can be known a priori not to be the subject of a priori knowledge. Recognizing, as we have just done, that knowledge claims are raised and decided upon in the course of argumentation and that this is undeniably so, one can now reconstruct the task of epistemology more precisely as that of formulating those propositions which are argumentatively indisputable in that their truth is already implied in the very fact of making an argument and so cannot be denied argumentatively; and to delineate the range of such a priori knowledge from the realm of propositions whose validity cannot be established in this way but require additional, contingent information for their validation, or that cannot be validated at all and so are mere metaphysical statements in the pejorative sense of the term metaphysical.

Yet what is implied in the very fact of arguing? It is to this question that our insight into the inextricable interconnection between the a priori of argumentation and that of action provides an answer. On a very general level, it cannot be denied argumentatively that argumentation presupposes action and that arguments, and the knowledge embodied in them, are those of actors. More specifically, it cannot be denied that knowledge itself is a category of action; that the structure of knowledge must be constrained by the peculiar function which knowledge fulfills within the framework of action categories; and that the existence of such structural constraints can never be disproved by any knowledge whatsoever.

It is in this sense that the insights contained in praxeology must be regarded as providing the foundations of epistemology. Knowledge is a category quite distinct from those explained earlier—from ends and means. The ends which we strive to attain through our actions and the means which we employ in order to do so are both scarce values. The values attached to our goals are subject to consumption and are exterminated and destroyed in consumption and thus must forever be produced anew. The means employed must be economized, too. It is not so, however, with respect to knowledge, regardless of whether one considers it a means or an end in itself. Of course, the acquisition of knowledge requires scarce means, at least one's body and time. Yet once knowledge is acquired, it is no longer scarce. It can neither be consumed, nor are the services that it can render as a means subject to depletion. Once there, it is an inexhaustible resource and incorporates an everlasting value (provided that it is not simply forgotten).[16] Yet knowledge is not a free good in the same sense as air, under normal circumstances, is a free good. Instead, it is a category of action. It is not only a mental ingredient of each and every action, quite unlike air, but more importantly, knowledge, and not air, is subject to validation, which is to say that it must prove to fulfill a positive function for an actor within the invariant constraints of the categorical framework of actions. It is the task of epistemology to clarify what these constraints are and what one can thus know about the structure of knowledge as such.

While such recognition of the praxeological constraints on the structure of knowledge might not immediately strike one as of great significance in itself, it does have some highly important implications.

---

[16]On this fundamental difference between economic (scarce) means and knowledge see also Mises, *Human Action*, pp. 128, 661.

282   *The Economics and Ethics of Private Property*

For one thing, with this insight one recurring difficulty of rationalist philosophy is eliminated. It has been a common quarrel with rationalism in the Leibniz-Kant tradition that it seemed to imply a sort of idealism. Realizing that a priori true propositions could not possibly be derived from observations, rationalism explained how a priori knowledge could then be possible by adopting the model of an active mind, as opposed to the empiricist model of a passive, mirror-like mind in the tradition of Locke and Hume. According to rationalist philosophy, a priori true propositions had their foundation in the operation of principles of thinking which one could not possibly conceive of as operating otherwise; they were grounded in categories of an active mind. However, as empiricists have been only too eager to point out, the obvious critique of such a position is that if this were indeed the case, it could not be explained why such mental categories would fit reality. Rather, one would be forced to accept the absurd idealistic assumption that reality would have to be conceived of as a creation of the mind in order to claim that a priori knowledge could incorporate any information about the structure of reality. Clearly, such an assertion seems to be justified when faced with programmatic statements of rationalist philosophers such as the following by Kant: "So far it has been assumed that our knowledge had to conform to reality," instead it should be assumed "that observational reality should conform to our mind."[17]

Recognizing knowledge as being structurally constrained by its role in the framework of action categories provides the solution to such a complaint, for as soon as this is realized, all idealistic suggestions of rationalist philosophy disappear, and an epistemology claiming that a priori true propositions exist becomes a realistic epistemology instead. Understood as constrained by action categories, the seemingly unbridgeable gulf between the mental on the one hand and

---

[17]Kant, *Kritik der reinen Vernunft*, p. 25. Whether or not such an interpretation of Kant's epistemology is indeed correct is a very different matter. Clarifying this problem is of no concern here, however. For an activist or constructivist interpretation of Kantian philosophy see Kambartel, *Erfahrung und Struktur*, chap. 3; also Hans-Hermann Hoppe, *Handeln und Erkennen* (Bern: Lang, 1976).

the real, outside physical world on the other is bridged. So constrained, a priori knowledge must be as much a mental thing as a reflection of the structure of reality since it is only through actions that the mind comes into contact with reality, so to speak. Acting is a cognitively guided adjustment of a physical body in physical reality. Thus, there can be no doubt that a priori knowledge, conceived of as an insight into the structural constraints imposed on knowledge qua knowledge of actors, must indeed correspond to the nature of things. The realistic character of such knowledge would manifest itself not only in the fact that one could not *think* it to be otherwise, but in the fact that one could not *undo* its truth.

Yet there are more specific implications involved in recognizing the praxeological foundations of epistemology, apart from the general one that in substituting the model of the mind of an actor acting by means of a physical body for the traditional rationalist model of an active mind, a priori knowledge immediately becomes realistic knowledge (so realistic indeed that it cannot be undone). More specifically, in light of this insight decisive support is given to those deplorably few rationalist philosophers who—against the empiricist Zeitgeist—stubbornly maintain on various philosophical fronts that a priori true propositions about the real world are possible.[18] Moreover, with the recognition of praxeological constraints on the structure of knowledge, these various rationalist endeavors become systematically integrated into one unified body of rationalist philosophy.

---

[18]In addition to the works mentioned in note 7 see Brand Blanshard, *The Nature of Thought* (London: Allen and Unwin, 1921); Morris Cohen, *Reason and Nature* (New York: Harcourt, Brace, 1931); idem, *Preface to Logic* (New York: Holt, 1944); A. Pap, *Semantics and Necessary Truth* (New Haven, Conn.: Yale University Press, 1958); Saul Kripke, "Naming and Necessity," in Donald Davidson and Gilbert Harman, eds., *Semantics of Natural Language* (New York: Reidel, 1972); Hugo Dingler, *Die Ergreifung des Wirklichen* (Frankfurt/M.: Suhrkamp, 1969); idem *Aufbau der exakten Fundamentalwissenschaft* (Munich: Eidos, 1964); Wilhelm Kamlah and Paul Lorenzen, *Logische Propädeutik* (Mannheim: Bibliographisches Institut, 1968); Paul Lorenzen, *Methodisches Denken* (Frankfurt/M.: Suhrkamp, 1968); idem, *Normative Logic and Ethics* (Mannheim: Bibliographisches Institut, 1969); Apel, *Transformation der Philosophie*.

When one understands that knowledge as displayed in argumentation is a peculiar category of action, the validity of the perennial rationalist claim that the laws of logic—beginning here with the most fundamental ones of propositional logic and of Junctors ("and," "or," "if-then," "not") and Quantors ("there is," "all," "some")—are a priori true propositions about reality and not mere verbal stipulations regarding the transformation rules of arbitrarily chosen signs, as empiricist-formalists would have it, becomes clear. They are as much laws of thinking as of reality because they are laws that have their ultimate foundation in action and can not be undone by any actor. In each and every action, an actor identifies some specific situation and categorizes it one way rather than another in order to be able to make a choice. It is this which ultimately explains the structure of even the most elementary propositions (like "Socrates is a man") as consisting of a proper name or some identifying expression for the naming or identifying of something and a predicate to assert or deny some specific property of the named or identified object. It is this which explains the cornerstones of logic: the laws of identity and contradiction. And it is this universal feature of action and choosing which also explains our understanding of the categories "there is," "all," "some," "and," "or," "if-then," and "not."[19] One can, say, of course, that

---

[19]On rationalist interpretations of logic see Blanshard, *Reason and Analysis*, chaps. VI, X; Paul Lorenzen, *Einführung in die operative Logik und Mathematik* (Frankfurt/M.: Akademische Verlagsgesellschaft, 1970); Kuno Lorenz, *Elemente der Sprachkritik* (Frankfurt/M: Suhrkamp, 1970); idem, "Die dialogische Rechtfertigung der effektiven Logik," in Friedrich Kambartel and Jürgen Mittelstrass, eds., *Zum normativen Fundament der Wissenschaft* (Frankfurt/M.: Athenaum, 1973).

On the propositional character of language and experience, in particular, see Kamlah and Lorenzen, *Logische Propädeutik*, chap. 1; Lorenzen, *Normative Logic and Ethics*, chap. 1. Lorenzen writes:

I call a usage a convention if I know of another usage which I could accept instead. However I do not know of another behavior which could replace the use of elementary sentences. If I did not accept proper names and predicators, I would not know how to speak at all. . . . Each proper name is a convention . . . but to use proper names at all is not a convention: it is a unique pattern of linguistic behavior.

something can be "a" and "non-a" at the same time, or that "and" means this rather than something else. But one cannot *undo* the law of contradiction and one cannot undo the real definition of "and." Simply by virtue of acting with a physical body in physical space we invariably affirm the law of contradiction and invariably display our true constructive knowledge of the meaning of "and" and "or."

Similarly, the ultimate reason for arithmetic's being an a priori and yet empirical discipline, as rationalists have always understood it, now also becomes discernible. The prevailing empiricist-formalist orthodoxy conceives of arithmetic as the manipulation of arbitrarily defined signs according to arbitrarily stipulated transformation rules

---

Therefore, I am going to call it "logical." The same is true with predicators. Each predicator is a convention. This is shown by the existence of more than one natural language. But all languages use predicators. (Ibid., p. 16)

See also J. Mittelstrass, "Die Wiederkehr des Gleichen," *Ratio*, 1966.

On the law of identity and contradiction, in particular, see Blanshard, *Reason and Analysis*, pp. 276ff., 423ff.

On a critical evaluation of 3- or more-valued logics as either meaningless symbolic formalisms or as logically presupposing an understanding of the traditional two-valued logic see Wolfgang Stegmüller, *Hauptströmungen der Gegenwartsphilosophie* (Stuttgart: Kröner, 1975), vol. 2, pp. 182–91; Blanshard, *Reason and Analysis*, pp. 269–75. Regarding the many-valued or open-textured logic proposed by Friedrich Waismann, Blanshard notes:

We can only agree with Dr. Waismann—and with Hegel—that the black-and-white distinctions of formal logic are quite inadequate to living thought. But why should one say, as Dr. Waismann does, that in adopting a more differentiated logic one is adopting an alternative system which is incompatible with black-and-white logic? What he has actually done is to recognize a number of gradations *within* the older meaning of the word "not." We do not doubt that such gradations are there, and indeed as many more as he cares to distinguish. But a refinement of the older logic is not an abandonment of it. It is still true that the colour I saw yesterday was either a determinate shade of yellow or not, even though the "not" may cover a multitude of approximations, and even though I shall never know which was the shade I saw. (Ibid., pp. 273–74)

and thus as entirely void of any empirical meaning. For this view, which evidently makes arithmetic nothing but play, however skillful it might be, the successful applicability of arithmetic in physics is an intellectual embarrassment. Indeed, empiricist-formalists would have to explain away this fact as simply being a miraculous event. That it is no miracle, however, becomes apparent once the praxeological or—to use here the terminology of the most notable rationalist philosopher-mathematician Paul Lorenzen and his school—the operative or constructivist character of arithmetic is understood. Arithmetic and its character as an a priori-synthetic intellectual discipline is rooted in our understanding of repetition—the repetition of action. More precisely, it rests on our understanding the meaning of "do this—and do this again, starting from the present result." Also, arithmetic deals with real things: with constructed or constructively identified units of something. It demonstrates what relations hold between such units because of the fact that they are constructed according to the rule of repetition. As Paul Lorenzen has demonstrated in detail, not all of what presently poses as mathematics can be constructively founded—and those parts then should of course be recognized for what they are: epistemologically worthless symbolic games. But all of the mathematical tools that are actually employed in physics (i.e., the tools of classical analysis), can be constructively derived. They are not empirically void symbolisms but rather true propositions about reality. They apply to everything insofar as it consists of one or more distinct units, and insofar as these units are constructed or identified as units by a procedure of "do it again, construct or identify another unit by repeating the previous operation."[20] Again, one can say that 2 plus 2

---

[20]On a rationalist interpretation of arithmetic see Blanshard, *Reason and Analysis*, pp. 427–31; on the constructivist foundation of arithmetic, in particular, see Lorenzen, *Einführung in die operative Logik and Mathematik*; idem, *Methodisches Denken*, chaps. 6, 7; idem, *Normative Logic and Ethics,* chap. 4; on the constructivist foundation of classical analysis see Paul Lorenzen, *Differential und Integral—Eine konstruktive Einführung in die klassische Analysis* (Frankfurt/M.: Akademische Verlagsgesellschaft, 1965); for a brilliant general critique of mathematical formalism see Kambartel, *Erfahrung und Struktur*, chap. 6, esp. pp. 236–42; on the irrelevance of the famous Gödel-theorem for a constructively founded arithmetic see Paul Lorenzen, *Metamathematik* (Mannheim:

is sometimes 4 but sometimes 2 or 5 units, and in observational reality, for lions plus lambs or for rabbits, this may even be true,[21] but in the reality of action, in identifying or constructing those units in repetitive operations, the truth that 2 plus 2 is never anything but 4 could not possibly be undone.

Further, the old rationalist claims that Euclidean geometry is a priori yet incorporates empirical knowledge about space becomes supported, too, in view of our insight into the praxeological constraints on knowledge. Since the discovery of non-Euclidean geometries and in particular since Einstein's relativistic theory of gravitation, the prevailing position regarding geometry is once again empiricist and formalist. It conceives of geometry as either being part of empirical, a posteriori physics, or as being empirically meaningless formalisms. That geometry is either mere play or forever subject to empirical testing seems to be irreconcilable with the fact that Euclidean geometry is the foundation of engineering and construction, and that nobody in those fields ever thinks of such propositions as only hypothetically true.[22] Recognizing knowledge as praxeologically

---

Bibliographisches Institut, 1962); also Charles Thiel, "Das Begründungsproblem der Mathematic und die Philosophie," in Kambartel and Mittelstrass, eds., *Zum normativen Fundament der Wissenschaft*, esp. pp. 99–101. Kurt Gödel's proof, which as a proof incidentally supports rather than undermines the rationalist claim of the possibility of a priori knowledge, only demonstrates that the early formalist Hilbert program cannot be successfully carried through because in order to demonstrate the consistency of certain axiomatic theories one must have a metatheory with even stronger means than those formalized in the object-theory itself. Interestingly enough, several years before Gödel's proof of 1931, the difficulties of the formalist program had led the old Hilbert to recognize the necessity of reintroducing a substantive interpretation of mathematics *à la* Kant, which would give its axioms a foundation and justification that was entirely independent of any formal consistency proofs. See Kambartel, *Erfahrung and Struktur*, pp. 185–87.

[21]Examples of this kind are used by Popper in order to "refute" the rationalist idea of rules of arithmetic being laws of reality. See Karl Popper, *Conjectures and Refutations* (London: Routledge and Kegan Paul, 1969), p. 211.

[22]See on this also Mises, *The Ultimate Foundation of Economic Science*, pp. 12–14.

constrained explains why the empiricist-formalist view is incorrect and why the empirical success of Euclidean geometry is no mere accident. Spatial knowledge is also included in the meaning of action. Action is the employment of a physical body in space. Without acting there could be no knowledge of spatial relations and no measurement. Measuring relates something to a standard. Without standards, there is no measurement, and there is no measurement which could ever falsify the standard. Evidently, the ultimate standard must be provided by the norms underlying the construction of bodily movements in space and the construction of measurement instruments by means of one's body and in accordance with the principles of spatial constructions embodied in it. Euclidean geometry, as again Paul Lorenzen in particular has explained, is no more and no less than the reconstruction of the ideal norms underlying our construction of such homogeneous basic forms as points, lines, planes and distances which are in a more or less perfect but always perfectible way incorporated or realized in even our most primitive instruments of spatial measurements such as a measuring rod. Naturally, these norms and normative implications cannot be falsified by the result of any empirical measurement. On the contrary, their cognitive validity is substantiated by the fact that it is they that make physical measurements in space possible. Any actual measurement must already presuppose the validity of the norms leading to the construction of one's measurement standards. It is in this sense that geometry is an a priori science and must simultaneously be regarded as an empirically meaningful discipline because it is not only the very precondition for any empirical spatial description, but it is also the precondition for any active orientation in space.[23]

---

[23]On the a prioristic character of Euclidean geometry see Lorenzen, *Methodisches Denken*, chaps. 8 and 9; idem, *Normative Logic and Ethics*, chap. 5; Hugo Dingler, *Die Grundlagen der Geometrie* (Stuttgart: Enke, 1933); on Euclidean geometry as a necessary presupposition of objective, intersubjectively communicable measurements and in particular of any empirical verification of non-Euclidean geometries (after all, the lenses of the telescopes which one uses to confirm Einstein's theory regarding the non-Euclidean structure of physical space must themselves be constructed according to Euclidean principles) see

In view of the recognition of the praxeological character of knowledge, these insights regarding the nature of logic, arithmetic and geometry become integrated and embedded into a system of epistemological dualism.[24] The ultimate justification for this dualist position (the claim that there are two realms of intellectual inquiry that can be understood a priori as requiring categorically distinct methods of treatment and analysis), also lies in the praxeological nature of knowledge. It explains why we must differentiate between a realm of objects which is categorized causally and a realm that is categorized teleologically instead.

I have already briefly indicated during my discussion of praxeology that causality is a category of action. The idea of causality—that there are constant, time-invariantly operating causes which allow one to project past observations regarding the relation of events into the future—is something (as empiricism since Hume has noticed) which has no observational basis whatsoever. One cannot observe the connecting link between observations. Even if one could, such an observation would not prove it to be a time-invariant connection. Instead, the principle of causality must be understood as implied in our

---

Kambartel, *Erfahrung und Struktur*, pp. 132–33; Peter Janich, *Die Protophysik der Zeit* (Mannhein: Bibliographisches Institut, 1969), pp. 45–50; idem, "Eindeutigkeit, Konsistenz und methodische Ordnung," in Kambartel and Mittelstrass, eds., *Zum normativen Fundament der Wissenschaft.*

Following the lead of Hugo Dingler, Paul Lorenzen and other members of the so-called Erlangen School have worked out a system of protophysics, which contains all a prioristic presuppositions of empirical physics, including, apart from geometry, also chronometry and hylometry (i.e., classical mechanics without gravitation, or rational mechanics).

> Geometry, chronometry and hylometry are a priori theories which make empirical measurements of space, time and material "possible." They have to be established before physics in the modern sense of an empirical science, with hypothetical fields of forces, can begin. Therefore, I should like to call these disciplines by a common name: protophysics. (Lorenzen, *Normative Logic and Ethics*, p. 60)

[24]On the fundamental nature of epistemological dualism see also Mises, *Theory and History*, pp. 1–2.

understanding of action as an interference with the observational world, made with the intent of diverting the natural course of events in order to produce a different, preferred state of affairs (of making things happen that otherwise would not happen), and thus presupposes the notion of events which are related to each other through time-invariantly operating causes. An actor might err with respect to his particular assumptions about which earlier interference produced which later result. But successful or not, any action, changed or unchanged in light of its previous success or failure, presupposes that there are constantly connected events as such, even if no particular cause for any particular event can ever be preknown to any actor. Without such an assumption it would be impossible to ever categorize two or more observational experiments as falsifying or confirming each other rather than interpreting them as logically incommensurable events. Only because the existence of time-invariantly operating causes *as such* is already assumed can one ever encounter particular instances of confirming or disconfirming observational evidence, or can there ever be an actor who can learn anything from past experience by classifying his actions as successful and confirming some previous knowledge or as unsuccessful and disconfirming it. It is simply by virtue of acting and distinguishing between successes and failures that the a priori validity of the principle of causality is established; even if one tried, one could not successfully refute its validity.[25]

---

[25]On the a prioristic character of the category of causality see Mises, *Human Action*, chap. 5; Hoppe, *Kritik der kausalwissenschaftlichen Sozialforschung*; idem, "Is Research Based on Causal Scientific Principles Possible in the Social Sciences?" (infra chap. 7); on the causality principle as a necessary presupposition in particular also of the indeterminacy principle of quantum physics and the fundamental misconception involved in interpreting the Heisenberg-principle as invalidating the causality principle see Kambartel, *Erfahrung and Struktur*, pp. 138–40; also Hoppe, "In Defense of Extreme Rationalism," footnote 36. In fact, it is precisely the indisputable praxeological fact that separate measurement acts can only be performed sequentially which explains the very possibility of irreducibly probabilistic—rather than deterministic—predictions as they are characteristic of quantum physics; however, in order to perform any experiments in the field of quantum mechanics, and in particular to repeat

In so understanding causality as a necessary presupposition of action, it is also immediately implied that its range of applicability must then be delineated a priori from that of the category of teleology. Indeed, both categories are strictly exclusive and complementary. Action presupposes a causally structured observational reality, but the reality of action which we can understand as requiring such structure, is not itself causally structured. Instead, it is a reality that must be categorized teleologically, as purpose-directed, meaningful behavior. In fact, one can neither deny nor undo the view that there are two categorically different realms of phenomena, since such attempts would have to presuppose causally related events qua actions that take place within observational reality as well as the existence of intentionally rather than causally related phenomena in order to interpret such observational events as meaning to deny something. Neither a causal nor a teleological monism could be justified without running into an open contradiction: in physically stating either position and in claiming to say something meaningful in so doing, the case is in fact made for an indisputable complementarity of both a realm of causal *and* teleological phenomena.[26]

Everything which is not an action must necessarily be categorized causally. There is nothing to be known a priori about this range of phenomena except that it is structured causally and that it is structured according to the categories of propositional logic, arithmetic and geometry.[27] Everything else there is to know about this range of phe-

----

two or more experiments and state this to be the case, the validity of the causality principle must evidently already be presupposed.

[26]On the necessary complementarity of the categories of causality and teleology see Mises, *Human Action*, p. 25; idem, *The Ultimate Foundation of Economic Science*, pp. 6–8; Hoppe, *Kritik der kausalwissenschaftlichen Sozialforschung*; idem, "Is Research Based on Causal Scientific Principles Possible in the Social Sciences?" (infra chap. 7); also Georg Henrik von Wright, *Norm and Action* (London: Routledge and Kegan Paul, 1963); idem, *Explanation and Understanding* (Ithaca, N.Y.: Cornell University Press, 1971); K.O. Apel, *Die Erklären: Verstehen Kontroverse in transzendental-pragmatischer Sicht* (Frankfurt/M.: Suhrkamp, 1979).

[27]More precisely still, it is structured according to the categories of logic, arithmetic, and protophysics (including geometry). See note 23 above.

nomena must be derived from contingent observations and thus represents a posteriori knowledge. In particular, all knowledge about two or more specific observational events being causally related or not is a posteriori knowledge. Obviously, the range of phenomena described in this way coincides (more or less) with what is usually considered to be the field of the empirical natural sciences.

In contrast, everything that is an action must be categorized teleologically. This realm of phenomena is constrained by the laws of logic and arithmetic, too. But it is not constrained by the laws of geometry as incorporated in our instruments of measuring spatially extending objects because actions do not exist apart from subjective interpretations of observable things. Therefore, they must be identified by reflective understanding rather than spatial measurements. Nor are actions causally connected events, but events that are connected meaningfully within a categorical framework of means and ends.

One can not know a priori what the *specific* values, choices and costs of some actor are or will be. This would fall entirely into the province of empirical, a posteriori knowledge. In fact, which particular action an actor is going to undertake would depend on his knowledge regarding the observational reality and/or the reality of other actors' actions. It would be manifestly impossible to conceive of such states of knowledge as predictable on the basis of time-invariantly operating causes. A knowing actor cannot predict his future knowledge before he has actually acquired it, and he demonstrates, simply by virtue of distinguishing between successful and unsuccessful predictions, that he must conceive of himself as capable of learning from unknown experiences in as yet unknown ways. Thus, knowledge regarding the particular course of actions is only a posteriori. Since such knowledge would have to include the actor's own knowledge—as a necessary ingredient of every action whose every change can have an influence on a particular action being chosen—teleological knowledge must also necessarily be reconstructive or historical knowledge. It would only provide *ex post* explanations which would have no systematic bearing on the prediction of future actions because future states of knowledge could never be predicted on the basis of constantly operating empirical causes. Obviously, such a delineation of a branch of a posteriori and reconstructive science of action fits the usual description of such disciplines as history and sociology.[28]

What *is* known to be true a priori regarding the field of action and what would then have to constrain any historical or sociological explanation is this: For one thing, any such explanation, which essentially would have to reconstruct an actor's knowledge, would invariably have to be a reconstruction in terms of knowledge of ends and means, of choices and costs, of profits and losses and so on. Second, since these are evidently the categories of praxeology as conceived of by Mises, any such explanation must also be constrained by the laws of praxeology. Since these laws are a priori laws, they must also operate as logical constraints on any future course of action. They are valid independent of any specific state of knowledge that an actor might have acquired, simply by virtue of the fact that whatever this state might be, it must be described in terms of action categories. And as referring to actions as such, the laws of praxeology must then be coextensive with all the predictive knowledge there can be in the field of the science of action. In fact, ignoring for the moment that the status of geometry as an a priori science is ultimately grounded in our understanding of action and in so far praxeology must be regarded as the more fundamental cognitive discipline, the peculiar role of praxeology proper within the entire system of epistemology can be understood as somewhat analogous to that of geometry. Praxeology is for the field of action what Euclidean geometry is for the field of observations (non-actions). As the geometry incorporated in our measuring instruments constrains the spatial structure of observational reality, so praxeology constrains the range of things that can possibly be experienced in the field of actions.[29]

---

[28]On the logic of history and sociology as reconstructive disciplines see, in addition to the works of Mises mentioned at the outset of this chapter, Hoppe, *Kritik der kausalwissenschaftlichen Sozialforschung,* chap. 2.

[29]On the categorical distinctiveness of praxeological theory and history (sociology) and the logical constraints that praxeology imposes on historical and sociological research as well as on social and economic predictions, see Mises, *Human Action,* pp. 51–59, 117–18; Hoppe, "In Defense of Extreme Rationalism"; idem, *Praxeology and Economic Science.*

IV.

In so establishing the place of praxeology proper, I have come full circle in delineating the system of rationalist philosophy as ultimately grounded in the action axiom. It has been my goal here to reaffirm Mises's claim that economics is praxeology; that the case for praxeology is an indisputable one; and that empiricist or historicist-hermeneuticist interpretations of economics are self-contradictory doctrines. It has also been my objective to indicate that the Misesian insight into the nature of praxeology provides the very foundation on which traditional rationalist philosophy can be successfully reconstructed and systematically integrated.

For the rationalist philosopher this would seem to imply that he must take account of praxeology, for it is precisely the insight into the praxeological constraints on the structure of knowledge which provides the missing link in an intellectual defense against skepticism and relativism. For the economist in the tradition of Mises it means that he should explicitly come to recognize the Misesian's place within the wider tradition of Western rationalism; and that he should incorporate the insights provided by this tradition in order to construct an even more impressive and profound case for praxeology and Austrian economics than the one made by the great Mises himself.

10

Is Research Based on Causal Scientific Principles Possible in the Social Sciences?

I.

The use of mathematical and statistical techniques is becoming more and more widespread in the social sciences. It is becoming all the more important, therefore, to demonstrate by a detailed description of these techniques that there are reasons to doubt their applicability in the field of the social sciences.

The aim of this paper is to offer such a demonstration with specific reference to the techniques which allow us to take a given set of data and determine the values of the constants by means of which a variable, interpreted as a dependent variable, can be brought into a law-governed relationship with other variables. It is irrelevant whether this relationship is linear or nonlinear, whether there is one or more than one independent variables, whether—as in time-series analyses—the dependent variables themselves also function (time-shifted) as independent variables, and whether the relationship is recursive or nonrecursive, deterministic or statistical. The critique applies to all techniques, from simple linear regression to the comparatively complex procedure of time-series analysis, insofar as such techniques are used to determine the value of constants (including

[Reprinted from *Ratio* 25, no. 1 (1983).]

those with values which vary according to some consistent pattern). It hardly needs pointing out that the use of such techniques is on the increase. In the field of economics, econometrics is steadily establishing its position as the home of these techniques,[1] despite criticism from the advocates of pure economics.[2] In sociology, too, the systematic introduction of econometric techniques is being seen increasingly as a universal panacea, a trend fostered above all by the works of Blalock.[3]

II.

To illustrate the following argument let us assume that the values of the constants b_1 and b_2 in the multiple regression equation

$$Y = a + b_1X_1 + b_2X_2 + e$$

have been determined on the basis of a given set of data. Y—the dependent variable—is interpreted as a linear function of the independent variables X_1 and X_2 and a magnitude of error e with a mean value of 0.

The b-constants in this equation can be interpreted in either of two ways. They can be given an innocuous, but completely unusual,

---

[1]See Mordecai Ezekiel and Karl Fox, *Methods of Correlation and Regression Analysis* (New York: John Wiley and Sons, 1966); P. Rao and R.L. Miller, *Applied Econometrics* (Belmont, Calif.: Wadsworth, 1971); Robert Pindyck and Daniel Rubinfeld, *Econometric Models and Economic Forecasts* (New York: McGraw-Hill 1976).

[2]See Lionel Robbins, *The Nature and Significance of Economic Science* (London: Macmillan, 1935); Ludwig von Mises, *Theory and History* (New Haven, Conn.: Yale University Press, 1957); idem, *The Ultimate Foundation of Economic Science* (Kansas City: Sheed Andrews and McMeel, 1978); idem, *Human Action: A Treatise on Economics* (Chicago: Regnery, 1966).

[3]Hubert Blalock, *Causal Inferences in Non-Experimental Research* (Chapel Hill: University of North Carolina Press, 1964); idem, *Theory Construction* (Englewood Cliffs, N.J.: Prentice Hall, 1969); N. Krishnan Namboodiri, F. Carter, and Hubert Blalock, *Applied Multivariate Analysis and Experimental Designs* (New York: McGraw-Hill, 1975); see also David Heise, *Causal Analysis* (New York: McGraw-Hill, 1975).

interpretation, or they can be given their normal interpretation. This second interpretation, however, is no longer innocuous. It involves assumptions which, as will be shown, are inappropriate in the social sciences.

According to the first innocuous interpretation, the partial regression coefficients represent nothing more than a verifiable statement of how best to predict the Y values on the basis of the X_1 and X_2 values (assuming both linearity and that one is dealing with additive effects). The constants are historico-mathematical facts. They have no significance beyond the historical data with respect to which their values were determined.

There can be no objection to this interpretation. It has the consequence, however, that setting up an equation of the kind given above becomes downgraded in importance. One would not be establishing a theoretical principle but merely providing a description of the facts, and what is more, a description of a kind that can be generated at will for any set of data simply by varying one's assumptions about the types of functions and by enlisting the aid of a computer.

It is improbable that anyone has ever performed a regression analysis intending to achieve only what is implied by this innocuous interpretation. The act of setting up the above equation is normally interpreted as formulating a general hypothesis which can be falsified by new data and which asserts that the relationship between Y, X_1 and X_2, determined by the constants in the equation is universally valid.

III.

The implicit assumptions demanded by this interpretation can be reconstructed by considering the following situation. Using fresh data, an attempt has been made to reproduce the results obtained by analysis of the initial set of data and formalized in the above equation using constants with precisely determined values. Let us assume that the outcome of this attempt is that the multiple linear regression analysis performed for both the Y and the X_1 and X_2 variables of this second set of data produces b constants which diverge significantly from those obtained for the first set of data. According to the innocuous interpretation of such equations, this result would not have any particular consequences. With the first set of data one has established a certain historico-mathematical fact, and with the second another fact. The two are different, and that is all there is to it. According to the normal interpretation, however, the failure to reproduce the results falsifies the hypothesis.

The prerequisite for being able to say "falsify" is the "constancy principle," the conviction that observable phenomena are in principle determined by causes which are constant and are time-invariant in the way in which they operate, and that in principle contingency plays no part in the way in which causes operate. Only if the constancy principle is assumed to be valid does it follow from any failure to reproduce a result that there is anything wrong with the original hypothesis.

Obviously, the constancy principle is not simply based on experience. As has been known since Hume, there is no observable link connecting events, and even if such a link existed, experience could not show whether it was time-invariant or not. The principle cannot be disproved by experience either, for once it is accepted, any event which appears to disprove it (such as a failure to duplicate a result) can be interpreted from the outset as if experience shows here merely that one *particular* variable is not the cause of another variable requiring explanation (otherwise the result would have been successfully duplicated). No conclusion can be drawn as to whether any *other* variable might actually be found which turns out to be time-invariant in the way it operates with respect to the dependent variable in which we are interested. To the extent that experience cannot exclude this possibility, the validity of the constancy principle cannot be disproved.

Although neither derived from nor disprovable by experience, the constancy principle is nevertheless a necessary condition for there being experiences which can be regarded as either confirming or falsifying each other (in contrast to the isolated and unconnected experiences connected with historical facts).[4] The failure to duplicate

---

[4]See on this point, for example, Friedrich Kambartel, *Erfahrung and Struktur* (Frankfurt/M.: Suhrkamp, 1968), chap. 3, in particular pp. 91ff.; also Hans-Hermann Hoppe, *Handeln und Erkennen* (Bern: Lang, 1976), pp. 85ff., and chap. 4.

results could be interpreted as falsifying the original hypothesis in accordance with the normal interpretation of the regression equation, and one might consequently feel prompted to explain the differing values of the b constants by asserting that in *one* sample one or more factors F were implicitly involved in causing Y which were not present in the *other* sample or did not operate in the same way. Finally, one might feel the need to explain these factors F hypothetically and to incorporate them in the initial hypothesis which assumed only the systematic operation of X_1 and X_2, thus replacing one hypothesis by a new one. But all this is only possible to the extent that one has already assumed the validity of the constancy principle for Y and all the factors causing Y.

IV.

We have asserted that there is a sphere of objective reality which cannot be regarded as determined by laws, and that, therefore, no equation describing its behavior (such as the regression equation given above) can be formulated which can be given a normal interpretation.

Since the validity of the constancy principle cannot be doubted on the evidence of external, sensory experience, it can only be on logical grounds that the principle can correctly be regarded as inapplicable in any particular sphere.

The constancy principle is an operational schema, a method. One does not experience and learn that there are causes which always operate in the same way, rather one establishes that phenomena have particular causes by following a particular type of investigative procedure, by refusing on principle to allow any exceptions (instances of inconstancy), and by being prepared to deal with them by producing a new hypothesis each time one is required. The world by itself is not sufficient to establish the constancy principle. It requires the existence of an active, perceiving subject. For his part, this active subject—the prerequisite for a world determined by causes having constant effects—cannot, for logical reasons, assume the validity of the constancy principle with respect to the states of his knowledge (and to the intentional actions which might draw on that knowledge). In

order to guarantee the unconditional validity of the constancy principle, the subject must himself be able to learn. He must start from the
assumption that he can assimilate falsifying experiences and replace
old hypotheses with new ones. If on the other hand one were to view
the state of one's knowledge as caused, and if (absurdly) one were to
treat anything not yet known as being predictable in principle, one
would deprive oneself of all possibility of using one's ability to learn,
that is, to form new, previously unknown hypotheses, as a way of
maintaining the law-governed nature of that sphere of reality, which
is *not* constituted by knowledge or actions drawing on that knowledge.

The result of this logical analysis of the constancy principle as the
principle of a nonempirically based operational schema underlying
causal investigation is that the principle can only be valid in that
objective sphere which is *not* constituted by one's own knowledge or
actions manifesting that knowledge. (In this sphere, the question of
whether there are law-governed constants on the basis of which it
becomes possible to make *ex ante* predictions is positively determined
independently of experience, and empirical factors play a role only in
the question of which concrete variables are causally linked to which
concrete effect variables and which are not.) In the sphere of knowledge and action, on the other hand, it cannot be valid. (In this sphere,
the question of whether or not there are constants is itself empirical
in nature and can only be decided for a given variable on the basis of
past experience, that is decided *ex post.*)

V.

For anyone who is capable of learning, his or her knowledge and
actions cannot logically be regarded as determined by a complex of
causes operating in a constant way (whether statistically or determin-
istically). There can only be constants in relation to the causes of
events where one is dealing with a world of nonlearning objects, or
more correctly, where one conceives of an objective sphere of reality
as a world of nonlearning objects. One cannot, however, think of oneself as nonlearning. Not only is an intellect functioning in accordance
with the constancy principle necessarily a learning intellect (we learn

about how objects conceived of as non-learning behave), but the statement "I can learn" also proves to hold true in other respects. It is in principle not falsifiable, for in order to falsify it one would need to be able to learn. And from another point of view, one cannot justifiably argue against the statement since, qua argument, there must be possible replies to it, and as the validity of an argument (as opposed to that of a stimulus) would be independent of the nature of the reply, such possible replies must be regarded as *contingent* reactions, and therefore it must be possible to learn.

No scientific advance can ever alter the fact that one must regard one's knowledge and actions as uncaused. One might hold this conception of "freedom" to be an illusion, and from the point of view of a "scientist" with cognitive powers substantially superior to any human, that is, from the point of view of God, such a description may well be correct. However, we are not God, and even if freedom is illusory from His standpoint, for us human beings it is a necessary illusion.[5] We cannot predict in advance the future states of our knowledge and the actions manifesting that knowledge on the basis of previous states; we can only reconstruct them after the event.[6]

VI.

Let us return to the regression equation given at the beginning of the discussion:

$$Y = a + b_1X_1 + b_2X_2 + e$$

---

[5] The same illusion would also arise in relation to God, if one assumed that He too could learn.

[6] Karl R. Popper, *Das Elend des Historizismus* (Tübingen: Mohr, 1971), p. xii, states in this connection that it is

> impossible for any scientific forecaster—whether human being or computer—to predict his or her or us own future results, no matter what methods are used. Any attempt to do so can only achieve its goal post festum.

On the methodological significance of this statement see also K.O. Apel, *Die Erklären: Verstehen Kontroverse in transzendental-pragmatischer Sicht* (Frankfurt/ M.: Suhrkamp, 1979), note 19, pp. 44ff.

and bring the argument full circle. Let the dependent variable Y in this equation be any intentional action (an action which attempts by some means to achieve a goal preferred over a starting point and other alternatives, and which in various ways manifests knowledge).

By setting up this equation or by determining the values of the constants for a particular set of data, if we accept the normal interpretation, we are making the following assertion:

There exists a complex of causes operating in a constant fashion which causes Y, and it is possible on the basis of our knowledge of this complex and of the way in which it operates (its function type) to predict the occurrence or nonoccurrence of the intentional act Y (conceived of as a dichotomic 0/1 variable). On the basis of experiences in connection with a particular set of data, the causal relationships explaining Y are described by a provisional hypothesis as in the above equation (with the values of the constants determined with respect to magnitude). New experiences may mean that these concrete assumptions about the causal variable and function types have to be revised. The equation may be replaced by others incorporating different assumptions. Some examples might be:

$$
\begin{aligned}
&(1) \quad Y = a + b_1X_1 + b_2X_2 + b_3X_3 + e \\
&(2) \quad Y = a + b_1Z + b_1X_1 + e \\
&(3) \quad Y = a + b_1 \log X_1 + b_2X_2 + e \\
&(4) \quad Y = a + b_1X_1 + b_2X_2 + b_3X_1X_2 + e
\end{aligned}
$$

In equation (1) it is assumed that X_3 is a causal variable as well as X_2. Equation (2) assumes that a variable Z (correlated with X_1) is the cause of Y and not X_1 as originally assumed. Equation (3) no longer assumes a linear relation in respect to the effect of X_1. Lastly, equation (4) assumes an interactive as well as an additive effect with regard to the two variables X_1 and X_2. No matter which equation is substituted for the original one, however, nor whether the original one is repeatedly found to be valid, it remains the case that Y can be predicted, however much one may argue about the precise details of the equation.

Our previous discussion demonstrated that this assertion is untenable. Y, qua intentional act, cannot in principle be predicted. This conclusion follows from the argument which we may summarize here:

(1) I and—as possible opponents in an argument—other people are able to learn.[7] (This statement cannot be challenged without implicitly admitting that it is correct. Above all, it must be assumed by anyone undertaking research into causes. To this extent, proposition (1) is valid a priori.)

(2) If it is possible to learn, one cannot know at any given time what one will know at any later time and how one will act on the basis of this knowledge. (If one did know at any given time what one will come to know at some later time, it would be impossible ever to learn anything—but see proposition (1) on this point.)

(3) The assertion that it is possible to predict the future state of one's own and/or another's knowledge and the corresponding actions manifesting that knowledge (i.e., to find the variables which can be interpreted as the causes) involves a contradiction. If the subject of a given state of knowledge or of an intentional act can learn, then there are no causes for this; however, if there are causes, then the subject cannot learn—but again see proposition (1).

The putative causes of Y qua intentional act and the putative constants by means of which Y and these causes are brought into a relationship with one another are in truth nothing more significant than variables which have been found in contingent, covariant relationships with Y at particular points in time. It is also a purely contingent historico-mathematical fact (but not a confirmation of a hypothesis!)

---

[7]The transition from one person to the other presupposes the indefensibility of solipsism. There can be no disputing that it is possible to argue with one another that solipsism cannot be defended, since by wanting to argue in its defense one has already thrown it overboard. See on this argument Karl R. Popper, *Conjectures and Refutations* (London: Routledge and Kegan Paul, 1969), pp. 293ff.; idem, *Objective Knowledge* (Oxford: Oxford University Press, 1972), pp. 119ff., 235ff. See also K.O. Apel, *Transformation der Philosophie* (Frankfurt/M.: Suhrkamp, 1973), vol. 2, part II, and Jürgen Habermas, *Legitimationsprobleme in Spätkapitalismus* (Frankfurt/M.: Suhrkamp, 1973), note 160, p. 1521.

if these covariant relationships were reproduced exactly or even merely approximately with new data. It is in principle only coincidence that people in the same situation defined by the same set of variables act in the same way (bring the same knowledge to bear). For if one is able to learn it is obviously impossible to predict whether a person will actually learn or not from one point in time to the next. It can only be ascertained post festum, as an already established fact. Ultimately, any change in these kinds of covariant relationships must be seen as a contingent fact (and not as a falsification of a hypothesis!). For if one can learn, then not only is it impossible to predict whether one will actually learn in any particular situation, but it is equally impossible to predict what, if anything at all, one will learn.

11

From the Economics of Laissez Faire to the Ethics of Libertarianism

I.

L udwig von Mises, without a doubt one of the most rigorous defenders of a social system of laissez faire unhampered by any governmental intervention in the history of economic thought, admits to two and only two deficiencies of a pure market system. While according to Mises it is generally true that a market economy produces the highest possible standard of living, this will not happen if any firm succeeds in securing monopoly prices for its goods, and the market cannot itself produce the goods of law and order. Law and order, or the protection of the legal framework underlying the market order, are considered by Mises, in current terminology, as "public goods," whose production must be undertaken by the state, which is not itself subject to the discipline of the market, but instead relies on coercion, in particular on compulsory taxation.

When Murray N. Rothbard entered the scene in 1962 with his *Man, Economy, and State,* he not only immediately became the foremost student of his revered teacher Ludwig von Mises, but standing

[Reprinted from *Man, Economy, and Liberty: Essays in Honor of Murray N. Rothbard,* Walter Block and Llewellyn H. Rockwell, Jr., eds., Auburn, Ala.: Ludwig von Mises Institute, 1988.]

on the shoulders of this giant, he also established himself at the age of 36 as an intellectual giant in his own right, going, in truly Misesian spirit, beyond Mises himself. He recognized Mises's position regarding the exceptional character of monopoly prices and public goods as incompatible with the very edifice of subjectivist economic theory laid down in *Human Action*, and presented for the first time a complete and fully consistent economic defense of a pure market system.

Regarding the problem of monopoly prices, Rothbard demonstrated that on the free market no price whatever can be identified as monopolistic or competitive, either by the "monopolist" himself or by any "neutral" outside observer. Economic orthodoxy, which includes Misesian Austrian economics, teaches that monopolistic prices are higher prices attained by restricting production, at which prices sales then bring higher returns than those to be gained by selling an unrestricted output at lower competitive prices. And, so the story continues, since such restrictive measures which the profit motive impels the monopolist to use would imply that the consumers would pay more for less, the existence of monopoly prices provides for the possibility of market failures.[1] As Rothbard points out, there are two related fallacies involved in this reasoning.[2]

First, it must be noted that every restrictive action must, by definition, have a complementary expansionary aspect. The factors of production which the monopolist releases from employment in some production line A do not simply disappear. Rather, they must be used otherwise: either for the production of other exchange goods or for an expansion in the production of the good of leisure for an owner of a labor factor. Now suppose the monopolist restricts production in line A at time k as compared with t_1, and prices and returns indeed go up. Following orthodoxy this would make the higher price at t_2 a monopoly price and the consumers worse off. But is this really the

---

[1]See Ludwig von Mises, *Human Action: A Treatise on Economics*, 3rd rev. ed. (Chicago: Regnery, 1966), pp. 357ff.; idem, "Profit and Loss," in *Planning for Freedom* (South Holland, Ill.: Libertarian Press, 1974), esp. p. 116. In this essay Mises takes a somewhat different, one might say, a proto-Rothbardian position.

[2]See Murray N. Rothbard, *Man, Economy, and State* (Los Angeles: Nash, 1972), chap. 10, esp. pp. 604–14.

case? Can this situation be distinguished from a situation in which the demand for the product in question changed from t_1 to t_2 (the demand curve shifted to the right)? The answer, of course, is no, since demand curves are never simply "given" for any good. Because of the change in demand for the good in question, the competitive price at t_1 has become subcompetitive at t_2, and the higher price at t_2 is simply a move from this subcompetitive to the new competitive price. The restrictive move of the monopolist also does not imply a worsening of the situation of the consumers since, by necessity, it must be coupled with a complementary expansionary move in other production lines. The monopolist's restrictive action could not be distinguished from any "normal" change in the production structure that was caused by relative changes in the consumer demand for various goods, including leisure. "There is no way whatever" writes Rothbard,

> to distinguish such a "restriction" and corollary expansion from the alleged "monopoly-price" situation.[3] But if a concept has no possible grounding in reality, then it is an empty and illusory, and not a meaningful, concept. On the free market there is no way of distinguishing a "monopoly price" from a "competitive price" or a "subcompetitive price" or of establishing any changes as movements from one to the other. No criteria can be found for making such distinctions. The concept is therefore untenable. We can speak only of the *free-market price*.[4]

Regarding the second alleged imperfection of markets, the problem of public goods and in particular of the good of law and order, Rothbard demonstrates that the advocates of this position do not succeed in establishing their claim that there are two categorically different types of economic goods—public and private—for which categorically different types of economic analysis would apply. Even if this distinction were assumed to hold water, they also can not furnish any

---

[3]Ibid., p. 607; emphasis added.

[4]Ibid., p. 614. See also Walter Block, "Austrian Monopoly Theory: A Critique," *Journal of Libertarian Studies* 1, no. 4 (1977); Hans-Hermann Hoppe, *Eigentum, Anarchie, und Staat* (Opladen: Westdeutscher Verlag, 1987), chap. 5; idem, *A Theory of Socialism and Capitalism* (Boston: Kluwer Academic Publishers, 1989), chap. 9.

economic reason why such public goods must be supplied by the state.[5] Orthodoxy holds that certain goods and services, of which law and order are usually considered to be the prototypes, have the special characteristic that their enjoyment cannot be restricted to those persons who actually finance their provision. Such goods are called public goods. As they cannot be provided by markets (at least not in sufficient quantity or quality) because of this "free rider" problem connected with them, but are nonetheless valued goods, the state has to jump in to secure their production, so the argument goes.[6] In his refutation of this reasoning Rothbard first makes us aware of the following: for something to be an economic good at all, it must be scarce and must be realized as scarce by someone. In other words,

---

[5]See Rothbard, *Man, Economy, and State*, pp. 883–90; idem, "The Myth of Neutral Taxation," *Cato Journal* (Fall, 1981).

[6]Mises is by no means a completely orthodox public goods theorist. He does not share their and the public choice theorists' commonly held naive view of the government being some sort of voluntary organization. Rather, and unmistakably so, he says, "the essential feature of government is the enforcement of its decrees by beating, killing, and imprisoning. Those who are asking for more government interference are asking ultimately for more compulsion and less freedom" (*Human Action*, p. 719). On this see also the refreshingly realistic assessment by Joseph Schumpeter (*Capitalism, Socialism and Democracy* [New York: Harper and Bros., 1942], p. 198), that "the theory which construes taxes on the analogy of club dues or the purchase of a service of, say, a doctor only proves how far removed this part of the social sciences is from scientific habits of minds." Nor does Mises overlook, as the public goods theorists almost invariably do, the multitude of fallacies involved in today's fashionable economic literature on "externalities" (*Human Action*, pp. 654–61). When Mises's position is classified as orthodox here, it is due to the fact that he, in this respect not unlike the rest of the public goods theorists, dogmatically assumes that certain goods (law and order, in his case) cannot be provided by freely competing industries; and that he, too, with respect to law and order at least, "proves" the necessity of a government by a non sequitur. Thus, in his "refutation" of anarchism he writes: "Society cannot exist if the majority is not ready to hinder, by the application or threat of violent action, minorities from destroying the social order. This power is vested in the state or government" (*Human Action*, p. 149). But clearly, from the first statement the second one does not follow. Why cannot private protection agencies do the job? And why would the government be able to do the job better than such agencies? Here the reader looks in vain for answers.

something is not a good-as-such, but goods are goods only in the eyes of some beholder. But when goods are never goods-as-such, when no physico-chemical analysis can establish something as an economic good, then there is also no fixed, objective criterion for classifying goods as public or private. They can never be private or public goods as such; their private or public character depends on how few or how many people consider them goods (or for that matter, bads), with the degree to which they are private or public changing as these evaluations change and ranging from 1 to infinity. Even seemingly completely private things like the interior of my apartment or the color of my underwear thus can become public goods as soon as somebody starts caring about them. And seemingly public goods like the exterior of my house or the color of my overalls can become extremely private goods as soon as other people stop caring about them. Moreover, every good can change its characteristics again and again; it can even turn from a public or private good to a public or private bad and vice versa, depending solely on the changes in this caring and uncaring. However, if this is so, no decision can be based on the classification of goods as private or public: in fact, if this were done, it would not only become necessary to ask virtually each individual person with respect to every single good, whether or not he happened to care about it, and if so, to what extent, in order to find out who might profit from what and should hence participate in its financing. It would also become necessary to monitor all changes in such evaluation continually, with the result being that no definite decision could ever be made regarding the production of anything, and all of us would be long dead as a consequence of such a nonsensical theory.

Second, even if all these difficulties were set aside, the conclusion reached by the public goods theorists is a glaring non sequitur, as Rothbard shows. For one thing, to come to the conclusion that the state has to provide public goods that otherwise would not be produced, one must smuggle a norm into one's chain of reasoning. Otherwise, from the statement that because of some special characteristics certain goods would not be produced, one could never reach the conclusion that these goods *should* be produced. With a norm required to justify their conclusion, the public goods theorists clearly have left the bounds of economics as a positive science and transgressed into the field of ethics. None of them, however, offers anything faintly resembling a clear system of ethics. Moreover, even the utilitarian reasoning employed by them is blatantly wrong. It might well be that it would be better to have these public goods than not to have them, though it should not be ignored that there is no a priori reason that even this must be so, as it is clearly possible, and even known to be a fact, that an anarchist exists who abhors any state action and would rather prefer not to have the so-called public goods at all if the alternative is to have them provided by the state. But even if the argument thus far is conceded, the conclusion drawn is still invalid. Since in order to finance the supposedly desirable goods resources must be withdrawn from possible alternative uses, the only relevant question is whether or not these alternative uses to which the resources could have been put are more valuable than the value that is attached to the public goods. The answer to this question is perfectly clear: In terms of consumer evaluations, the value of the public goods is relatively lower than that of the competing private goods because if one leaves the choice to the consumers, they evidently will prefer different ways of spending their money (otherwise no coercion would have been necessary in the first place). This proves that the resources used up for the provision of public goods are wasted in providing consumers with goods and services which are at best only of secondary importance. In short, even if one assumes that public goods exist, they will stand in competition to private ones. To find out if they are more urgently desired or not and to what extent, there is only one method: analyzing the profit and loss accounts of freely competing private enterprises. Hence, regarding the provision of law and order, the conclusion is reached that even if it is a public good, the only way to make sure that its production does not take place at the expense of more highly valued private goods and that the kind of law and order that is supplied is indeed the most highly valued one, law and order, like any other good, must be provided by a market of freely competing firms.[7] Rothbard sums it up as follows:

---

[7]On the specific problem of a free-market provision of law and order see Murray N. Rothbard, *For A New Liberty*, rev. ed. (New York: Macmillan, 1978), chap. 12; idem, *Power and Market* (Kansas City: Sheed Andrews and McMeel,

[The] view [that free-market action must be brought back into optimality by corrective State action] completely misconceives the way in which economic science asserts that free-market action is *ever* optimal. It is optimal, not from the standpoint of the personal ethical view of an economist, but from the standpoint of the free, voluntary actions of all participants and in satisfying the freely expressed needs of the consumers. Government interference, therefore, will necessarily and always move *away* from such an optimum.[8]

II.

Yet Rothbard is not content with having developed a full-fledged economic defense of a pure market system. Culminating in 1982 with his second *magnum opus, The Ethics of Liberty*, he proceeds to provide us with a comprehensive system of ethics to complement and complete the task of justifying laissez faire.

Mises, along with most social scientists, accepts the Humean verdict that reason is and can be no more than the slave of the passions. That is to say reason or science can do no more than inform us whether or not certain means are appropriate for bringing about certain results or ends. It is beyond the powers of reason, though, to teach us what ends we should choose or what ends can or cannot be justified. Ultimately, what ends are chosen is arbitrary from a scientific point of view; they are a matter of emotional whim. To be sure, Mises, like most other economists, is committed to a sort of utilitarianism. He favors life over death, health over sickness, abundance over poverty. And insofar as such ends, in particular the goal of achieving the highest possible standard of living for everyone, are

---

1977), chap. 1; also Gustave de Molinari, "The Production of Security," Occasional Paper No. 2 (1849; reprint, New York: Center for Libertarian Studies, 1977).

[8]Rothbard, *Man, Economy, and State,* p. 887; see on the above also Walter Block, "Public Goods and Externalities: The Case of Roads," *Journal of Libertarian Studies* 7, no. 1 (1983); Hoppe, *Eigentum, Anarchie, und Staat,* chap. 1; idem, *A Theory of Socialism and Capitalism,* chap. 10.

indeed shared by other people, as he assumes they generally are, as
an economic scientist Mises recommends that the correct course of
action to choose is a policy of laissez faire.[9] And doubtlessly, insofar
as economics can say this much, the case for laissez faire is a highly
important one. However, what if people do not consider prosperity to
be their ultimate goal? As Rothbard points out, economic analysis
only establishes that laissez faire will lead to higher standards of living in the long run. In the long run, however, one will be dead. Why
then would it not be quite reasonable for a person to argue that while
one perfectly agreed with everything economics had to say, one was
still more concerned about one's welfare in the short run and there,
clearly for no economist to deny, a privilege or a subsidy would be the
nicest thing? Moreover, why should social welfare in the long run be
one's first concern at all? Couldn't people advocate poverty, either as
an ultimate value in itself or as a means of bringing about some other
ultimate value such as equality? The answer, of course, is that such
proposals are made. However, whenever they are, not only has economics nothing to say, but according to Mises and other utilitarians
there is nothing more to be said at all, since no reasonable, scientific
way of choosing between conflicting values exists, as ultimately they
are all arbitrary.[10]

Against this position Rothbard takes sides with the philosophical
tradition of rational ethics claiming that reason is capable of yielding
cognitive value statements regarding man's proper ends.[11] More

---

[9]On this see Mises, *Human Action*, pp. 153–55.

[10]For Rothbard's Mises-critique see Murray N. Rothbard, *The Ethics of Liberty* (Atlantic Highlands, N.J.: Humanities Press, 1982), pp. 205–12.

[11]For various cognitivist approaches towards ethics see Kurt Baier, *The Moral Point of View: A Rational Basis of Ethics* (Ithaca, N.Y.: Cornell University Press, 1961); Marcus Singer, *Generalization in Ethics* (New York: A. Knopf, 1961); Paul Lorenzen, *Normative Logic and Ethics* (Mannheim: Bibliographisches Institut, 1969); Stephen Toulmin, *The Place of Reason in Ethics* (Cambridge: Cambridge University Press, 1970); Friedrich Kambartel, ed., *Praktische Philosophie and konstruktive Wissenschaftstheorie* (Frankfurt/M: Athenäum, 1974); Alan Gewirth, *Reason and Morality* (Chicago: University of Chicago Press, 1978).

specifically, he aligns himself with the natural law or natural rights tradition of philosophic thought which holds that universally valid norms can be discerned by means of reason as grounded in the very nature of man.[12] The *Ethics of Liberty* presents the full case for the libertarian property norms being precisely such rules.

Agreeing with Rothbard on the possibility of a rational ethic and, more specifically, on the fact that only a libertarian ethic can indeed be morally justified, I propose a different, non-natural-rights approach to establishing these two related claims. It has been a common quarrel with the natural rights position, even on the part of sympathetic readers, that the concept of human nature is far "too diffuse and varied to provide a determinate set of contents of natural law."[13] Furthermore, its description of rationality is equally ambiguous in that it does not seem to distinguish between the role of reason in establishing empirical laws of nature on the one hand and normative laws of human conduct on the other.[14] Avoiding such difficulties from the outset, I claim the following approach to be both more straightforward and more rigorous as regards its starting point as well as its methods of deriving its conclusions. Moreover, as I will explain later, my approach also seems to be more in line with Rothbard's when it comes to justifying the specific norms of libertarianism than the rather vague methodological prescriptions of the natural rights theorists.[15]

---

[12]On the natural rights tradition see John Wild, *Plato's Modern Enemies and the Theory of Natural Law* (Chicago: University of Chicago Press, 1953); Henry Veatch, *Rational Man: A Modern Interpretation of Aristotelian Ethics* (Bloomington, Ind.: Indiana University Press, 1962); idem, *For An Ontology of Morals: A Critique of Contemporary Ethical Theory* (Evanston, Ill.: Northwestern University Press, 1971); idem, *Human Rights: Fact or Fancy?* (Baton Rouge: Louisiana State University Press, 1985).

[13]Alan Gewirth, *Law, Action, and Morality*, in Rocco Porreco, ed., *Georgetown Symposium on Ethics: Essays in Honor of Henry B. Veatch* (New York: University Press of America, 1984), p. 73.

[14]See the discussion in Veatch, *Human Rights*, pp. 620–67.

[15]To disassociate myself from the natural rights tradition is not to say that I could not agree with its critical assessment of most of contemporary ethical theory—indeed I do agree with Veatch's complementary refutation of all desire—

Let me start by asking what is wrong with the position taken by Mises and so many others that the choice between values is ultimately arbitrary? First, it should be noted that such a position assumes that at least the question of whether or not value judgments or normative statements can be justified is itself a cognitive problem. If this were not assumed, Mises could not even say what he evidently says and claims to be the case. His position simply could not exist as an arguable intellectual position.

At first glance this does not seem to take one very far. Indeed, it still seems to be a far cry from this insight to the actual proof that normative statements can be justified and that it is only the libertarian ethic which can be defended. This impression is wrong, however, and there is already much more won here than might be suspected. The argument shows us that any truth claim, the claim connected with any proposition that it is true, objective or valid (all terms used synonymously here), is and must be raised and settled in the course of an argumentation. Since it cannot be disputed that this is so (one cannot communicate and argue that one cannot communicate and argue), and since it must be assumed that everyone knows what it means to claim something to be true (one cannot deny this statement without claiming its negation to be true), this very fact has been aptly called "the a priori of communication and argumentation."[16]

Arguing never consists of just free-floating propositions claiming to be true. Rather, argumentation is always an activity, too. However,

---

(teleological, utilitarian) ethics as well as all duty (deontological) ethics (ibid., chap. 1). Nor do I claim that it is impossible to interpret my approach as falling in a "rightly conceived" natural rights tradition after all (see also footnote 17 below). What is claimed, though, is that the following approach is clearly out of line with what the natural rights approach has actually come to be, and that it owes nothing to this tradition as it stands.

[16]See K.O. Apel, "Das Apriori der Kommunikationsgemeinschaft und die Grundlagen der Ethik," in idem, *Transformation der Philosophie* (Frankfurt/M.: Suhrkamp, 1973), vol. 2; also Jürgen Habermas, "Wahrheitstheorien," in Helmut Fahrenbach, ed., *Wirklichkeit und Reflexion* (Pfullingen: Neske, 1974); idem, *Theorie des kommunikativen Handelns* (Frankfurt/M.: Suhrkamp, 1981), vol. 1, pp. 44ff.; idem, *Moralbewusstsein und kommunikatives Handeln* (Frankfurt/M.: Suhrkamp, 1983).

given that truth claims are raised and settled in argumentation and that argumentation, aside from whatever it is that is said in its course, is a practical affair, it follows that intersubjectively meaningful norms must exist—precisely those which make some action an argumentation—which have a special cognitive status in that they are the practical preconditions of objectivity and truth.

Hence, one reaches the conclusion that norms must indeed be assumed to be justifiable as valid. It is simply impossible to argue otherwise, because the ability to argue so would in fact already presuppose the validity of those norms which underlie any argumentation whatever. In contradistinction to the natural rights theorists, though, one sees that the answer to the question of which ends can or cannot be justified is not to be deduced from the wider concept of human nature but from the narrower one of argumentation.[17] With this, then, the peculiar role of reason in determining the contents of ethics can be given a precise description. Contrary to the role of reason in establishing empirical laws of nature, in determining moral laws reason can claim to yield results which can be shown to be valid a priori. It only makes explicit what is already implied in the concept of argumentation itself, and in analyzing any actual norm proposal its task is merely confined to analyzing whether or not it is logically consistent with the very ethics which the proponent must presuppose as valid insofar as he is able to make his proposal at all.[18]

---

[17]Of course, since the capability of argumentation is an essential feature of human nature—one could not even say anything about the latter without the former—it could also be argued that norms which cannot be defended effectively in the course of argumentation are also incompatible with human nature.

[18]Methodologically this approach exhibits a close resemblance to what Gewirth has described as the "dialectically necessary method" (*Reason and Morality*, pp. 42–47)—a method of a priori reasoning modelled after the Kantian idea of transcendental deductions. Unfortunately though, in his important study Gewirth chooses the wrong starting point for his analyses. He attempts to derive an ethical system not from the concept of argumentation but from that of action. However, surely this cannot work, because from the correctly stated fact that in action an agent must, by necessity, presuppose the existence of certain values or goods, it does not follow that such goods are universalizable and hence should

But what are the strictures of the ethics-implied-in-argumentation whose validity cannot be disputed because disputing it would implicitly presuppose it? Quite normally it has been observed that argumentation implies that a proposition claims universal acceptability or should it be a norm proposal, that it be "universalizable." Applied to norm proposals, this is the idea, as formulated in the Golden Rule of ethics or in the Kantian Categorical Imperative, that only those norms can be justified that can be formulated as general principles which without exception are valid for everyone.[19] Indeed as it is implied in argumentation that everyone who can understand an argument must in principle be able to be convinced by it simply because of its argumentative force, the universalization principle of ethics can now be understood and explained as implied in the wider a priori of communication and argumentation.[20] Yet the universalization principle only provides one with a purely formal criterion for morality. To be sure, checked against this criterion, all proposals for valid norms which would specify different rules for different classes of people

---

be respected by others as the agent's goods by right. Gewirth might have noticed the ethical "neutrality" of action had he not been painfully unaware of the existence of the well-established "pure science of action" or "praxeology" as espoused by Mises. Incidentally, an awareness of praxeology might also have spared him from many mistakes that derive from his faulty distinction between "basic," "additive" and "non-subtractive" goods (ibid., pp. 53–58). Rather, the idea of truth or of universalizable rights or goods only emerges with argumentation as a special subclass of actions, but not with action as such, as is clearly revealed by the fact that Gewirth, too, is not engaged simply in action but more specifically in argumentation when he wants to convince us of the necessary truth of his ethical system. However, with argumentation being recognized as the one and only appropriate starting point for the dialectically necessary method, a libertarian (i.e., non-Gewirthian) ethic follows, as will be seen.

On the faultiness of Gewirth's attempt to derive universalizable rights from the notion of action see also the perceptive remarks by Alasdair MacIntyre, *After Virtue: A Study in Moral Theory* (London: Duckworth, 1981), pp. 64–65; Habermas, *Moralbewusstsein und kommunikatives Handeln*, pp. 110–11; and Veatch, *Human Rights*, pp. 159–60.

[19]See the works cited in footnotes 11 and 12 above.

[20]See the works cited in footnote 16 above.

could be shown to have no legitimate claim of being universally acceptable as fair norms, unless the distinction between different classes of people were such that it implied no discrimination but could instead be accepted as founded in the nature of things again by everybody. However, while some norms might not pass the test of universalization, if enough attention were paid to their formulation, the most ridiculous norms (and what is more relevant even openly incompatible norms) could easily and equally well pass it. For example, "everybody must get drunk on Sundays or else he will be fined" or "anyone who drinks any alcohol will be punished" are both rules that do not allow discrimination among groups of people and thus could both claim to satisfy the condition of universalization.

Clearly then, the universalization principle alone would not provide one with any positive set of norms that could be demonstrated to be justified. However, there are other positive norms implied in argumentation apart from the universalization principle. In order to recognize them, it is only necessary to call to mind three interrelated facts. First, that argumentation is not only a cognitive but also a practical affair. Second, that argumentation, as a form of action, implies the use of the scarce resource of one's body. And third, that argumentation is a conflict-free way of interacting—not in the sense that there is always agreement on the things said, but in the sense that as long as argumentation is in progress, it is always possible to agree at least on the fact that there is disagreement about the validity of what has been said. This is only to say that a mutual recognition of each person's exclusive control over his own body must be assumed to exist as long as there is argumentation (note again that it is impossible to deny this and claim this denial to be true without implicitly having to admit its truth).

Hence, one would have to conclude that the norm implied in argumentation is that everybody has the right to exclusively control his own body as his instrument of action and cognition. It is only as long as there is at least an implicit recognition of each individual's property right in his or her own body that argumentation can take place.[21]

---

[21]It might be noted here that only because scarcity exists is there even a problem of formulating moral laws; insofar as goods are superabundant (free

The Economics and Ethics of Private Property

Only if this right is recognized is it possible for someone to agree to what has been said in an argument and can what has been said be validated, or is it possible to say no and to agree only on the fact that there is disagreement. Indeed, anyone who would try to justify any norm would have to presuppose the property right in one's body as a valid norm, simply in order to say this is what I claim to be true and objective. Any person who would try to dispute the property right in one's own body would become caught up in a contradiction.

Thus it can be stated that whenever a person claims that some statement can be justified, he at least implicitly assumes the following norm to be justified: "nobody has the right to uninvitedly aggress against the body of any other person and thus delimit or restrict anyone's control over his own body." This rule is implied in the concept of argumentative justification. Justifying means justifying without having to rely on coercion. In fact, if one formulated the opposite of this rule (i.e., everybody has the right to uninvitedly aggress against other people [a rule, by the way, that would formally pass the universalization test!]), then it is easy to see that this rule is not and never could be defended in argumentation. To do so would presuppose the validity of precisely its opposite (i.e., the aforementioned principle of nonaggression).

It may seem that with this justification of a property norm regarding a person's body not much is won, as conflicts over bodies, for whose possible avoidance the nonaggression principle formulates a

---

goods), no conflict over the use of goods is possible and no action-coordination is needed. Hence, it follows that any ethic, correctly conceived, must be formulated as a theory of property, i.e., a theory of the assignment of rights of exclusive control over scarce means, for only then does it become possible to avoid otherwise inescapable and unresolvable conflicts. Unfortunately, moral philosophers in their widespread ignorance of economics have hardly ever seen this clearly enough. Rather, like Veatch (*Human Rights*, p. 170), for instance, they seem to think that they can do without a precise definition of property and property rights only to then necessarily wind up in a sea of vagueness and ad-hoceries.

On human rights as property rights see also Rothbard, *The Ethics of Liberty*, chap. 15.

universally justifiable solution, make up only a small portion of all possible conflicts. However, this impression is not correct. To be sure, people do not live on air and love alone. They need a smaller or greater number of other goods as well simply to survive—and only he who survives can sustain argumentation, let alone lead a comfortable life. With respect to all of these other goods norms are needed too, as it could come to conflicting evaluations regarding their use. In fact, any other norm now must be logically compatible with the non-aggression principle in order to be justified and, *mutatis mutandis*, every norm that could be shown to be incompatible with this principle would have to be considered invalid. In addition, as the things for which norms have to be formulated are scarce goods—just as a person's body is a scarce good—and as it is only necessary to formulate norms at all because goods are scarce and not because they are particular kinds of scarce goods, the specifications of the nonaggression principle, conceived as a special property norm referring to a specific kind of good, must already contain those of a general theory of property.

I will first state this general theory of property as a set of rulings applicable to all goods, with the goal of helping to avoid all possible conflicts by means of uniform principles, and I will then demonstrate how this general theory is implied in the nonaggression principle. According to the nonaggression principle a person can do with his body whatever he wants as long as he does not thereby aggress against another person's body. Thus, that person could also make use of other scarce means, just as one makes use of one's own body, provided these other things have not already been appropriated by someone else but are still in a natural unowned state. As soon as scarce resources are visibly appropriated—as soon as somebody "mixes his labor" with them, as John Locke phrased it,[22] and there are objective traces of this—then property (the right of exclusive control), can only be acquired by a contractual transfer of property titles from a previous to a later owner, and any attempt to unilaterally

---

[22]John Locke, *Two Treatises on Government*, ed. Peter Laslett (Cambridge: Cambridge University Press, 1970), esp. vols. II, V.

delimit this exclusive control of previous owners or any unsolicited
transformation of the physical characteristics of the scarce means in
question is, in strict analogy with aggressions against other people's
bodies, an unjustifiable action.[23]

The compatibility of this principle with that of nonaggression can
be demonstrated by means of an *argumentum a contrario*. First, it
should be noted that if no one had the right to acquire and control
anything except his own body (a rule that would pass the formal universalization test), then we would all cease to exist and the problem
of the justification of normative statements simply would not exist.
The existence of this problem is only possible because we are alive,
and our existence is due to the fact that we do not, indeed cannot
accept a norm outlawing property in other scarce goods next to and
in addition to that of one's physical body. Hence, the right to acquire
such goods must be assumed to exist. Now if this is so and if one does
not have the right to acquire such rights of exclusive control over
unused, nature-given things through one's own work (by doing something with things with which no one else has ever done anything
before), and if other people have the right to disregard one's ownership claim to things which they did not work on or put to some particular use before, then this is only possible if one can acquire property titles not through labor (i.e., by establishing some objective,
intersubjectively controllable link between a particular person and a
particular scarce resource), but simply by verbal declaration, by
decree.[24] However, the position of property titles being acquired

----

[23]On the nonaggression principle and the principle of original appropriation
see also Rothbard, *For A New Liberty*, chap. 2; idem, *The Ethics of Liberty*, chaps.
6–8.

[24]This is the position taken by Jean-Jacques Rousseau, when he asks us to
resist attempts to privately appropriate nature-given resources by, for example,
fencing them in. He says in his famous dictum; "Beware of listening to this
impostor, you are undone if you once forget that the fruits of the earth belong
to us all, and the earth itself to nobody" ("Discourse upon the Origin and
Foundation of Inequality Among Mankind," in Jean-Jacques Rousseau, *The
Social Contract and Discourses*, ed. G.D.H. Cole [New York: 1950], p. 235).
However, to argue so is only possible if it is assumed that property claims can be
justified by decree. How else could "all" (even those who never did anything

through declaration is incompatible with the above justified non-aggression principle regarding bodies. For one thing, if one could indeed appropriate property by decree, this would imply that it would also be possible for one to simply declare another person's body to be one's own. Clearly enough, this would conflict with the ruling of the nonaggression principle which makes a sharp distinction between one's own body and the body of another person. Furthermore, this distinction can only be made in such a clear-cut and unambiguous way because for bodies, as for anything else, the separation between "mine and yours" is not based on verbal declarations, but on action. The observation is based on some particular scarce resource that had in fact—for everyone to see and verify because objective indicators for this existed—been made an expression or materialization of one's own will or, as the case may be, of somebody else's will. More importantly, to say that property could be acquired not through action but through a declaration would involve an obvious practical contradiction because nobody could say and declare so unless his right of exclusive control over his body as his own instrument of saying anything was in fact already presupposed, in spite of what was actually said.

As I intimated earlier, this defense of private property is essentially also Rothbard's. In spite of his formal allegiance to the natural rights tradition, Rothbard, in what I consider his most crucial argument in defense of a private property ethic, not only chooses essentially the same starting point—argumentation—but also gives a justification by means of a priori reasoning almost identical to the one just developed. To prove the point I can do no better than simply quote:

> Now, *any* person participating in any sort of discussion, including one on values, is, by virtue of so participating, alive and affirming life. For if he were *really* opposed to life, he would have no business continuing to be alive. Hence, the *supposed* opponent of life is really affirming it in the very process of discussion, and hence the

---

with the resources in question) or "nobody" (not even those who made use of it) own something unless property claims were founded by mere decree?

preservation and furtherance of one's life takes on the stature of an incontestable axiom.[25]

III.

So far it has been demonstrated that the right of original appropriation through actions is compatible with and implied by the non-aggression principle as the logically necessary presupposition of argumentation. Indirectly, of course, it has also been demonstrated that any rule specifying different rights cannot be justified. Before entering a more detailed analysis, though, of *why* it is that any alternative ethic is indefensible, a discussion which should throw some additional light on the importance of some of the stipulations of the libertarian theory of property, a few remarks about what is and what is not implied by classifying these latter norms as justified is in order.

In making this argument, one would not have to claim to have derived an "ought" from an "is." In fact, one can readily subscribe to the almost generally accepted view that the gulf between "ought" and "is" is logically unbridgeable.[26] Rather, classifying the rulings of the libertarian theory of property in this way is a purely cognitive matter. It no more follows from the classification of the libertarian ethic as "fair" or "just" that one ought to act according to it, than it follows from the concept of validity or truth that one should always strive for it. To say that it is just also does not preclude the possibility of people proposing or even enforcing rules that are incompatible with this principle. As a matter of fact, the situation with respect to norms is

---

[25]Rothbard, *The Ethics of Liberty*, p. 32; on the method of a priori reasoning employed in the above argument see also, idem, *Individualism and the Philosophy of the Social Sciences* (San Francisco: Cato Institute, 1979); Hans-Hermann Hoppe, *Kritik der kausalwissenschaftlichen sozialforschung. Untersuchungen zur Grundlegung von Soziologie und Ökonomie* (Opladen: Westdeutscher Verlag 1983); idem, "Is Research Based on Causal Scientific Principles Possible in the Social Sciences? *Ratio* (1983); supra chap. 7; idem, *A Theory of Socialism and Capitalism*, chap. 6.

[26]On the problem of deriving "ought" from "is" see W.D. Hudson, ed., *The Is-Ought Question* (London: Macmillan 1969).

very similar to that in other disciplines of scientific inquiry. The fact, for instance, that certain empirical statements are justified or justifiable and others are not does not imply that everybody only defends objective, valid statements. On the contrary, people can be wrong, even intentionally. But the distinction between objective and subjective, between true and false, does not lose any of its significance because of this. Instead, people who would do so would have to be classified as either uninformed or intentionally lying. The case is similar with respect to norms. Of course there are people, lots of them, who do not propagate or enforce norms that can be classified as valid according to the meaning of justification I have given above. However, the distinction between justifiable and nonjustifiable norms does not dissolve because of this, just as that between objective and subjective statement does not crumble because of the existence of uninformed or lying people. Rather, and accordingly, those people who would propagate and enforce such different, invalid norms would again have to be classified as uninformed or dishonest, insofar as one had made it clear to them that their alternative norm proposals or enforcements cannot and never will be justifiable in argumentation. There would be even more justification for doing so in the moral case than in the empirical one, since the validity of the nonaggression principle and that of the principle of original appropriation through action as its logically necessary corollary must be considered to be even more basic than any kind of valid or true statements. For what is valid or true has to be defined as that upon which everyone—acting according to this principle—can possibly agree. As I have just shown, at least the implicit acceptance of these rules is the necessary prerequisite to being able to be alive and argue at all.

Why is it then that other nonlibertarian property theories fail to be justifiable? First, it should be noted, as will become clear shortly, that all of the practiced alternatives to libertarianism and most of the theoretically proposed nonlibertarian ethics would not even pass the first formal universalization test and would fail for this fact alone! All these versions contain norms within their framework of legal rules which have the form, "some people do, and some people do not." However, such rules that specify different rights or obligations for different classes of people have no chance of being accepted as fair by every potential participant in an argument for simply formal reasons. Unless the distinction made between different classes of people happens to be such that it is acceptable to both sides as grounded in the nature of things, such rules would not be acceptable because they would imply that one group is awarded legal privileges at the expense of complementary discriminations against another group. Some people, either those who are allowed to do something or those who are not, would not be able to agree that these were fair rules.[27] Since most alternative ethical proposals, as practiced or preached, have to rely on the enforcement of rules such as "some people have the obligation to pay taxes, and others have the right to consume them," or "some people know what is good for you and are allowed to help you get these alleged blessings even if you do not want them, but you are not allowed to know what is good for them and help them accordingly," or "some people have the right to determine who has too much of something and who too little, and others have the obligation to accept that," or even more plainly, "the computer industry must pay to subsidize the farmers, the employed for the unemployed, the ones without kids for those with kids," or vice versa. They all can be discarded as serious contenders to the claim of being a valid theory of norms qua property norm, because they all indicate by their very formulation that they are not universalizable.

What is wrong with a nonlibertarian ethic if this is resolved and there is indeed a theory formulated that contains exclusively universalizable norms of the type "nobody is allowed to" or "everybody can?" Even then the validity of such proposals could never hope to be proven—not because of formal reasons but because of their material specifications. Indeed, while the alternatives that can be refuted easily as regards their claim to moral validity on simple formal grounds can at least be practiced, the application of those more sophisticated versions that would pass the universalization test would prove for material reasons to be fatal: even if one tried to, they simply could never be implemented.

---

[27]See Rothbard, *The Ethics of Liberty*, p. 45.

There are two related specifications in the libertarian property theory with at least one of which any alternative theory comes into conflict. According to the libertarian ethic, the first such specification is that aggression is defined as an invasion of the *physical* integrity of other people's property.[28] There are popular attempts to define it as an invasion of the *value* or *psychic integrity* of other people's property. Conservatism, for instance, aims at preserving a given distribution of wealth and values and attempts to bring those forces which could change the status quo under control by means of price controls, regulations, and behavioral controls. Clearly, in order to do so property rights to the value of things must be assumed to be justifiable, and an invasion of values, *mutatis mutandis*, would have to be classified as unjustifiable aggression. Not only does conservatism use this idea of property and aggression; redistributive socialism does, too. Property rights to values must be assumed to be legitimate when redistributive socialism allows me, for instance, to demand compensation from people whose chances or opportunities negatively affect mine. The same is true when compensation for committing psychological, or "structural violence" is requested.[29] In order to be able to ask for

---

[28]On the importance of the definition of aggression as physical aggression see also Rothbard, ibid., chaps. 8–9; idem, "Law, Property Rights and Air Pollution," *Cato Journal* (Spring, 1982).

[29]On the idea of structural violence as distinct from physical violence see Dieter Senghass, ed., *Imperialismus und strukturelle Gewalt* (Frankfurt/M.: Suhrkamp, 1972). The idea of defining aggression as an invasion of property *values* also underlies both the theories of justice of John Rawls and Robert Nozick, however different these two authors may have appeared to be to many commentators. For how could Rawls think of his so-called difference-principle ("Social and economic inequalities are to be arranged so that they are reasonably expected to be to everyone's—including the least advantaged ones—advantage or benefit," John Rawls, *A Theory of Justice* [Cambridge, Mass.: Harvard University Press 1971], pp. 60–83, 75ff.), as justified unless he believes that simply by increasing his relative wealth a more fortunate person commits an aggression, and a less fortunate one then has a valid claim against the more fortunate person only because the former's relative position in terms of value has deteriorated?! And how could Robert Nozick claim it to be justified for a "dominant protection agency" to outlaw competitors, regardless of what their actions would have been like? (Robert Nozick, *Anarchy, State, and Utopia* [New York:

such compensation, what one must have done, namely affect my opportunities, my psychic integrity, or my feeling of what is owed to me, would have to be classified as an aggressive act.

Why is this idea of protecting the value of property unjustifiable? First, while every person, at least in principle, can have full control over whether or not his actions cause the *physical* characteristics of something to change and hence can also have full control over whether or not those actions are justifiable, control over whether or not one's actions affect the *value* of somebody else's property does not rest with the acting person but rather with other people and their subjective evaluations. Thus, no one could determine *ex ante* if his actions would be qualified as justifiable or unjustifiable. One would first have to interrogate the whole population to make sure that one's planned actions would not change another person's evaluations regarding his own property. Even then nobody could act until universal agreement was reached on who is supposed to do what with what, and at which point in time. Clearly, because of all the practical problems involved, everyone would be long dead and nobody could argue any longer, well before agreement could be reached.[30] Even more decisively, this position regarding property and aggression could not even be effectively *argued* because arguing in favor of any norm implies that there is conflict over the use of some scarce resources; otherwise, there would simply be no need for discussion.

Basic Books, 1974], pp. 55f.) Or how could he believe it to be morally correct to outlaw so-called nonproductive exchanges, i.e., exchanges where one party would be better off if the other one did not exist at all or at least had nothing to do with it (as, for instance, in the case of a blackmailee and a blackmailer), regardless of whether or not such an exchange involved physical invasion of any kind (ibid., pp. 83–86) unless he thought that the right to have the integrity of one's property values (rather than its physical integrity) preserved existed? For a devastating critique of Nozick's theory in particular see Rothbard, *The Ethics of Liberty*, chap. 29; on the fallacious use of the indifference curve analysis, employed both by Rawls and Nozick, idem, *Toward a Reconstruction of Utility and Welfare Economics* (New York: Center for Libertarian Studies, Occasional Paper Series, No. 3, 1977).

[30]See also Rothbard, *The Ethics of Liberty*, p. 46.

However, in order to argue that there is a way out of such conflicts it must be presupposed that actions must be allowed *prior* to any actual agreement or disagreement because if they were not, one could not even argue so. Yet if one can do this, and insofar as it exists as an argued intellectual position the position under scrutiny must assume that one can, then this is only possible because of the existence of *objective* borders of property—borders which anyone can recognize as such on his own without having to agree first with anyone else with respect to his system of values and evaluations. Such a value-protecting ethic, too, in spite of what it says, must in fact presuppose the existence of objective property borders rather than of borders determined by subjective evaluations, if only in order to have any surviving persons who can make its moral proposals.

The idea of protecting value instead of physical integrity also fails for a second related reason. Evidently, one's value, for example on the labor or marriage market, can be and indeed is affected by other people's physical integrity or degree of physical integrity. Thus, if one wanted property values to be protected, one would have to allow physical aggression against people. However, it is only because of the very fact that a person's borders—that is the borders of a person's property in his own body as his domain of exclusive control that another person is not allowed to cross unless he wishes to become an aggressor—are *physical* borders (intersubjectively ascertainable, and not just subjectively fancied borders) that everyone can agree on anything independently (and agreement means agreement among independent decision-making units!). Only because the protected borders of property are objective (i.e., fixed and recognizable as fixed prior to any conventional agreement), can there be argumentation and possibly agreement of and between independent decision-making units. Nobody could argue in favor of a property system defining borders of property in subjective, evaluative terms because simply to be able to say so presupposes that, contrary to what theory says, one must in fact be a physically independent unit saying it.

The situation is no less dire for alternative ethical proposals when one turns to the second essential specification of the rulings of the libertarian theory of property. The basic norms of libertarianism are characterized not only by the fact that property and aggression are defined in physical terms; it is of no less importance that property is defined as private, individualized property and that the meaning of original appropriation, which evidently implies making a distinction between prior and later, has been specified. It is with this additional specification as well that alternative, nonlibertarian ethics come into conflict. Instead of recognizing the vital importance of the prior-later distinction in deciding between conflicting property claims, they propose norms which in effect state that priority is irrelevant for making such a decision and that late-comers have as much of a right to ownership as first-comers. Clearly, this idea is involved when redistributive socialism makes the natural owners of wealth and/or their heirs pay a tax so that the unfortunate late-comers can participate in its consumption. It is also involved when the owner of a natural resource is forced to reduce (or increase) its present exploitation in the interest of posterity. Both times it only makes sense to do what one does when it is assumed that the person accumulating wealth first, or using the natural resource first, has thereby committed an aggression against some late-comers. If they had done nothing wrong, then the late-comers should have no such claim against them.[31]

What is wrong with this idea of dropping the prior-later distinction as morally irrelevant? First, if the late-comers (those who did not do something with some scarce goods), indeed had as much of a right to them as the first-comers (those who did do something with the scarce goods), then nobody would ever be allowed to do anything with anything, as one would have to have all of the late-comers' consent prior to doing what one wanted to do. Indeed, as posterity would include one's children's children—people who come so late that one could not possibly ask them—to advocate a legal system that does not make use of the prior-later distinction as part of its underlying property theory is simply absurd because it implies advocating death but must presuppose life to advocate anything. Neither we, nor our

[31]For an awkward philosophical attempt to justify a late-comer ethic see James P. Sterba, *The Demands of Justice* (Notre Dame, Ind.: Notre Dame University Press, 1980), esp. pp. 58ff., 137ff.; on the absurdity of such an ethic see Rothbard, *Man, Economy, and State*, p. 427.

forefathers, nor our progeny could, do, or will survive and say or argue anything if one followed this rule. In order for any person—past, present or future—to argue anything it must be possible to survive now. Nobody can wait and suspend acting until everyone of an indeterminate class of late-comers happens to come around and agree to what one wants to do. Rather, insofar as a person finds himself alone, he must be able to act, to use, to produce, and to consume goods straightaway, prior to any agreement with people who are simply not around (and perhaps never will be). Insofar as a person finds himself in the company of others and there is conflict over how to use a given scarce resource, he must be able to resolve the problem at a definite point in time with a definite number of people instead of having to wait unspecified periods of time for unspecified numbers of people. Simply in order to survive, then, which is a prerequisite to arguing in favor or against anything, property rights cannot be conceived of as being timeless and nonspecific regarding the number of people concerned. Rather, they must be thought of as originating through acting at definite points in time for definite acting individuals.[32]

Furthermore, the idea of abandoning the prior-later distinction would simply be incompatible with the nonaggression principle as the practical foundation of argumentation. To argue and possibly agree with someone (if only on the fact that there is disagreement) means to recognize the prior right of exclusive control over one's own body. Otherwise, it would be impossible for anybody to say anything at a definite point in time and for someone else to be able to reply, for neither the first nor the second speaker would be a physically independent decision-making unit anymore at any time. Eliminating the

---

[32]It should be noted here that only if property rights are conceptualized as private property rights originating in time does it then become possible to make contracts. Clearly enough, contracts are agreements between enumerable physically independent units which are based on the mutual recognition of each contractor's private ownership claims to things acquired prior in time to the agreement and which then concern the transfer of property titles to definite things from a definite prior to a definite later owner. No such thing as contracts could conceivably exist in the framework of a late-comer ethic!

prior-later distinction, then, is tantamount to eliminating the possibility of arguing and reaching agreement. However, as one cannot argue that there is no possibility for discussion without the prior control of every person over his own body being recognized and accepted as fair, a late-comer ethic that does not make this distinction could never be agreed upon by anyone. Simply *saying* that it could be would imply a contradiction, for one's being able to say so would presuppose one's existence for an independent decision-making unit at a definite point in time.

Hence, one is forced to conclude that the libertarian ethic not only can be justified and justified by means of a priori reasoning, but that no alternative ethic can be defended argumentatively.

12

The Justice of
Economic Efficiency

The central problem of political economy is how to organize society so as to promote the production of wealth. The central problem of political philosophy is how to arrange society so as to make it a just social order.

The first question regards matters of efficiency: What means are appropriate for achieving a specific result, in this case, wealth?

The second question falls outside the realm of the so-called positive sciences. It asks whether or not the goal political economy assumes to be given can be justified as a goal, and whether or not, then, the means which political economy recommends can be regarded as efficient means for just ends.

In the following I present an a priori justification for the thesis that those means recommended by political economy are indeed efficient means for just ends.

I begin by describing the means recommended by political economy and explain the systematic reasons the production of wealth attained by adopting them is greater than that produced by choosing any other means. Since my main task is to demonstrate the justice of

[Reprinted from the *Austrian Economics Newsletter* (Winter, 1988). Also reprinted in volume 3 of *Austrian Economics*, edited by Stephen Littlechild (London: Edward Elgar, 1990).]

these means of producing wealth, my description and explanation of economic efficiency will be brief.

Political economy begins with the recognition of scarcity. It is only because we do not live in the Garden of Eden that we are concerned about the problem of economic efficiency. According to political economy, the most efficient means of alleviating, if not overcoming, scarcity is the institution of private property. The rules underlying this institution have been correctly identified for the most part by John Locke. They are as follows:

Every person owns his own body as well as all scarce goods which he puts to use with the help of his body before anyone else does. This ownership implies the right to employ these scarce goods however one sees fit so long as in so doing one does not aggress against anyone else's property, i.e., so long as one does not uninvitedly change the physical integrity of another's property or delimit another's control over it without his consent. In particular, once a good has first been appropriated or homesteaded by mixing one's labor with it (Locke's phrase) then ownership in it can only be acquired by means of a contractual transfer of property title from a previous to a later owner.

The reason this institution leads to the greatest possible production of wealth is straightforward. Any deviation from this set of rules implies, by definition, a redistribution of property titles (and hence of income) away from user-producers and contractors of goods and onto non-user-producers and noncontractors. As a consequence, any such deviation implies that there will be relatively less original appropriation of resources whose scarcity is realized, there will be less production of new goods, less maintenance of existing goods, and less mutually beneficial contracting and trading. This naturally implies a lower standard of living in terms of exchangeable goods and services. Further, the provision that only the first user (not a later one) of a good acquires ownership assures that productive efforts will be as high as possible *at all times*. Further, the provision that only the physical integrity of property (not property values) be protected guarantees that every owner will undertake the greatest possible *value*-productive efforts, i.e., efforts to promote favorable changes in property values and to prevent or counter any unfavorable changes in property values (as they might result from another person's actions regarding his property). Thus, any deviation from these rules also implies reduced levels of value productive efforts at all times.

Now on to my main task of demonstrating that the institution of private property as just characterized is just—in fact, that only this institution is just and that any deviation from it is not only economically inefficient but unethical as well.

First, however, let me clarify an essential similarity between the problem facing political economy and that facing political philosophy—a similarity that political philosophers in their widespread ignorance of economics generally overlook only to wind up in endless *ad hoceries*. The recognition of scarcity is not only the starting point for political economy; it is the starting point of political philosophy as well. Obviously, if their were a superabundance of goods, no economic problem whatsoever would exist. With a superabundance of goods such that my present use of them would neither reduce my own future supply nor the present or future supply of them for any other person, ethical problems of right or wrong, just or unjust would not emerge either since no conflict over the use of such goods could possibly arise. Only insofar as goods are scarce are economics and ethics required. In the same way, just as the answer to the problem of political economy must be formulated in terms of rules constraining the possible uses of resources qua scarce resources, political philosophy too must answer in terms of property rights. In order to avoid inescapable conflicts, it must formulate a set of rules assigning rights of exclusive control over scarce goods. (Note that even in the Garden of Eden, a person's body, the space occupied by that body, and time would still be scarce and to that extent political economy and philosophy would still have a task, however limited, to fulfill.)

Now to the actual proof of the thesis that out of the infinitely conceivable ways of assigning rights of exclusive ownership to people, only the previously described rules of private property are actually justifiable. I will present my argument in a step-by-step fashion.

First, while scarcity is a necessary condition for the emergence of the problem of political philosophy, it is not sufficient. For obviously, we could have conflicts regarding the use of scarce resources with, let us say, an elephant or a mosquito, yet we would not consider it possible to resolve these conflicts by means of proposing property norms. In such cases, the avoidance of possible conflicts is merely a technological, not an ethical, problem. For it to become an ethical problem, it is also necessary that the conflicting actors be capable, in principle, of argumentation. In fact, this is undeniably so because we are also engaged in argumentation here. Denying that political philosophy presupposes argumentation is contradictory, as the very denial would itself be an argument. Only with argumentation does the idea of validity and truth emerge and by no means only the idea of truth in ethical matters but of truth in general. Only within argumentation are truth claims of any kind made, and it is only in the course of argumentation that truth claims are decided. This proposition, it turns out, is itself undeniably true: one cannot argue that one cannot argue, and one cannot dispute knowing what it means to make a truth claim without implicitly claiming at least the very negation of this proposition to be true. My very first step in the following chain of reasoning, then, has been called "the a priori of argumentation" by such philosophers as Jürgen Habermas and K.O. Apel.[1]

In the same way as it is undeniably true that ethics requires argumentation, it is also undeniably true that any argument requires an arguing person. Arguing does not consist of free-floating propositions. It is an activity. If aside from whatever is said in its course, however, argumentation is also a practical affair and if argumentation is the presupposition of truth-claiming and possibly true propositions, then it follows that intersubjectively meaningful norms must exist—namely those which make an action argumentation—which must have a special cognitive status in that they are the practical preconditions of truth. Once more, this is true a priori, so that anyone, such as an empiricist-positivist-emotivist who denied the possibility of a rational ethics and who declared the acceptance or rejection of norms an arbitrary affair would invariably get caught in a practical

---

[1]K.O. Apel, "Das Apriori der Kommunikationsgemeinschaft und die Grundlagen der Ethik," in idem, *Transformation der Philosophie* (Frankfurt/M., 1973), vol. II; Jürgen Habermas, *Moralbewusstsein und kommunikatives Handeln* (Frankfurt/M. 1983).

contradiction. For contrary to what he would say, he would in fact have to presuppose the norms which underlie any argumentation whatsoever as valid simply in order to say anything at all.

With this step I lose, once and for all, the company of philosophers like Habermas and Apel.[2] Yet, as will become clear immediately, it is directly implied in the previous step. That Habermas and Apel are unable to take this step is, I submit, due to the fact that they, too, suffer, as do many other philosophers, from a complete ignorance of economics, and a corresponding blindness towards the fact of scarcity. The step is simply this: To recognize that argumentation is a form of action and does not consist of free-floating sounds implies the recognition of the fact that all argumentation requires that a person have exclusive control over the scarce resource of his body. As long as there is argumentation, there is mutual recognition of each other's property right in his own body. It is this recognition of each other's exclusive control over one's own body, presupposed by all argumentation, which explains the unique feature of verbal communication that while one may disagree about what has been said, it is still possible to agree at least on the fact that there is such disagreement. Again, such a property right in one's own body must be said to be justified a priori, for anyone who would try to justify any norm whatsoever would already have to presuppose the exclusive right to control over his body as a valid norm simply in order to say "I propose such and such." Further, any person who tried to dispute the property right in his body would become caught up in a practical contradiction since arguing in this way would already imply acceptance of the very norm which he was disputing. He would not even open his mouth if he were right.

The final argument extends the idea of private property as justified, and justified a priori, from the very prototype of a scarce good (a person's body) to other goods. It consists of two parts. I first

---

[2]Apel and Habermas are essentially silent on the all-decisive question of what ethical prescription actually follows from the recognition of the "a priori of argumentation." However, there are remarks indicating that they both seem to believe some sort of participatory social democracy is implied in this a priori. The following explains why nothing could be further from the truth.

demonstrate that argumentation, and argumentative justification of anything, presupposes not only the right to exclusively control one's body but the right to control other scarce goods as well, for if no one had the right to control anything except his own body, then we would all cease to exist and the problem of justifying norms—as well as all other human problems—simply would not exist. We do not live on air alone; hence, simply by virtue of the fact of being alive, property rights to other things must be presupposed to be valid, too. No one who is alive could argue otherwise.

The second part of the argument demonstrates that only the Lockean idea of establishing property claims through homesteading is a just principle of property acquisition. The proof employs a simple *argumentum a contrario*: If a person did not acquire the right of exclusive control over other, nature-given goods by his own work, that is, if other people, who had not previously used such goods, had the right to dispute the homesteader's ownership claim, then this would only be possible if one would acquire property titles not through labor, i.e., by establishing some objective link between a particular person and a particular scarce resource, but simply by means of verbal declaration. This solution—apart from the obvious fact that it would not even qualify as a solution in a purely technical sense in that it would not provide a basis for deciding between rivaling declarative claims—is incompatible with the already justified ownership of a person over his body. For if one could indeed appropriate property by decree, this would imply that it would also be possible for one to simply declare another person's body to be one's own. However, as we have seen, to say that property is acquired not through homesteading action but through declaration involves a practical contradiction: nobody can say and declare anything, unless his right to use his body is already assumed to be valid simply because of the very fact that regardless of what he says, it is he, and nobody else, who has homesteaded it as his instrument of saying anything.

With this, my a priori justification of the institution of private property is essentially complete. Only two supplementary arguments may be needed in order to point out why and where all other ethical proposals (let me call them socialist) are argumentatively indefensible.

According to the private property ethics, scarce resources that are under the exclusive control of their owners are defined in physical terms, and, *mutatis mutandis*, aggression, is defined as an invasion of the physical integrity of another person's property. As indicated, the economic effect of this provision is that of maximizing value productive efforts. A popular deviation from this is the idea of defining aggression as an invasion of the value or psychic integrity of another person's property instead. This idea underlies John Rawls's "difference principle" that all inequalities have to be expected to be to everyone's advantage regardless of how such inequalities have come about,[3] Robert Nozick's claim that a "dominant protection agency" has the right to outlaw competitors regardless of their actual actions, and his related claim that "nonproductive exchanges" in which one party would be better off if the other one did not exist may be outlawed, again regardless of whether or not such exchange involved any physical aggression.[4]

Such proposals are absurd as well as indefensible. While every person can have control over whether or not his actions cause the physical integrity of something to change, control over whether or not one's actions affect the value of someone's property to change rests with other people and their evaluations. One would have to interrogate and come to an agreement with the entire world population to make sure that one's planned actions would not change another person's evaluations regarding his property. Everyone would be long dead before this could ever be accomplished. Moreover, the idea that property value should be protected is argumentatively indefensible, for even in order to argue, it must be presupposed that actions must be allowed prior to any actual agreement because if they were not, one could not even argue so. Yet if one can, then this is only possible because of objective borders of property, i.e., borders which every person can recognize as such on his own, without having to agree first with anyone else with respect to one's system of values and

---

[3]John Rawls, *A Theory of Justice* (Cambridge, Mass.: Harvard University Press, 1971), p. 60, pp. 75f., 83.

[4]Robert Nozick, *Anarchy, State, and Utopia* (New York: Basic Books, 1974), pp. 55f., 83–86.

evaluations. Rawls and Nozick could not even open their mouths if it were otherwise. The very fact, then, that they do open them proves what they say is wrong.

The second popular deviation, equally absurd and indefensible, is this: Instead of recognizing the vital importance of the prior-later distinction in deciding between conflicting property claims—as the private property ethics does, thereby assuring value productive efforts to be as high as possible at all times—the claim is made, in essence, that priority is irrelevant and that late-comers have rights to ownership just as first-comers do. Again, with his belief in the rights of future generations, just savings rates and such things, Rawls may be cited as an example. However, if late-comers indeed had legitimate ownership claims to things, then literally no one would be allowed to do anything with anything as one would have to have all of the later-comers' consent prior to ever doing what one wanted to do. Neither we, nor our forefathers, nor our progeny could, do or will survive if one followed this rule. However, in order for any person—past, present, or future—to argue anything it must evidently be possible to survive then and now. Moreover, in order to do just this—and even people behind a Rawlsian "veil of ignorance" would have to be able to survive—property rights cannot be conceived of as being timeless and non-specific regarding the number of people concerned. Rather, they must necessarily be thought of as originating through acting at specific points in time for specific acting individuals. Otherwise, it would be impossible for anyone to first say anything at a definite point in time and for someone else to be able to reply. Simply saying, then, that the prior-later distinction can be ignored implies a contradiction, as one's being able to say so must presuppose one's existence as an independent decision-making unit at a given point in time.

Hence, I conclude that any socialist ethic is a complete failure. Only the institution of private property, which also assures the greatest possible production of wealth, can be argumentatively justified, because it is the very precondition of argumentation.

13

On the Ultimate Justification of the Ethics of Private Property

L
udwig von Mises, in his masterpiece *Human Action*, presents and explains the entire body of economic theory as implied in, and deducible from, one's conceptual understanding of the meaning of action (plus that of a few general, explicitly introduced assumptions about the empirical reality in which action is taking place). He calls this conceptual knowledge the "axiom of action," and he demonstrates in which sense the meaning of action from which economic theory sets out, i.e., of values, ends, and means, of choice, preference, profit, loss, and cost, must be considered a priori knowledge. It is not derived from sense impressions but from reflection (one does not see actions but rather interprets certain physical phenomena as actions!). Most importantly, it cannot possibly be invalidated by any experience whatsoever, because any attempt to do so would already presuppose the existence of action and an actor's understanding of the categories of action (experiencing something is, after all, itself an intentional action!).

Thus having reconstructed economics as, in the last resort, derived from an a priori true proposition, Mises can claim to have provided an ultimate foundation of economics. He terms a so-founded

[Reprinted from *Liberty* 2, no. 1 (1988).]

economics "praxeology," the logic of action, in order to emphasize the fact that its propositions can be definitively proven by virtue of the indisputable action-axiom and the equally indisputable laws of logical reasoning (such as the laws of identity and contradiction)—completely independent, that is, of any kind of empirical testing (as employed, for instance, in physics). However, though his idea of praxeology and his construction of an entire body of praxeological thought places him among the greats of the modern Western tradition of rationalism in its search for certain foundations, Mises does not think that another claim of this tradition can be made good: the claim that there are also foundations in ethical matters. According to Mises there exists no ultimate justification for ethical propositions in the same sense as there exists one for economic propositions. Economics can inform us whether or not certain means are appropriate for bringing about certain ends, yet whether or not the ends can be regarded as just can neither be decided by economics nor by any other science. There is no justification for choosing one rather than another end. In the last resort, which end is chosen is arbitrary from a scientific point of view and is a matter of subjective whim, incapable of any justification beyond the mere fact of simply being liked.

Many libertarians have followed Mises on this point. Like Mises, they have abandoned the idea of a rational foundation of ethics. As he does, they make as much as possible out of the economic proposition that the libertarian private property ethic produces a higher general standard of living than any other one; that most people actually prefer higher over lower standards of living; and hence, that libertarianism should prove highly popular. But ultimately, as Mises certainly knew, such considerations can only convince somebody of libertarianism who has already accepted the "utilitarian" goal of general wealth maximization. For those who do not share this goal, they have no compelling force at all. Thus, in the final analysis, libertarianism is based on nothing but an arbitrary act of faith.

In the following I outline an argument that demonstrates why this position is untenable, and how the essentially Lockean private property ethic of libertarianism can ultimately be justified. In effect, this argument supports the natural rights position of libertarianism as espoused by the other master thinker of the modern libertarian movement, Murray N. Rothbard—above all in his *Ethics of Liberty*. However, the argument establishing the ultimate justification of private property is different from the one typically offered by the natural rights tradition. Rather than this tradition, it is Mises, and his idea of praxeology and praxeological proofs, who provides the model.

I demonstrate that only the libertarian private property ethic can be justified argumentatively, because it is the praxeological presupposition of argumentation as such; and that any deviating, nonlibertarian ethical proposal can be shown to be in violation of this demonstrated preference. Such a proposal can be made, of course, but its propositional content would contradict the ethic for which one demonstrated a preference by virtue of one's own act of proposition-making, i.e., by the act of engaging in argumentation as such. For instance, one can say "people are and always shall be *indifferent* towards doing things," but this proposition would be belied by the very act of proposition-making, which in fact would demonstrate subjective *preference* (of saying this rather than saying something else or not saying anything at all). Likewise, nonlibertarian ethical proposals are falsified by the reality of actually proposing them.

To reach this conclusion and to properly understand its importance and logical force, two insights are essential.

First, it must be noted that the question of what is just or unjust—or for that matter the even more general question of what is a valid proposition and what is not—only arises insofar as I am, and others are, capable of propositional exchanges, i.e., of argumentation. The question does not arise vis-à-vis a stone or fish because they are incapable of engaging in such exchanges and of producing validity claiming propositions. Yet if this is so—and one cannot deny that it is without contradicting oneself, as one cannot argue the case that one cannot argue—then any ethical proposal as well as any other proposition must be assumed to claim that it is capable of being validated by propositional or argumentative means. (Mises, too, insofar as he formulates economic propositions, must be assumed to claim this.) In fact, in producing any proposition, overtly or as an internal thought, one demonstrates one's preference for the willingness to rely on argumentative means in convincing oneself or others of something. There is then, trivially enough, no way of justifying anything unless it is a justification by means of propositional exchanges and arguments. However, then it must be considered the ultimate defeat for an ethical proposal if one can demonstrate that its content is logically incompatible with the proponent's claim that its validity be ascertainable by argumentative means. To demonstrate any such incompatibility would amount to an impossibility proof, and such proof would constitute the most deadly defeat possible in the realm of intellectual inquiry.

Second, it must be noted that argumentation does not consist of free-floating propositions but is a form of action requiring the employment of scarce means; and that the means which a person demonstrates as preferring by engaging in propositional exchanges are those of private property. For one thing, no one could possibly propose anything, and no one could become convinced of any proposition by argumentative means, if a person's right to make exclusive use of his physical body were not already presupposed. It is this recognition of each other's mutually exclusive control over one's own body which explains the distinctive character of propositional exchanges that, while one may disagree about what has been said, it is still possible to agree at least on the fact that there is disagreement. It is also obvious that such a property right to one's own body must be said to be justified a priori, for anyone who tried to justify any norm whatsoever would already have to presuppose the exclusive right of control over his body as a valid norm simply in order to say, "I propose such and such." Anyone disputing such a right would become caught up in a practical contradiction since arguing so would already imply acceptance of the very norm which he was disputing.

Furthermore, it would be equally impossible to sustain argumentation for any length of time and rely on the propositional force of one's arguments if one were not allowed to appropriate in addition to one's body other scarce means through homesteading action (by putting them to use before somebody else does), and if such means and the rights of exclusive control regarding them were not defined in objective physical terms. For if no one had the right to control anything at all except his own body, then we would all cease to exist and the problem of justifying norms simply would not exist. Thus, by virtue of the fact of being alive, property rights to other things must be presupposed to be valid. No one who is alive could argue otherwise.

Moreover, if a person did not acquire the right of exclusive control over such goods by homesteading action, i.e., by establishing an objective link between a particular person and a particular scarce resource before anybody else had done so, but if instead late-comers were assumed to have ownership claims to goods, then no one would be allowed to do anything with anything as one would have to have all of the late-comers' consent prior to ever doing what one wanted to do. Neither we, nor our forefathers, nor our progeny could, do, or will survive if one were to follow this rule. In order for any person—past, present, or future—to argue anything it must be possible to survive then and now, and in order to do just this property rights cannot be conceived of as being timeless and nonspecific regarding the number of people involved. Rather, property rights must be thought of as originating as a result of specific individuals acting at definite points in time. Otherwise, it would be impossible for anyone to first say anything at a definite point in time and for someone else to be able to reply. Simply saying that the first-user-first-owner rule of libertarianism can be ignored or is unjustified implies a contradiction, for one's being able to say so must presuppose one's existence as an independent decision-making unit at a given point in time.

Finally, acting and proposition-making would also be impossible if the things acquired through homesteading were not defined in objective, physical terms (and if correspondingly, aggression were not defined as an invasion of the physical integrity of another person's property), but in terms of subjective values and evaluations. While every person can have control over whether or not his actions cause the physical integrity of something to change, control over whether or not one's actions affect the value of someone's property rests with other people and their evaluations. One would have to interrogate and come to an agreement with the entire world population to make sure that one's planned actions would not change another person's evaluations regarding his property. Surely, everyone would be long dead before this was accomplished. Moreover, the idea that property values should be protected is argumentatively indefensible, for even in order to argue so it must be presupposed that actions must be permitted prior to any actual agreement. (If they were not one could not even make this proposition.) If they are permitted, however, this is

344 The Economics and Ethics of Private Property

only possible because of objective borders of property, i.e., borders which every person can recognize as such on his own without having to agree first with anyone else with respect to one's system of values and evaluations.

By being alive and formulating any proposition, one demonstrates that any ethic except the libertarian private properly ethic is invalid. If this were not so and late-comers had to have legitimate claims to things or things owned were defined in subjective terms, no one could possibly survive as a physically independent decision-making unit at any given point in time. Hence, no one could ever raise any validity-claiming proposition.

This concludes my a priori justification of the private property ethic. A few comments regarding a topic already touched upon earlier, the relationship of this "praxeological" proof of libertarianism to the utilitarian and to the natural rights position, shall complete the discussion.

As regards the utilitarian position, the proof contains its ultimate refutation. It demonstrates that simply in order to propose the utilitarian position, exclusive rights of control over one's body and one's homesteaded goods already must be presupposed as valid. More specifically, as regards the consequentialist aspect of libertarianism, the proof shows its praxeological impossibility: the assignment of rights of exclusive control cannot be dependent on certain outcomes. One could never act and propose anything unless private property rights existed prior to a later outcome. A consequentialist ethic is a praxeological absurdity. Any ethic must instead be "aprioristic" or instantaneous in order to make it possible that one can act here and now and propose this or that rather than having to suspend acting until later. Nobody advocating a wait-for-the-outcome ethic would be around to say anything if he took his own advice seriously. Also, to the extent that utilitarian proponents are still around, they demonstrate through their actions that their consequentialist doctrine is and must be regarded as false. Acting and proposition-making require private property rights now and cannot wait for them to be assigned only later.

As regards the natural rights position, the praxeological proof, generally supportive as it is of the former's position concerning the possibility of a rational ethic and in full agreement with the conclusions reached within this tradition (specifically, by Murray N. Rothbard), has at least two distinctive advantages. For one thing, it has been a common quarrel with the natural rights position, even on the part of otherwise sympathetic observers, that the concept of human nature is far too diffuse to allow the derivation of a determinate set of rules of conduct. The praxeological approach solves this problem by recognizing that it is not the wider concept of human nature but the narrower one of propositional exchanges and argumentation which must serve as the starting point in deriving an ethic. Moreover, there exists an a priori justification for this choice insofar as the problem of true and false, of right and wrong, does not arise independent of propositional exchanges. No one, then, could possibly challenge such a starting point without contradiction. Finally, it is argumentation which requires the recognition of private property, so an argumentative challenge of the validity of the private property ethic is praxeologically impossible.

Second, there is the logical gap between "is-" and "ought-statements" which natural rights proponents have failed to bridge successfully—except for advancing some general critical remarks regarding the ultimate validity of the fact-value dichotomy. Here the praxeological proof of libertarianism has the advantage of offering a completely value-free justification of private property. It remains entirely in the realm of is-statements and never tries to derive an "ought" from an "is." The structure of the argument is this: (a) justification is propositional justification—a priori true is-statement; (b) argumentation presupposes property in one's body and the homesteading principle—a priori true is-statement; and (c) then, no deviation from this ethic can be argumentatively justified—a priori true is-statement. The proof also offers a key to an understanding of the nature of the fact-value dichotomy: Ought-statements cannot be derived from is-statements. They belong to different logical realms. It is also clear, however, that one cannot even state that there are facts and values if no propositional exchanges exist, and that this practice of propositional exchanges in turn presupposes the acceptance of the private property ethic as valid. In other words, cognition and truth-seeking as such have a normative foundation, and the normative foundation on which cognition and truth rest is the recognition of private property rights.

14

Austrian Rationalism in the Age of the Decline of Positivism

I. RATIONALISM AND RELATIVISM IN THE NATURAL AND SOCIAL SCIENCES

Philosophical rationalism claims that man is capable of recognizing ultimate foundations and principles of knowledge. It recognizes that all knowledge which must be presupposed insofar as one argues about any knowledge claim whatsoever (and thus cannot be meaningfully disputed because it is the precondition of meaningful doubt) is ultimately justified or a priori valid. The law of contradiction is an example of such knowledge. Moreover, philosophical rationalism asserts that based on the recognition of such ultimate truths, man is capable of systematic scientific progress.

Relativism denies the existence of absolute foundations of knowledge and the possibility of scientific progress.

There appears to be little or no evidence in support of relativism in the natural sciences. It is undeniable that the history of the natural sciences has been one of continuous progress, and that man has achieved mastery over nature far surpassing that of bygone ages. Moreover, disciplines such as propositional logic, arithmetic, Euclidean

[Reprinted from volume 17 of *Austrian Economics: Perspectives on the Past and Prospects for the Future*, edited by Richard M. Ebeling (Hillsdale, Mich.: Hillsdale College Press, 1991).]

geometry, rational mechanics (classical mechanics without gravitation), and chronometry, all of which have been termed "protophysics," provide perfect examples of the rationalist idea of ultimately founded knowledge. Logic and protophysics must be presupposed if one is to say anything meaningful at all, or if one is to make any empirical measurement of space, time, and material and thus cannot possibly be invalidated by human experience or measurement. (Euclidean geometry, for instance, cannot be said to have been falsified by the theory of relativity because the establishment of the theory of relativity presupposes the validity of Euclidean geometry in the construction of the measurement instruments.)

On the contrary, in full agreement with the claims of rationalism, it appears that it is precisely the status of logic and protophysics as absolutely a priori justified theories which makes progress in the empirical natural sciences systematically possible.[1]

This view of the natural sciences and their development has come under criticism in the wake of Thomas Kuhn's much celebrated book, *The Structure of Scientific Revolutions*.[2] In detailed analyses of central episodes in the history of the empirical natural sciences, Kuhn therein challenged the view that the process of scientific development

---

[1]On this in particular Paul Lorenzen, *Methodisches Denken* (Frankfurt/M.: Suhrkamp, 1968); idem, *Normative Logic and Ethics* (Mannheim: Bibliographisches Institut, 1969),

> Geometry, chronometry and hylometry [rational mechanics] are a priori theories which make empirical measurement of space, time and material "possible." They have to be established before physics in the modern sense of all empirical science, with its hypothetical fields of forces, can begin. Therefore, I should like to call these three disciplines by the common name: *protophysics*. The true sentences of protophysics are those sentences which are defendable on the basis of logic, arithmetic and analysis, definitions and the ideal norms which make measurements possible. (p. 60)

See also Peter Janich, *Die Protophysik der Zeit* (Mannheim: Bibliographisches Institut, 1969); Friedrich Kambartel, *Erfahrung und Struktur* [Frankfurt/M.: Suhrkamp, 1968]).

[2]Chicago: University of Chicago Press, 1970; also Imre Lakatos and Alan Musgrave, eds., *Criticism and the Growth of Knowledge* (Cambridge: Cambridge University Press, 1970).

could be described as gradually progressing towards truth through a series of hypothetical conjectures, crucial experiments, and the elimination of experimentally falsified theories, with every future generation knowing more than the previous one. Instead, according to Kuhn it has been a noncumulative, nonteleological process. Different "paradigms" or fundamental views of the essence of nature followed and supplanted one another as temporary orthodoxies, with each paradigm immune from, and irrefutable by, experience, and different paradigms incommensurable with each other. Shifts of paradigms were not motivated by incontrovertible experiences but were akin to religious conversions. Old paradigms died out as the scientists who had promoted them died away; new ones took their place as new generations of scientists, infected by conversion fever, grew up, with each generation gaining new knowledge from the adoption of a new creed as well as losing old knowledge in having abandoned the paradigms of past generations.

Does Kuhn's work, then, call for a revision of the rationalist interpretation of the natural sciences and establish a case for relativism? While Kuhn is inclined to think so, and while others, most notably Paul Feyerabend, have even radicalized Kuhn's relativistic aspirations to a "methodological anarchism" with the battle cry "anything goes,"[3] there can be little doubt that neither Kuhn, Feyerabend, nor anyone else has successfully persuaded the general public outside of the ivory towers of academia to accept a relativistic model of the natural sciences. Now as before, the general public is convinced of the views of rationalism, and justly so.

This is not to say that there is not some partial truth contained in Kuhn's and Feyerabend's often fascinating investigations. It is certainly true, and noteworthy, that losses of knowledge can occur even in the natural sciences, and that it is therefore profitable to study not only the most recent publications in one's field but also the writings of authors long past and forgotten. It is also true that motives such as power, prestige, income, animosity, and friendship do not become

---

[3]See Paul Feyerabend, *Against Method* (London: New Left Books, 1975); idem, *Science in a Free Society* (London: New Left Books, 1978); idem, *Wissenschaftals Kunst* (Frankfurt/M.: Suhrkamp, 1984).

inoperative once people turn to the study of nature. (Who, for instance, is ready to abandon a theory to whose development he has committed his entire life's work only because the world around is increasingly defecting to another incompatible paradigm?) Indeed, as an economist one can go even further and admit the possibility of scientific regression: A process of capital consumption, followed by lower general standards of living, a reduced population, a disintegration of markets, and the division of labor, as has repeatedly occurred in the history of mankind, would inevitably result in a decrease in man's knowledge of nature.

Yet even when all this is said, rationalism's claims are not affected in the least. For one thing, Kuhn's and Feyerabend's relativism surely cannot be extended to logic and protophysics. If one wants to make a meaningful proposition, or any measurement at all, "anything" does *not* go. Such disciplines, which incidentally have remained largely outside the scope of Kuhn's and Feyerabend's considerations, are *absolutely* indispensable for *any* empirical natural science (and not merely irrefutable paradigms capable of substitution by other, incommensurable ones). However, once this is recognized, and once it is understood that proposition-making, counting, the construction of measurement instruments, and measuring, all of which make the empirical natural sciences possible, are purposeful activities, it immediately becomes clear that the paradigms of the natural sciences must be conceived of as means toward some universal, indispensable human end, and that they must be commensurable as regards their efficiency in attaining this end.[4]

The relativistic impression of the development of the empirical natural sciences that Kuhn and Feyerabend try to convey can be traced to the fact that they both misconceive of scientific theories as mere systems of verbal propositions and systematically ignore their foundation in the reality of action. Only if one regards theories as being completely detached from action does any single theory not only become immunizable, but any two rival theories whose respective

---

[4]See on this also Hans-Hermann Hoppe, "On Praxeology and the Praxeological Foundation of Epistemology and Ethics," in Jeffrey Herbener, ed., *The Meaning of Ludwig von Mises* (Boston: Kluwer Academic Publishers, 1991).

terms cannot be reduced to and defined in terms of each other must then appear completely incommensurable so as to exclude any rational choice between them. However, this affects neither the refutability of any one theory, nor the commensurability of rival paradigms, on the entirely different level of applying them in the reality of action, of using them as instruments for the attainment of a practical purpose. On the level of mere words, paradigms may be irrefutable and incommensurable, but in practice they never can be. In fact, one could not even state that any single paradigm was irrefutable or any two paradigms were incommensurable and in what respect, unless one presupposed a common categorical framework that could serve as the basis for such an assessment or comparison. It is this *practical* refutability and commensurability of the paradigms of the empirical natural sciences that explains the possibility of technological progress.

In systematically ignoring the fact that theories and theoretically interpreted observations are those of an actor, built and made in order to act successfully, Kuhn and Feyerabend have deprived themselves of the very criterion against which all knowledge concerning nature is continually tested and commensurated: the criterion of successfully reaching a set goal by applying knowledge in a given situation, or of failing to do so. Without the criterion of instrumental success, relativism would be inescapable. Yet in each of our actions vis-à-vis nature, we confirm the claim of rationalism that one can identify a range of applications for some theoretical knowledge and test it for its success within this range, and hence, that competing theories must be considered commensurable as regards such ranges of application and success. No situation is conceivable in which it would be rational to give up an intellectual tool which had once proven successful in a range of applications if no better tool were available. Yet if a superior tool were available, for example, a theory or paradigm that allowed one to reach a goal that could not be reached equally successfully by applying another, incompatible theory, it would be irrational for an actor not to adopt it. To be sure, such irrational behavior is empirically possible. However, whoever chose it would have to pay a price for doing so. He would deprive himself of the ability to achieve goals that he otherwise could accomplish, and isolated from all social contexts which might offer other, socio-psychological reasons not to adopt it, alone vis-à-vis nature, no one capable of distinguishing between successful and unsuccessful action would ever want to pay such a price. It is this which explains the unacceptability of a relativist view of the natural sciences and the possibility of the actually observable continuous—if at times for socio-psychological reasons somewhat erratic—progress in man's mastery of nature, which Kuhn and Feyerabend would declare nonexistent, although all the while it seems to be staring them in the face.[5]

The situation is very different if one turns from the natural to the social sciences. Here the claims of rationalism seem to find far less support, and relativism has gained widespread public acceptance.[6]

Foremost among the indicators cited in support of relativism is the observation that there is nothing in the development of the social sciences resembling the progress which has been achieved in the natural sciences. While our predictive powers and instrumental control over nature have dramatically increased since the times of Plato and Aristotle, the development of the empirical social sciences has been characterized by a standstill. In spite of the availability of all sorts of technical gadgets, such as high-speed computers, it appears that we are in no better position today to predict social events or to planfully bring about social change than were Plato or Aristotle in their days. (One might note that even if the validity of this observation is admitted, the relativistic conclusion to which it allegedly leads does not directly follow. It only follows if it is presupposed that the criteria for progress in the social sciences are indeed identical to those in the natural sciences. Proponents of social relativism take this for granted, yet it is by no means obvious why this should be so. On the contrary, in the natural sciences the object of knowledge [nature] and the subject of this knowledge [an actor] are different separate entities. In the social

---

[5]See also Hans-Hermann Hoppe, "In Defense of Extreme Rationalism," *Review of Austrian Economics* 3 (1989): esp. 190–92; Wolfgang Stegmüller, *Hauptströmungen der Gegenartsphilosophie* (Stuttgart: Kröner, 1975), vol. 2, chap. 5, esp. pp. 523ff.

[6]See Martin Hollis and Steven Lukes, eds., *Rationality and Relativism* (Oxford: Basil Blackwell, 1982).

sciences, on the other hand, the objects of knowledge and research are themselves knowers and researchers. In light of this categorical difference, it would seem anything but clear why the methodology appropriate for the natural and the social sciences could possibly be one and the same. In fact, it is entirely unsurprising that when it comes to predicting predictors, or instrumentally controlling instrumental controllers, there *cannot* be any systematic progress of the kind observed in the natural sciences![7]

Moreover, proponents of relativism usually point out, apparently there is no analogue in the social sciences to the role played by logic and protophysics as the a prioristic foundations of the empirical natural sciences. The rationalist claim, associated in particular with the "natural law" tradition, that such an analogue is provided by economics and ethics,[8] has either been forgotten and disappeared from public consciousness or is dismissed out of hand: Economics, it is held, is an empirical science very much like physics, with the objective of producing predictive knowledge, but unlike physics it fails to deliver the promised goods. As regards the observation that prosperous as well as poor societies exist, which would seem to make room for economic explanations after all—though not for explanations of the kind offered by physics—the proponents of social relativism contend that such differences have no *economic* reasons but are due to different degrees of *technological* knowledge. Rich societies are rich because of their advanced state of technology; poverty is due to a lack of natural-scientific know-how. Two objections to this view appear obvious: (1) The description of the facts is false. Do not the

---

[7]See Hans-Hermann Hoppe, *Kritik der kausalwissenschaftlichen Sozialforschung. Untersuchungen zur Grundlegung von Soziologie und Ökonomie* (Opladen: Westdeutscher Verlag, 1983), esp. pp. 30–32; on methodological dualism see also Ludwig von Mises, *Human Action: A Treatise on Economics* (Chicago: Regnery, 1966), p. 18; idem, *Theory and History: An Interpretation of Social and Economic Evolution* (Auburn, Ala.: Ludwig von Mises Institute, 1985), pp. 1–2, 38–41; further, K.O. Apel, *Die Erklären: Verstehen Kontroverse in transzendental-pragmatischer Sicht* (Frankfurt/M.: Suhrkamp, 1979).

[8]See Mises, *Theory and History*, pp. 44ff.

underdeveloped societies send their future scientists and engineers in large numbers to the universities of the advanced countries, and do not these poor societies then have access to the *same* knowledge upon their return as the rich ones? (2) More important still, technological know-how can only have a material impact if it is utilized. However, in order to do this, there must be savings and investment. It is not the availability of technical or scientific knowledge that imposes limits on a society's prosperity; rather, it is the amount of savings and investment that imposes limits on the exploitation of actually available knowledge and on scientific progress, insofar as research activities, too, must be supported by saved-up funds. Hence, contrary to relativistic views, economics seems to have something to do with prosperity and poverty after all![9]

Nor, it is claimed, does ethics offer support for anything but relativism, for does not the fact of continuous and, so it seems, ineradicable differences of opinion in the field of contemporary politics prove the case of ethical relativism conclusively? Does not social anthropology, the study of societies such as the Fidshi islanders, or the natives of New Guinea, for instance, add still more evidence in support of relativistic conclusions? There are institutions such as cannibalism or slavery which a relativist might be hard pressed to defend. However, according to ethical relativists, regarding these practices as counter-evidence is the result of a misconception. The problem with these institutions is not that they invalidate relativism but that societies adopting them are still under the spell of social rationalism. That is, they still falsely believe in an absolutely founded ethic. Ethical relativism, its proponents claim, rules out intolerant practices such as these and implies a pluralism of values. (But is it not obvious that this doctrine is entirely fallacious? Without an absolute, a priori foundation, a value pluralism is itself just another unfounded ideology, and there is no compelling reason to adopt it over any other one. Only if a priori valid reasons could be given for adopting pluralism

---

[9]See Murray N. Rothbard, *Man, Economy, and State* (Los Angeles: Nash, 1970), p. 749.

could it claim to safeguard tolerance and could cannibalism or slavery then be ruled out as acceptable social practices.[10])

II. POSITIVISM AND THE RELATIVISTIC DESTRUCTION OF ETHICS AND ECONOMICS

No other philosophical doctrine in modern times has contributed more to the spread of relativism than positivism. Rooted in the tradition of the classical empiricism of Locke and Hume, it emerged first in Vienna around the turn of the century and then established itself, in particular in the wake of the emigration of its intellectual leaders to the U.S. during the 1930s, as the dominant philosophical creed of the Western world.[11]

While the basic tenets of positivism amount to a denial of the claims of rationalism as applied to the natural as well as the social sciences, its impact has been particularly strong in the latter. To be sure, there can be no doubt that even the natural sciences, and especially logic and protophysics, have suffered from the influence of positivism.[12] However, for reasons already mentioned, to derail rationalism within this field would be extremely difficult. Adopting a relativist viewpoint would ultimately amount to forsaking the intellectual means for one's own successful handling of nature, and no one capable of distinguishing between success and failure has a systematic interest in paying such a price. In the social sciences matters are different. While up to now the purely intellectual case for social relativism has hardly appeared better founded than the case for the natural sciences, and

---

[10]See Henry Veatch, *Rational Man: A Modern Interpretation of Aristotelian Ethics* (Bloomington: Indiana University Press, 1962), esp. pp. 37–46; Hoppe, "In Defense of Extreme Rationalism," pp. 84–85.

[11]See Viktor Kraft, *Der Wiener Kreis* (Vienna: Springer, 1968); Stegmüller, *Hauptströmungen der Gegenwartsphilosophie* (Stuttgart: Kroner, 1965), vol. 1, chaps. IX–X.

[12]See Kambartel, *Erfahrung und Struktur*, esp. chap. 6; see also note 18 below.

while I demonstrate it in the following to be entirely baseless, advocating and adopting relativism in the social sciences is not self-defeating in the same sense as it is in the sciences of nature. If one were to deny the existence of absolute laws of economics and/or ethics and the possibility of social progress, a price would have to be paid, too. However, the price would not necessarily have to be paid directly, and would not invariably be borne in full by whoever adopted and acted on this view. Rather, he who adopted it could externalize the costs of his views onto others; hence, insofar as relativism can serve as a means for increasing one's own well-being at the expense of reducing that of others, individuals could have an interest in advocating social relativism.[13]

It is this which explains why the influence of positivism has made itself felt in the social sciences in particular. Whether this had been intended by the positivists or not, their philosophical message was quickly recognized by the powers that be as a mighty ideological weapon in the pursuit of their own goal of increasing their control over others and of enriching themselves at the expense of others. Accordingly, lavish support was bestowed on the positivist movement, and this movement returned the favor by destroying economics and ethics in particular as the traditional bastions of social rationalism and eradicating from public consciousness a vast body of knowledge that had once constituted a seemingly permanent part of the heritage of Western thought and civilization.[14]

The first and most fundamental tenet of positivism is this: Knowledge regarding reality, or *empirical* knowledge, must be verifiable or

---

[13]See Mises, *Human Action*, chap. III.

[14]See Mises, *Human Action*, part 7; idem, *The Ultimate Foundation of Economic Science* (Kansas City: Sheed Andrews and McMeel, 1978), esp. chaps. 5–8, which conclude with the statement:

> As far as the empiricist principle of logical positivism refers to the experimental methods of the natural sciences, it merely asserts what is not questioned by anybody. As far as it rejects the epistemological principles of the sciences of human action, it is not only entirely wrong. It is also knowingly and intentionally undermining the intellectual foundations of Western civilization. (p. 133)

at least falsifiable by experience; that whatever is known by experience could have been otherwise, or, put differently, that nothing about reality can be known to be true a priori; that all a priori true propositions are *analytical* statements which have no factual content whatsoever but are true by convention, representing merely tautological information about the use of symbols and their transformation rules; that all statements are either empirical or analytical, but never both; and hence, that normative statements, because they are neither empirical nor analytical, cannot legitimately contain any claim to truth, but must be regarded as mere expressions of emotions, saying, in effect, no more than "wow" or "grrr."[15]

The second tenet of positivism formulates the extension or rather the application of the first one to the problem of scientific explanation. According to positivism, to explain a real phenomenon is to formulate a statement of either the type "if A, then B" or, should the variables allow quantitative measurement, "if an increase (or decrease) in A, then an increase (or decrease) in B." As a statement referring to reality (with A and B being real phenomena, that is), its validity can never be established with certainty by examining the proposition alone or any other proposition from which the one in question could in turn be logically deduced, but will always remain hypothetical and dependent on the outcome of future experiences which cannot be known in advance. Should experience confirm a hypothetical explanation, i.e., should one observe an instance where B indeed followed A, as predicted, this would not prove that the hypothesis is true, since A and B are general, abstract terms ("universals, as opposed to proper names") which refer to phenomena or events of which there are (or, at least *might*, in principle be) an indefinite number of instances, and hence later experiences could still possibly falsify it. And if an experience falsified a hypothesis, i.e., if one observed an instance of A that was not followed by B, this would not be decisive either, as it would still be possible that the hypothetically related phenomena were indeed connected and that some other

---

[15]See in particular Alfred J. Ayer, *Language, Truth, and Logic* (New York: Dover, 1946).

previously neglected and uncontrolled circumstance or variable had simply prevented the hypothesized relationship from being actually observed. A falsification would only prove that the particular hypothesis under investigation was not completely correct as it stood and needed some refinement, some specification of additional variables which one would have to control in order to be able to observe the hypothesized relationship between A and B. However, a falsification would never prove once and for all that a relationship between some given phenomena did not exist.[16]

Finally, positivism claims that these two related tenets apply universally, to all fields of knowledge (the thesis of "the unity of science"): No a priori knowledge of nature nor of the social reality of human actions and knowledge exists; and the structure of scientific explanations is the same regardless of the subject matter.[17]

Assuming for the moment this doctrine to be correct, it is easy to recognize its relativistic implications. Ethics is not a cognitive discipline. Any normative statement is just as well-, or rather, ill-founded as any other one. But then, what is wrong with everyone trying to impose on others whatever one wishes? Surely nothing. Everything is allowed. Ethics is reduced to the question "what can I get away with?" What better message could there be for those in power: for the cannibal king, for the slave owner, or for the holders of government office! It is precisely what they want to hear: might is and makes right.

Similarly, they must be thrilled about the message of positivism as regards the positive sciences. In the natural sciences, the positivist doctrine is relatively harmless. Disciplines such as logic and protophysics, whose propositions are generally considered a priori true

---

[16]See Karl R. Popper, *The Logic of Scientific Discovery* (New York: Basic Books, 1959); idem, *Conjectures and Refutations* (London: Routledge and Kegan Paul, 1969); Carl G. Hempel, *Aspects of Scientific Explanations* (New York: Free Press, 1970); Ernest Nagel, *The Structure of Science* (New York: Harcourt, Brace and World, 1961).

[17]See Paul Oppenheim and Hilary Putnam, "Unity of Science as a Working Hypothesis," in H. Feigl, ed., *Minnesota Studies in the Philosophy of Science* (Minneapolis: University of Minnesota Press, 1967), vol. 2.

(nonfalsifiable by experience), are interpreted by positivists as containing no "real" knowledge at all, as empirically empty formalisms. This view has helped legitimize and further the degeneration of parts of logic and mathematics into meaningless symbolic games, of which the general public has remained largely ignorant due to the arcane nature of the subject.[18] But it has not, nor could it have, changed the fact that at least some propositions of logic and mathematics are employed as the very foundation of the empirical natural sciences, and hence are actually treated as containing empirical information, though of a nonhypothetical kind.[19] Nor is there much harm in the positivist view of the empirical natural sciences, such as physics. Its methodology, according to which one can never definitively establish whether a hypothesized relationship between two or more variables exists or not, offers the possibility that one might cling to one's

------

[18]See Kambartel, *Erfahrung und Struktur*, esp. pp. 236–42. The rationalist conception of logic and mathematics is summarized by Gottlob Frege's dictum that "it follows from the truth of the axioms, that they do not contradict each other." The positivist-formalist interpretation, on the other hand, is formulated by the young D. Hilbert: "If the arbitrarily assumed axioms do not lead to contradictory implications, then they are true, and the objects defined by the axioms exist" (quoted from Kambartel, p. 239).

The advance of formalism, then, explains Kambartel, has far-reaching consequences.

> The retreat of mathematics from all practical justification, and from the corresponding epistemological justification of formalism, is itself a practical decision of the utmost importance. It is the abandonment of practical justification and, since formal systems without a meaningful interpretation of their starting point cannot justify anything, ultimately of the justification of propositions altogether. (p. 241)

In consequence,

> many formal analyses become a high-bred game of an interested few, although without the public noticing it, because of its inability to attain the level of discussion that is required here to determine the borderline between theory and game. (p. 238)

[19]See Hans Lenk, "Logikbegründung und Rationaler Kritizismus," *Zeitschrift für Philosophische Forschung* 24 (1970); K.O. Apel, *Transformation der Philosophie*, vol. II, pp. 406–10.

hypotheses regardless of all seemingly falsifying experiences, for one could always blame a previously neglected variable for one's predictive failures. However, as explained above no one trying to produce some given physical event would systematically prefer finding excuses for not reaching this goal over actually reaching it because he alone would have to pay the price for such stubbornness.

In the realm of the social sciences, however, where the costs of one's actions can be externalized onto others, this possibility of immunizing one's hypotheses from falsification offers welcome opportunities to those in power.

Consider some typical economic propositions: Whenever an exchange is not voluntary but is coerced, such as highway robbery or taxation, one exchange party profits at the expense of the other. Or: Whenever minimum wage laws are enforced that require wage rates to be higher than existing market wages, involuntary unemployment will result. Or: Whenever the quantity of money is increased while the demand for money is unchanged, the purchasing power of money will fall. Or: Any supply of money is "optimal" such that no increase in the supply of money can raise the overall standard of living (while it can have redistributive effects). Or: Collective ownership of all factors of production makes cost-accounting impossible, and thus leads to a lower output in terms of consumer evaluations. Or: Taxation of income producers raises their effective time preference rate, and thus leads to a lower output of goods produced. Apparently, these propositions contain knowledge about reality, yet they do not seem to be falsifiable but are true by definition.[20] However, according to positivism this cannot be so. Insofar as they claim to be empirically meaningful statements, they must be hypotheses subject to empirical confirmation or falsification. One can formulate the very opposite of the above propositions without thereby stating anything that could be recognized from the outset, a priori, as false (and nonsensical). Experience would have to decide the matter. Thus, in assuming the

---

[20]See on this the two foremost economic treatises of our times: Mises's *Human Action*, and Rothbard's *Man, Economy, and State.*

positivist doctrine, the highway robber, taxman, union official or the Federal Reserve Board would act legitimately, from a scientific point of view, in claiming that taxation benefits the taxed and increases productive output, minimum wage laws increase employment, and the creation of paper money generates all-around prosperity. As a good positivist, one would have to admit that these are merely hypotheses, too. With the predicted effects being benevolent, however, surely they should be put into effect and tried out. After all, one should not close one's eyes to new experience, and one should always be willing to react flexibly and open-mindedly, depending on the outcome of such an experience. However, if the outcome is not as hypothesized, and the robbed or taxed do not appear to benefit, employment actually decreases, or economic cycles rather than all-around prosperity ensue, the possibility of immunizing one's hypotheses becomes a real, almost irresistibly tempting option. For why would the robber, the taxman, or the Federal Reserve Board *not* want to continuously play down all apparently falsifying experiences as merely accidental, so long as he can personally profit from conducting their robbing-, taxing-, or money-creating experiment? Why would he *not* want to interpret all apparent falsifications as experiences that had been produced by some unfortunately neglected circumstance and that would disappear and turn into their very opposite, revealing the true relationship between taxes, minimum wage laws, the creation of money, and prosperity once these circumstances were controlled?

In fact, whatever empirical evidence one presents against these hypotheses, as soon as one adopts positivism and rejects the idea of formulating a *principled* case either for or against them as ill-conceived, the robber's or the taxman's case is safe from decisive criticism because any failure can be ascribed to an as yet uncontrolled intervening variable. Not even the most perfectly controlled experiment could change this situation. For it would never be possible to control all variables that might conceivably have an influence on the variable to be explained or the result to be produced. In practice, this would involve controlling literally all of the universe, and in theory no one even knows what all the variables which make up this universe *are*. No matter what the charges brought against the robber, the taxman, or the Federal Reserve Board, within the boundaries of the positivist methodology they will always be able to preserve and rescue the "hard-core" of their "research program" as the neo-Popperian positivist Lakatos would have called it. Experience only tells us that a particular experiment did not reach its goal, but it can never tell us if a slightly different one will produce any different results, or if it is possible to reach the goal of generating all-around prosperity by means of *any* form of robbery, taxation, or paper money creation.

The attitude toward positive economics that positivism fuels and that has indeed become characteristic of most contemporary power elites and their subsidized intellectual bodyguards is that of a relativist social engineer whose motto is "nothing can be known with certainty to be impossible in the realm of social phenomena and there is nothing that one might not want to try out on one's fellowmen, so long as one keeps an open mind."[21]

The fact that positivism supports the mentality of social relativism does not prove it wrong. However, suspicion regarding its validity seems appropriate. It certainly is not obvious that there should be no rational ethical standard at all and that literally "anything goes." Nor is it intuitively plausible that economics should be either an empirically meaningless symbolic game (a system of analytic propositions), or a set of hypothetical, empirically falsifiable predictions concerning the outcome of human actions and interactions. In the former case it would be nothing but a waste of time, and in the latter economics would obviously be impotent and hence irrelevant (if anything, the baker in ancient Athens could have predicted the behavior of his fellowmen *better and with a higher degree of confidence* than his modern counterpart!). However, economic propositions such as those mentioned above are apparently neither meaningless nor irrelevant. Indeed, in light of the self-serving implications of positivism for those in power, it may well be suspected that positivism might come to be

---

[21]See also Hans-Hermann Hoppe, *A Theory of Socialism and Capitalism* (Boston: Kluwer Academic Publishers, 1989), chap. 6; idem, "The Intellectual Cover for Socialism," *Free Market* (February 1988).

accepted even if it were false, and that it might continue even if its falsehoods were exposed—as they surely have been.

Each of the three interrelated premises of positivism is demonstrably false.[22]

Regarding positivism's supposedly exhaustive classification of analytic, empirical, and emotive propositions one must ask: What, then, is the status of this very axiom? It must be either an analytical or an empirical proposition, or it must be an expression of emotions. If it is taken to be analytical, then it is merely empty verbal quibble, saying nothing about anything real, but only defining one sound or symbol by another. Hence, one would simply have to shrug one's shoulders and reply "so what?" The same response would be appropriate if the positivist argument were taken to be an empirical proposition. If this were the case, it would have to be admitted that the proposition might well be wrong and that one would be entitled to know the criterion on the basis of which one would have to decide whether or not it was. More decisively, as an empirical proposition it could merely state a historical fact and would thus be entirely irrelevant in determining whether or not it would be possible to ever produce propositions that were empirical and yet nonfalsifiable, or normative, yet nonemotive. Finally, if the positivist line of reasoning were assumed to be an emotive proposition, then according to its own doctrine it is cognitively meaningless and contains no claim to truth whatsoever, and one would not need to pay any more attention to it than to a barking dog.

Thus, one must conclude from the outset that positivism is an utter failure. It does not prove that there can be no rational ethic.

----

[22]See on the following Mises, *The Ultimate Foundation of Economic Science*; Murray N. Rothbard, *Individualism and the Philosophy of the Social Sciences* (San Francisco: Cato, 1979); Hans-Hermann Hoppe, *Praxeology and Economic Science* (Auburn, Ala.: Ludwig von Mises Institute, 1988); idem, "On Praxeology and the Praxeological Foundations of Epistemology and Ethics"; also Martin Hollis and Edward Nell, *Rational Economic Man* (Cambridge: Cambridge University Press, 1975), Introduction.

Nor can it even be considered an epistemology, a justifiable theory of knowledge. For if it were, then positivism's most basic premise would have to be a synthetic a priori statement (empirical, but unfalsifiable), whose existence positivism denies. Thus, one would have landed in the camp of social rationalism.

Similarly, positivism's claim that all scientific explanations are hypothetical is self-defeating. (For what is the status of this explanation?)[23] In order to see this, let it be assumed that an explanation relating two or more events has been found to fit one set of data, and that it is then applied to a second data set, presumably to undergo further empirical testing. Now one must ask: What is the presupposition which must be made in order to relate the second experience to the first one as either confirming or falsifying it? It might seem that if in the second instance of experience the observations of the first were repeated this would be a confirmation, and if not, a falsification. Clearly, the positivist methodology assumes this to be obvious. But this is not true. Experience only reveals that two or more observations regarding the temporal sequence of two or more types of events can be "neutrally" classified as "repetition" or "nonrepetition." A neutral repetition only becomes a "positive" confirmation and a nonrepetition a "negative" falsification if independent of what can actually be discovered by experience, it is assumed that there are constant, time-invariantly operating causes. If, contrary to this, it is assumed that causes in the course of time might operate sometimes this way and sometimes that way, then these repetitive or nonrepetitive occurrences simply are and remain neutrally registered experiences, completely independent of one another. They are not in any way logically related to each other as confirming or falsifying one another. There is one experience and there is another, they are the same or they are different, but that is all there is to it; nothing else follows.

---

[23]See on the following also Hoppe, *Kritik der kausalwissenschaftlichen Sozialforschung*; see also supra chap. 7.

Thus, the presupposition of being able to say "falsify" or "confirm" is the constancy principle: the conviction that observable phenomena are in principle determined by causes that are constant and time-invariant in the way they operate. Only if the constancy principle is assumed to be valid does it follow from any failure to reproduce a result that there is something wrong with an original hypothesis; and only then can a successful reproduction indeed be interpreted as a confirmation. Obviously, this constancy principle is not itself based on or derived from experience. There is not only no observable link connecting events, but even if such a link existed, experience could not reveal whether or not it was time-invariant. The principle cannot be disproved by experience either, since any event which might appear to disprove it (such as a failure to duplicate some result) could be interpreted from the outset as if experience had shown here merely that one *particular* type of event was not the cause of another. However, to the extent that experience cannot exclude the possibility that *another* set of events might actually be found which would turn out to be time-invariant in its way of operating, the validity of the constancy principle cannot be disproved.

Nonetheless, although neither derived from nor disprovable by experience, the constancy principle is nothing less than the logically necessary presupposition for experiences which can be regarded as either confirming or falsifying each other (in contrast to isolated, logically unconnected experiences). Hence, since positivism assumes the existence of such logically related experiences, it must be concluded that it also assumes the existence of nonhypothetical knowledge about reality. It must assume that there are indeed time-invariantly operating causes, and it must assume this to be the case although experience could never possibly prove or disprove it. Once again, positivism turns out to be an inconsistent, contradictory philosophy. There exist nonhypothetical explanations of real things.

Finally (and by now not surprisingly), the positivist thesis of the unity of science turns out to be self-contradictory. Positivism claims that actions, just as any other phenomenon, can and must be explained by means of hypotheses which can be confirmed or refuted by experience. If this were the case, then—contrary to its own doctrine that there can be no a priori knowledge about reality—positivism would be forced to assume that with respect to actions time-invariantly operating causes exist. In order to proceed as positivism wants us to proceed—to relate different experiences regarding sequences of events as either confirming or falsifying each other—a constancy over time in the operation of causes must be presupposed (as has already been explained). However, if this were true and actions could indeed be conceived of as governed by time-invariantly operating causes, what about explaining the explainers, i.e., those who carry on the very process of hypothesis creation, of verification and falsification; all of us, that is, who act the way the positivists tell us to act? Evidently, to do all this—to assimilate confirming or falsifying experiences, to replace old hypotheses with new ones—one must assumedly be able to learn. However, if one can learn from experience, and the positivist is compelled to admit this, then one cannot know at any given time what one will know at later times and how one will act based on this knowledge. Rather, one can only reconstruct the causes of one's actions after the event, since one can only explain one's knowledge after one already possesses it. Thus, the positivist methodology applied to the field of knowledge and action, which contains knowledge as its necessary ingredient, is simply contradictory—a logical absurdity.

The constancy principle can and indeed must be assumed within the sphere of natural objects, i.e., for phenomena that are *not* constituted by one's own knowledge or actions manifesting that knowledge (in this sphere the question of whether there are law-governed constants on the basis of which it becomes possible to make *ex ante* predictions is positively determined independent of experience, and empirical factors play a role only in determining which concrete variables are causally linked to which concrete effect variables, and which are not). With respect to knowledge and action, on the other hand, the constancy principle cannot be valid (in this sphere of phenomena, the question of whether or not there are constants is itself empirical in nature and can only be decided for a given variable on the basis of past experience, that is, *ex post*). And all this, which is definitely knowledge about something real, can be known apodictically. Hence, a methodological *dualism* rather than the positivist monism must be accepted and admitted as absolutely a priori true.

III. THE AUSTRIAN SCHOOL OF ECONOMICS AND THE PROSPECTS OF A RATIONALIST RECONSTRUCTION OF ETHICS AND ECONOMICS

The fact that positivism was quickly refuted as a self-contradictory philosophical system naturally did not *help* its cause. However, due to the self-serving nature of the positivist doctrine for those in positions of governmental power it also did little to reduce positivism's popularity. Much more was needed to defeat positivism than to prove it logically false: It took decades of social experimentation, of trying on an ever-increasing scale to prove world-wide and within each nation state that there are no ethical and economic laws, that nothing is taboo, and that everything is possible. It took the economic stagnation of the Western welfare democracies beginning in the late 60's and early 70's; the enduring impoverishment of the Third World nations decades after their decolonization; and the gradual, and since the late 80's—after more than 70 years of experimenting—the breathtakingly rapid economic collapse of the socialist East Bloc countries.[24] Outside of the real world, in academia, that is, it took the temporary disappearance of ethics and political theory, and their substitution by linguistic analysis, operationally meaningless moonshine talk, or interest group politics and bargaining theories.[25] It required the degeneration of economics into either empirically meaningless symbolic exercises, with no resemblance whatsoever to what had once been the subject matter of the classics of economic thought (except for some occasional, economically sounding term[26] produced by, at best, second-rate

---

[24]For an interpretation of the twentieth century as the apogee of the philosophy of social engineering and relativism see Paul Johnson's magnificent *Modern Times* (New York: Harper and Row, 1983).

[25]See also Veatch, *Rational Man*; idem, *For an Ontology of Morals: A Critique of Contemporary Ethical Theory* (Evanston, Ill.: Northwestern University Press, 1971); idem, *Human Rights: Facts or Fancy?* (Baton Rouge: Louisiana State University Press, 1985).

[26]For example, Gary North suggests one

> take a look at any page by the 1983 economics [Nobel] prize winner, Gerald Debreu, *Theory of Value: An Axiomatic Analysis of Economic Equilibrium*, which was in its eighth printing in 1979—a testimony to

mathematicians for no actual audience at all, but only to collect dust in the tax-supported libraries of this world); or it required its degeneration into a mighty econometric forecasting industry, whose futility was painfully obvious to everyone, including the politicians and government bureaucrats who subsidized it so as to employ it for purposes of "scientific legitimation."[27] It required the default of the Keynesian system, with the advent of the allegedly impossible phenomenon of stagflation in the mid-70's; the breakdown of the monetarist paradigm, after a long series of patently false predictions from the late 70's on through the 80's; and the complete, worldwide bankruptcy of Marxist economics.[28]

Still positivism is not dead. However, since the mid-70's the price of decades of social relativism and engineering has become too high to be ignored or simply explained away. Gradually, a philosophical crisis situation has emerged. Not surprisingly, with positivism finally losing ground other varieties of relativism, which had been submerged during the positivist reign, have resurfaced and are trying to fill the widening ideological vacuum. Associated with names such as hermeneutics, rhetoric, ultra-subjectivism, and deconstructionism, an academic movement of sorts is underway that is trying to revive the old message of nihilism—that there is no such thing as truth—and

------

the honors of graduate study in economics. The only hint of reality in the entire book appears on p. 29, the words, "No. 2 Red Winter Wheat." (Gary North, "Why Murray Rothbard Will Never Win the Nobel Prize!," in Walter Block and Llewellyn H. Rockwell, Jr., eds., *Man, Economy, and Liberty, Essays in Honor of Murray N. Rothbard* [Auburn, Ala.: Ludwig von Mises Institute, 1988], pp. 89–90)

[27]On the degeneration of the social sciences in particular see the brilliant observations by Stanislav Andreski, *Social Science as Sorcery* (New York: St. Martin's Press, 1972); Charles Sykes, *ProfScam: Professors and the Demise of Higher Education* (Washington, D.C.: Regnery, 1988).

[28]See also Murray N. Rothbard, *For a New Liberty* (New York: Macmillan, 1978), chap. 9; idem, "The Hermeneutical Invasion of Philosophy and Economics," *Review of Austrian Economics* 3 (1989): 54–55; idem, "Is There Life After Reaganomics," in Llewellyn H. Rockwell, Jr., ed., *The Free Market Reader* (Auburn, Ala.: Ludwig von Mises Institute, 1988), esp. p. 378; idem, "Ronald Reagan; An Autopsy," *Liberty* II, no. 4 (March 1989).

which ascribes the failure of positivism not to its relativism, but to the fact that it is not relativistic enough in continuing to allow for *empirical* (hypothetical) truths rather than for no truths at all.[29]

But the crisis has also brought back the philosophy of social rationalism that has long since demonstrated the falsity of positivism but fell into oblivion during the decades of positivist supremacy. Sparked by the Nobel-prize award in 1974 to Friedrich August von Hayek, the arch-rationalist Austrian School of economics, in the tradition of Carl Menger, Eugen von Böhm-Bawerk and, above all, Ludwig von Mises, Hayek's teacher, and Murray N. Rothbard, has experienced a resounding revival. Removed for decades from the higher reaches of subsidized academia because of its unpalatable implications for those in power and relegated to an unobtrusive existence in the underworld of non-University, real-world intellectuals, the Austrian School has steadily gained momentum and grown into a genuine mass movement, with an increasing number of academic bastions as well as a continuously swelling grass roots support. In fact, spearheaded by the Ludwig von Mises Institute, founded in the mid-80's, the movement has taken on an international dimension with a rapidly spreading Mises-renaissance among intellectual circles in the countries of Eastern Europe. Faced with the total collapse of socialism and the exhaustion of all governmental authority and legitimacy, and confronted with the task of the immediate and radical reconstruction of their countries, the advice that empirically meaningless mathematical economics, or econometrics, can give or that can be derived from Keynesianism, Monetarism, Rational Expectationism or, worse still, Hermeneuticism, can only appear to them as ridiculously inappropriate. In their emergency situation, only the Austrian School offers an unambiguous, radical, and constructive answer: Not only do

---

[29]For a critical evaluation of the new nihilism see Henry Veatch, '"Deconstruction in Philosophy: Has Rorty Made It the Denouement of Contemporary Analytical Philosophy?," *Review of Metaphysics* 39 (1985); Jonathan Barnes, "A Kind of Integrity," *London Review of Books* (November 6, 1986); Rothbard, "The Hermeneutical Invasion of Philosophy and Economics"; Hoppe, "In Defense of Extreme Rationalism."

truths exist in the social sciences, but there exist a priori, nonhypothetical truths which no one is capable of undoing. The truth is as simple as fundamental: that private property and private property rights is an indisputably valid, absolute principle of ethics and the basis for continuous "optimal" economic progress; and that in order to arise from the ruins of socialism, nothing will suffice but an uncompromising privatization of each and all property and the return to a contractual society based on the recognition of the absoluteness of private property rights.[30]

Indeed, the Austrian School represents the most ambitious of all forms of social rationalism with its unyielding contention that non-hypothetical a priori empirical knowledge within the field of the social sciences exists, and that it is ethics and economics (which contain this knowledge) which are analogous to logic and protophysics as the absolutely indispensable foundation of all empirical social research. Furthermore, the Austrian School alone has substantiated this contention by offering a completely developed, consistent, and all-comprehensive *positive* theory of ethics and economics.[31]

Indirectly, the basic claim of Austrianism has already been established. During the above refutation of positivism it was demonstrated that while knowledge and actions cannot be conceived of as caused (i.e., predictable on the basis of time-invariantly operating effect variables), any action, by virtue of trying to bring about some given goal, presupposes a causally structured physical reality. Obviously, this insight itself represents a perfect example of the possibility of non-hypothetical social knowledge: it formulates knowledge about actions which no actor could possibly discover to be false, because any such discovery would actually presuppose its validity. Austrianism in fact merely claims that there is much more implied in our reflectively

---

[30]For a critical assessment of the revolution in Eastern Europe see Hans-Hermann Hoppe, "The Collapse of Socialism and the Future of Eastern Europe," *Kwasny Economics* II, no. 6 (October 30, 1989); idem, *Desocialization in a United Germany* (Auburn, Ala.: Ludwig von Mises Institute, 1991).

[31]See in particular Mises, *Human Action*; Rothbard, *Man, Economy, and State*; idem, *The Ethics of Liberty* (Atlantic Highlands: Humanities Press, 1982).

gained knowledge of what it is to act than this, which no actor can thus possibly falsify.

The Austrian theory sets out from two systematically interrelated axioms, both of which are nonhypothetically true. The first is the "axiom of action": the proposition that humans act, or more precisely, that I am acting now. It cannot be denied that this proposition is true, since the denial would itself be an action. Nor can anyone intentionally *not* act, because this, too, would be an action. Thus the truth of the axiom literally cannot be undone.[32]

The second axiom is the "a priori of argumentation." What we have done here all along—I in writing this study and the reader in reading it—is engaged in argumentation. If it were not for argumentation there would be no debate about the truth or falsity of social relativism or rationalism and the status of ethics and economics. There would only be silence or meaningless noise. Only with argumentation does the idea of validity and truth emerge. Whether or not something is true, false, or undecidable; whether or not it has been justified; what is required in order to justify it; whether I, someone else, or no one is right—all of this must be decided in the course of argumentation and propositional exchanges. This proposition is a priori true, too, because it cannot be denied without affirming it in the act of denying it. One cannot argue that one cannot argue, and one cannot dispute knowing what it means to raise a validity claim without implicitly claiming at least the negation of this proposition to be true. This is the *a priori of argumentation*,[33] and both axioms are related as logically necessary interwoven strands of a priori knowledge. On the one hand, actions are more fundamental than argumentation because argumentation is only a subclass of action. On the other hand, to state what has just been stated about action and argumentation and their relationship to each other already requires argumentation, so epistemologically argumentation must be considered to be more fundamental than nonargumentative action.

---

[32]See Mises, *Human Action*, part 1.
[33]See in particular Apel, *Transformation der Philosophie*, vol II.

Ethics, or more specifically, the Austrian private property ethic, is derived from the a priori of argumentation, and it is from its nature as a nonhypothetically true axiom that ethics derives its own status as absolutely true.[34]

With the a priori of argumentation established as an axiomatic starting point of epistemology, it follows that anything that must be presupposed in the act of proposition-making cannot be propositionally disputed again. It would be meaningless to ask for a justification of presuppositions which make the production of meaningful propositions possible in the first place. Instead, they must be regarded as ultimately justified by every proposition maker. Any specific propositional content that disputed their validity must be understood as implying a performative or practical contradiction.

Further, in the same way as it is undeniably true that one cannot argue that one cannot argue, and that it must be assumed that everyone engaging in argumentation must know what it means to claim something to be true, it is also true that any argument requires an arguing person, an actor. Arguing never just consists of free-floating propositions but is always an activity, too. Given that truth claims must be raised and decided upon in the course of argumentation, and that argumentation, aside from whatever is said in its course is also a practical affair, it follows that intersubjectively meaningful norms must exist. These norms are precisely those which make an action argumentation, and they have a special cognitive status in that they are the practical preconditions of truth. In fact, neither the empirical-fact/emotive-value dichotomy so dear to the positivists, nor their distinction between empirical and analytical statements, could be claimed to be valid unless the norms underlying argumentation (in the course of which these distinctions are made) were themselves regarded as valid. It is simply impossible to argue otherwise because in doing so one would in fact presuppose their validity.

Now, as a necessarily practical affair, any propositional exchange requires a proposition-maker's exclusive control (property) over

---

[34]See on the following Hoppe, *A Theory of Socialism and Capitalism*, chaps. 2, 7.

some scarce means. No one could possibly propose anything, and no one could possibly become convinced of any proposition, if one's right to make exclusive use of one's physical body were not already presupposed. It is one's recognition of another's mutually exclusive control over his body which explains the distinctive characteristic of propositional exchanges: that while one may disagree about what has been said, it is still possible to agree at least on the fact that there is disagreement. It is obvious, too, that such a property right in one's own body must be said to be justified a priori, for anyone who would try to justify any norm whatsoever must already presuppose an exclusive right of control over his body simply to say, "I propose such and such." Anyone disputing such a right would become caught up in a practical contradiction, since in arguing so one would already implicitly have accepted the very norm that one was disputing.

Finally, it would be equally impossible to engage in argumentation, if one were not allowed to appropriate in addition to one's body other scarce means through homesteading, i.e., by putting them to use before someone else does, or if such means were not defined in objective, physical terms.

For if no one had the right to control anything at all, except his own body, then we would all cease to exist and the problem of justifying norms—as well as all other human problems—simply would not exist. The fact that one is alive presupposes the validity of property rights to other things. No one who is alive could argue otherwise.

And if a person did not acquire the right of exclusive control over such goods by homesteading, by establishing some objective link between a particular person and a particular physical resource before anyone else had done so, but instead late-comers were assumed to have ownership claims to things, then literally *no one would be allowed to do anything with anything at any time* unless he had the prior consent of all late-comers. Neither we nor our forefathers nor our progeny could survive or will survive if we were to follow this rule. Yet in order for any person—past, present or future—to argue anything it must evidently be possible to survive. And in order for us to do this, property rights cannot be conceived of as timeless and nonspecific regarding the number of people concerned. Rather, property rights must necessarily originate through action at definite places and times for specific acting individuals. Otherwise, it would be impossible for anyone to say anything at a definite tine and place and for someone else to reply. To assert that the first-user-first-owner rule of private property can be ignored or is unjustified implies a contradiction. One's assertion of this proposition presupposes one's existence as a physically independent decision-making unit at a given point in time, and the validity of the homesteading principle as an absolute principle of property acquisition.

Economics, or in Mises's terminology praxeology, and its status as a nonhypothetical, a priori true social science is derived from the axiom of action.[35]

With every action an actor pursues a goal, and whatever his goal may be, the fact that it is pursued by an actor reveals that he places a relatively higher value on it than on any other goal of action he could conceive of at the start of his action.

In order to achieve this goal an actor must interfere or decide not to interfere (which is also an interference) at an earlier point in time to produce a later result, and this interference implies the use of some scarce means (at least those of the actor's body, its standing room, and the time used by the interference).

These means must also have value for an actor—a value derived from that of the goal—because the actor must regard their employment as necessary in order to achieve the goal effectively. Further, actions can only be performed sequentially and always involve making a choice, i.e., taking up one course of action which at some given point in time promises the most highly valued result to the actor and excluding at the same time the pursuit of other, less valued goals.

In addition, when acting an actor not only invariably aims to substitute a more for a less satisfactory state of affairs and demonstrates a preference for higher over lower values; he also invariably considers

---

[35]See on the following Mises, *Human Action*, chap. IV; Rothbard, *Man Economy, and State,* chap. 1; idem, "Praxeology: The Methodology of Austrian Economics," in Edwin Dolan, ed., *The Foundations of Modern Austrian Economics* (Kansas City: Sheed and Ward, 1976); Hoppe, *Praxeology and Economic Science*; also Lionel Robbins, *The Nature and Significance of Economic Science* (New York: New York University Press, 1982).

when in the future his goals will be reached and demonstrates a universal preference for earlier over later results. Since every action requires time and man must occasionally consume something, time is always scarce. Hence, present or earlier results are, and invariably must be, valued more highly than future or later ones, and man will only exchange a present value against a future one if he thereby anticipates *increasing* his future well-being.

Furthermore, as a consequence of having to choose and give preference to one goal over another, of not being able to realize all goals simultaneously, and of being constrained by time preference, each and every action implies the incurrence of costs, i.e., the forsaking of the value attached to the most highly valued alternative goal that cannot be realized or whose realization must be postponed because the means necessary to effect it are bound up in the production of another, even more highly valued goal.

Finally, it is implied in our knowledge of what it is to act, that at its starting point every goal of action must be considered worth more to the actor than its cost and capable of yielding a profit, i.e., a result whose value is ranked higher than that of the foregone opportunities. However, every action is also invariably threatened by the possibility of a loss if in retrospect an actor finds that contrary to expectations the result actually achieved has a lower value than the relinquished alternative would have had.

All of these categories which we know to be the very heart of economics—values, means, choice, preference, time preference, cost, profit and loss—are implied in the axiom of action. Like the axiom itself, they incorporate nonhypothetically true knowledge. Any attempt to disprove this knowledge would itself have to be an action, aimed at a goal, requiring means, excluding other courses of action, incurring costs, subjecting the actor to the possibility of achieving or not achieving the desired goal, and thus leading to a profit or a loss.

All true economic propositions, and this is what the Austrian conception of economics is all about, can be deduced by means of formal logic from this incontestably true material knowledge regarding the meaning of action and its categories. More precisely, all true economic theorems consist of: (a) an understanding of the meaning of action; (b) a situation or situational change—assumed to be given or identified as being given—and described in terms of action-categories; and (c) a logical deduction of the consequences—again in terms of such categories—which result for an actor from this situation or situational change. For instance, the law of marginal utility, one of the most basic laws of economics, follows from our indisputable knowledge of the fact that every actor always prefers what satisfies him more over what satisfies him less, plus the assumption that he is faced with an increase in the supply of a good (a scarce means) whose units he regards as of equal serviceability by one additional unit. From this it follows with logical necessity that this additional unit can only be employed as a means for the removal of an uneasiness that is deemed less urgent than the least valuable goal previously satisfied by a unit of such a good.

The combination of ethics as implied in the axiom of argumentation and of economics as implied in that of action yields what might be called Austrian welfare economics.[36]

If and insofar as actors choose to act in accordance with the indisputably valid principle of the private property ethic, social welfare—defined in terms of Pareto-optimality—will invariably be optimized: A person's original appropriation of unowned resources, as demonstrated by this very action, increases his utility or welfare (at least *ex ante*). At the same time, it makes no one worse off because in appropriating them he takes nothing away from others. Obviously, others could have homesteaded these resources, too, if only they had perceived them as scarce, and hence, valuable. However, they did not do so, which demonstrates that they attached no value to them whatsoever, and thus they cannot be said to have lost any utility on account of this act. Proceeding from this basis, any further act of production utilizing homesteaded resources is equally Pareto-optimal on demonstrated preference grounds, provided only that it does not uninvitedly

---

[36]See also Murray N. Rothbard, *Toward a Reconstruction of Utility and Welfare Economics* (New York: Center for Libertarian Studies, Occasional Paper Series no. 3, 1977); idem, *Power and Market* (Kansas City: Sheed, Andrews and McMeel, 1977); idem, "The Myth of Neutral Taxation," *Cato Journal* 1, no. 2 (1981); Hoppe, *A Theory of Socialism and Capitalism*; idem, "*Man, Economy, and Liberty*: Review Essay," *Review of Austrian Economics* 4 (1990).

impair the physical integrity of the resources homesteaded or produced with homesteaded means by others. Finally, every voluntary
exchange starting from this basis must also be regarded as a Pareto-
optimal change because it can only take place if both parties expect
to benefit from it.

Operating according to the rules just described always, and invariably so, leads to the greatest possible production of wealth, for any
deviation from this set of rules implies, by definition, a redistribution
of property titles, and hence of income, away from user-producers
and contractors of goods onto non-users-producers and noncontractors. Consequently, any such deviation implies that there will be relatively less original appropriation of resources whose scarcity is recognized, there will be less production of new goods, less maintenance
of existing goods, and less mutually beneficial contracting and trading. This in turn implies a lower standard of living in terms of
exchangeable goods and services. Furthermore, the provision that
only the *first* user of a good acquires ownership assures that productive efforts will be as high as possible *at all times*. The provision that
only the physical integrity of property (not property values) is protected guarantees that every owner will undertake the greatest possible *value*-productive efforts to promote favorable changes in property
values and to prevent or counter any unfavorable changes in property
values (as they might result from another person's actions regarding
his property). Thus, any deviation from these rules also implies
reduced levels of value productive efforts at all times.

The radical simplicity of this Austrian theory of ethics and economics, indeed the fact that it has been fully elaborated—foremost in
Ludwig von Mises's epochal *Human Action*, and in Murray N. Rothbard's *Man, Economy, and State* and *The Ethics of Liberty*—to a rig-
orously consistent as well as architectonically beautiful edifice of ethical and economic thought explains why the social rationalism of the
Austrian School could be driven underground during the heyday of
positivism but could never be entirely uprooted and eradicated. Its
truth is too obvious to be consistently ignored among men of intellectual curiosity and common sense, for is it not natural that every
person should own his own body as well as all scarce goods which he
puts to use with the help of this body before anyone else does? Is it

not obvious that every owner should have the right to employ these goods as he sees fit so long as in so doing he does not uninvitedly change the physical integrity of another's property? Is it not obvious that once a good has first been homesteaded or produced with homesteaded means, then ownership of it can only be acquired by means of a contractual, voluntary transfer of a property title from a previous to a later owner? And is it not intuitively clear that only if, and insofar as, these rules are in effect, the greatest possible production of social wealth and welfare will ensue?[37]

This so obviously true theory has the most radical practical-political implications. It refutes as ethically unjustifiable and economically counterproductive actions such as taxation, the legislative redistribution of private property rights, the creation of fiat money, fractional reserve banking, and ultimately, the very institution of state government. It demands instead a pure private property society, an anarchy of private property owners, regulated exclusively by private property law.[38] By virtue of this, the Austrian School is brought into fundamental opposition to any exercise of governmental power. Recognizing it as their natural and most dangerous intellectual enemy, those in power have done everything possible to stamp out its memory and substitute statolatry for ethics and economics. As Mises writes:

> Despots and democratic majorities are drunk with power. They must reluctantly admit that they are subject to the laws of nature. But they reject the very notion of economic law. Are they not the supreme legislator? . . . It is impossible to understand the history of economic thought if one does not pay attention to the fact that economics as such is a challenge to the conceit of those in power. An economist can never be a favorite of autocrats and demagogues. With them he is always the mischief-maker, and the more

---

[37]See on the idea of a natural sense of justice also Gustave de Molinari, *The Production of Security* (Burlingame, Calif.: Center for Libertarian Studies, Occasional Paper Series No. 2, 1977).

[38]On this also Rothbard, *Man, Economy, and State*; idem, *Power and Market*, idem, *For A New Liberty*; idem, *The Ethics of Liberty*; Hans-Hermann Hoppe, *Eigentum, Anarchie, und Staat* (Opladen: Westdeutscher Verlag, 1987); idem, *A Theory of Socialism and Capitalism*.

they are inwardly convinced that his objections are well founded, the more they hate him.[39]

In the present situation of a worldwide crisis of governmental legitimacy, of the collapse of East Bloc Socialism, and of the enduring stagnation of the Western Welfare States, the chance for Austrian rationalism to fill the philosophical vacuum that has appeared with the retreat of positivism and to become the paradigm of the future is as good or better than ever.[40] Now as before it requires moral courage as much as intellectual integrity to propound the Austrian social theory—the opposing statist battalions still represent a formidable majority and are in control of a far larger share of resources. Nonetheless, with the total breakdown of socialism and the concept of social ownership staring everyone in the face, the antithetical Austrian theory of private property, free markets and laissez faire cannot but gain attractiveness and win support. Austrians have reason to believe that the time has come when they may succeed in bringing about a fundamental change in public opinion, by reclaiming ethics and economics from the hands of the positivists and the engineering powerful and by restoring public recognition of private property rights and free markets based on such rights as ultimate, absolute principles of ethics and economics.

---

[39]Mises, *Human Action*, p. 67.

[40]For a strategic assessment of the present age from an Austrian perspective see Murray N. Rothbard, "Left and Right: The Prospects for Liberty," and "Ludwig von Mises and the Paradigm of Our Age," in idem, *Egalitarianism as a Revolt Against Nature and Other Essays* (Washington, D.C.: Libertarian Review Press, 1974).

15

Rothbardian Ethics

THE PROBLEM OF SOCIAL ORDER

Robinson Crusoe, alone on his island, can do whatever he pleases. For him, the question concerning rules of orderly human conduct—social cooperation—simply does not arise. Naturally, this question can only arise once a second person, Friday, arrives on the island, yet even then, the question remains largely irrelevant so long as no *scarcity* exists. Suppose the island is the Garden of Eden. All external goods are available in superabundance. They are "free goods," such as the air that we breathe is normally a "free" good. Whatever Crusoe does with these goods, his actions have repercussions *neither* with respect to his own future supply of such goods, nor with regard to the present or future supply of the same goods for Friday (and vice versa). Hence, it is impossible that there could ever be a conflict between Crusoe and Friday concerning the use of such goods. A conflict becomes possible only if goods are scarce, and only then can there arise a problem of formulating rules which make orderly, conflict-free social cooperation possible.

In the Garden of Eden only two scarce goods exist: the physical body of a person and its standing room. Crusoe and Friday each have only one body and can stand only at one place at a time. Hence, even in the Garden of Eden conflicts between Crusoe and Friday can arise: Crusoe and Friday cannot both simultaneously occupy the same standing room without coming thereby into physical conflict with each other. Accordingly, even in the Garden of Eden rules of orderly social conduct must exist—rules regarding the proper location and movement of human bodies. Outside the Garden of Eden, in the realm of scarcity, there must be rules that regulate not just the use of personal bodies but of *everything* scarce so that *all* possible conflicts can be ruled out. This is the problem of social order.

THE SOLUTION: THE IDEA OF ORIGINAL APPROPRIATION AND PRIVATE PROPERTY

In the history of social and political thought many proposals have been advanced as an alleged solution to the problem of social order, and this variety of mutually inconsistent proposals has contributed to the fact that today the search for a single "correct" solution is frequently deemed illusory. Yet as I will demonstrate, a correct solution *exists*; hence, there is no reason to succumb to moral relativism. I did not discover this solution, nor did Murray Rothbard, for that matter. Rather, the solution has been known for hundreds of years if not for much longer. Murray Rothbard's claim to fame is "merely" that he rediscovered this old and simple solution and formulated it more clearly and convincingly than anyone before him.

Let me begin by formulating the solution—first for the special case represented by the Garden of Eden and subsequently for the general case represented by the "real" world of all-around scarcity—and then proceed to the explanation of why this solution, and no other one, is correct.

In the Garden of Eden, the solution is provided by the simple rule stipulating that everyone may place or move his own body wherever he pleases, *provided only that no one else is already standing there and occupying the same space*. Outside of the Garden of Eden, in the realm of all-around scarcity, the solution is provided by this rule: Everyone is the proper owner of his own physical body as well as of all places and nature-given goods that he occupies and puts to use by means of his body, *provided only that no one else has already occupied or used the same places and goods before him*. This ownership of "originally appropriated" places and goods by a person implies his right to use and transform these places and goods in any way he sees fit, *provided only that he does not thereby uninvitedly change the physical integrity of places and goods originally appropriated by another person*. In particular, once a place or good has been first appropriated by (in John Locke's phrase) "mixing one's labor" with it, ownership in such places and goods can be acquired only by means of a voluntary contractual transfer of its property title from a previous to a later owner.

In light of widespread moral relativism, it is worthwhile to point out that this idea of original appropriation and private property as a solution to the problem of social order is in complete accordance with our moral "intuition." Isn't it simply absurd to claim that a person should *not* be the proper owner of his body and the places and goods that he originally, i.e., *prior to anyone else*, appropriates, uses and/or produces by means of his body? Who else, if not he, should be their owner? Isn't it also obvious that the overwhelming majority of people, including children and primitives, act according to these rules, and do so unquestioningly and as a matter of course?

As important as it is, a moral intuition is not a proof. Yet there does exist proof that our moral intuition is correct.

The proof can be provided in a twofold manner. On the one hand, such proof can be provided by spelling out the consequences that follow if one were to deny the validity of the institution of original appropriation and private property: If a person A were *not* the owner of his own body and the places and goods originally appropriated and/or produced with this body as well as of the goods voluntarily (contractually) acquired from another previous owner, then only two alternatives exist. Either *another* person B must be recognized as the owner of A's body as well as the places and goods appropriated, produced or acquired by A, or else *all* persons, A *and* B, must be considered equal co-owners of all bodies, places and goods.

In the first case, A would be reduced to the rank of B's slave and object of exploitation. B is the owner of A's body and all places and goods appropriated, produced, and acquired by A, but A in turn is not the owner of B's body and the places and goods appropriated, produced and acquired by B. Hence, under this ruling two categorically distinct classes of persons are created—*Untermenschen* such as A and *Übermenschen* such as B—to whom different "laws" apply. Accordingly, such a ruling must be discarded as a human ethic equally applicable to everyone *qua* human being (rational animal). From the very outset, any such ruling can be recognized as not universally acceptable and thus cannot claim to represent law. For a rule to aspire to the rank of a law—a *just* rule—it is necessary that such a rule apply equally and universally to everyone.

Alternatively, in the second case of universal and equal co-ownership, the requirement of equal law for everyone is fulfilled. However, this alternative suffers from another even more severe deficiency, for if it were applied, all of mankind would instantly perish. (And since every human ethic must permit the survival of mankind, this alternative must be rejected.) Every action of a person requires the use of some scarce means (at least the person's body and its standing room), but if all goods were co-owned by everyone, then no one, at no time and no place, would be allowed to do anything unless he had previously secured every other co-owner's consent to do so. However, how could anyone grant such consent if he were not the exclusive owner of his own body (including his vocal cords) by means of which his consent must be expressed? Indeed, he would first need others' consent in order to be allowed to express his own, but these others cannot give their consent without having first his, etc.

This insight into the praxeological impossibility of "universal communism," as Rothbard referred to this proposal, brings us immediately to an alternative way of demonstrating the idea of original appropriation and private property as the only correct solution to the problem of social order. Whether or not persons have any rights and, if so, which ones, can only be decided in the course of argumentation (propositional exchange). Justification—proof, conjecture, refutation—is *argumentative* justification. Anyone who denied this proposition would become involved in a performative contradiction because his denial would itself constitute an argument. Even an ethical relativist must accept this first proposition, which has been referred to as the *a priori of argumentation*.

From the undeniable acceptance—the axiomatic status—of this a priori of argumentation, two equally necessary conclusions follow. First, it follows under what circumstances *no* rational solution to the problem of conflict arising from scarcity exists. Suppose in my earlier scenario of Crusoe and Friday that Friday was not the name of a man but of a gorilla. Obviously, just as Crusoe can run into conflict regarding his body and its standing room with Friday the man, so he might do so with Friday the gorilla. The gorilla might want to occupy the same space that Crusoe occupies. In this case, at least if the gorilla is the sort of entity that we know gorillas to be, there is in fact no rational solution to their conflict. Either the gorilla wins, and devours, crushes, or pushes Crusoe aside (that is the gorilla's solution to the problem) or Crusoe wins, and kills, beats, chases away, or tames the gorilla (that is Crusoe's solution). In this situation, one may indeed speak of moral relativism. One may concur with Alasdair MacIntyre, a prominent philosopher of the relativist persuasion, who asks as the title of one of his books, *Whose Justice? Which Rationality?*—Crusoe's or the gorilla's? Depending on whose side one chooses, the answer will be different. However, it is more appropriate to refer to this situation as one in which the question of justice and rationality simply does not arise: as an extra-moral situation. The existence of Friday the gorilla poses for Crusoe merely a technical problem, not a moral one. Crusoe has no other choice but to learn how to manage and control the movements of the gorilla successfully just as he must learn to manage and control the inanimate objects of his environment.

By implication, only if both parties to a conflict are capable of engaging in argumentation with one another can one speak of a moral problem and is the question of whether or not there exists a solution meaningful. Only if Friday, regardless of his physical appearance (i.e., whether he looks like a man or like a gorilla), is capable of argumentation (even if he has shown himself to be so capable only once), can he be deemed rational and does the question whether or not a correct solution to the problem of social order exists make sense. No one can be expected to give an answer to someone who has never raised a question or, more to the point, to someone who has never stated his own relativistic viewpoint in the form of an argument. In that case, this "other" cannot but be regarded and treated like an animal or plant, i.e., as an extra-moral entity. Only if this other entity can in principle pause in his activity, whatever it might be, step back so to speak, and say "yes" or "no" to something one has said, do we owe this entity an answer and, accordingly, can we possibly claim that our answer is the correct one for both parties involved in a conflict.

Second, it follows from the a priori of argumentation that everything that must be presupposed in the course of an argumentation—as the logical and praxeological precondition of argumentation—cannot in turn be argumentatively disputed as regards its validity without one becoming thereby entangled in an internal (performative) contradiction. Propositional exchanges are not made up of free-floating propositions but constitute a specific human activity. Argumentation between Crusoe and Friday requires that both possess, and mutually recognize each other as possessing, exclusive control over their respective bodies (their brain, vocal cords, etc.) as well as the standing room occupied by their bodies. No one could propose anything and expect the other party to convince himself of the validity of this proposition or else deny it and propose something else unless his and his opponent's right to exclusive control over their respective bodies and standing rooms were already presupposed and assumed to be valid. In fact, it is precisely this mutual recognition of the proponent's as well as the opponent's property in his own body and standing room which constitutes the *characteristicum specificum* of all propositional disputes: that while one may not agree regarding the validity of some specific proposition one can agree nonetheless on the fact that one disagrees.

Moreover, this right to property in one's own body and its standing room must be considered a priori (or indisputably) justified by proponent and opponent alike. Anyone who wanted to claim any proposition as valid vis-à-vis an opponent would already have to presuppose his and his opponent's exclusive control over their respective body and standing room simply in order to say "I claim such and such to be true, and I challenge you to prove me wrong."[1]

---

[1]So much for John Rawls's claim, in his celebrated *Theory of Justice*, that we cannot but "acknowledge as the first principle of justice one requiring an equal

Furthermore, it would be equally impossible to engage in argumentation and rely on the propositional force of one's arguments if one were not allowed to own (exclusively control) other scarce means (besides one's body and its standing room). If one did not have such a right, then we would all immediately perish and the problem of justifying rules simply would not exist. Hence, by virtue of the fact of being alive property rights to other things must be presupposed as valid, too. No one who is alive could possibly argue otherwise.

And if a person were not permitted to acquire property in these goods and spaces by means of an act of original appropriation, i.e., by establishing an objective (intersubjectively ascertainable) link between himself and a particular good and/or space prior to anyone else, but if instead property in such goods or spaces were granted to late-comers, then no one would be permitted to ever begin using any good unless he had previously secured such late-comers' consent. Yet how can a late-comer consent to the actions of an early-comer? Moreover, every late-comer would in turn need the consent of other still later-comers, and so on. That is, neither we, nor our forefathers, nor our progeny would have been or will be able to survive if one were to follow this rule. However, in order for any person—past, present, or future—to argue anything it must be possible to survive then and now, and in order to do just this property rights cannot be conceived of as being timeless and unspecific with respect to the number of persons concerned.

Rather, property rights must necessarily be conceived of as originating as a result of definite individuals acting at definite points in time and space. Otherwise, it would be impossible for anyone to ever say anything at a definite point in time and space and for someone

---

distribution (of all resources)," and his comment that "this principle is so obvious that we would expect it to occur to anyone immediately." What I have demonstrated here is that any egalitarian ethic such as this proposed by Rawls is not only *not* obvious but must be regarded instead as absurd, i.e., as self-contradictory nonsense. If Rawls were right and all resources were indeed equally distributed, then he literally would have no leg to stand on and support him in proposing the very nonsense that he does pronounce.

else to be able to reply. Simply saying that the first-user-first-owner rule of the ethics of private property can be ignored or is unjustified implies a performative contradiction, for one's being able to say so must presuppose one's existence as an independent decision-making unit at a given point in time and space.

SIMPLE SOLUTION, RADICAL CONCLUSIONS: ANARCHY AND STATE

As simple as the solution to the problem of social order is and as much as people in their daily lives intuitively recognize and act according to the ethics of private property just explained, this simple and undemanding solution implies some surprisingly radical conclusions. Apart from ruling out as unjustified all activities such as murder, homicide, rape, trespass, robbery, burglary, theft, and fraud, the ethics of private property is also incompatible with the existence of a state defined as an agency that possesses a compulsory territorial monopoly of ultimate decision-making (jurisdiction) and/or the right to tax.

Classical political theory, at least from Hobbes onward, had viewed the state as the very institution responsible for the enforcement of the ethics of private property. In regarding the state as unjust—indeed, as "a vast criminal organization"—and reaching anarchist conclusions instead, Rothbard did not deny the necessity of enforcing the ethics of private property. He did not share the view of those anarchists, ridiculed by his teacher and mentor Mises, who believed that all people, if only left alone, would be good and peace-loving creatures.

To the contrary, Rothbard wholeheartedly agreed with Mises that there will always be murderers, thieves, thugs, con-artists, etc., and that life in society would be impossible if they were not punished by physical force. Rather, what Rothbard categorically denied was the claim that it followed from the right and need for the protection of person and property that protection rightfully should or effectively could be provided by a monopolist of jurisdiction and taxation. In making this claim, classical political theory had to present the state as the result of a contractual agreement among private property owners. Rothbard argued this was false and an impossible undertaking. No state can possibly arise contractually; accordingly, it can be demonstrated that no state is compatible with the rightful and effective protection of private property.

Private-property ownership, as the result of acts of original appropriation, production, or exchange from prior to later owner, implies the owner's right to exclusive jurisdiction regarding his property; and no private property owner can possibly surrender his right to ultimate jurisdiction over and physical defense of his property to someone else unless he sold or otherwise transferred his property (in which case someone else would have exclusive jurisdiction over it). To be sure, every private property owner may partake of the advantages of the division of labor and seek more or better protection of his property through cooperation with other owners and their property. That is, every property owner may buy from, sell to, or otherwise contract with anyone else concerning more or better property protection, and every property owner may at any time unilaterally discontinue any such cooperation with others or change his respective affiliations. Hence, in order to meet the demand for protection, it would be rightfully possible and economically likely that specialized individuals and agencies would arise to provide protection, insurance, and arbitration services for a fee to voluntarily paying clients.

While it is easy to conceive of the contractual origin of a system of competitive security suppliers, it is inconceivable how private property owners could possibly enter a contract that entitled another agent irrevocably (once and for all) with the power of ultimate decision-making regarding his own person and property and/or the power to tax. That is, it is inconceivable how anyone could ever agree to a contract that allowed someone else to determine permanently what he may or may not do with his property, for in so doing this person would have effectively rendered himself defenseless vis-à-vis such an ultimate decision maker. Likewise, is it inconceivable that anyone would ever agree to a contract that allowed one's protector to determine unilaterally, without consent of the protected, the sum that the protected must pay for his protection.

Orthodox, i.e., statist, political theorists, from John Locke to James Buchanan and John Rawls, have tried to solve this difficulty through makeshift "tacit," "implicit," or "conceptual" agreements, contracts, or state constitutions. All of these characteristically tortuous and confused attempts, however, have only added to the same unavoidable conclusion drawn by Rothbard: That it is impossible to derive a justification for government from explicit contracts between private property owners, and hence, that the institution of the state must be considered unjust, i.e., the result of moral error.

THE CONSEQUENCE OF MORAL ERROR:
STATISM AND THE DESTRUCTION OF LIBERTY AND PROPERTY

All errors are costly. This is most obvious with errors concerning laws of nature. If a person errs regarding laws of nature this person will not be able to reach his own goals. However, because the failure of doing so must be borne by each erring individual, there prevails in this realm a universal desire to learn and correct one's errors. Moral errors are costly, too. Unlike in the former case, however, their cost must not, at least not necessarily, be paid for by each and every person committing the error. In fact, this would be the case only if the error involved were that of believing that *everyone* had the right to tax and the right of ultimate decision-making regarding the person and property of *everyone* else. A society whose members believed *this* would be doomed. The price to be paid for this error would be universal death and extinction. However, matters are distinctly different if the error involved is one of believing that only *one agency—the state*—has the right to tax and the right to ultimate decision-making (rather than *everyone*, or else, and correctly so, no one). A society whose members believed *this*—that is, that there must be different laws applying unequally to masters and serfs, taxers and taxed, legislators and legislatees—*can* in fact exist and endure. This error must be paid for, too. But not everyone holding this erroneous belief pays for it equally. Rather, *some* people will have to pay for it, while others—the agents of the state—actually benefit from the same error. Hence, in this case it would be mistaken to assume a universal desire to learn and correct one's errors. To the contrary, in this case it must be assumed that rather than learning and promoting the truth, some people have a constant motive to lie, i.e., to maintain and promote falsehoods even if they themselves recognize them as such.

In any case, what are the "mixed" consequences of, and what is the unequal price to be paid for, the error and/or lie of believing in the justice of the institution of a state?

Once the principle of government—judicial monopoly and the power to tax—is incorrectly admitted as just, any notion of restraining government power and safeguarding individual liberty and property is illusory. Instead, under monopolistic auspices the price of justice and protection will continually rise and the quality of justice and protection fall. A tax-funded protection agency is a contradiction in terms—an expropriating property protector—and will inevitably lead to more taxes and less protection. Even if, as some classical liberal statists have proposed, a government limited its activities exclusively to the protection of pre-existing private property rights, the further question of *how much* security to produce would arise. Motivated (like everyone) by self-interest and the disutility of labor but endowed with the unique power to tax, a government agent's response will invariably be the same: To *maximize expenditures on protection*—and almost all of a nation's wealth can conceivably be consumed by the cost of protection—and at the same time to *minimize the production of protection*. The more money one can spend and the less one must work to produce, the better off one will be.

Moreover, a judicial monopoly will inevitably lead to a steady deterioration in the quality of justice and protection. If no one can appeal to justice except to government, justice will be perverted in favor of the government, constitutions and supreme courts notwithstanding. Constitutions and supreme courts are state constitutions and agencies, and all limitations to state action they might contain or find are invariably decided by agents of the very institution under consideration. Predictably, the definition of property and protection will continually be altered and the range of jurisdiction expanded to the government's advantage until, ultimately, the notion of universal and immutable human rights—and in particular property rights—will disappear and be replaced by that of law as government-made legislation and rights as government-given grants.

The results, all of which were predicted by Rothbard, are before our eyes, for everyone to see. The tax load imposed on property owners and producers has continually increased, making the economic burden even of slaves and serfs seem moderate in comparison. Government debt—and hence, future tax obligations—has risen to breathtaking heights. Every detail of private life, property, trade, and contract is regulated by ever higher mountains of paper laws. However, the only task that government was ever supposed to assume—of protecting our life and property—it does not perform. To the contrary, the higher the expenditures on social, public, and national security have risen, the more our private property rights have been eroded, the more our property has been expropriated, confiscated, destroyed, and depreciated. The more paper laws have been produced, the more legal uncertainty and moral hazard has been created, and lawlessness has displaced law and order. Instead of protecting us from domestic crime and foreign aggression, our government, equipped with enormous stockpiles of weapons of mass destruction, aggresses against ever new Hitlers and suspected Hitlerite sympathizers anywhere and everywhere outside of its "own" territory. In short, while we have become ever more helpless, impoverished, threatened, and insecure, our state rulers have become increasingly more corrupt, arrogant, and dangerously armed.

The Restoration of Morality: On Liberation

What to do, then? Rothbard has not only reconstructed the ethics of liberty and explained the current morass as the result of statism; he has also shown us the way toward a restoration of morals.

First and foremost, he has explained that states, as powerful and invincible as they might seem, ultimately owe their existence to ideas, and since ideas can in principle change instantaneously, states can be brought down and crumble practically over night.

The representatives of the state are always and everywhere only a small minority of the population over which they rule. The reason for this is as simple as it is fundamental: one hundred parasites can live comfortable lives if they suck out the life blood of thousands of productive hosts, but thousands of parasites cannot live comfortably off of a host population of just a hundred. Yet if government agents are merely a small minority of the population, how can they enforce their will on this population and get away with it? The answer given by

Rothbard as well as de la Boétie, Hume, and Mises before him is only by virtue of the voluntary cooperation of the majority of the subject population with the state. Yet how can the state secure such cooperation? The answer is only because and insofar as the majority of the population believes in the *legitimacy* of state rule. This is not to say that the majority of the population must agree with every single state measure. Indeed, it may well believe that many state policies are mistaken or even despicable. However, the majority of the population must believe in the justice of the institution of the state as such, and hence, that even if a particular government goes wrong, these mistakes are merely accidents which must be accepted and tolerated in view of some greater good provided by the institution of government.

Yet how can the majority of the population be brought to believe this? The answer is with the help of the intellectuals. In the old days that meant trying to mold an alliance between the state and the church. In modern times and far more effectively, this means through the nationalization (socialization) of education: through state-run or state-subsidized schools and universities. The market demand for intellectual services, in particular in the area of the humanities and social sciences, is not exactly high and none too stable and secure. Intellectuals would be at the mercy of the values and choices of the masses, and generally the masses are uninterested in intellectual-philosophical concerns. The state, on the other hand, notes Rothbard, accommodates their typically overinflated egos and "is willing to offer the intellectuals a warm, secure, and permanent berth in its apparatus, a secure income, and the panoply of prestige." Indeed, the modern democratic state in particular, has created a massive oversupply of intellectuals.

This accommodation does not guarantee "correct"—statist—thinking, of course; and as well and generally overpaid as they are, intellectuals will continue to complain how little their oh-so-important work is appreciated by the powers that be. But it certainly helps in reaching the "correct" conclusions if one realizes that without the state—the institution of taxation and legislation—one might be out of work and may have to try one's hands at the mechanics of gas pump operation instead of concerning oneself with such pressing problems as alienation, equity, exploitation, the deconstruction of gender and sex roles, or the culture of the Eskimos, the Hopis, and the Zulus. Furthermore, even if one feels underappreciated by this or that incumbent government, one still realizes that help can only come from another government, and certainly not from an intellectual assault on the legitimacy of the institution of government as such. Thus, it is hardly surprising that, as a matter of empirical fact, the overwhelming majority of contemporary intellectuals are far-out lefties and that even most conservative or free market intellectuals such as Friedman or Hayek, for instance, are fundamentally and philosophically statists.

From this insight into the importance of ideas and the role of intellectuals as bodyguards of the state and statism, it follows that the most decisive role in the process of liberation—the restoration of justice and morality—must fall on the shoulders of what one might call anti-intellectual intellectuals. Yet how can such anti-intellectual intellectuals possibly succeed in delegitimizing the state in public opinion, especially if the overwhelming majority of their colleagues are statists and will do everything in their power to isolate and discredit them as extremists and crackpots? Time permits only a few brief comments on this fundamental question.

First, one must reckon with the vicious opposition from one's colleagues. In order to withstand it, it is of utmost importance to ground one's case not in economics and utilitarianism, but in ethics and moral arguments, for only moral convictions provide one with the courage and strength needed in ideological battle. Few are inspired and willing to accept sacrifices if what they are opposed to is mere error and waste. More inspiration and courage can be drawn from knowing that one is engaged in fighting evil and lies. (I'll return to this shortly.)

Second, it is important to recognize that one does not need to convert one's colleagues, i.e., to persuade mainstream intellectuals. As Thomas Kuhn has shown, this is rare enough even in the natural sciences. In the social sciences, conversions among established intellectuals from previously held views are almost unheard of. Instead, one should concentrate one's efforts on the not-yet intellectually committed young, whose idealism makes them also particularly receptive to moral arguments and moral rigorism. Likewise, one should circumvent academia and reach out to the general public (i.e., to the educated laymen), which entertains some generally healthy anti-intellectual prejudices into which one can easily tap.

Third, returning to the importance of a moral attack on the state, it is essential to recognize that there can be no compromise on the level of theory. To be sure, one should not refuse to cooperate with people whose views are ultimately mistaken and confused, *provided* that their objectives can be classified clearly and unambiguously as a step in the right direction of the de-statization of society. For instance, one would not want to refuse cooperation with people who seek to introduce a flat income tax of 10 percent (although one would not want to cooperate with those who would want to combine this measure with an increased sales tax in order to achieve revenue neutrality, for instance). However, under no circumstances should such cooperation lead to or be achieved by compromising one's own principles. Either taxation is just or it is not. Once it is accepted as just, how is one to oppose any increase in it? The answer is of course that one cannot!

Put differently, compromise on the level of theory, as we find it, for instance, among moderate free-marketeers such as Hayek or Friedman or even among the so-called minarchists, is not only philosophically flawed but is also practically ineffective and indeed counterproductive. Their ideas can be—and in fact are—easily co-opted and incorporated by the state rulers and statist ideology. Indeed, how often do we hear nowadays from statists and in defense of a statist agenda cries such as "even Hayek (Friedman) says," or, "not even Hayek (Friedman) denies that such and such must be done by the state!" Personally, they may not be happy about this, but there is no denying that their work lends itself to this purpose, and hence, that they actually contributed to the continued and unabated growth of state power.

In other words, theoretical compromise or gradualism will only lead to the perpetuation of the falsehood, evils, and lies of statism, and only theoretical purism, radicalism, and intransigence can and will lead first to gradual practical reform and improvement and then possibly to final victory. Accordingly, as an anti-intellectual intellectual in the Rothbardian sense, one can never be satisfied with criticizing various government follies although one might have to begin with this, but one must always proceed from there to a fundamental attack on the institution of the state as a moral outrage and its representatives as moral as well as economic frauds, liars, and impostors—as emperors without clothes.

Specifically, one must never hesitate to strike at the very heart of the legitimacy of the state: its alleged indispensable role as producer of private protection and security. I have already shown how ridiculous this claim is on theoretical grounds: how can an agency that may expropriate private property possibly claim to be a protector of private property? It is hardly less important to attack the legitimacy of the state in this regard on empirical grounds by pointing out and hammering at the fact that states, which are supposed to protect us, are the very institutions responsible for an estimated 170 million deaths in the twentieth century alone—more than the victims of private crime in all of human history! And this number of victims of private crimes, from which government did not protect us, would have been much lower if governments everywhere and at all times had not undertaken constant efforts to disarm their own citizens so that the governments in turn could become ever more effective killing machines!

Instead of treating politicians with respect, then, one's criticism of them should be significantly stepped up. Almost to a man they are not only thieves but mass murderers. How dare they demand our respect and loyalty?

But will a sharp and distinct ideological radicalization bring the desired results? I have no doubt. Indeed, only radical and indeed radically simple ideas can possibly stir the emotions of the dull and indolent masses and delegitimize government in their eyes.

Let me quote Hayek to this effect (and in doing so, I hope to indicate also that my rather harsh earlier criticism of him should not be misunderstood as implying that one cannot learn anything from authors who are fundamentally wrong and muddled):

> We must make the building of a free society once more an intellectual adventure, a deed of courage. What we lack is a liberal Utopia, a programme which seems neither a mere defence of things as they are nor a diluted kind of socialism, but a truly liberal

radicalism which does not spare the susceptibilities of the mighty
... which is not too severely practical and which does not confine
itself to what appears today as politically possible. We need intellectual leaders who are prepared to resist the blandishments of
power and influence and who are willing to work for an ideal,
however small may be the prospects of its early realization. They
must be men who are willing to stick to principles and to fight for
their full realization, however remote. . . . Free trade and freedom
of opportunity are ideas which still may arouse the imaginations
of large numbers, but a mere "reasonable freedom of trade" or a
mere "relaxation of controls" is neither intellectually respectable
nor likely to inspire any enthusiasm. . . .

Unless we can make the philosophic foundations of a free society
once more a living intellectual issue, and its implementation a task
which challenges the ingenuity and imagination of our liveliest
minds, the prospects of freedom are indeed dark. But if we can
regain that belief in the power of ideas which was the mark of liberalism at its best, the battle is not lost.[2]

Hayek did not heed his own advice and provide us with a consistent and inspiring theory. His Utopia, as developed in his *Constitution
of Liberty*, is the rather uninspiring vision of the Swedish welfare
state. Instead, it is Rothbard who has done what Hayek recognized as
necessary for a renewal of classical liberalism; and if there is anything
that can reverse the seemingly unstoppable tide of statism and
restore justice and liberty, it is the personal example set by Murray
Rothbard and the spread of Rothbardianism.

---

[2]Hayek, F.A., "The Intellectuals and Socialism," in idem, *Studies in
Philosophy, Politics, and Economics* (New York: Simon and Schuster, 1969), p.
194.

Appendix:
Four Critical Replies

I. Demonstrated Preference and Private Property[1]

Professor Osterfeld, after generously acknowledging the "path-breaking" nature of my a priori defense of the ethics of private property, concentrates on four objections to my arguments.

I will comment on all four objections that Professor Osterfeld addresses. However, since they depend on a correct understanding of my central argument and its logical force, I will first restate my case in the briefest possible way.

As Osterfeld correctly notices, I give a praxeological proof for the validity of the essentially Lockean private property ethic. More precisely, I demonstrate that only this ethic can be argumentatively justified because it is the praxeological presupposition of argumentation, and any deviating ethical proposal can hence be shown to be in violation of demonstrated preference. Such a proposal can be raised, but its propositional content would contradict the ethic for which one would demonstrate a preference by virtue of one's own act of

---

[1]Reply to David Osterfeld, "Comment on Hoppe," *Austrian Economics Newsletter* (Spring/Summer, 1988).

proposition-making, i.e., by the act of engaging in argumentation. In the same way as one can say "I am and always shall be indifferent towards doing things" though this proposition contradicts the act of proposition-making, which reveals subjective *preferences* (saying this rather than saying something else or not saying anything at all), deviationist ethical proposals are falsified by the reality of actually proposing them.

To reach this conclusion and properly understand its importance, two insights are essential.

First, the question of what is just or unjust (or what is valid or not) only arises insofar as I am and others are capable of propositional exchanges—of argumentation. The question does not arise for a stone or fish because they are incapable of producing validity-claiming propositions. Yet if this is so—and one cannot deny that it is without contradicting oneself, for one cannot argue the case that one cannot argue—then any ethical proposal, or indeed any proposition, must be assumed to claim it can be validated by propositional or argumentative means. In producing any proposition, overtly or as an internal thought, one demonstrates one's preference for the willingness to rely on argumentative means to convince oneself or others of something. There is then no way of justifying anything unless it is a justification by means of propositional exchanges and arguments. It must be considered the ultimate defeat for an ethical proposal if one can demonstrate that its content is logically incompatible with the proponent's claim that its validity be ascertainable by argumentative means. To demonstrate such incompatibility would amount to an impossibility proof, and such proof is deadly in the realm of intellectual inquiry.

Second, the means with which a person demonstrates preference by engaging in argumentation are those of private property. Obviously, no one could propose anything or become convinced of any proposition by argumentative means if a person's right to exclusive use of his physical body were not presupposed. Furthermore, it would be equally impossible to sustain argumentation and rely on the propositional force of one's arguments if one were not allowed to appropriate other scarce goods through homesteading action, by putting them to use before somebody else does, or if such goods and the right of exclusive control regarding them were not defined in objective physical terms. If such a right were not presupposed, or if latecomers had legitimate claims to things, or things owned were defined in subjective evaluative terms, no one could survive as a physically independent decision-making unit; hence, no one could ever raise any validity-claiming proposition.

Thus, by being alive and formulating propositions, one demonstrates that any ethic except that of private property is invalid.

Osterfeld's fourth objection states that my argument is an instance of ethical naturalism, but that I then fall afoul of the naturalistic fallacy of deriving an "ought" from an "is." The first part of this proposition is acceptable, but not the second. What I offer is an entirely value-free system of ethics. I remain exclusively in the realm of is-statements and nowhere try to drive an "ought" from an "is." The structure of my argument is this: (a) justification is propositional or argumentative (a priori true is-statement); (b) argumentation presupposes the recognition of the private property ethic (a priori true is-statement); (c) no deviation from a private property ethic can be justified argumentatively (a priori true is-statement). Thus, my refutation of all socialist ethics is a purely cognitive one. That Rawls or other socialists may still advocate such ethics is completely beside the point. That one plus one equals two does not rule out the possibility that someone says it is three, or that one ought not attempt to make one plus one equal three the arithmetic law of the land. However, this does not affect the fact that one plus one still *is* two. In strict analogy to this, I "only" claim to prove that whatever Rawls or other socialists say is false and can be understood as such by all intellectually competent and honest men. It does not change the fact that incompetence or dishonesty and evil still may exist and may even prevail over truth and justice.

The second objection suffers from the same misunderstanding of the value-free nature of my defense of private property. Osterfeld agrees that argumentation presupposes the recognition of private property. But then he wonders about the source of this right. Yet how can he raise such a question? Only because he, too, is capable of argumentation. Without argumentation there would be nothing but silence or meaningless noise. The answer is that the source of human rights is and must be argumentation as the manifestation of our rationality. It is impossible to claim anything else to be the starting point for the derivation of an ethical system because claiming so would once again have to presuppose one's argumentative capability. Could rights not be derived from a contract behind a "veil of ignorance" asks Osterfeld? Yes and no. Of course, there can be rights derived from contracts, but in order for a contract to be possible, there must already be private owners and private property; otherwise there would be no physically independent contractors and nothing to contractually agree upon. And "no": no rights can be derived "from behind a veil of ignorance" because no one lives behind such a thing except epistemological zombies, and only a Rawlsian zombie ethic can be derived from behind it. Can rights emerge from tradition a la Hume or Burke? Of course, they always do. But the question of the factual emergence of rights has nothing to do with the question of whether or not what exists can be justified.

In his third objection, Osterfeld claims that I construct an alternative between either individual ownership or world community ownership but that such an alternative is not exhaustive. This is a misrepresentation. Nowhere do I say anything like this. In the section to which Osterfeld refers, I am concerned with explaining the entirely different alternative between property as defined in physical terms and as originating at definite points in time for definite individuals in contrast to property as defined in value terms and nonspecific with respect to its time of origin, and the refutation of the latter as absurd and self-contradictory. I do not at all rule out the possibility of ownership of "intermediate communities." However, such ownership presupposes individual private ownership. Collective ownership requires contracts, and contracts are only possible if there are already prior noncontractually acquired ownership claims. Contracts are agreements between physically independent units which are based on the mutual recognition of each contractor's private ownership claim to things acquired prior to the agreement and which concern the transfer of these property titles from a specific prior to a specific later owner or owners.

Regarding Osterfeld's first objection, I did not write that the fundamental goals of political economy and political philosophy are "complementary" ones. What I said is that they are different. No one trying to answer 'What is just?" is logically committed to insisting that his answer must also contribute to the greatest possible production of wealth (at least I don't contend anywhere that there is any such logical commitment!). Hence, it is no valid objection to my remarks on the relationship between political philosophy and economy that Hobbes, Rousseau, and others suggest that political systems do not increase wealth but rather scarcity. Their claim that such systems are just cannot be made good, and as it turns out, the ethic which alone can be justified indeed helps maximize wealth production. Fortunately, this is a matter of fact. It does not change in the least the fact that political philosophy and political economy are concerned with completely separate issues.

This and only this has been my thesis: While political philosophers as such need not be concerned with the problem of alleviation of scarcity, political philosophy and economy have in common the fact that without scarcity neither discipline would make any sense. There would be no interpersonal conflict over anything, and no question as to what norms should be accepted as just in order to avoid such possible clashes! It is no stretching of the point to say that political philosophers have invariably been concerned with the assignment of rights of exclusive control over scarce goods. Such is the case when a Lockean proposes to accept the private property ethic, and no less when a Hobbesian suggests, instead, to make some person the supreme Führer, whose commands everyone else must follow.

II. UTILITARIANS AND RANDIANS VS. REASON[2]

It is neither possible nor worthwhile to address all of the points brought up in the foregoing discussion. I will concentrate on those critics who come out most vehemently against my argument—all of them utilitarians of sorts. I will then comment briefly on the Randian type of reaction.

---

[2]Reply to "Symposium on Hoppe's Argumentation Ethic," *Liberty* (November 1988).

Amazingly, Friedman, Yeager, Steel, Waters, Virkkala, and Jones believe I must have overlooked the fact that all existing societies are less than fully libertarian (that there is slavery, the gulag, or that husbands own wives, etc.), and that this somehow invalidates my argument. Obviously, I would hardly have written this article if it had been my opinion that libertarianism were already prevalent. Thus, it should have been clear that it was precisely this nonlibertarian character of reality which motivated me to show something quite different: why such a state of affairs cannot be *justified*. Citing facts like slavery as a counter-example is roughly on a par with refuting the proof that 1+1=2 by pointing out that someone has just come up with 3 as an answer—and about as ridiculous.

To restate my claim: Whether or not something is true, false, or undecidable; whether or not it has been justified; what is required in order to justify it; whether I, my opponents, or none of us is right—all of this must be decided in the course of argumentation. This proposition is true a priori, because it cannot be denied without affirming it in the act of denying it. One cannot argue that one cannot argue, and one cannot dispute knowing what it means to raise a validity claim without implicitly claiming at least the negation of this proposition to be true.

This has been called "the a priori of argumentation," and it was because of the axiomatic status of this proposition, analogous to the "action axiom" of praxeology, that I invoked Mises in my article. (Virkkala's outrage over this disqualifies itself because I explicitly stated that Mises thought what I was trying to do was impossible. Moreover, it is his understanding of Mises that is amusing. While it is true that praxeology talks *about* marginalism, it is obviously not the case that praxeology as a body of propositions is in any way affected by marginal choices. Praxeology contains universally true propositions, and whether or not we choose to accept them does not affect this at all. It is beyond me why that should be any different when it comes to ethical propositions. Virkkala might just as well attack Mises for a "retreat from marginalism" because of his claim that praxeology is *true*.)

With the a priori of argumentation established as an axiomatic starting point, it follows that anything that must be presupposed in the act of proposition-making cannot be propositionally disputed again. It would be meaningless to ask for a justification of presuppositions which make the production of meaningful propositions possible in the first place. Instead, they must be regarded as ultimately justified by every proposition maker. Any specific propositional content that disputed their validity could be understood as implying a performative contradiction (in the sense explained by David Gordon), and hence, as ultimately falsified.

The law of contradiction is one such presupposition. One cannot deny this law without presupposing its validity in the act of denying it. But there is another such presupposition. Propositions are not free-floating entities. They require a proposition maker who in order to produce any validity claiming proposition whatsoever must have exclusive control (property) over some scarce means defined in objective terms and appropriated (brought under control) at definite points in time through homesteading action. Thus, any proposition that would dispute the validity of the homesteading principle of property acquisition or that would assert the validity of a different incompatible principle would be falsified by the act of proposition making in the same way as the proposition "the law of contradiction is false" would be contradicted by the very fact of asserting it. As the praxeological presupposition of proposition making, the validity of the homesteading principle cannot be argumentatively disputed without running into a performative contradiction. Any other principle of property acquisition can then be understood—reflectively—by every proposition maker as ultimately incapable of propositional justification. (Note, in particular, that this includes all proposals which claim it is justified to restrict the range of objects which may be homesteaded. They fail because once the exclusive control over *some* homesteaded means is admitted as justified, it becomes impossible to justify any restriction in the homesteading process—except for a self-imposed one—without thereby running into a contradiction. For if the proponent of such a restriction were consistent, he could have justified control only over some physical means which he would not be allowed to employ for any additional homesteading. Obviously, he could not interfere with another's extended homesteading simply because of his own lack of physical means to do anything about it justifiably. But if he did interfere, he would thereby inconsistently extend his ownership claims beyond *his* own justly homesteaded means. Moreover, in order to justify this extension he would have to invoke a principle of property acquisition incompatible with the homesteading principle whose validity he would already have admitted.)

My entire argument, then, claims to be an impossibility proof. It is not, as the mentioned critics seem to think, a proof that means to show the impossibility of certain empirical events so that it could be refuted by empirical evidence. Instead, it is a proof that it is impossible to justify nonlibertarian property principles propositionally without falling into contradictions. Whatever such a thing is worth (and I'll come to this shortly), it should be clear that empirical evidence has absolutely no bearing on it. So what if there is slavery, the gulag, taxation? The proof concerns the issue that claiming such institutions can be justified involves a performative contradiction. It is purely intellectual in nature, like logical, mathematical, or praxeological proofs. Its validity, like theirs, can be established independent of any contingent experiences. Nor is its validity in any way affected, as several critics—most notoriously Waters—seem to think, by whether or not people like, favor, understand, or come to a consensus regarding it, or whether or not they are actually engaged in argumentation.

Since considerations such as these are irrelevant in order to judge the validity of a mathematical proof, for instance, so are they beside the point here. In the same way as the validity of a mathematical proof is not restricted to the moment of proving it, so is the validity of the libertarian property theory not limited to instances of argumentation. If correct, the argument demonstrates its universal justification. (Of all utilitarian critics only Steele takes up the challenge that I had posed for them: that the assignment of property rights cannot be dependent on any later outcome because in this case no one could ever know before the outcome what he was or was not justified to do; and that in advocating a consequentialist position utilitarianism is [strictly speaking] no ethic at all if it fails to answer the all-decisive question "what am I justified to do now?" Steele solves this problem in the same way as he proceeds throughout his comment: by misunderstanding what it is. He misconceives my argument as subject to empirical testing and misrepresents it as claiming to show that "I favor a libertarian ethic" follows from "I am saying something," while in fact it claims that entirely independent of whatever people happen to favor or utter "the libertarian ethic can be given an ultimate propositional justification" follows from "I claim such and such to be valid, i.e., capable of propositional justification." His response to the consequentialist problem is yet another stroke of genius: No, says Steele, consequentialism must not involve a praxeologically absurd waiting-for-the-outcome ethic. His example: Certain rules are advocated first, then implemented, and later adjusted depending on outcomes. While this is indeed an example of consequentialism, I fail to see how it should provide an answer to "what are we justified in doing now?" and so escape the absurdities of a waiting-for-the-outcome ethic. The starting point is unjustified [Which rules? Not only the outcome depends on this!]; and the consequentialist procedure is unjustified, too. [Why not adopt rules and stick to them regardless of the outcome?] Steele's answer to the question "what am I justified in doing?" is "that depends on whatever rules you start out with, then on the outcome of whatever this leads to, and finally on whether or not you care about such an outcome." Whatever this is, it is no ethic.)

The reaction from the other Randian side, represented by Rasmussen, is different. He has fewer difficulties recognizing the nature of my argument but then asks me in turn "So what? Why should an a priori proof of the libertarian property theory make any difference? Why not engage in aggression anyway?" Why indeed?! But then, why should the proof that $1+1=2$ make any difference? One certainly can still act on the belief that $1+1=3$. The obvious answer is "because a propositional justification exists for doing one thing, but not for doing another." But why should we be reasonable, is the next comeback. Again, the answer is obvious. For one, because it would be impossible to argue against it; and further, because the proponent raising this question would already affirm the use of reason in his act of questioning it. This still might not suffice and everyone knows that it would not, for even if the libertarian ethic and argumentative reasoning must be regarded as ultimately justified, this still does not preclude that people will act on the basis of unjustified beliefs either because they don't know, they don't care, or they prefer not to know. I fail to see why this should be surprising or make the proof somehow defective. More than this cannot be done by propositional argument.

Rasmussen seems to think that if I could get an "ought" derived from somewhere (something that Yeager claims I am trying to do though I explicitly denied this), then things would be improved. But this is simply an illusory hope. For even if Rasmussen had proven the proposition that one *ought* to be reasonable and *ought* to act according to the libertarian property ethic, this would still be just another propositional argument. It can no more assure that people will do what they ought to do than my proof can guarantee that they will do what is justified. Where is the difference, and what is all the fuss about? There is and remains a difference between establishing a truth claim and instilling a desire to act upon the truth—with "ought" or without it. It is surely great if a proof can instill this desire. But even if it does not, this can hardly be held against it. It also does not subtract anything from its merit if in some or even many cases a few raw utilitarian assertions prove more successful in persuading anyone of libertarianism than it can do. A proof is still a proof and social psychology remains social psychology.

III. INTIMIDATION BY ARGUMENT[3]

Loren Lomasky was intimidated and angered by my book *A Theory of Socialism and Capitalism*. For one, because the book is more ambitious than its title indicates. "It is," he laments, "no less than a manifesto for untrammeled anarchism." So be it. But so what? As explained in my book but conveniently left unmentioned by Lomasky, untrammeled anarchism is nothing but the name for a social order of untrammeled private property rights, i.e., of the absolute right of self-ownership and the absolute right to homestead unowned resources, of employing them for whatever purpose one sees fit so long as this does not affect the physical integrity of others' likewise appropriated

---

[3]Reply to Loren Lomasky, "The Argument From Mere Argument," *Liberty* (September 1989).

resources, and of entering into any contractual agreement with other property owners that is deemed mutually beneficial. What is so horrifying about this idea? Empirically speaking, this property theory constitutes the hard core of most people's intuitive sense of justice and so can hardly be called revolutionary. Only someone advocating the trammeling of private property rights would take offense, as does Lomasky, with my attempt to justify a pure private-property economy.

Lomasky is not only enraged at my conclusions, however. His anger is further aggravated because I do not merely try to provide empirical evidence for them, but a rigorous proof, Lomasky chides, "validated by pure reason and uncontaminated by any merely empirical likelihoods." It is not surprising that an opponent of untrammeled private property rights, such as Lomasky, should find this undertaking doubly offensive. Yet what is wrong with the idea of *a priori-theorizing* in economics and ethics? Lomasky points out that failed attempts to construct a priori theories exist. But so what? This only reflects on those particular theories. Moreover, it actually presupposes the existence of a priori reasoning in that the refutation of an a priori theory must itself be a proof. For Lomasky, however, nothing but intellectual hyperbole can possibly be responsible for "eschewing the low road of empiricism, soaring instead with Kant, and von Mises through the realm of a priori necessities." A book on political philosophy or economy, then, should never come up with unambiguous conclusions as to what to do or what rules to follow. Everything should be left vague and at a nonoperational stage of conceptual development, and no one should ever try to prove anything but instead should follow the forever open-minded empiricist approach of trial and error, of tentative conjectures, of refutations, and of confirmations. Such, for Lomasky, is the proper path, the low and humble road, along which one is to travel. Sure enough, most contemporary political philosophers seem to have wholeheartedly followed this advice on their way to fame. Taking the high road instead, I present an unambiguous thesis, stated in operational terms, and attempt to prove it by axiomatic-deductive arguments. If this makes my book the ultimate insult in some philosophical circles, so much the better. Apart from other advantages, such that this might actually be the only appropriate method of inquiry, it at least forces one to say something specific and to open oneself up wide to rigorous logical-praxeological criticism instead of producing, as Lomasky and his fellow low roaders, meaningless nonoperational moonshine talk and distinctions.

Besides finding fault with the arrogance of someone writing a book that presents a praxeologically meaningful and easily understandable thesis concerning the central problems of political philosophy and economy, and that vigorously defends it to the point of excluding any other answers as false, Lomasky also has some specific nits to pick. As might be expected from an intimidated low roader, they are either unsystematic cheap shots, or they display a complete miscomprehension of the problem.

I am criticized for not paying enough attention to Quine, Nozick, and entire bodies of philosophic thought. Maybe so, though Nozick, if only in a footnote as Lomasky notes indignantly, is actually systematically refuted. However, one would like to know why that should have made a difference for my argument. Mere reading suggestions are all too easy to come up with in these times. I am criticized for misinterpreting Locke by not mentioning his famous proviso, but I am not engaged in an interpretation of Locke. I construct a positive theory and in so doing employ Lockean ideas; and assuming my theory correct for the sake of argument, there can be no doubt as to my verdict on the proviso. It is false, and it is incompatible with the homesteading principle as the central pillar of Locke's theory. Lomasky does not demonstrate that it is not so. He is annoyed at my dissolution of the public goods problem as a pseudo-problem without so much as mentioning my central contention regarding the matter, i.e., that the notion of objectively distinct classes of private vs. public goods is incompatible with subjectivist economics and so must fall by the wayside along with all distinctions based on it. He finds my arguments in support of the thesis of the ever-optimality of free markets wanting because they must rely on the assumption of "the universal optimality of voluntary transactions." They must indeed. I never claimed anything else. Yet this assumption happens to be true—in fact, as I argue, indisputably true. So what then? Or is Lomasky willing to take on the task of proving it to be false?! How dare I—in a footnote—criticize Buchanan and Tullock for Orwellian double-talk, Lomasky complains. Only he forgets to mention that I give rather specific reasons for this characterization: among others, the use of the notion of "conceptual" agreements and contracts in their attempt to justify a state when according to ordinary speech, such agreements and contracts are nonagreements and noncontracts. Noncontracting means contracting! Similarly, for my oh-so-disrespectful remarks regarding Chicago-style property theories I give reasons (their assumption of the measurability of utility, for instance), which Lomasky simply suppresses. The rest, regarding my theory of justice, is either miscomprehension or deliberate misrepresentation. From reading Lomasky's reconstruction of my central argument, which revealingly employs no direct quotes, no one would grasp its main thrust and structure: Without scarcity there can be no interpersonal conflict and hence no ethical questions (what am I justified doing and what not?). Conflicts are the result of incompatible claims regarding scarce resources, and there is but one possible way out of such predicaments: through the formulation of rules that assign mutually exclusive ownership titles regarding scarce, physical resources so as to make it possible for different actors to act simultaneously without thereby generating conflict. (Like most contemporary philosophers, Lomasky gives no indication that he has grasped the elementary yet fundamental point that any political philosophy which is not construed as a theory of property rights fails entirely in its own objective and thus must be discarded from the outset as praxeologically meaningless moonshine.)

Yet scarcity, and the possibility of conflicts, is not sufficient for the emergence of ethical problems. Obviously, one could have conflicts regarding scarce resources with an animal, yet one would not consider it possible to resolve these conflicts by means of proposing property norms. In such cases, the avoidance of conflicts is merely a technical, not an ethical, problem. For it to become an ethical problem, it is also necessary that the conflicting actors be capable, in principle, of argumentation. (Lomasky's mosquito example is thus silly: Animals are no moral agents, because they are incapable of argumentation. My theory of justice explicitly denies its applicability to animals and, in fact, implies that they have no rights!)

Further, that there can be no problem of ethics without argumentation is indisputable. Not only have I been engaged in argumentation all along, but it is impossible, without falling into a contradiction, to deny that whether or not one has any rights and, if any which ones, must be decided in the course of argumentation. Thus, there can be no ethical justification of anything, except insofar as it is argumentative. This has been called "the a priori of argumentation." (Insofar as Lomasky has at all understood this, he most definitely appears to be unaware of the axiomatic status of this proposition, i.e., of the fact that the a priori of argumentation provides an absolute starting point, neither capable of, nor requiring, any further justification!)

Arguing is an activity and requires a person's exclusive control over scarce resources (one's brain, vocal cords, etc.). More specifically, as long as there is argumentation, there is a mutual recognition of each other's exclusive control over such resources. It is this which explains the unique feature of communication: that while one may disagree about what has been said, it is still possible to independently agree at least on the fact that there is disagreement. (Lomasky does not seem to dispute this. He claims, however, that it merely proves the *fact* of mutually exclusive domains of control, not the *right* of self-ownership. He errs. Whatever [the law of contradiction, for instance] must be presupposed insofar as one argues cannot be meaningfully disputed because it is the very precondition of meaningful doubt; hence, it must be regarded as indisputable or *a priori valid*. In the same vein, the fact of self-ownership is a praxeological precondition of argumentation. Anyone trying to prove or disprove anything must be a self-owner. It is a self-contradictory absurdity to ask for any further-reaching justification for this fact. Required, of necessity, by all meaningful argumentation, self-ownership is an absolutely and ultimately *justified* fact.)

Finally, if actors were not entitled to own physical resources other than their bodies, and if they as moral agents—categorically different from Lomasky's mosquitoes—were to follow this prescription, they would be dead and no problem whatsoever would exist. For ethical problems to exist, then, ownership in other things must be justified. Further, if one were not allowed to appropriate other resources through homesteading action, i.e., by putting them to use before anybody else does, or if the range of objects to be homesteaded were somehow limited, this would only be possible if ownership could be acquired by mere decree instead of by action. However, this does not qualify as a solution to the problem of ethics, i.e., of conflict-avoidance, even on purely technical grounds, for it would not allow one to decide what to do if such declarative claims happened to be incompatible. More decisive still, it would be incompatible with the already justified self-ownership, for if one could appropriate resources by decree, this would imply that one could also declare another person's body to be one's own. Thus, anyone denying the validity of the homesteading principle—whose recognition is already implicit in arguing two persons' mutual respect for each other's exclusive control over his own body—would contradict the content of his proposition through his very act of proposition making. (For one thing, in a stroke of genius, Lomasky finds fault with the fact that the first part of this argument provides no justification for unlimited homesteading. True. But then it also does not claim to do any such thing. The second part—the *argumentum a contrario*—does. Regarding my argument in its entirety Lomasky claims that I have only shown the validity of the nonaggression principle for the act of argument itself and not beyond . . . it does not extend to the object of discussion. At best, this objection indicates a total failure to grasp the nature of performative contradictions: If justification of anything is argumentative justification, and if what must be presupposed by any argumentation whatsoever must be considered ultimately justified, then any validity claiming proposition whose content is incompatible with such ultimately justified facts is ultimately falsified as involving a performative contradiction. And that is that.)

Philosophic and economic theorizing is indeed serious work.

IV. ON THE INDEFENSIBILITY OF WELFARE RIGHTS[4]

David Conway claims that my argument intending to show the unrestricted validity of the homesteading principle, i.e., the

---

[4]Reply to David Conway, "A Theory of Socialism and Capitalism," *Austrian Economics Newsletter* (Winter/Spring, 1990).

first-use-first-own rule regarding unowned, nature-given resources, is flawed, and that he can demonstrate the defensibility of welfare rights. I remain unconvinced and contend that it is his counterargument which is faulty.

While I have no quarrel with his presentation of my argument, I will first briefly restate my proof. Second, I will point out the central errors in his reply. Third, I wish to offer an explanation for Conway's rejection of my argument as resulting from a rather common misconception regarding the logic of ethical reasoning.

Whether or not one has any rights, and, if any, which ones, can only be decided in the course of argumentation. It is impossible to deny the truth of this without falling into a contradiction. Arguing requires a person's exclusive control (ownership) over scarce resources (one's brain, vocal cords, etc.). Denying this would again merely prove the point. Further, a person must have acquired this ownership simply by virtue of the fact that he began using these resources before anyone else had done so; otherwise, he could never say or argue anything to begin with. Thus, anyone denying the validity of the homesteading principle at least with respect to *some* resources would contradict the content of his proposition through his very act of proposition making. So far, it appears, Conway would agree. But he would impose limitations on the range of objects that may legitimately be homesteaded. Unfortunately for Conway's case, however, once exclusive control over some homesteaded means is admitted as justified, it becomes impossible to justify any restrictions in the homesteading process—except for a self-imposed, voluntary one—without thereby running into contradictions. For if the proponent of such a restriction were consistent, he could have justified control only over some, albeit limited, scarce resources which he would not be allowed to employ for additional homesteading. Yet obviously, he could not then interfere with another's extended homesteading simply because of his own lack of means to do anything about this. And if he did interfere, he would thereby (inconsistently) extend his ownership claims beyond his own justly homesteaded resources. Moreover, in order to justify his interference he would have to invoke a principle of property acquisition incompatible with the homesteading principle: He would have to claim (inconsistently) that a person who extends his homesteading, and who does so in accordance with a principle that no one can argue to be generally invalid, is, or at least can be, an aggressor (even though in doing so this person could not possibly be said to have taken anything away from anyone because he would have merely appropriated *previously unowned resources*, i.e., things that no one up to that point had even recognized as scarce and which anyone else could have appropriated as well if only he had recognized their scarcity earlier, including anyone such as Conway, who was concerned about the fate of late-comers and wanted to preserve these resources for their later benefit). Furthermore, that a person who interferes with such an action and who does so in accordance with a principle that no one could possibly argue to be generally valid is, or at least can be, acting legitimately (even though he would always take something away from someone whose appropriations had occurred at no one's expense).

The central error in Conway's rejection of this argument is his refusal to acknowledge the logical incompatibility of his idea of welfare rights on the one hand—the notion that one can have enforceable claims against homesteaders—and of the homesteading principle on the other. Either the first idea is right or the second is. However, the first cannot be said to be right because in order for anyone to say so, the second one must be presupposed as valid. There can be no such thing as a right to life, then, in Conway's sense of a right to having one's life sustained by others. There can only be each person's right to own his physical body, and everything homesteaded with its help, and to engage in mutually beneficial exchanges with others. Suppose, for instance, that I am terminally ill and the only way for me to survive is to have my brain short-circuited with Conway's. Does he have the right to refuse? I think so, and I am sure that he thinks so, too. But he cannot have this right on welfare grounds (assuming that his life would not be threatened by such an operation), but only on the basis of the homesteading principle as the precondition of one's existence as an independently reasoning and arguing physical being. Further, his claim that welfare rights are "every bit as objective" as those implied by mixing one's labor with scarce resources (contrary to my thesis that the former are subjective, arbitrary, verbal, derived out of thin air) is fallacious. Through homesteading an objective link between a *particular person* and a *particular resource* is created. But how in the world can one say that my need can give rise to a claim regarding any specific resource or resource owner X, rather than Y, or Z, if I had not homesteaded or produced either one?! Not only is neediness incapable of objective identification or measurement: Who determines who is or is not needy? Everyone for himself? But what if I happened to disagree with someone's self-assessment? People have died from love-sickness. Do they have a right to a lover-conscript? People have survived by eating grass, bark, rats, roaches, or others' garbage. Are there no needy people then so long as there is enough grass or garbage to eat? If not, why not? For how long would the support for the needy have to last? Forever? And what about the rights of the supporters who would thereby become permanently enslaved to the needy? Or what if my support for the needy caused me to become needy myself, or somehow increased my own future needs? Would I still have to continue to support them? And how much work can I expect the destitute to perform in return for my support, given the fact that one is not dealing here with a mutually beneficial employment relation or voluntary charity to begin with? As much as the needy feel is appropriate?

Moreover, even if all these difficulties were overcome, more are lying in the wings because need does not connect the needy with any resource or resource owner in particular, yet it must invariably be particular resources that provide relief. The needy may be needy without any fault of their own, but the non-needy may be non-needy without any fault of theirs, too. So how can the needy claim support from me rather than from you? Surely that would be utterly unfair toward me in particular! In fact, either the needy can have a claim against no one in particular, which is to say they have no claim whatsoever; or else their claim would have to be directed equally against each one of the world's non-needy.

Yet how can the needy possibly enforce such a claim? After all, they lack resources. For this to be possible, an all-resourceful, worldwide operating agency would be required. The owners of such an agency obviously would have to be classified as among the non-needy and could hence have no direct claim against anyone. Supposedly, only need creates such claims. In fact, this agency would have to be considered one of the foremost debtors to the needy, and it could only legitimately act against other non-needy if it had previously voluntarily paid *its* share of welfare debts *and* the needy had contractually entrusted it with such an enforcement task. Hence, the welfare problem would have to wait for a solution until this institution arrived. So far it has not arrived, and there is nothing to indicate that it will arrive in the near future. Even if it did, welfare rights would still be incompatible with the homesteading rule as an indisputably valid, axiomatic principle.

The explanation for Conway's refusal to accept the homesteading ethic lies in a misconception regarding the nature of ethical theory. Instead of recognizing ethics as a logical theory, deductively derived from incontestable axioms (akin to praxeology), Conway implicitly shares a popular, empiricist-intuitionist (or gut-feeling) approach toward ethics. Accordingly, an ethical theory is *tested* against moral experience such that if the theory yields conclusions at variance with one's moral intuitions, it should be regarded as falsified. However, this view is entirely mistaken and, much like in economics, the role of theory and experience in ethics is almost precisely the opposite: It is the very function of ethical theory to provide a rational justification for our moral intuitions, or to show why they have no such basis and make us reconsider and revise our intuitive reactions. This is not to say that intuitions can never play a role in the building of ethical theory. In fact, counterintuitive theoretical conclusions may well *indicate* a theoretical error. But if after one's theoretical reexamination errors are found neither in one's axioms nor in one's deductions, then it is one's intuitions that must go, not one's theory.

In fact, what strikes Conway as a counterintuitive implication of the homesteading ethic, and then leads him to reject it, can easily be interpreted quite differently. It is true, as Conway says, that this ethic would allow for the possibility of the entire world's being homesteaded. What about newcomers in this situation who own nothing but their physical bodies? Cannot the homesteaders restrict access to their property for these newcomers and would this not be intolerable? I fail to see why. (Empirically, of course, the problem does not exist: if it were not for governments restricting access to unowned land, there would still be plenty of empty land around!)

These newcomers normally come into existence somewhere as children born to parents who are owners or renters of land (if they came from Mars, and no one wanted them here, so what?; they assumed a risk in coming, and if they now have to return, tough luck!). If the parents do not provide for the newcomers, they are free to search the world over for employers, sellers, or charitable contributors, and a society ruled by the homesteading ethic would be, as Conway admits, the most prosperous one possible! If they still could not find *anyone* willing to employ, support, or trade with them, why not ask what's wrong with *them*, instead of Conway's feeling sorry for them? Apparently *they* must be intolerably unpleasant fellows and should shape up, or they deserve no other treatment. Such, in fact, would be my own intuitive reaction.

Subject Index

A posteriori knowledge, 267, 287, 292–93
A priori knowledge, 280–83, 287, 339, 358, 365, 371
A priori reasoning, 13, 18, 315, 321–22, 330, 409
A priori synthetic propositions, 274, 276, 286
Absolute growth of GNP, 38
Absolutist (government), 61–62, 128
Accounting, 78, 80, 159, 177, 180, 218, 255, 360
Accumulation (of capital), 101–02, 119, 123, 134, 148–49, 243–44, 261
Action Committee for Europe, 114
Africa, 72, 112
Aggression, 13, 17–20, 25, 31–32, 54–55, 73–74, 88, 100, 102, 105–06, 221, 320, 325–28, 337, 343, 392, 407
  foreign, 100–01, 105, 392
  physical, 13, 221, 325, 327, 337
American revolution, 61
American Wild West, 26–27
Amsterdam, 58
Anarchism, 19, 55, 269, 308, 349, 408
Anarchist, 13, 16, 310, 388
Anarchy, 26, 55–67, 104, 378, 388–90
Arbitration, 26, 28–29, 389
Argumentation, 13, 18, 29, 257, 279–81, 284, 314–19, 321–23, 327, 329, 334–38, 341–42, 345, 371–73, 376, 384–87, 399–406, 411–14
Arithmetic (and praxeology and episte-mology), 285–87, 289, 291–92, 347–48, 401

Asia, 112
Athens, 362
Austrian economics/Austrian School, 117, 124, 126, 128, 138–39, 205, 230, 294, 306, 367–79
Austrian Rationalism, 347–79
Austrian theory of ethics, 370–79
Axiom of action, 275–79, 339, 371, 374–75
Axioms, 275, 280, 417

Bank and business elites, 108, 110, 112, 124, 132, 362
Bank for International Settlement, 112
Bank fraud, 83–84
Banking elites, 112
Banking Federation of the European Community, 114
Banks, 79–83, 90–97, 107–09, 111, 114–16, 132, 135, 183, 186, 194–95, 200–01, 204, 217–18, 224, 228, 230–34, 239–42, 250–51
Barter, 77–81, 109, 176–80, 187, 230
Basel Committee, 114
Berlin, 72
Berlin Wall, xi
Bank for International Settlement (BIS), 112, 115–16
Boom-bust cycle, 82–83, 93, 153–55, 168, 172, 196, 199, 202, 204, 244, 251
British Guiana, 106
Brooklyn Polytechnic Institute, ix

Name Index

Abshire, David M., 114
Acton, Lord John, 58–59, 127
Agnelli, G., 115
Agnelli, U., 115
Alchian, Armen, 11
Anderson, Terry, 27
Andreski, Stanislav, 72, 270, 368
Apel, K.O., 283, 291, 301, 303, 314,
   334–35, 353, 359, 371
Aquinas, 58, 104
Atkinson, A.B., 41
Ayer, Alfred, 357

Baechler, Jean, 57, 104
Bachrach, Peter, 97
Bagehot, J., 165
Baier, Kurt, 312
Bailyn, Bernard, 31
Balladour, E., 115
Baran, Paul A., 97, 113, 117
Baratz, Morton, 97
Barnes, Jonathan, 270, 369
Bauer, Peter T., 72
Baumol, William, 4–5, 44, 47
Benda, Julien, 65
Bendix, Reinhard, 67
Blalock, Hubert, 296
Blanshard, Brand, 272, 283–86
Blaug, Mark, 267
Blinder, Alan, 5, 44, 47
Block, Walter, 4, 6, 9, 11, 13, 75, 146,
   194, 201, 205–06, 222, 305, 307, 311,
   368

Blumenthal, W. Michael, 114
Blumert, Burt S., xii
Boettke, Peter, 270
Böhm-Bawerk, Eugen v., 96–97, 121,
   146, 369
Boétie, Etienne de la, 75, 393
Brady, N., 115
Bramsted, Ernest K., 61
Break, George F., 41
Brown, Harold, 114
Brzezinski, Zbigniew, 114
Buchanan, James M., 4, 6, 12, 16,
   22–23, 51, 85, 87, 131, 389, 411
Bull, John, 165
Bush, George (President), 114

Cairnes, John E., 271
Callaghan, J., 115
Cantillon, Richard, 61
Carlucci, Frank C., 114
Carstens, K., 115
Carter, F., 296
Carter, James E. ("Jimmy"), 114
Cipolla, C.M., 59
Clemence, Richard, 137
Coase, Ronald, 7, 11
Coffey, P., 115
Cohen, Morris, 283
Cole, G.D.H., 320
Comte, Charles, 96, 125
Conway, David, 413–18
Cooper, R.N., 114

Copleston, Frederick C., 58
Cuzán, Alfred G., 55–56

Davidson, Donald, 283
Davignon, E., 115
Davis, Lance E., 70, 104
Deflassieux, J., 115
Delors, J., 115
Demsetz, Harold, 11
d'Estaing, V.G., 115
Dicey, A.V., 64
Dingler, Hugo, 283, 288–89
Dolan, Edwin, 61, 178, 271, 374
Domhoff, G. William, 97
Dunoyer, Charles, 96, 125
Dusenberg, W., 115
Dworkin, Ronald, 11

Ebeling, Richard, 199, 206, 239, 347
Ekelund, Robert, 44
Ekirch, Arthur E., 64
Engels, Friedrich, 117, 119, 137
Evans, Peter, 55, 99, 134
Ezekiel, Mordecai, 296

Fabius, L., 115
Fahrenbach, Helmut, 314
Fama, Eugene, 182
Feigl, H., 358
Fetter, Frank, 122, 146
Feyerabend, Paul, 349–52
Fisher, Irving, 176, 179
Fisher, Stanley, 44
FitzGerald, G., 115
Fourtou, J.R., 115
Fox, Karl, 296
Frege, Gottlob, 359
Friedman, Milton, 10, 140, 176–79,
184–88, 191–94, 199, 204, 267, 394–95,
404
Fusfeld, Daniel R., 44

Garrison, Roger, 146, 154–55, 237, 240
Gewirth, Alan, 312–16

Gödel, Kurt, 286–87
Goodhart, C., 115
Gordon, David, xii, 270, 405
Graham, Benjamin, 178
Graham, Frank D., 178
Greaves, Percy, 124
Grice-Hutchinson, Marjorie, 61
Greenleaf, W.H., 64
Greenspan, Alan, 114
Groseclose, Elgin, 82
Grotius, Hugo, 58, 104
Guimbretiere, P., 115
Guth, W., 115

Habermas, Jürgen, 138, 273, 303, 314,
316, 334–35
Haig, A., 114
Halevy, Elie, 64
Hansen, Alvin, 155, 168
Harman, Gilbert, 283
Harris, Seymour P., 155
Hart, David M., 125
Hayek, Friedrich A., 10, 62, 71, 81–82,
130, 144, 154, 176, 178, 191, 197,
239–40, 255–62, 369, 394–97
Hazlitt, Henry, 111, 113, 155, 157–58,
160, 164–65, 167, 171, 242
Heath, E., 115
Heise, David, 296
Hempel, Carl G., 358
Herbener, Jeffrey M., 265, 350
Herbert, Auberon, 50
Higgs, Robert, 63–64, 70, 99, 134
Hilbert, D., 287, 359
Hilferding, Rudolf, 97
Hill, Peter J., 27
Hobbes, Thomas, 388, 403
Hollis, Martin, 271, 352, 363
Hoppe, Hans-Hermann, 13, 27, 44, 50,
65, 73, 75, 85, 87–88, 104, 123, 126,
131–32, 135, 140, 153–54, 202, 205,
208–10, 221–22, 232–34, 241–45, 249,
261, 265–66, 269–71, 274, 282, 290–91,
293, 298, 307, 311, 322, 350, 352–53,

Selgin, George, 176, 199–226, 230–50
Senghass, Dieter, 325
Senior, Nassau W., 271
Sheehy, P., 116
Singer, Marcus, 312
Skousen, Mark, 139
Solana, L., 115
Solomon, Anthony M., 114
Solvay, J., 116
Sombart, Werner, 269
Spencer, Herbert, 50
Stegmüller, Wolfgang, 285, 352, 355
Sterba, James P., 328
Stiglitz, Joseph E., 41
Stockman, David A., 114
Strigl, Richard von, 82, 146, 154
Suarez, Francisco, 58, 104
Sweezy, Paul M., 97, 117
Sykes, Charles, 368

Tannehill, Linda, 21, 32
Tannehill, Morris, 21, 32
Tansill, Charles, 107
Taylor, J.P., 63
Terborgh, George, 168
Thiel, Charles, 286
Tigar, Michael, 59
Tilly, Charles, 55, 99, 134, 137
Tollison, Robert, 44
Toulmin, Stephen, 312
Tuck, Richard, 58
Tucker, Jeffrey, 115–16
Tullock, Gordon, 4, 12, 16, 23, 51–52, 85, 131, 411
Turgot, A.J., 61, 206

Vance, Cyrus, 114
Veatch, Henry, 59, 270, 313, 316, 318, 355, 367, 369
Vogel, H.J., 115
Volcker, Paul A., 114

Wagner, Richard, 22
Waismann, Friedrich, 285
Wallace, Neil, 182
Warren, Bill, 137
Webber, Carolyn, 60, 66
Weinberger, Caspar, 114
Weinburg, Mark, 125
Weinstein, James, 94, 133
Weischedel, W., 275
Wetter, G., 117
White, Lawrence, 176, 182, 199–226, 230–50
Whitehead, J.C., 114
Wicksell, Knut, 12
Wieser, Friedrich, 271
Wild, John, 313
Wildavsky, Aaron, 60, 66
Will, George, 114
Woolridge, W.C., 21
Wright, Georg Henrik von, 291

Yamey, B.S., 72
Young, Andrew, 114

Zijlstra, J., 116